Essential Primary Scier

Second Edition

Essential Primary Science

Second Edition

Alan Cross and Adrian Bowden

Open University Press

Open University Press
McGraw-Hill Education
McGraw-Hill House
Shoppenhangers Road
Maidenhead
Berkshire
England
SL6 2QL

email: enquiries@openup.co.uk
world wide web: www.openup.co.uk

and Two Penn Plaza, New York, NY 10121-2289, USA

First published 2009
First published in this second edition 2014

A catalogue record of this book is available from the British Library

ISBN-13: 978-0-335-26334-9
ISBN-10: 0-335-26334-8
eISBN: 978-0-335-26335-6

Library of Congress Cataloging-in-Publication Data
CIP data applied for

Typesetting and e-book compilations by
RefineCatch Limited, Bungay, Suffolk

Fictitious names of companies, products, people, characters and/or data that may be used herein (in case studies or in examples) are not intended to represent any real individual, company, product or event.

Printed and bound by CPI Group (UK) Ltd, Croydon, CR0 4YY

Praise for this book

"This book is a really useful 'one stop shop' handbook outlining some of the key ideas in primary science – an essential reference guide for trainee teachers, full of handy tips about spotting misconceptions, linked to the new primary curriculum, practical suggestions ideas for how to communicate basic concepts and signposts to websites for further ideas."
    Claire Seeley, Member of Association of Science Education, Primary Committee

"The book is a veritable 'manual of primary science'. It is an extremely valuable resource that is both accessible and user-friendly while remaining an authoritative academic text. The book includes a wealth of information that exemplifies and illuminates outstanding classroom practice. It will be of support for the generalist teacher wishing to develop their understanding of the nature and practice of science as well as the novice trainee attempting their first classroom investigation. The content is effectively supported by reference to key research which gives credibility to the text and the practice exemplified within the writing."
    Elizabeth Briten, BA Programme Leader, Kingston University, UK

"This is a very useful, clear and well-informed book that is an invaluable resource for both practising teachers and teachers in training. It covers the key subject knowledge and also gives ideas for teaching all areas of the 2014 science curriculum. It uses a helpful structure for each subject area: what the teacher needs to know and understand; what the pupil needs to know at each Key Stage and ways to teach for that understanding. It sets out clear learning objectives for each suggested pupil activity, which is a real bonus for lesson planning.

In order to teach science well at primary school, the teacher needs to understand and enjoy the subject. This book will really help teachers to do just that. It will help build their confidence in the subject and give a wealth of knowledge about how and what to teach. I recommend this book highly."
    Helen Wilson, Principal Lecturer of Science Education,
    Oxford Brookes University, UK

"For me, the format of the book is very teacher friendly and can be read as a whole book to strengthen teacher confidence or dipped into when the need arises. I particularly like the clear format of 'what the children need to know' and 'How to teach it' parts as this is easily accessed by teachers who are usually rushed off their feet and have little time to wade through lots of information. Many of the suggestions for teaching are original fresh ideas that give the teachers ideas to develop further. I think this is what helps the book to stand out from others that attempt to do the same job.

The background knowledge for teachers is also a very valuable part to the book as any teacher or classroom assistant can read this information secure in the knowledge that it is sound and once read can feel more confident to be able to teach and answer children's questions. In my experience having all this background information in one, easily accessed and clearly organised way can help a nervous, unsure teacher have the confidence to teach a new subject to their class.

I have absolutely no hesitation in continuing to promote this book to all the teachers I train as the companion book that every school should have to help the less confident and/or seasoned teacher create better science learning experiences for their children."

Hester Binge, Primary Science Consultant working as part of a small team called Primarily Science

To Sue and Sara
for their support, encouragement, and suggestions

Contents

Acknowledgements

The authors wish to thank the copyright holders of the following material for permission to reproduce artwork in *Essential Primary Science.*

Data Harvest Group Ltd., 1 Eden Court, Leighton Buzzard, Bedfordshire LU7 4FY
Figure 4.14 Hand-held data logger
Figure 5.17 An electronic pulse sensor

Millgate House Education Ltd., Unit 1, Zan Industrial Park, Wheelock, Sandbach CW11 4QD
Figure 4.11 Concept cartoon

The University of Manchester Children's University, The University of Manchester, Oxford Road, Manchester M13 9PL
Figure 11.8 Page from a website simulation – shadows

Sherston Publishing Group, Angel House, Sherston, Malmesbury, Wiltshire SN16 0LH
Figure 4.2 A simple drawing of a flowering plant
Figure 4.5 A section through a leaf
Figure 5.4 The human skeleton
Figure 5.5 Structure of the human knee joint
Figure 5.6 The human heart
Figure 5.8 Components of human blood
Figure 5.14 A human tooth
Figure 5.15 The digestive system
Figure 11.1 Eight planets and Pluto (dwarf planet) orbit our Sun to make up our Solar System

TTS Group Ltd., Park Lane Business Park, Kirkby-in-Ashfield, Nottinghamshire NG17 9GU
Figure 2.10 Stereo microscope

The authors also wish to thank Gary Holmes for redrawing the artwork for all other figures.

1

Knowledge and understanding of science

In this book, we recognise that as a teacher or student teacher you may have to move quickly from a low level of personal knowledge and understanding of science to a much higher level, as well as learn how to teach it to others! The following chapters are based on the three things you need to know:

- what science the teacher needs to know and understand;
- what science the pupils need to learn; and
- effective ways to teach that science in primary classes.

In England, this means that pupils have opportunities to learn the science required by the National Curriculum (DfE, 2013a) or the curriculum adopted by their school. For you as a teacher, we take that science further so that the book complies with the Teachers' Standards (DfE, 2013b) for subject teaching (Standards 1–6) and suggests ways to teach and assess science, including many references to science investigations (working scientifically). This means that you can approach the teaching of primary science with increasing confidence. In this chapter, we outline basic principles and ideas about teaching science that will set you on the right path to help you experience early success. The most important contributors to this success will be your own commitment to learn, reflect, and act to further maximum progress in pupil learning.

Following an explanation of the structure and background of the book, this chapter will summarise several key ideas or principles that you can use to guide your own learning and teaching of science. Teaching includes all those things a teacher does which influence the learning of pupils in classrooms (Stenhouse, 1975). In this book, we focus on the personal knowledge and understanding of science required by primary teachers and the actions planned and taken by teachers in classrooms to provide primary pupils with the opportunities for learning science. Classroom teaching is cyclic in that teachers begin with ideas about what pupils should learn, find out what the pupils already know, understand and can do, design experiences for pupils that will provide opportunities to learn, and then lead the review of that learning before considering the next steps. Our intention is to help you to develop a growing confidence through your command of science education. You will derive much of this from your personal science knowledge and understanding, your ability to provide effective experiences for pupils in science, and your enthusiasm for the subject. If you are a trainee teacher in England, you must ensure that your science teaching reaches the standards set out by the DfE (2013b). This includes your personal understanding, knowledge of common misconceptions and of teaching safe science for learning. We have included aspects of physical processes in Key Stage 1 (5- to 7-year-olds) not included in the National Curriculum (DfE, 2013a) as we feel these can be learned by this age range, forming a firm foundation for Key Stage 2. The areas we have included are light, sound, forces as pushes and pulls, and simple electrical circuits. If you are teaching Lower Key Stage 2, check whether your learners have covered these aspects of science at Key Stage 1. If you need to, you can use our suggested activities. Some schools are adapting the curriculum to suit the needs of their learners. As part of this they are choosing to include these areas of physics for 5- to 7-year-olds. We have additionally placed extra emphasis on environmental science, including climate change, as we take the view that primary teachers should have a growing knowledge and understanding of the science behind environmental issues.

Two important clarifications are required. First, our chapter subheadings include the phrase 'know and understand', as we recognise that no book can guarantee complete understanding of all these science topics. Each chapter will help to increase your awareness of your personal knowledge and understanding in science. In a similar vein, we recognise that we cannot include all possible teaching methods, but do include examples that previously have worked well in primary classrooms. These will give you a great starting point, although we encourage you to adapt and develop the suggestions to suit you, your pupils, and the particular learning that is your objective. Second, although we have a chapter on investigative science and refer to it in sections of the book, you will need to further strengthen your background knowledge, understanding, and practice of science investigation. We recommend materials such as those available in resources and books, including *It's Not Fair – or is it?* (Turner *et al.*, 2011), *Making Sense of Primary Science Investigations* (Goldsworthy and Feasey, 1997) and chapter 2 of Peacock (1998) or chapter 3 of Sharp *et al.* (2000), which are practical and highly readable. Your understanding of the teaching of primary science will be further enhanced by reference to other well-presented and relevant educational research, which is usefully summarised by several authors (Harlen, 1999; Sharp, 2004; Roden, 2005).

Organisation of the book

The first three chapters deal with important over-arching professional topics including working scientifically (DfE, 2013a) and assessment of learners. Following this, each chapter deals with a significant section of science understanding for both you as teacher and your pupils. The length of the chapters varies depending on the science involved; for example, materials is an important part of science in the National Curriculum (DfE, 2013a), so this is reflected in the length of Chapter 8. After a short summary of the content, each chapter reviews the essential science background knowledge you require in 'What the teacher needs to know and understand'. In addition to reading the text, please complete the activities provided in these sections and make use of the recommended internet links. We know these will assist your learning greatly and ideas can often be adapted to work with pupils. You might also consider them if you find yourself supporting colleagues. Each chapter then summarises 'What the pupils need to know' by the end of either Key Stage 1 (5–7 years) or Key Stage 2 (7–11 years). These short sections are based on the National Curriculum (DfE, 2013a). Occasionally, we have added other items we feel are appropriate, for example, optional learning objectives for physical processes in Key Stage 1. Third, each chapter suggests 'Ways to teach . . . [the science topic]'. Here you will find a selection of effective explanations, demonstrations, and approaches from which you can select ones that you feel are appropriate for your pupils. You will find a range of pupil activities, including suggestions that will enable development of pupils' investigative skills. We include ideas for discussions – both whole-class and small-group discussions – which themselves can lead to questions the pupils can investigate. Where investigative elements are increasingly pupil-led, science can become even more meaningful. It is widely accepted that pupils who learn science through hands-on investigations learn more effectively and that learning stays with them longer (Wenham, 1995). Icons in the margins indicate links within science to other subjects and highlight sections which deal with safety.

The suggested activities do not necessarily constitute lessons but may be part of a lesson. Each activity includes a learning objective that can be adapted but should be the focus of your teaching, as this helps pupils understand why they are doing an activity. These, like the activities, can be rewritten to suit your objectives. Activities are not presented in a particular order, so you should consider borrowing and adapting ideas from one section to another and from one key stage to another. Some include a little repetition so ensure that you actively use and adapt the most useful ones for your learners.

In these sections, boxes are inserted that refer to what Driver (1983) and we prefer to call 'alternative understandings'. However, we have adopted the language used more often in school and so these are entitled 'common misconceptions'. Each misconception is stated in speech marks, as if a pupil has stated it. This draws attention to the fact that it may not be correct. After a brief explanation, we have usually suggested an activity or discussion point to help challenge the misconception. In the margin of the pages you will find boxes to indicate that the text includes a link to another part of science, an issue about safety (ASE, 2010) or options that use computing or information and communication technology, including the internet. Science education presents many opportunities for the learning of literacy and numeracy; a selection is indicated in the margin along with references to other subjects. Science can enhance learning in these subjects and learning in science can itself be enhanced if pupils are more literate and numerate.

At the end of each chapter you will find a short summary of content and a list of common misconceptions. These could be used within a science development diary (Appendix 3) which you might use to review your learning. Can you see ways to challenge these misconceptions? Are they ones you once held? You might reveal other areas of uncertainty by utilising the short multi-choice self-test questions at the end of the chapter. These short self-tests are representative not comprehensive and so are only indicators of your learning.

Rationale

Spiritual

The natural world is a wonderful place. Almost all of us have stared into a flower or at the night sky with awe and wonder. As far as we know, we are the first living creatures to have sought to explain the universe and where we fit into it. Science provides one of the most effective tools for doing so.

This book is founded on the need for all learners to engage with their science learning. Science can be daunting for teacher and pupils. The approach advocated here is to be honest about the challenges and the rewards of learning science. Primary science teaching can utilise learners' interest in the world, encourage questions in the classroom and an active engagement with each person's understanding and skill in science. Primary science provides many opportunities for the use of key numeracy and literacy skills, for example presenting the results of an investigation to an audience.

Numeracy and literacy

It is worth reminding ourselves that as primary teachers our concern is science education and, as part of that, science itself. By this we mean that while in school we and our pupils engage in scientific behaviour; however, the reason we do this is not for science enquiry or discovery alone, but also so that our pupils will learn about science and the world. What you as a teacher understand and know about science and science education is crucial to this learning. An important part of the special knowledge you require as a teacher is pedagogical knowledge. Alexander (2004) summarises pedagogy as the 'act and discourse of teaching'. This book will assist you with examples of some of the best ways to teach science. It is our hope that by reflecting on and thinking about your learning and the learning of your pupils, you will engage in a personal discourse about the ways you teach science most effectively. During your training and afterwards, your growing confidence should allow you to gain even more as a teacher through, for example, discussion with others.

Part of this knowledge of science is the nature of science. Take a look at Table 1.1 and consider the ways in which you view science and how as a teacher you

Table 1.1 Views of science?

Science is not:	Science is:
dull	interesting
closed	expanding, creative
exclusive	inclusive
magic	real
always straightforward	sometimes complex
always as it seems	sometimes counter-intuitive
able to solve all problems	a way we can tackle problems
able to answer all questions	a powerful way to seek answers
only for one group of people	for all

convey science. Unfortunately, society sometimes encourages a stereotypical or negative view of science (Driver, 1983). As a primary teacher you are in a powerful position to affect the long-term view that pupils take of science. Can you see ways to present a positive view of science to your pupils? Although this book will assist you, it is best to be explicit with pupils about the nature of science from the start.

Guiding principles

As well as knowing what you understand about science, as a teacher you also need to be clear about what your weaker areas are and the ways that you might take that learning forward. This approach to learning is known as 'metacognitive' learning, which can be defined as thinking about thinking (Flavell *et al.*, 1977). Thus a metacognitive learner is self-aware, reflective, and proactive about what they know and understand and how they learn. Key indicators of effective adult learners are that they are self-motivated and self-directed. We hope that you will take on these ideas about your own learning and accept that all sources, from internet simulations to concept maps, audits and tests, are useful tools for you as a learner. This book provides many pedagogical ideas (ideas relating to teaching children). We accept that adults and pupils learn in similar but not necessarily identical ways. For example, you are likely to be more experienced at reading diagrams than an average 8-year-old and may therefore gain more from studying them. Alternatively, you may know that you find diagrams less helpful and therefore know that you must seek other sources to learn from effectively. You might also recognise that you need to strengthen your capacity to deal with diagrams.

Learning is different for all learners. In science, each learner starts from where they are, thus your first act as a teacher should always be to find out or elicit what the pupils already know and can do. Reference to assessment records and pupils' science books is essential, as is helping pupils to review their own learning to date. This elicitation can be the first stage in what is referred to as the 'constructivist approach', which is based on the idea that pupils construct their own learning. Social constructivists see this as occurring alongside others, including other pupils and adults, in social settings such as classrooms (Vygostky, 1988). After initial orientation of the learner with the aspect of science, and elicitation, the teacher is advised to provide learning experiences that will challenge any misconceptions held and seek to move pupils towards the scientifically accepted view. These ideas have much to offer teachers and to this we add the important notion of pupil engagement. To utilise powerful ideas such as constructivism, the pupils must be engaged in their science and their learning. You, as their teacher, require a growing repertoire of ideas to gain and maintain the attention and involvement of pupils.

Vygotsky's (1988) view was that learners require a 'knowledgeable other' to guide them through ideas and experiences so that they have the best opportunity to learn. This occurred, he suggested, in a 'zone of proximal development', where learners are guided and supported to a point where that guidance is no longer required. These ideas are linked to those of pupil autonomy, which recognise the need for pupils to become more autonomous or 'self-governing' (Baud, 1987). As teacher you are the 'knowledgeable other'. Individual pupils require varying amounts of support, which can include, for example, the teacher guiding with questions or modelling science language and behaviour.

You might extend metacognitive approaches to your knowledge of teaching, in this case of teaching science. What is your present knowledge and understanding of teaching science? What have you learned about teaching science for learning? What have you learned from experienced practitioners? In which circumstances do you learn best about teaching science? How do you make best use of your experiences?

As teachers we should be interested in the teaching methods that are the most effective. John Hattie (2009), Geoff Petty (2009) and others have presented evidence from meta-analysis of research studies from around the world which indicate the effectiveness of teaching and other methods adopted by schools. The approach is referred to as 'evidence-based teaching'. This provides the strongest scientific evidence base for us as teachers and so we would recommend these works which might aid you in developing your own professional agenda.

The teaching ideas provided in each chapter of this book aim to increase your repertoire of options for teaching for learning. These have the potential to turn satisfactory lessons into good or very good lessons. By very good in this context we mean lessons in which all pupils learn well. The book does not, however, provide a complete scheme of work. Rather, it provides high-quality guidance. This guidance includes the following principles, which might underpin your teaching for learning in science:

- finding out (eliciting) what children already understand, know, and can do;
- making lessons memorable;
- including elements to capture and hold pupils' attention;
- making science fun by including both enjoyment and challenge;
- ensuring learning in science is based on pupil interaction;
- making science questions a key focus;
- ensuring teacher and pupils pose and seek to answer 'why' questions;
- providing a considerable emphasis on language (including scientific) and communication;
- ensuring a high level of engagement with science and purposeful practical science activity;
- ensuring investigations are increasingly pupil-led – that is, initiated and planned by pupils;
- involving pupils in self-review, assessment, and reflection about their learning in science.

If, as a teacher, you can gain the full attention of an individual, they can learn from your teaching. Without their attention, you will simply be background noise. The ideas provided in this book have been tried and tested over many years by the authors. What works for one learner will almost certainly not work for all learners. This links to a problem that all science teachers experience, that we often ask pupils to generalise from an instance (McGuigan and Schilling, 1997). That is, we provide an experience, say thermal insulation of warm beakers with different materials, and hope pupils will learn from that experience – that is, to be able to talk about and ideally explain what is happening and apply this learning to other examples of thermal insulation. For many learners, that one instance is insufficient to fully cement the learning. Thus, you should consider options to conduct or at least illustrate and discuss other instances of, in this case, thermal insulation. One simple approach that could provide other instances is to utilise your pupils' senses (sight, sound, touch, taste, and smell). Most science lessons can utilise the first three safely. If you consider the use of sight, sound, and touch when teaching difficult ideas, you can have some confidence that at least one will work for a proportion of children and another with another group in the class. Ensure pupils have time to observe the phenomenon, to see posters or simulations, to talk about and hear different ideas and views, and handle the materials. A practical investigation by the pupils might offer all of these opportunities for learning.

It is also worth considering that different teachers might teach equally success-fully in different ways. Thus you may find that teaching methods that a colleague finds less successful are an overwhelming success for your pupils' learning. Remember that classes vary considerably. You should therefore see your pupils as the most important variable when considering what approach to take, but also be mindful of other varia-bles, including: the particular science topic; your personal strengths, including your science and pedagogic knowledge and understanding; the need to stress investigations in science; the resources and the time available.

When thinking about how to approach a science lesson, consider the following:

- How and when will I express the learning objective(s)?
- What teaching methods, including pupil activities, should I employ?
- How will I introduce and encourage the pupils to use the science language?
- Will these lessons engage pupils?
- How can I involve pupils more?
- How will pupils be able to develop investigative skills?
- How will pupils further their understanding of their own learning in science?
- To what extent do these pupils need to see, do or hear things?
- How can I play to the strengths of my resources and my skills?

For pupils to feel part of their own learning in science, you might take complemen-tary approaches. First, give them increased autonomy in science investigations and, second, share with them ideas such as those of constructivism and metacognition. These approaches support 'thinking about thinking', which offers a powerful way to make science learning more personal. This approach fits very well with important emphases in primary education, including personalisation of learning and Assessment for Learning (AfL) (DCSF, 2008).

For more information on metacognition, visit:
http://www.gse.buffalo.edu/fas/shuell/cep564/Metacog.htm

We will refer throughout to learning tools such as internet-based and other science simulations, which we believe should complement learning but never take the place of hands-on experience of, say, magnets. Simulations can assist learners and their teachers by representing ideas, utilising language, and reviewing, introducing and challenging ideas, but they cannot replace essential personal experience of, for example, the strength of different magnets.

Language/literacy and science

It is a basic tenet of primary education that language is central. Language is also very important in science and science education. Some science ideas and concepts can be expressed mathematically, but to a far greater extent the medium of learning science in classrooms is language. Therefore, as much emphasis as possible should be placed on pupils engaging with and using appropriate language in their science education (Yore *et al.*, 2003). Words are often used very precisely in science, so point out to pupils that they will come across words such as 'force' that are used in all sorts of ways, such as air force, storm force, and Parcel Force, but in science its meaning is special, focused, and limited to pushes and pulls.

Speaking and listening are major vehicles for learning in science, as are the different forms of writing and drawing. Pupils' learning will benefit when given very regular opportunities to talk and discuss as well as to write about their science. The idea of do, talk, and record applies well here – that is, pupils doing things, talking about them and what they mean, and then recording what has occurred and their thoughts. Written science can occur on classroom posters, books, text, diagrams, interactive whiteboards, internet sites, blogs, and resources published by others as well as those written by pupils. The development of literacy in science presents a wealth of opportunities for pupils to strengthen language and language skills in a very meaningful context.

The importance of questions

There is a possibly apocryphal story of an apple falling on Isaac Newton's head, which was the trigger for him to think about why things fall to Earth. Whether or not an apple ever fell on Newton's head, he was very interested in falling objects as an example of objects moving in relation to one another (in this case, the apple and the Earth). His key word was, of course, 'why'? Armed with a question that can be investigated, the scientist has made the first, and perhaps the most essential, step towards the answer.

Questions are at the heart of science and of science education. The teacher and pupils should together be asking questions and seeking answers. Your understanding of the different questions that can be asked by pupils and teachers and the ways these can be handled will allow you to utilise questions rather than fear them.

As a teacher, you should develop the following skills yourself so that you can best enable pupil learning of science. Questioning skills for teachers include:

- using questions in all aspects of science (for example, focusing attention, establishing links, making things explicit; utilising predictions, seeking explanations and motivating);
- learning to pose questions about the world;
- learning to pose questions that can be investigated scientifically;
- understanding that pupils often misunderstand our questions;
- using the power of questions in your science teaching, including Elstgeet's (1985):
  - open and closed questions,
  - productive questions,
  - attention-focusing questions,
  - measuring and counting questions,
  - comparison questions,
  - action questions,
  - problem-posing questions,
  - children's how and why questions.

Pupils' questions often provide a potential starting point in science, although you will often have to help pupils form questions: 'As we can't all agree which material will be the strongest, could we ask a question that would help us to find the answer?' The questions posed by pupils at this point often need reworking, for example they might ask, 'Which material is best?' Part of our science teaching is to ensure that pupils learn to pose questions that can be investigated. Thus, such a pupil question might need to be adjusted. 'What do we mean by "best"?' You might then consider if you can employ any useful 'w' words, such as 'which', 'when', 'where' or 'why', as these can often improve a science question. The most challenging science questions often begin with the words 'why' or 'how'.

You can further improve your teaching by ensuring that alongside other questions you pose 'why' questions; for example, 'You predicted that the large parachute would fall the slowest and that is what happened. Why did that happen?' This question challenges everyone in the classroom to move towards an explanation. The pupils' attempts to explain may require rewording so that they become even more useful.

Pupil #1: 'It's because of air.'
Teacher: 'But what is the air doing?'
Pupil #2: 'There's more air hitting it.' [pupil uses hand to demonstrate]
Teacher: 'That's right. The bigger parachute canopy hits or catches more air. So there is more . . .?'
Pupil #2: 'There is more air resistance?'
Teacher: 'You're right, the bigger canopy creates more air resistance.'

Explaining what pupils observe is perhaps the hardest part of science for them. They may appear to know the background science and the observation they have made may appear to you to be clearly linked and obvious. However, you may be dismayed when pupils struggle to link the science to what they have seen. This is perhaps another example of the difficulty of generalising from an instance. Annual reviews published in England (QCA, 2004, accessed at: http://www.naa.org.uk/naa_19199.aspx), based on analysis of pupils' responses to the English national Standard Assessment Tests (SATs), repeatedly illustrate the difficulty. A survey entitled 'Maintaining Curiosity' (Ofsted, 2013) concluded that in the best schools visited, teachers ensured that learners understood the big ideas in science. They made sure that learners 'mastered the investigative and practical skills that underpin the development of scientific knowledge and could develop for themselves the relevance and usefulness of those ideas'.

Dealing with pupils' questions

One common area of anxiety for non-specialist primary teachers is what they anticipate will be difficult science questions from pupils. Teachers can understandably be concerned first about whether they will know the answer and only second with the options for responding. We hope that as you gain confidence in your subject knowledge and understanding and in your pedagogical skills, you will become more concerned about the options you have for responding rather than about whether or not you know the answer. You should always show that you are pleased that the question has been asked, perhaps by pausing and offering praise while thinking about the options for your response. You might like to use the question to:

- find out more about what the pupils know – 'What do you think? Do any of us have any ideas?' Explore the topic – 'Have you seen that happen? Is this similar to anything else you have seen?'

- find out more about their understanding – 'Can you tell me why you ask that? Do you think there is an answer?'

- stimulate interest – use the pupils' own questions to fire their enthusiasm for science: 'What a great question, how could we find out?' 'Could we investigate this ourselves?' 'Could a book help us?'

- scaffold learning – for example, assist pupils in making links – 'Have you seen this before? What did we learn about this last term/yesterday?'

Sheila Jelly (1985) suggested a useful approach that included, among other ideas, an analysis of the question and a consideration of whether the question can be turned to a practical activity. With all age ranges it is helpful for the teacher to encourage questions, such as setting up an 'our questions' poster on the classroom wall. These questions do not have to be answered at once. Pupils can try themselves to find out the answers to the questions on the wall by doing their own research. Try a 'Wiki' poster headed by the pupil's question and encourage others to assist with explanations or suggestions, perhaps on Post-it® notes (you will need to monitor this for misconceptions). Another idea is to do this in the format of a computer-based 'blog'.

One word of caution, although this will not occur very often, if a pupil asks a 'why' question and responds to your answer with another 'why' question, you will soon find yourself at PhD-level science. For example, you respond to a simple question about an object falling with 'it falls because of gravity pulling it towards the centre of the Earth'. If the pupil then comes back with another question, for example 'Why does gravity do that?', you are now approaching the limits of current scientific theory, as there is no complete accepted explanation of what gravity actually is and how it works. At this level, most specialist science educators would be unable to give a complete answer. Accept this and focus on praising the question poser, being honest and taking things forward positively; for example, 'We can learn a great deal in the class about the effect of the force of gravity on different objects'.

Teacher confidence

We hope this book will have a dramatically positive effect on your confidence to teach science. It is intended to encourage you to engage with two essential ingredients for increased confidence to teach: (1) your own knowledge and understanding of science and (2) your repertoire of ideas for teaching science. Just as we advocate gaining and holding pupils' interest, it is necessary for you to become actively engaged in your own learning in science and hopefully very much engaged with ideas in science.

Your repertoire of teaching methods includes much of what Lee Schulman (1987) called 'pedagogical content knowledge'. This knowledge of the most effective ways to teach a topic was to him the essential knowledge of a teacher. For example, pupils' misconceptions or alternative ideas can mistakenly be seen as bad, as ideas to be purged as quickly as possible. A more realistic view is that they are inevitable, to be expected, and to be recognised and challenged. Misconceptions are themselves a good example of Schulman's pedagogical content knowledge. The recognition and anticipation of common difficulties, including errors and misconceptions, will allow you to strengthen teaching and learning (Table 1.2).

As a teacher of primary science you will 'collect' common errors and misconceptions in science, remembering from term to term and year to year those aspects of a topic that caused difficulties. Teachers encounter these misconceptions informally when chatting to colleagues, 'discovering' them with pupils in the classroom, spotting them in test results, being taught about them on courses or when reading research. Recently in a science lesson one pupil was observed to say, 'I think that the plant was unhealthy because I think it was drowned in the darkness'. While most such statements are incorrect, they often contain some truth. This pupil clearly has a sense of continued darkness being bad for the plant. Her teacher might ask her to explain what she means, and then challenge the pupil's statement by asking her about darkness and establishing that it is the absence of light and that perhaps this can help us to explain the plant's condition.

Knowledge of common errors and misconceptions in science will give you confidence as you anticipate and, even better, plan to deal with them and learn to use them in lessons to promote learning. For example, when preparing for lessons about dissolving, it will help to know that many learners confuse dissolving and melting (see Chapter 8 on materials). Share the idea of misconceptions and errors with pupils: 'Some people find this easy, some find it puzzling, some think . . .'.

Table 1.2 Examples of common errors or misconceptions

Aspect of science	Difficulty, error or misconception	Possible approach
Rocks and soils	Soil is just dirt	Question is posed – 'What is soil made from?' Pupils examine soil samples with magnifier to observe mineral content, organic content, and living content
Earth in space	Learner states incorrectly that the Sun orbits the Earth	Observation of shadows moving demonstrates the apparent movement of the Sun across the sky but this alone is not evidence of the Earth orbiting the Sun. Models can be used comprising a globe and a ball as the Sun. This, alongside posters and web-based simulations, can illustrate the accepted scientific view of the relative movement of the Sun and the Earth
Scientific investigation	Learner fails to see the need to repeat an experiment	The experiment is likened to a test to determine which of two footballers is better at scoring from penalties. If we give each of them one attempt, will the result be reliable? Should we give them 3 attempts to score or 10 or 100? Which would be the most reliable result?

Another very powerful influence on your confidence will be your enthusiasm and enjoyment of teaching science. Be aware of those aspects of science and science education which interest you and you enjoy, and share these with pupils. Importantly, make sure that you sound positive about all of science.

The importance of practical work

It is worth saying here that not all authors and researchers agree exactly about what we mean by practical work and studies have tended to focus on secondary age pupils and on the amount of practical work and not its quality. Several research studies of secondary education are quite negative about the quality of practical work undertaken. Research into secondary teachers' understanding of practical work has identified teacher knowledge as a limiting factor (Pekmez *et al.*, 2005).

We understand practical work to include engagement in which pupils manipulate materials and experience phenomena in science lessons. Smith and Peacock (1995) recognise four sub-categories of practical science activity: learning a practical skill; exploring; observation of a demonstration; and investigation. Although not necessarily required as part of a practical activity, we feel that more often than not in primary classrooms practical work will involve working with others.

In recognising practical activity, early writers discussed aspects of primary education (Piaget, 1973; Rousseau, 1979) as fundamental to learning. However, the need for, or value of, practical work in science has been questioned by some like Gott and Duggan (1995) and Hodson (1998), who, for example, question the time devoted to practical work, note the proportion of time pupils have been observed off-task during practical work, and the confusion that they have observed in classrooms with the teacher pursuing an educational objective and pupils becoming sidetracked or simply misunderstanding the purpose of the work. Researchers and writers recognise potential positive outcomes of practical work, including the opportunity to aid science learning, as a context for literacy (Gipps *et al.*, 2000) and numeracy learning in action, to teach and assess skills, and to practise and develop skills in Science 1. If for no other reason than there is limited time in primary schools for science, primary educationalists should be clear about exactly what are the benefits and drawbacks of practical work. There are clearly aspects of science that cannot be taught practically, such as aspects of space science and the working of the organs of the human body.

Wellington (1998) questioned student teachers about the purpose of practical science in primary classrooms and summarised their responses into three categories:

- cognitive arguments – helping them to learn;
- affective arguments – motivating and exciting;
- skills arguments – developing scientific and other transferable skills.

Wellington considered that these are reasonable arguments but, like other authors, does not accept them at face value. Pupils and teachers when asked to justify practical work often respond in terms of motivation of pupils; unfortunately, there is no research evidence to link pupils' interest and motivation in science with the amount of practical work completed (Harlen, 1999). Harlen usefully concludes that practical work is a 'means to various ends and not an end in itself'.

We might conclude that practical activity is not of itself a good thing, rather it is the communication and reflection before, during, and after that is educational: 'we learn not by simply carrying out practical work but by reflecting on the experience it yields in the light of previous experience' (Peacock, 1998). For most researchers, it is the combination of practical work and pupil talk that leads to learning (Mercer, 1995). Barnes (1976) pointed to clear links he perceived between pupil talk and pupil thinking: 'The more a learner controls his own language strategies and the more he is enabled to talk aloud, the more he can take responsibility for forming explanatory hypotheses and evaluating them.'

Assessment, self-assessment, and feedback

More examples of how to carry out assessment are given in Chapter 3. Here it is useful to ask why must schoolteachers assess pupils' learning in science? The answer is because they must be able to inform themselves, the pupil, the school, and others of pupils' achievements. Our focus here is on the teacher and the learner. The teacher needs to know about pupils' achievements to plan future lessons and inform others; pupils should be engaged with their own learning so that they want feedback on what they have learned and how they can learn more. Thus pupils benefit from teacher assessment and their own personal self-assessment, supporting their thinking about thinking or knowing about knowing (metacognition). Teachers' assessment of pupils and pupils' self-assessment are most effective when they work alongside one another. The two will hopefully overlap with the clearest expression of this being teacher feedback to pupils during and after lessons.

Perhaps the single most powerful tool in lessons is the clear expression of sharp learning objectives. These can be expressed and utilised in different ways, including learning outcomes, perhaps in the form of 'We are learning to . . .', or success criteria (Table 1.3), framed perhaps as 'What I am looking for . . .'. Such clarity assists your assessment of pupils' achievement in science and pupils' self- and peer assessment. This clarity will have a positive effect on the feedback you give to pupils both orally and written so that you can comment on whether they have achieved the objective and how they might improve.

Elicitation of pupil understanding at the start of a science topic has already been mentioned in this chapter. This is a form of assessment but with a particular purpose – to inform teaching for learning. Teachers use a variety of methods to obtain evidence to make a judgement. In addition to explicit tests and assessment questions, they will observe pupils and their work during lessons followed by review of the pupils' responses. This means that activities designed to progress learning also provide evidence for assessment, including concept cartoons, concept maps, games, DARTs (see example in Table 4.1), POE (three prompts: Predict, Observe, Explain), and so on, most of which are legitimate teaching methods but all of which can reveal something of the learners' achievements. Teaching methods such as these are exemplified throughout this book. They should be recognised for their value in eliciting or revealing pupils' learning so that a pupil or teacher can then assess (i.e. judge) the extent of learning. The assessment is driven by the teacher and utilised by teacher and learner to reflect on and analyse what has been learned, what has been partially learned, and what has not been learned.

Establishing and maintaining interest

Pupils are almost always interested in themselves and the extent to which they are learning. To encourage pupils' interest in science lessons, identify aspects of science or contexts that link to pupils' lives or interests. Most primary-aged pupils are

Table 1.3 Example of a learning objective and success criteria

Learning objective	Success criteria
To name the main external parts of a flowering plant	On a diagram correctly label flower, stem, leaf, and root

enthusiastic about protecting the environment and love animals; they may also be interested in the human body or in sports, and are highly engaged by unusual phenomena. Learn to think how they think. Keep abreast of the news and media, news stories about exploration, the natural world, and so on, which will be of interest to pupils. Establish a notice board in the classroom with newspaper and magazine clippings. Be aware of current crazes among pupils, as simply adding the name or image of a popular superhero or character can often hook their interest. Give otherwise routine activities extra interest by linking to the real world or an occupation of interest to pupils. You could try teaching the science of materials through a forensic approach to, for example, 'the scene of the crime'. The simple strategy of linking the science to the real world at least in the lesson introduction and plenary usually raises interest and adds greatly to a lesson's relevance. For example, 'Now that we know which material causes the most friction, if you wanted non-slippery shoes what would you ask for in the shoe shop?'

Your own apparent interest in the world and science will be highly influential. We therefore suggest that as well as considering your pupils' interests, you are mindful of your own. If a teacher is not highly engaged by the science or by how it is being taught, there is much less chance of the pupils being interested.

Make science lessons interesting with a new material, a new angle or new teaching methods. Simply moving furniture, working in different groupings, moving to a different room or outside can have a big effect. Plan elements to capture and hold pupils' attention, and consider at least one significant stimulus per topic: a visit, a visitor to school, a challenge, a competition, a special day. The simple strategy of getting every child to become involved at the front of the class at some point means they expect to be involved and enjoy being, and seeing classmates being, involved. Make science fun by including both enjoyment and challenge. Game-like activities can make some parts of science enjoyable, and you may remember your own sense of delight when you mastered a tricky idea. Make sure you challenge pupils with harder concepts in science. Perhaps inspire them with some of the really big ideas in science, such as the size of space. Visit, for example, http://www.wimp.com/bluedot/ to find out about Carl Sagan's famous Pale Blue Dot photograph.

Challenge yourself by saying that your lessons will be memorable; include features and elements that will stay with a pupil for years. Examples in this book, including edible rocks (Chapter 9), the dance/drama simulation of the movement of the Earth and Moon (Chapter 11), and the role-play of a food chain (Chapter 7), will be just that. Consider the development of the pupils' enthusiasm for science as a long-term target in your teaching. We can all imagine a situation where pupils score very well on tests but have been turned off the subject for life. This, if it occurs, is a travesty. Pupils who enjoy a topic learn more about that topic. It ought to be possible to steer a more productive path, resulting in pupils achieving as well as they can and maintaining interest in, or better, enthusiasm for, or even better love of, the subject and learning.

Conclusion

As a primary teacher you are a primary science teacher. Your attitude, growing understanding and knowledge of science, and how to teach it, are very powerful factors in generating interest, and even love, of science learning. This book will provide an opportunity to think about what you know about science and aspects of science education. By engaging with your own learning in science, you will undergo a process that your pupils will need to experience if they are to learn and become more aware of their own learning and achievement. Make it your aim that pupils will learn as much as possible and that at the end of term they will be looking forward to more.

2

Working scientifically

The language surrounding practical science in primary school can be a little imprecise, with teachers sometimes using the words 'investigation', 'enquiry' and 'practical' interchangeably to describe differing approaches.

The term 'practical' in science is very broad and can refer to almost anything where some kind of scientific equipment or enquiry skill is used in a primary classroom. Teachers are often in agreement that learners benefit from practical work, but as this refers to anything from a teacher demonstration of a kettle boiling to a nature walk, it is a vague term at best. For us, working scientifically (DfE, 2013a) is about being increasingly scientific, by working as a scientist might. For this to happen teachers need to plan experiences which will allow pupils to develop science skills alongside knowledge and understanding.

What does the National Curriculum for England require?

Teachers are expected to enable learning about working scientifically (DfE, 2013a) through all aspects of science, by teaching skills and involving learners in different forms of investigations. Working scientifically suggests that pupils act as scientists, building up a repertoire of skills and increasing their knowledge of how actual scientists work. To avoid merely teaching 'scientific content', you might consider in each lesson having two objectives, one for science knowledge and understanding and one for working scientifically. The statutory guidance for science (DfE, 2013a) includes the following:

Working scientifically

Key Stage 1

During years 1 and 2, pupils should be taught to use the following practical scientific methods, processes and skills through the teaching of the programme of study content:

- asking simple questions and recognising that they can be answered in different ways

- observing closely, using simple equipment
- performing simple tests
- identifying and classifying
- using their observations and ideas to suggest answers to questions
- gathering and recording data to help in answering questions.

(DFE, 2013a)

Lower Key Stage 2

During years 3 and 4, pupils should be taught to use the following practical scientific methods, processes and skills through the teaching of the programme of study content:

- asking relevant questions and using different types of scientific enquiries to answer them
- setting up simple practical enquiries, comparative and fair tests
- making systematic and careful observations and, where appropriate, taking accurate measurements using standard units, using a range of equipment, including thermometers and data loggers
- gathering, recording, classifying and presenting data in a variety of ways to help in answering questions
- recording findings using simple scientific language, drawings, labelled diagrams, keys, bar charts, and tables
- reporting on findings from enquiries, including oral and written explanations, displays or presentations of results and conclusions
- using results to draw simple conclusions, make predictions for new values, suggest improvements and raise further questions
- identifying differences, similarities or changes related to simple scientific ideas and processes
- using straightforward scientific evidence to answer questions or to support their findings.

(DFE, 2013a)

Upper Key Stage 2

During years 5 and 6, pupils should be taught to use the following practical scientific methods, processes and skills through the teaching of the programme of study content:

- planning different types of scientific enquiries to answer questions, including recognising and controlling variables where necessary
- taking measurements, using a range of scientific equipment, with increasing accuracy and precision, taking repeat readings when appropriate
- recording data and results of increasing complexity using scientific diagrams and labels, classification keys, tables, scatter graphs, bar and line graphs
- using test results to make predictions to set up further comparative and fair tests

- reporting and presenting findings from enquiries, including conclusions, causal relationships and explanations of and degree of trust in results, in oral and written forms such as displays and other presentations
- identifying scientific evidence that has been used to support or refute ideas or arguments.

(DFE, 2013a)

The following sections will give you ideas to make this programme of study a reality for all your learners.

Science enquiry skills

'Practical science' often involves the introduction or practice of scientific enquiry skills, which are valuable activities, but are not full blown 'scientific investigations'. Examples of this would include: a nature walk to record plant species in the school grounds; observing and drawing a range of seeds; sorting materials into pairs of opposites (hard versus soft, strong versus weak, rough versus smooth). These all involve a range of important enquiry skills, so let us look at the skills one at a time.

Classifying by comparing similarities and differences

In the above mentioned sorting activity, pupils begin to see how materials can differ and so can be selected for various different uses. For example, when stuffing a cushion the softest materials would be preferable to the harder materials. They can also look at similarities, for example, wood and plastic can both be used to make cooking spoons because they are smooth and don't conduct heat that well. Wood and metal can both be used for school climbing frames because they are both hard and strong. By getting pupils to examine different materials and focus on their properties, we help them to organise their own ideas into a more coherent scientific framework. Sorting hoops can be used for organising pairs of opposite properties, which emphasises differences, for example, flexible versus rigid, or opaque versus transparent. They can also be used to sort for similarities, for example three sorting hoops for solid, liquid and gas and a range of substances to classify (e.g. sand, washing up liquid, wood, silly putty, glycerine, bottle labelled 'air').

These relatively straightforward cases are part of the suite of evidence-based teaching techniques, reviewed by Robert Marzano (Marzano *et al.*, 2003) as a very effective teaching tool. Sometimes things don't fit into a discrete category and so the pupils could place such an item halfway between two sorting hoops. In the solid, liquid and gases sorting exercise a fizzy drink could be placed between liquid and gas, because it consists of both.

Observation

Observation is the ability of a learner to look carefully at a scene or object in front of them. Much can be revealed if time is taken to give more than just a cursory glance. On a nature walk it can take time and practice to seek out all the plant species that are around. For example, some plants might be hidden under the shade of others and some might be very small. Seeds provide another context for the development of observation skills. If pupils examine seeds closely, perhaps with a magnifying glass, they will see all sorts of features they may have overlooked at first and can make a note of these.

Observational drawing allows the pupils to appreciate subtle features, as only by looking really closely can they capture all the aspects of what is in front of them. For example, perhaps a seed is not wholly one colour, perhaps it is not perfectly round, or it may have a rough or wrinkled surface, or even tiny hairs. Such features can give a valuable clue as to which plant it has come from and perhaps adaptations it has to help it survive and grow. Larger seeds have more food energy stored inside and can grow quicker but could be a tasty meal for an animal. Smaller, darker seeds might easily be overlooked and so can grow undisturbed. Drawing, shading and colouring force the pupils to pay very close attention to all these features.

In experiments when something is changed we know to look for the effect of that change. We principally observe using our eyes, but we can also use our sense of hearing, smell and touch to detect changes. The observation of the effect can either be qualitative (a bulb is brighter or dimmer) or quantitative (a measurable numbered change, e.g. 10 cm long, a temperature of 35°C, or a sound level of 80 decibels).

Qualitative effects are measured using our senses alone. So a change in a bulb could be recorded as *bright, brighter, brightest* or *dim, dimmer, dimmest*. A change in sound could be classed as *loud, louder, loudest* or *quiet, quieter, quietest*. A change in temperature can be classified as *cool* to *warm*. Estimates of distance or height can be made as *nearest* to *furthest* and *shortest* to *tallest*. Younger pupils will often observe qualitative changes such as those outlined above, but they do have their value with older pupils too.

Quantitative effects are measured using a range of simple instruments. As pupils get older, through practice their ability develops to be able to measure accurately and use scientific units correctly. The instruments need not be complicated: thermometers to measure outdoor temperature or how hot indoor liquids are, rulers to measure plant growth or how far a toy car has travelled along a carpet. More complex measuring devices such as data loggers to measure light, and sound meters to measure sound volume require more direct teaching of how to use them, and extended pupil practice in using them correctly.

Comparative Tests

We might do a simple comparative test based on the observation of an event. For example, we may ask "If I drop this tennis ball, what will happen?" The pupils make the prediction "It will bounce back up." We drop the ball and make the observation, "It bounced high". Then we get a golf ball and say "Which will bounce the highest, the tennis ball or the golf ball?" This is a comparative test where the children can directly compare their observations of how high each ball bounces. Further comparisons can be made, for example using other balls such as a football and a basketball. We could then easily rank the balls in order of height of bounce, from smallest bounce to largest bounce. In doing so, we would have answered the question as to which ball bounces the highest.

These comparative tests, together with the predictions we make, are useful but lack any sophistication. Perhaps their greatest value for primary educators is that they are an easy entry step into science for young children, but importantly they also allow us to discuss 'unfairness' in a test. In the above example we are not really comparing 'like with like'. In this case, what makes a ball bounce highest? Is it the material the ball is made of, the size of the ball or whether it is solid throughout or has air inside it? This lack of control of the different variables means that we cannot explain why a particular ball has the highest bounce out of all those compared. As teachers, we can ask learners to challenge the test and suggest ways to make it fair. In Key Stage 1 this is often best done initially as a shared activity between teacher and children.

Recording data

Pupils may not know the name of each species they see on a nature walk, but they could record them by sketching them, photographing them or making up a suitable descriptive name, for example, 'spiky leaf plant'. They may simply count the number of different species present when comparing a playing field to a flowerbed. A higher number of different plant species means a habitat has a greater biodiversity of plants and animals, and so this is a very simple but effective technique. This skill of recording the variety of species is invaluable in modern-day nature conservation and ecology.

Gathering data in a meaningful way helps pupils to understand it. For example, when measuring the temperature of warm water cooling, they may take the temperature every two minutes and enter the figure into a table. The figures in the table would show a pattern of decreasing value, which would clearly help the pupils explain what has happened to the water since the start of the experiment. By plotting the temperature data against time in a graph, a pattern would emerge. If they then conducted an experiment where they measured the temperature of water with ice cubes floating in it, and entered the data into a table and then used it to plot a graph, this again would help them to see patterns emerge. In both cases, the warm and the chilled water will reach room temperature if left long enough.

Evaluating evidence

Pupils will learn to evaluate how accurate data from their experiments is. They learn to take a measurement or a reading more than once if necessary. To evaluate the accuracy of a secondary source, such as a book or television programme, can be tricky for children and adults alike. Pupils often believe that anything written in a book must be true. Likewise anything seen on television or the internet is similarly imbued with truth by them. In getting them to evaluate claims, we can ask pupils to look at the source of the claim. If they are watching a television programme, they can look at the end to see who made it. A trusted broadcaster like the BBC seeks to produce professional programmes, and employs experts to check any facts used. Contrast this with something on YouTube where anyone can put up content, and make any claim. Likewise advertisers often use scientific sounding terms or ideas, which are deliberately misleading. (For example, television advertisements for cosmetic and hair products use scientific sounding terms that don't really mean anything.) Even school library books can make dubious claims, you might contrast the *Guinness Book of Records* with Ripley's *Believe it or Not*.

Teacher demonstration of science skills

Sometimes the teacher will carry out a practical science demonstration in front of the whole class. This has both benefits and drawbacks. Let's look at the benefits first. Sometimes it is necessary for the teacher to do a demonstration because it is not safe for the class to do it. Two instances might be boiling water in a kettle, and watching a large candle burn.

Boiling water is an obvious hazard because there is the chance of scalding, but if a teacher does it with the class observing at a safe distance, then useful things can be shown. Using questioning the teacher can draw out the class knowledge, helping make sense of their observations and building new concepts on top of existing ones. If a kettle is used with a clear side panel, then the pupils could be asked about the effects they are observing: 'Why are bubbles forming in the water?' 'What can we see coming out of the top of the kettle?' 'What can we hear as the water comes to the boil?' They can be asked questions which clarify concepts: 'What happens to the steam when it goes into the air?' 'Why are the windows going "misty" on the inside when it's cold outside?'

With the candle demonstration the teacher poses the following questions when the candle is lit – 'What colour is the flame?' 'Can we smell anything?' – and to clarify concepts: 'What happens to the melted wax when I blow the candle out?' 'What happens to the smoke?'

A further demonstration could be making toast with the teacher asking them to observe the effects – 'What is causing the smell?' – and to clarify concepts – 'Is making toast a reversible change, if we scrape off the toasted part?'

The benefits of such simple, but vivid examples are very useful for eliciting information from the pupils. They have in front of them real, concrete phenomena that can lead to more questions and discussion. We may assume that everyone has seen a kettle boil, or a candle burn, or toast being made, but many pupils have not really watched these things closely, or connected what they are seeing to the scientific concepts they are learning about. These demonstrations give them an opportunity to organise their scientific knowledge in their own minds, through 'concrete' examples.

The drawback of overusing teacher demonstrations is that it deprives the pupils of a chance to have a go and engage with doing experiments themselves. Many pupils enjoy the experience of working like scientists, and with a full investigation it allows them to appreciate the joy and the difficulties of real world science.

For example, when teaching about seeds and growth, a teacher may be tempted to merely plant a seed in a pot on the window ledge and nominate a pupil to water it each day. This would be a teacher demonstration, as described above, but it is really a missed opportunity for a full scientific investigation that could be carried out by the pupils. Planting seeds is fun, relatively simple to do and an enormously rewarding practical activity. A good investigation could be carried out to see if bigger seeds produce bigger seedlings, or the effects of over-watering or under-watering on seeds.

After reading the above descriptions of experiments, we may ask 'why is a teacher demonstration not a full investigation?' To turn the practical activity 'growing seeds' into a full investigation the following steps need to be taken. The investigation needs to be posed in terms of a question, for example, 'Do larger seeds grow into larger seedlings?' The pupils should make a prediction as an answer to this question, before carrying out the experiment. Next, they need to set up a fair test. This is done by keeping all the variables the same (same amount of water, compost, place in the class-room) except the variable they are testing (the size of seed). They then measure the outcome (the height of the seedlings, each day). They put their results into a table or graph that shows these measurements. Finally, they need to answer the question they started with, using their results. With these components in place – a question to be answered, a prediction, a fair test, an observation of the results and finally an answer to their question – we can be sure they have carried out a full investigation. Contrast between how we use the word investigation in the everyday sense, and how we use it in a scientific sense to mean an experiment carried out to answer a question.

Full scientific investigations

There are certain key terms that pupils need to understand as they plan and carry out full scientific investigations. For the youngest pupils, much of the planning might have been supported by the teacher, but by Upper Key Stage 2 a pupil who has carried out investigations throughout school will be quite able to plan their own. However, they need that earlier experience in order to have the skills to do so.

Let's consider the individual components of an investigation, and see how they can be put together. Each investigation should have: a question that can be answered, a prediction, a fair test, some outcome that can be observed and measured, the opportunity to check accuracy, an opportunity to identify patterns in the data, and an answer to the original question posed.

Constructing a question to be answered

For the youngest pupils the teacher may be the one to initiate the investigation with a question, for example 'Are bigger magnets stronger than smaller ones?' or 'Which is the most absorbent paper for cleaning up a spill?' However, there is no reason, once younger pupils get the idea that questions can be tested scientifically, that they shouldn't suggest their own. The problem is that selecting a question that can be answered requires some skill, and like all skills it improves with practice and careful support from a teacher.

Teaching pupils how to ask a scientific question that can be answered with an investigation first requires the pupils to spot one that can be answered scientifically, in the classroom, from one that can't. The teacher may run a session on this, giving the pupils a set of cards they can sort into 'can answer this in a classroom experiment' and 'cannot answer this in a classroom experiment'. So for example, 'Which materials block light the best?', 'How far away can we hear a paper clip hit the floor?', 'Who is the tallest person in Manchester?', 'Does temperature affect plant growth?', 'If a cheetah and a leopard had a race which would win?', 'Which biscuit can you dunk the longest?'. Although the pupils would find both the tallest person and the big cat race interesting, and they both do have scientific answers, they need to be able to recognise what they, as pupil scientists, can and can't do. They can't race a leopard and a cheetah in the classroom but they could answer the question using secondary science sources such as an encyclopedia or science website.

Once they have a question they want answering, it may need to be refined to make it one that is truly testable. For example, 'Which coat enables us to be seen the best at night?' could be changed to 'Which coat is the most reflective?' and then to the truly testable 'Which material reflects the most light?'

A friction investigation, 'Which material generates the most friction?', could be tested as 'Which material slows a moving toy car down most quickly?' An investigation into thermal insulators 'How can I stop this ice pop from melting?' could become 'Which material wrapped around the ice pop keeps it frozen for the longest time?'

Pupils sometimes have unrealistic expectations about which questions they could answer for themselves, and which they could not. To tackle this you could have the pupils, in pairs, write down their own questions. Each question could be written on a postcard. They should try to think of questions that could be answered in class (or in school) and those that can't. Then have each pair team up with a second pair and swap cards. Do they agree with the original authors' ideas about which questions they could answer, and which they could not? Ask the pupils to select their favourite 'possible' and 'not possible' examples as a class. It may be dispiriting that they can't answer some of their more exciting questions, but emphasise that this is the same problem that all scientists have – they have to attract big research money to answer big questions.

As an example, you might ask the pupils to do some internet research about the international science laboratory CERN. Here a huge team of scientists are exploring the mysteries of the smallest particles in the world, some of which have not been seen since the Big Bang. The questions they are asking are 'What are the first ever particles created in the universe?' and 'How did the universe go from being a very hot, tiny thing, to an enormous cold thing with lots of stars and planets in?' This project is something that no country, and certainly no person, could afford to do on their own. With over 3000 people employed there, plus another 10,000 visiting scientists from around the world, it is a massive project.

> http://www.cernland.net/ helps pupils understand the work done at CERN.

There will be some things the pupils may want to try themselves, because they find practical enquiry and investigative work so motivating. An example which won a Royal Society of Chemistry award saw a group of children testing the question, 'Are spiders really afraid of conkers?' In the UK many people leave conkers (the large seed of the horse chestnut tree) around their homes to deter spiders. The children devised various experiments to test the idea. One group of children devised a bridge made of conkers and a bridge of wood. Would the spiders be equally happy to walk over either? Are you interested in the answer? For the results go to http://www.rsc.org/AboutUs/News/PressReleases/2010/Conkerswin.asp, but make your prediction first! In this experiment the children had a variable that they changed (the material the bridge was made of) and observed what happened (i.e. would the spiders prefer one type of bridge to another).

The spider experiment may seem a little ambitious, especially for teachers that have in the past not had much knowledge or enthusiasm for science. But like any skill or any body of knowledge, the more we as teachers practise it, the more confident we get. So learning to ask a question is a real skill. Throughout this book you will find a list of readymade questions, because every one of our investigation boxes (labelled 'Pupil investigation skills') begins with a scientific question that pupils will be able to answer if they do the experiment.

Predictions

Every question can have an answer. In an investigation we always make a prediction first as to what we think the answer will be. This allows us to really focus on the task in hand, looking carefully at our results to see if they are what we predicted. Younger children especially love to get an answer right (even if they don't know why they got it right) but older children will also be engaged by this process. It may be that the pupils in the class as a whole don't agree on their predictions, which would make the experiment even more interesting.

It is important to get the pupils to write down their prediction on their planning sheets, as younger ones often will forget what they predicted and just say they predicted the correct results when they see them!

Fair test

This is the key idea in any investigation in the classroom and in the real-world experiments carried out by scientists. Scientists work in a number of ways, for example, they carry out surveys, make careful observations, identify and classify research using secondary sources and more, but in primary science we see the design and use of fair tests as pivotal for the learner. It is the objectivity presented by the manipulation of variables which marks this method out. Educationally the steps in designing a fair test present a fantastic opportunity for scaffolded learning to an impressive level when learners can design and carry out their own tests.

There are many things that can be varied or changed in an experiment. We call the things we can change 'variables' (or 'factors'). The pupils must understand that they can only change one variable and keep all the other variables constant. This is so they can measure the effect of the variable they have changed. The idea to get across is 'change one thing, try to keep everything else the same'. For example, if measuring how much light we can observe coming through different materials, the thing we are changing is the material selected, for example, printer paper, coloured paper, tracing paper. The things to keep the same are the size and thickness of paper, the light source used, and the distance it is from the materials.

This idea can be introduced in Key Stage 1, but by Lower Key Stage 2 the pupils should become increasingly familiar with the concept and be able to check that their investigation is a fair test.

A common misconception among younger pupils is 'It was a fair test because we all took turns and everyone had a go'. Here the pupil is using the word 'fair' in its social sense. Like many words and terms there is an everyday sense and a scientific sense. A discussion of what is meant by a fair test might be built on the pupils' concept of fairness. For example, when seeing how far different shaped balloons travel along a string, the children could be asked how much air should be put into each balloon. If a round shaped balloon has two big blows of air put in it, how many blows of air should be put in a long shaped balloon? Younger pupils often find the idea quite tricky, saying one blow, or three blows or even more. If the question is posed differently, in terms of sweets, the pupils often grasp the idea more quickly. If two children have to share sweets, and one has two sweets, how many should the other have? The pupils often immediately grasp that the idea should be two each, they don't think the other child should have only one or even three sweets.

If you explain the sweet analogy, you are then in a good position to re-pose the original question about the balloons. Then the pupils often grasp that the balloons should each receive two big blows to be fair.

A result that can be observed or measured

With younger learners we may do more direct *observing* of changes; for example, for sound we may use comparative words like loud, louder, loudest or quiet, quieter, quietest. These are qualitative changes and are easy for the pupils to understand. For light we could use 'bright, brighter, brightest' or 'dim, dimmer, dimmest'; for measuring seedling growth we could use 'smallest' and 'tallest'; for absorbing liquid using paper we could use 'most' and 'least'.

For older learners, they would look to observe and *measure* the changes. These are termed quantitative changes. So they need to be able to use equipment to give simple measurements such as rulers, measuring cylinders, thermometers, sound meters, and data loggers.

Checking for accuracy

A group of pupils are investigating how far a toy car will travel over different surfaces. They roll a car down a ramp and measure how far it travels from the base of the ramp until it stops. How many times should they check this result before changing the surface and making a new measurement? Many pupils just want to do the experiment once, before changing the surface. They are reluctant to take another reading because they have 'already done it'.

What the teacher needs to convey is the importance of checking this result and making sure it is accurate. Lots of things could have caused the result to be inaccurate. Perhaps the surface had not been smoothed out enough, and a bump stopped the car. Perhaps the car was not placed at the top of the ramp. The point is the pupils should check their result at least three times before moving on to the next surface or material. This allows them to check they are being accurate. If they make three measurements that are very similar, they can be confident of their accuracy.

Many pupils know to make a measurement 'three times', but they often don't know why they do it. If asked the question, 'Why must we do this three times?', the most frequent incorrect answer given is 'We do it again to make sure it's a fair test'. In fact, many teachers think this too. But checking accuracy is *not* the same thing as fair testing. Of course, in our example, variables must be kept constant, the car must start off from the same place on the ramp each time, the ramp must be the same height each time, and so on, so perhaps this is where the confusion arises. It is the accuracy of the results that we are trying to guarantee by repeating the measurements.

Sometimes pupils cannot make repeated measurements in their experiments. For example, if they are measuring how much a seedling grows each day, they don't need to measure that seedling three times! However, with the teacher's help, they could aggregate their data as a class, so that inaccuracies are ironed out. Any widely inaccurate measurement would be seen as an outlier in the class data. Useful practice would be, for example, teaching the pupils to look at a scatter diagram and spotting data that might not be accurate because it is so far away from the rest.

Presenting results

Pupils might present their results in a number of ways. At the simplest level they could draw or write about the results of their experiments. They could construct a results table. As they get older and have data to show, they need to construct bar and line graphs. Bar graphs are the easier of the two to construct and understand, and are often suitable for Lower Key Stage 2 investigations. Line graphs require more skill to construct and interpret, and are more suitable for Upper Key Stage 2.

Knowing whether to construct a bar graph or line graph requires some explicit knowledge. In general younger pupils are more familiar with bar graphs than line graphs. To get used to dealing with each type of graph, pupils need to focus on the variable they are changing and the variable they are observing.

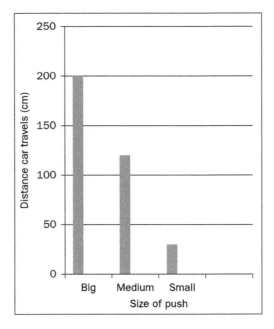

Figure 2.1 A graph to show distance a car travels with different sizes of push

When considering the variable to be changed and the variable to be observed, if one is qualitative and the other is quantitative then a bar graph is called for. Consider the question, 'How does the size of push (small, medium or big) affect how far a toy car travels?' The variable we are changing is qualitative (small, medium or big push) and the variable we are observing is quantitative (the distance the car travels in centimetres).

A line graph is called for if the variable being changed and the variable being observed are both qualitative, particularly so if we are not dealing with whole numbers. For the investigation question, 'When we move an object towards a lamp, what happens to the size of its shadow?', the pupils will measure the distance from the lamp to the object in centimetres (the variable they are changing) and the size of the shadow in centimetres (the variable they are observing). The graph (Figure 2.2) shows that as the object and lamp gets closer together, the size of the shadow increases.

Spotting patterns

Analysing results is a skill, and getting the pupils to look for a pattern is not always easy. Like all skills, correctly interpreting results improves with practice. Similarly, constructing result tables and reading results from them is also a skill that needs to be taught and practised.

Bar graphs are relatively easy for pupils to interpret. They can easily spot the largest bar and smallest bar and work out what they mean. Line graphs are more tricky for pupils to understand. If we get the pupils to start to recognise shapes of line graph

Figure 2.2 A graph showing size of shadow and distance between object and lamp

then they will find it easier to construct their own, and to work out what their graphs are telling them.

The graphs below have no numbers on their axis, but again this does not matter as we are looking at general trends and shapes, giving pupils a 'feel' for visual data interpretation (see Goldsworthy *et al.*, 1999).

For example if they examine the graph in Figure 2.3, can they interpret what is going on in a pan of water left on a lit stove? The graph shows that as time passes, the temperature of the water rises. Notice that the temperature of water does not start at zero, but part way up the y axis, around room temperature. Challenge the pupils to continue the line of a graph, once the heat has been switched off. (The temperature would fall over time, giving a line that is opposite to the one above. The reality may be more complex, with the graph showing a curve rather that a straight line, but the pupils' ability to spot trends and patterns is what is being assessed here.)

Fun graphs can be constructed, such as the one in Figure 2.4 showing the length of a breadstick during the time it is being eaten. Ask the pupils why the graph is 'stepped' (the answer is that each bite removes a piece of breadstick, and time is taken for chewing and swallowing before the next bite is taken).

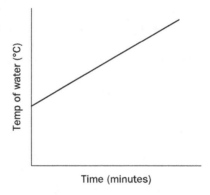

Figure 2.3 A graph of temperature of water changing with time

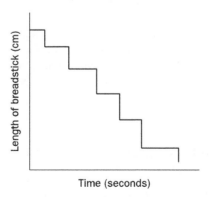

Figure 2.4 Graph to show how length of breadstick varies with time

Adapted from Goldsworthy *et al.* (1999).

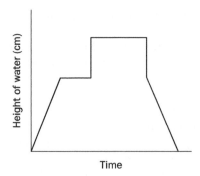

Figure 2.5 A graph of level of water varying with time

In the graph in Figure 2.5, we can see what happens to the depth of water in a bath. As the water is run into the bath, the height of water rises as can be seen by the steep slope at the start of the graph. When the taps are switched off the level of water stays steady for a while. The sudden jump up is someone getting in the bath causing the water to rise. While they stay in the bath the height of water stays the same, and then drops suddenly to its previous level when they get out. Finally, the water is let out and the level falls as it drains down the plug hole, eventually reaching zero again.

The approach to graphs we have discussed in this section was pioneered by Goldsworthy *et al.* (1999) and more examples can be seen by consulting their book *AKSIS Investigations: Getting to Grips with Graphs*.

Has the question been answered?

By the time an investigation is finished, pupils may have forgotten what the original question was! They need to be redirected back to it and then look back at the pattern of their results, to see if they can answer the original question. Challenge them to answer the question in a sentence or two. They can expand on their answer in a short paragraph using their knowledge and understanding of science to explain what has happened.

In summary, pupils need a mix of scientific enquiry activities and full scientific investigations. We cannot expect them to just be able to carry out the tasks competently and completely – the skills need be taught and practiced if they are to develop expertise. 'Full' investigations take time, so we would advise at least one whole investigation per term. A 'full' investigation may be heavily supported by teachers and teaching assistants for pupils who have not had as much opportunity for practice.

Progression in scientific enquiry and investigation skills – working scientifically

By reorganising the new statutory guidance statements (DfE, 2013a), we can see how the skills progress from Key Stage 1 to Lower Key Stage 2 and then Upper Key Stage 2.

Spotting similarities and differences
- KS1: identifying and classifying
- Lower KS2: identifying differences, similarities or changes related to simple scientific ideas and processes
- Upper KS2: classification keys

Asking questions
- KS1: asking simple questions and recognising that they can be answered in different ways
- Lower KS2: asking relevant questions and using different types of scientific enquiries to answer them
- Upper KS2: planning different types of scientific enquiries to answer questions, including recognising and controlling variables where necessary

Observing and measuring
- KS1: observing closely, using simple equipment
- Lower KS2: making systematic and careful observations and, where appropriate, taking accurate measurements using standard units, using a range of equipment, including thermometers and data loggers
- Upper KS2: taking measurements, using a range of scientific equipment, with increasing accuracy and precision, taking repeat readings when appropriate

Testing
- KS1: performing simple tests
- Lower KS2: setting up simple practical enquiries, comparative and fair tests
- Upper KS2: using their test results to make predictions to set up *further* comparative and fair tests

Gathering, using and presenting data
- KS 1: gathering and recording data to help in answering questions.
- Lower KS2: gathering, recording, classifying and presenting data in a variety of ways to help in answering questions
- Lower KS2: recording findings using simple scientific language, drawings, labelled diagrams, keys, bar charts, and tables
- Upper KS2: recording data and results of *increasing complexity* using scientific diagrams and labels, classification keys, tables, scatter graphs, bar and line graphs

Answering questions using scientific knowledge, experimental knowledge and secondary source knowledge
- KS1: using their observations and ideas to suggest answers to questions
- KS1: gathering and recording data to help in answering questions
- Lower KS2: reporting on findings from enquiries, including oral and written explanations, displays or presentations of results and conclusions
- Lower KS2: using results to draw simple conclusions, make predictions for new values, suggest improvements and raise further questions
- Upper KS2: using test results to make predictions to set up *further* comparative and fair tests

- Upper KS2: reporting and presenting findings from enquiries, including conclusions, causal relationships and explanations of and degree of trust in results, in oral and written forms such as displays and other presentations

Using a framework to plan and carry out an investigation

Planning frameworks can be a useful planning tool for pupils, giving them a scaffold to slot their various ideas into, and a structure they can follow in a step by step manner. In literacy lessons you will be familiar with pupils planning a story with a 'writing framework'. For science we could call the frameworks we use for investigations 'thinking frameworks' (Cross and Board, 2014). One familiar framework is the 'rocket', used by Key Stage 1 pupils. In this there are just four slots on the rocket to fill, which give a general guidance for the pupils (see Figure 2.6).

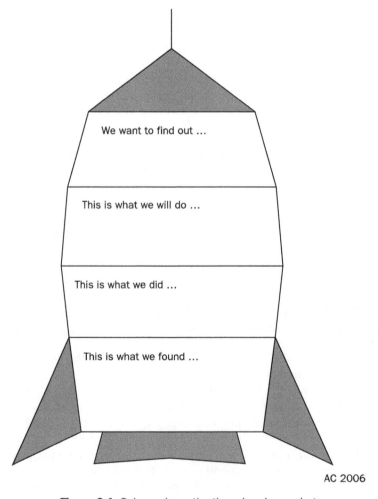

We want to find out …

This is what we will do …

This is what we did …

This is what we found …

AC 2006

Figure 2.6 Science investigation planning rocket

More complex thinking frameworks for Key Stage 1 include Discovery Dog™ (licensed by Creative Classroom), which has many more slots to fill and introduction of more complex science terms such as 'our prediction', 'we will change' and 'we will observe'. One of the most useful thinking frameworks for older pupils is the sticky notes investigation framework, which is described below.

Sticky notes investigations

Sometimes called the Post It™ investigation (originated by Goldsworthy and Feasey, 1997), the sticky notes investigation framework is a great way for Upper Key Stage 2 pupils to plan their own investigations. The pupils select the variable they are going to change and write it on a sticky note. They then select the variable they are going to observe and write this on a second sticky note. These two sticky note variables can then be actively moved through the investigation sheets, including being used to label results tables and graphs.

By looking at a worked example, we can see how effective this framework is. Let's take the investigation 'How can we make sugar dissolve faster?'. Get the pupils to write the question at the top of their first sheet. This helps them really focus on what the investigation is about. The pupils first have to decide what they will change. Each variable they could change can be written on a separate sticky note and stuck onto the 'THINKING ABOUT VARIABLES' sheet in the 'Things I could change (or vary)' section. Perhaps they come up with three ideas. They could change the temperature of the water, or the number of stirs, or volume of water (see Figure 2.7).

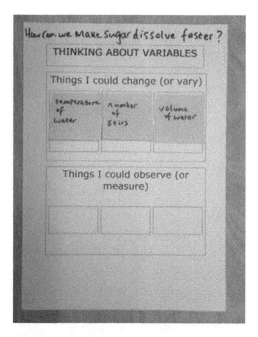

Figure 2.7 Thinking about variables that could be changed

Based on Goldsworthy and Feasey (1997).

Next, they have to think about which variable they are going to observe (or measure). They could observe the time taken for sugar to fully dissolve, or how much sugar remains after one minute. They put these onto the 'THINKING ABOUT VARIABLES' sheet in the 'Things I could observe (or measure)' section (see Figure 2.8).

The pupils then decide which variable they are going to change, and which to observe, selecting from the above choices. Let's say they decide to change 'number of stirs' and observe 'time taken for sugar to dissolve fully'. They then put these in the appropriate boxes on the 'PLANNING A FAIR TEST' sheet. The other variables that could be changed can now be put on in the 'I will keep these the same' boxes – and these are the control variables. So in this instance we can put 'temperature of water' and 'volume of water' into this section, and make sure we do keep these things the same in each test (see Figure 2.9).

They can now progress to the 'PREDICTING' sheet, placing the variable being changed and the variable being observed in their boxes, and so forming the sentence: 'When I change the number of stirs what will happen to the time taken for the sugar to fully dissolve'. The pupils can write the answer to their prediction in the space on the sheet 'I think that . . .' (see Figure 2.10).

The sticky notes can then be transferred to the 'RESULTS TABLE' sheet, and the pupils can fill in their results in the table underneath the two variables columns (see Figure 2.11).

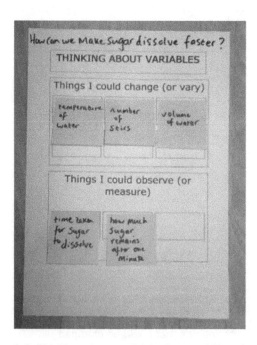

Figure 2.8 Thinking about variable that could be observed

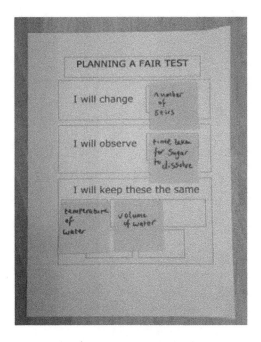

Figure 2.9 Planning a fair test

Figure 2.10 Predicting outcomes

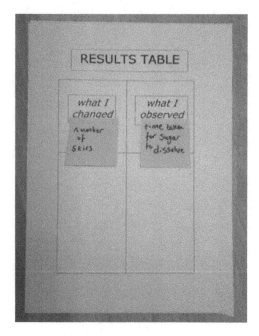

Figure 2.11 Results table

The sticky notes can then be transferred to a RESULTS GRAPH and the variables placed on the axes. Then the graph can be plotted (see Figure 2.12). Graph paper or squared paper could be stuck onto the sheet.

Finally, they can use the 'FINDING PATTERNS IN THE RESULTS' sheet (Figure 2.13), and place the sticky notes in the correct place to give them a question which they should now be able to answer, using the data they have generated.

The final sentence of the above sheet states 'I found out that . . .' and here the pupil can write an explanation of their findings. A better statement might be 'This can be explained by . . .' again prompting the pupils to discuss their findings using their knowledge and understanding of science.

At first glance, if you are unfamiliar with the sticky notes method, it may look difficult. With practice it becomes a very easy tool for the pupils to use. If Upper Key Stage 2 are to plan their own investigations (a statutory requirement of the National Curriculum for this age) then this is a great thinking framework for them. It enables them to come up with their own questions, manipulate the variables by themselves and put their data into appropriate tables and graphs, and finally answer their investigation question with confidence. If this approach is introduced in Lower Key Stage 2, then with support the pupils should be able to use it. At Lower Key Stage 2 it will be the teacher frequently introducing the question to be answered and modelling the selection of variables, but once the pupils get the hang of this framework it will free up their thinking so they can concentrate on setting their own questions and variables.

The sticky notes/Post It™ method was originally developed by Goldsworthy and Feasey (1997) however it has been adapted many times by teachers over the years.

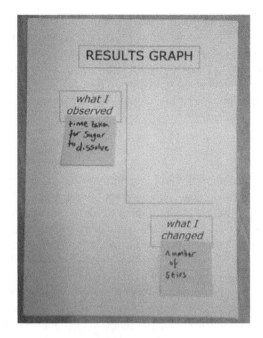

Figure 2.12 Results graph

Figure 2.13 Finding patterns in the results

Templates can be downloaded from http://www.primaryresources.co.uk/science, click through to science investigation section. There are various versions of this resource online that can easily be modified. Some appear as Word™ documents, others as PowerPoint™ presentations that you can talk the pupils through. Interestingly we might consider that our objective with Upper Key Stage 2 is to make such methods redundant as by then pupils might be so conversant with variables etc. that they could plan much more independently.

Conclusion

This chapter has outlined approaches to the teaching of the important skills of science. You will have seen that these skills can usefully be taught in isolation but when taught within a whole investigation they may appear more relevant. Specific approaches have been illustrated which provide scaffolding for learners and real support for teachers who may be non-specialists. As you work through other sections of this book and science topics you teach, remember that you need to identify opportunities for pupils to work as scientists, developing these important skills. We have made suggestions within each chapter for opportunities for pupils to work scientifically. Make sure you put aside lesson time for whole investigations and that in other science lessons you emphasise the development of specific science skills. Because you teach this part of science in every science topic, this is where you are likely to see most learning over the year, so do enjoy your pupils' successes as they become more skilful and independent investigators.

Web resources

http://www.bbc.co.uk/radio4/features/sywtbas/
   (website from BBC Radio 4 showing science experiments thought up by everyday people (who are *not* scientists) and entered for a competition)

http://www.cernland.net/
   (helps pupils understand the work done at CERN)

http://www.nationalstemcentre.org.uk/elibrary
   (has a range of resources to use for investigations. The site requires registration to download the resources, but is completely free to use)

http://www.primaryresources.co.uk/science
   (a wealth of free science templates and worksheets, including sticky notes investigation templates)

http://www.rsc.org/AboutUs/News/PressReleases/2010/Conkerswin.asp
   (the experiments done by primary pupils to show if spiders are scared of conkers or not, which won a Royal Society of Chemistry award. Video footage of some different experimental approaches used by the pupils)

Discovery Dog investigations templates and interactive CDs are available from http://www.creativeclassroom.co.uk/discoverydog.html

3

Assessment in primary science

Assessment of pupils' learning can be used for a number of purposes. It can be used to inform teaching, to measure educational attainment, to inform learners, parents and carers, and to help form judgements about schools and schooling. Assessment of science learning ensures that we, as teachers, know who in our class is grasping the often challenging concepts and skills we teach, who is part-way there and who is struggling. This knowledge means that we can then respond by tailoring further lessons to suit the individual learners. Science assessment in a classroom and a school is likely to include a number of elements or layers. These might include elicitation, in-class teacher assessment, marking, pupil self-assessment, peer assessment, and paper tests. The latter are rather limited as they can only test certain parts of science. They can however make a contribution to assessment overall.

Chapter 1 referred to metacognition, that is, cognition about cognition or thinking about thinking. Learners need to know what they know and understand, what they don't fully grasp, and what and how they learn. Clearly assessment (including self-assessment) has the potential to contribute to the learner's understanding of themselves as learners. As learners we learn better if we are engaged with our own learning processes. This ties in well with science as we often take a little time to fully appreciate ideas and concepts, so it can be helpful to adopt a reflective approach to our own learning. Do I really understand that? Could I explain this to others? As a teacher you have to be able to explain to others and provide them with experiences which lead them to learning.

Forms of assessment

Formative and summative assessments

As a primary teacher of science you need to know a little about some basic principles around assessment. You will have encountered these elsewhere in your life. Most assessment taking place in school is *formative*, that is, it is used to inform the teacher and child about learning. The child is informed so that she or he can respond personally, the teacher is informed so that she or he can adapt lessons which will follow.

Assessment which occurs at the end of a period of learning can be *summative*. That is, it tells all those involved what the learner has learned at that point. Summative assessment often occurs at the end of an exam course or at the end of a stage of education, for example, Key Stage 2.

Formative assessment tends to inform us about learner achievement, that is, the educational progress of that learner over time against the learning criteria. It encapsulates the personal learning of the learner. Summative assessment tends to assess attainment, that is, where is the learner up to at a particular point? All this means that your assessment of science learning will dramatically help the inclusivity of your teaching because it will enable your tailoring of science education to suit the learners.

Criterion- and norm-referenced assessment

Assessment tends to be either *criterion* or *norm* referenced. Criterion-referenced assessment uses a number of statements about the desired learning outcomes to be assessed. This is seen in a driving test. Can the driver complete a safe emergency stop? Can they parallel park safely? If 100 candidates are tested it is possible that all 100 will pass or indeed all fail. Norm-referenced assessment is quite different. Here a test may be set, scores are collected and then a distribution of scores is examined. The examiners then decide where, this time, the pass mark will be. Thus the learner is compared not to an objective but to a group of their peers.

Criterion-referenced assessment tells you whether you know or understand things, whereas norm-referenced assessment tells you where you are in a ranking with other people. Both have value but most classroom teachers find criterion-referenced assessment more useful as it readily informs future teaching. Of course, these categories of assessment are not mutually exclusive and do overlap, for example, national testing uses assessment criteria in the marking guidance but also employs norm referencing.

Teachers routinely use criterion-referenced assessment in classrooms, for example, when sharing learning objectives or success criteria towards the start of a lesson. Teachers usually use this or some other device to show what the learners might learn in the lesson. School curricula can be written in different ways but can be viewed as a large set of objectives which it is hoped will be mastered by learners. Some school curricula are set out in high-level overarching terms leaving it to the teacher to formulate lesson objectives which will lead towards these higher level objectives.

As you assess the learning of science lesson by lesson you will gain more and more information about each learner. As you assess their knowledge, understanding and science skill development you will be able to differentiate more and more accurately, personalising the experience of the learners, for example, perhaps focusing on the skill of 'question formation' for some and the skill of 'explaining experimental results' for others. In addition you will be increasingly aware of their learning style and how you can tailor aspects of your science lessons to suit groups and individuals.

Some people can develop negative views of assessment and this is understandable. Children in our schools today are some of the most examined learners in UK history. Assessment, like most things, can have negative and positive affects. Used well it is part of the teaching cycle and informs those involved. Formative assessment can be a natural part of a lesson conclusion or introduction which enables learners to consider and reconsider what they know and understand and how they might take their own learning forward. Were we to rely solely on either summative or norm-referenced assessment we would deny ourselves the rich range of information available in lessons.

Assessment in science classes

For some teachers assessment of science can raise a number of challenges. Challenges occur when the area of science is not fully understood by the teacher. They also occur if the learners are working in pairs or groups, or if learners are 'talking and doing' rather than writing. Confidence in your own science knowledge and skills will help you enormously. If you have to assess whether children understand dissolving, you need to understand it yourself. This will allow you to spot misconceptions when they occur.

Subject knowledge is perhaps the most straightforward aspect of science assessment. For example, ask a class of 5-year-olds to sing the action song 'Heads, shoulder knees and toes' and see if they point to the right body parts. If they do, then it is clear that they know where these body parts are. Lots of other science activities reveal this kind of knowledge. Science understanding is a little more difficult, for example, we may ask the class 'How does air resistance affect the way objects fall?' Whenever we ask for an explanation rather than simply recall of knowledge, learners are more likely to experience difficulty. Here we might ask specific questions or more simply ask the child to explain something orally to another child, or to create an explanatory poster. Skills are best assessed when observing learners. We can borrow assessment methods from Early Years. For example you might have a classroom wall poster or grid on which you note when you see learners display a skill such as measuring light levels. Of course the learners know whether

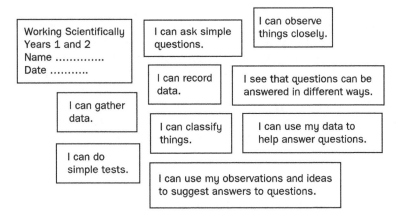

Figure 3.1 Pupils self-assessment record: working scientifically

Figure 3.2 Science investigation role badges

they know, understand or can do things so pupil self-assessment can save you a great deal of time.

Where you have learners working collaboratively in science it can be difficult to determine whether each person has developed a specific skill. Different approaches can be taken. One is to assign roles to each person in the group so that you can assess them in their role. For example, see the set of possible badges in Figure 3.2. Another is to identify one child in the group who is typical of that group, assess them in detail and then check that the others are at the same point.

When learners are talking and doing things, the evidence of their knowledge, understanding and skills is fleeting and it may not be recorded. Options to address this include:

- keeping notes in the lesson;
- making notes immediately after the lesson;
- taking photographs;

- making audio recordings;
- using mini plenaries and plenaries to check learners' achievement;
- employing forms of pupil self-assessment and peer assessment.

Vehicles for assessment of science

Elicitation

We advocate elicitation at the start of each topic. For example, when approaching a science topic on forces you might ask learners to complete a concept map (see Figure 3.5) or discuss a concept cartoon (see Figure 3.4), so that you know what they already know about forces. Or you may give them a simple investigation which involves pushing objects on a table with a force meter. Your observation will give you the opportunity to find out, elicit, what the learners know or don't know and so later teach accordingly. There is little point in planning and delivering three or four science lessons on a topic if they already know everything you wish to teach. Better to elicit their present understanding and then move them on. This might require more challenge, going back over basics or shifting the emphasis more to science investigation. Elicitation is in fact just another form of formative assessment but one which is used specifically, for example, at the start of a topic to inform planning.

Games

Games or game-like activities have great capacity to assist learning but also to tell us what children know, understand and can do. Examples include: 'feely bags' (can the pupils describe the material in the bag, by touch alone?); 'blindfold games' (can a blindfolded pupil explain why they can tell which direction the sound of keys being rattled is coming from, and how close the keys are?); and miming games (can the class guess what scientific idea a pupil has in mind, when he drops a pencil on to the floor (gravity) or rubs his hands together (friction)? A very active example is 'Flappy Fish', where children have cardboard rectangles which they use to flap and push along paper fish from a starting line to a finishing line on the floor. We can ask the children to talk about how the fish is moved, involving concepts of pushes, pulls and air resistance, and thus gain a picture of their understanding. In this example we could easily use the game to ask about ways to answer a scientific question such as 'Do paper fish move faster on carpet in the classroom, on a wood floor in the hall or on tarmac on the playground?' Thus we can assess how the children are able to work as scientists, by getting them to pose and answer a scientific question.

Songs

Can the children invent their own song about a science topic to a well known tune? Could they rewrite the song 'Them Bones' ('the head bone's connected to the . . .') by including the correct names for bones or body parts they now know? Could they explain the flow of electricity around a circuit to the tune of 'Row, row, row your boat'? ('Flow, flow, flow the electrons, moving through the wire . . .')?

Quizzes

The teacher can of course write a quiz. However, it may be far more revealing to have each table in a class write one or two questions for a quiz, for example, on electricity. Can they grade the questions they come up with from easy to hard, and award points accordingly?

Tests

In a similar way you might use published tests and even create your own tests but there is huge value in asking learners to write their own test questions and the answer sheet. The multi-choice format offers some advantages but of course quizzes and tests rely on the learners being able to read adequately.

Here is the answer, what is the question?

This is a very simple and revealing approach. For example, we may ask the pupils 'If the answer is "deciduous", what is the question?' The response will usually give an indication about the learners' understanding of deciduous and evergreen plants.

Figure 3.3 is an example for the topic of 'Space':

Here are the answers, what are the questions?

The question is ...

The question is ...

Sun

Pluto

The question is ...

The question is ...

orbit

moon

The question is

Venus

24

The question is ...

The question is ...

Figure 3.3 What is the question?

KWL chart

Here the learners complete three columns as appropriate. In the first column the learners note what they already know. They then list the things they would like to know and finally perhaps at the end of the unit of work they write about the things that they have now learnt.

What I know	What I would like to know	What I have learned

Concept cartoons

Learners can create their own cartoon or work with one you provide. The idea is to have cartoon figures examine a science phenomenon such as a burning candle. The characters have speech bubbles where they make various statements, as can be seen in Figure 3.4. Learners consider each statement and think about why the character says this and whether it is correct or not.

Concept map

Here learners begin with a set of words relating to a concept. They tick the words they feel they know and then use them to create a chart as in Figure 3.5 using lines, arrows and words to join words and represent their learning.

Role play

Role playing can also reveal knowledge and understanding in science. A classic example would be a class in the school hall modelling the solar system. To represent the different planets children might hold balls, labels or posters. Up to nine children 'orbit' one child who represents the Sun. Learners might be asked to produce a commentary for the model, or instructions on how to make it work. They might be asked to describe the motion of Jupiter in relation to the Sun and the other planets. The use or

Figure 3.4 Concept cartoon

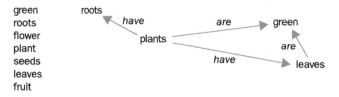

Figure 3.5 Concept map about plants

misuse of terms like spin, turn, rotate, year and orbit can tell us a lot (see a discussion of the correct and incorrect use of these words in Chapter 11, 'Earth in Space'). Of course some children will not have the language but will be able to show you that they understand by acting out the role. This means that role plays can be used to great advantage for assessment.

Another example would be to challenge the class, in groups of around eight pupils, to form parts of a tree. Some could be the roots, some the stem and branches, and others the surrounding bark. Can they fit themselves together to be a whole tree? Can they role-play the journey of water, from soil to leaf tip?

Directed activities related to texts (DARTs)

Directed activities related to texts include all sorts of diagrams, charts and tables, and are used a lot in science education to illustrate, represent and clarify parts of science. Asking learners to cut out and stick on labels is one simple way of using DARTs for assessment. Learners can be asked to label, improve, complete, create and interpret figures, diagrams, tables and charts. These all reveal something of their understanding. Approaches like this work best if supported by time for discussion.

Written tests

Written tests have a place in primary classrooms, as another layer in the assessment approach you might take. They might be published tests, tests written by yourself or written by the class. Questions can include:

- true/false statements;
- link a word to a word or picture or definition;
- label all or part of a diagram;
- select which drawing/diagram is correct;
- fill in the missing word;
- say what will happen next;
- multiple choice;
- explain why something happens.

These can be very time-consuming to produce so most teachers would look for a published scheme of questions which ideally would cover most aspects of science, have been trialled, have a marking scheme, have a diagnostic element and not be over-facing.

The big disadvantages are that written tests rely heavily on the learner's reading skills, cannot assess some aspects of science (e.g. some science skills), cannot assess some aspects of science well (e.g. understanding of the relative motion of Earth, Sun and Moon), and they can present science as a rather dull paper-based exercise. Overemphasis of written assessment can begin to put some learners off learning. Used with care they can provide useful back-up to the other methods adopted.

Assessing science investigation skills

Science skills are best assessed while they are being demonstrated, so a notebook or poster can be invaluable as the teacher moves from group to group perhaps noting the outliers in relation to the lesson objectives, for example, who is struggling, who is excelling?

A great aid to this can be to ensure that in each science lesson you include a learning objective which specifically relates to a science investigation skill (this could also be done with target setting). Thus both you and the learners will be clear about the skill you are focusing on and whether individuals are displaying the skill.

Target setting

Target setting means different things to different people. One form of group target setting is the lesson objective or learning outcome. Another would be a target or set of targets about science given on a poster to a whole class. These could be given termly or even weekly. While you might write individual targets in science for each individual, such an approach would be unlikely to be efficient use of your time. It would be better to have clear class targets, with perhaps so called, stretch targets for the higher achievers, but towards which all of the class can aim. The question to keep in mind is, 'If I ask a child what they need to focus on to develop their personal science learning, could they give a meaningful answer?' A set of targets would give each child a real focus.

Feedback

A key feature of good teaching is effective feedback. Your assessment will feedback to your lesson planning but very importantly will inform pupils of your feedback. You will do this through written feedback (marking in books and targets for groups) and oral feedback to individuals and groups. It is most important that learners are clear about their achievement and how they can now improve. Make sure that you:

- keep marking up to date;
- mark clearly and accurately;
- confirm when objectives have been achieved;
- provide guidance about future approach/focus.

If science is only taught once or twice a week you will need to plan your feedback differently to that for subjects taught every day. Make sure you use your time effectively with a combination of personal written feedback in books, written feedback to groups in the form of targets, and oral feedback to individuals and groups.

Differentiation

One reason we assess as teachers is so that we can progressively tailor our lessons to the learners. As the year goes by you will keep teaching and assessing aspects of working scientifically (DfE, 2013a) so that you will soon be able to identify those who need to be stretched and others who need more support.

Differentiation in science can mirror differentiation in other subjects. Approaches could include variation in expectations, resources provided, amount of support, difficulty of tasks, and level of challenge. Unique to science is the expectation that learners will work scientifically. Learning to work like a scientist is part of each half-term's work and so provides lots of potential for getting to know the learners' achievement and for differentiation. See Chapter 2 for a comprehensive exploration of pupils 'working scientifically' in line with the National Curriculum (DfE, 2013a).

Challenge

A word of caution about differentiation in science. For some groups, for example, lower achievers, differentiation can create a glass ceiling of expectation. For example, if your assessment tells you that some learners need support, you might always provide this and thus these learners might not develop any autonomy. Avoid this by:

- providing a stretch objective for all;
- using target setting to raise expectations;
- having them work independently at times;
- having them work in groups based on science achievement at times;
- using science investigation to make the science more challenging;
- ensuring that your expectations are high for everyone in the class.

Recording assessment

In order for you to monitor progress in science learning we would suggest a record of assessment against the learning objectives for science (science content and working scientifically). This does not need to be elaborate but a simple record of:

- any learners with specific needs;
- the half-term's science learning objectives;
- a record of those who have been absent, those who have not achieved the objectives, and those who have gone further.

Conclusion

The different approaches to assessment, coupled with your use of what you discover about learners, offers you as a teacher of science the most powerful tool for raising expectations about pupil learning in science. We would encourage you to be transparent with learners about assessment processes in science, and encourage them to be increasingly reflective about their learning of science and how they themselves learn science. Science offers learners a fantastic window on their world. The knowledge, understanding and skills they develop will enable learning in other areas and allow them to gain from all that science has to offer. Your teaching of science will benefit from being well informed about your learners. You will be able to respond in different ways, for example, if at the start of the topic you discover they already know the science, move them on to new and/or more challenging content.

4

Life processes – plants

About this chapter

This chapter is about plants. We first summarise the main groups found in the plant kingdom and deal with the identification of common wild and garden plants. The chapter then describes the main parts of a flowering plant, the structure of flowers, and how pollination, fertilisation, seed formation, seed dispersal, and germination are part of the life cycle of the flowering plant. We describe the basic life processes of plants, plant cells, and a number of tissues found within plants, as well as factors that affect the health of a plant. The second part of the chapter highlights what pupils need to learn about and in the final part we suggest some of the best ways to teach pupils about the life processes of plants, including common misconceptions.

What the teacher needs to know and understand

Alive, dead, and never alive

A basic distinction to be made in the study of the natural world by young children is between those things that are alive, those that are dead, and those that have never been alive. As a teacher you need to make yourself aware of these things and be able to make the distinction with the harder examples, for example, a piece of wood. We can add other harder examples, such as coal which is made from plant materials that have been changed over time following burial.

Does the exception prove the rule?

Because there is so much variety in the biological world, whenever humans try to make a statement about plants there is almost always an exception to the rule. For example, is it true that 'all plants are green'? Can you identify plants that are not green?

There are a few, for example the Japanese red maple tree. Plants that are not green still have chlorophyll (which normally makes a plant green) but it is being masked by other non-green pigments. There are also plants whose leaves have a grey or silvery appearance.

Plants are widespread and exhibit great variety

Plants are living things; they begin life, grow, reproduce, and eventually die. Some plants live for a few months whereas others live much longer. Some of the oldest trees on the planet could be over 4000 years old. These are the very long-lived species of bristlecone pine. In the United Kingdom, we have yew trees that are over 2000 years old. Parasitic plants such as some species of dodder, which can be seen in the UK, live on other plants and literally suck sugars from their host. Mistletoe is an example of a partial parasite. It is parasitic but because it contains chlorophyll it can also photosynthesise.

The plant kingdom

The plant kingdom is vast and amazing in its diversity. Plants have adapted or evolved to exploit all but the very harshest environments on Earth, from the frozen tundra to deserts and from the local park to the deepest ocean. Classification of organisms is complex; it is a science on its own.

The easiest way to understand the breadth of the plant kingdom is to split it into four main groups: mosses and liverworts; ferns; conifers; and flowering plants. These groups are a simplification, but a fairly accurate one.

The simplest types of plants are mosses and liverworts. They have very primitive leaves and stems. Mosses often grow in damp places such as moorland, but can also be found on roofs and in lawns. Liverworts are less common than mosses and form mats of small lobe-like or disc-like leaves on the surface of soils and rocks. You may have seen them in very damp, shady places, for example by the side of a stream or waterfall. The next group, the ferns, is one people are more familiar with. Ferns often have large leaves and a more complex internal structure than mosses and liverworts. They have larger stems and vessels inside to carry water and nutrients through them. They include the very common plant we know as bracken, which grows in the country on hillsides. You may well be familiar with the third group, conifers. These are cone-bearing plants, and familiar examples include the spruce tree (often used as a Christmas

| mosses and liverworts | ferns | conifers | flowering plants |
| e.g. club moss | e.g. maidenhair fern | e.g. Douglas fir | e.g. tulip |

Figure 4.1 Simplified plant kingdom

tree), Douglas fir, and Scots pine. Most of these are evergreen and do not lose their small, needle-like leaves, but some are not, such as the larch. The final group are the flowering plants. These include small plants we all know such as bluebells and daisies, but also larger ones like ash and lime trees, whose flowers may not be as obvious.

Spend a few minutes in a local park or garden (remember it is illegal to pick flowers, this is only allowed in a private garden) and try to find examples from each of the above groups.

A simple pocket guide to wild flowers and trees will give you great insight into the diversity of plants. Several websites will assist in this way. Try the following:

http://www.ukwildflowers.com/Web_pages_intros_indexes/english_index.htm

Organisms often confused with plants

Algae (including seaweeds) are not plants. Scientists used to classify them as plants, but more recently they have been shown to be markedly different. Like plants they are able to make their own food by photosynthesis, but unlike plants they do not contain specialist organs and structures. Seaweeds are a more complicated type of algae, but are still very primitive organisms. Algae are part of a group called the 'Protoctista'.

Fungi are not included in the plant kingdom because they do not photosynthesise, and they too are classified separately in their own group (imaginatively titled 'Fungi'). Lichens are not plants because they are made of a combination of algae and fungi, neither of which are part of the plant kingdom.

Observation and identification of plants

As a teacher you can't be expected to be able to identify all plants. But you need to begin learning to identify common plants including trees and be able to show learners how to identify ones we don't know. In order to identify plants we are interested in the following features:

- overall form, shape and size of the plant;
- leaf colour, shape, texture and distribution;
- stem colour, shape and texture;
- flower colour, shape, number of petals and distribution;
- fruit, berries or seed pod colour and shape;
- habitat in which a plant is found.

This sort of observation is an important part of working scientifically (DfE, 2013a). Teach learners to use their eyes and fingers and to use magnifying glasses. Explain that we will try never to damage plants in order to observe and identify them and that picking wild plants is against the law. However it is acceptable to collect small amounts of plant material from the school grounds.

You need to learn the common names of a selection of trees, wild flowers and garden plants. The lists below are starting points, you will know others and once you start to notice plants you will soon learn more.

Trees

Deciduous – horse chestnut, sycamore, hawthorn, flowering cherry, birch, oak

Evergreen – holly, Douglas fir, Scots pine

Use resources such as these:

http://apps.kew.org/trees/?page_id=17
(Kew gardens tree identifier)

http://www.nhm.ac.uk/nature-online/british-natural-history/urban-tree-survey/
identify-trees/tree-key/index.html#tree-s1
(Natural History Museum Tree identifier)

http://www.opalexplorenature.org/Identification
(free posters)

As you get better at this, realise that you can identify some trees from a distance by their shape, or at least you can make an educated guess and you might even learn to identify fruit, berries, seed pods and the bark of some trees, for example, the silver birch.

Wild flowers – buttercup, daisy, dandelion, clover, dock, nettle, honeysuckle, poppy, snowdrop, bluebell, thistle.

Resources:

http://wildflowerfinder.org.uk
(allows you to search by flower colour, number of petals and other features)

http://www.british-wild-flowers.co.uk/index%20flowers.htm
(comprehensive alphabetic catalogue with pictures)

Garden plants – rose, daffodil, tulip, clematis, red hot poker, lily, geranium, peony, primrose, sweet pea (notice that some of these are cultivated versions of wild flowers, some native and some from other countries).

More important than knowing many plants is to know how to identify them. There are numerous pocket guides which school might have in the school library as well as the websites listed above and free apps you can use on smart devices. This use of secondary sources is an important part of working scientifically (DfE, 2013a).

Structure of a flowering plant

You should be very familiar with the basic structure of a flowering plant. You should be able to draw a plant with its main parts. Try to draw a generic plant including some of the parts listed in Table 4.1. Then compare your picture with the figures in this chapter. Try also unravelling the sentences in Table 4.1.

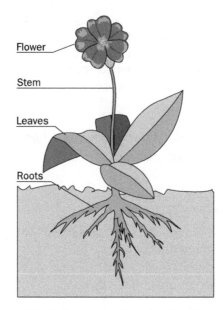

Figure 4.2 A simple drawing of a flowering plant

Table 4.1 DARTs activity

A muddled sentence DART (based on Wellington and Osbourne, 2001)

A root	is	the	using energy from sunlight
The stem	anchors	the	female part of the flower
Each leaf	holds	the	plant to the ground
The stigma	makes	sugar	plant upright

For more information and illustrations about plants, visit
www.saps.org.uk/primary

What do plants need to survive?

Write a short list of the things plants require to survive. You should have listed air, light, warmth, space, water, and nutrients. Individual species may have become adapted to survive on small amounts of the above. For example, cacti can grow in areas of very low rainfall. They rarely have what we would recognise as leaves, since these would increase their surface area and thus water loss.

These requirements allow plants to carry out their life processes (the mnemonic MRS NERG may help you recall these): movement (limited in plants), respiration, sensitivity, nutrition, excretion, reproduction, and growth.

Table 4.2 The seven life processes in plants

Life processes	Examples
Movement (limited)	Plants grow towards the light; flowers open in sunlight; some flowers track the Sun during the day
Respiration	Air moves into and out of leaves; sugars react with oxygen in plant cells to produce energy for the life of the cell and for growth
Sensitivity	Plants respond to changes in light intensity and changes in temperature
Nutrition	Most plants make their own food using carbon dioxide, water, and energy from sunlight
Excretion	Most plants excrete oxygen as a by-product of photosynthesis, and carbon dioxide and water vapour as by-products of respiration
Reproduction	Some plants can reproduce sexually and asexually
Growth	Plants grow, in many cases, throughout their lives

Movement

Movement for plants is different to that of animals. Place a potted plant by a window and over the following days its leaves will turn towards the light (phototropism). If a potted plant is knocked over and left it will do what comes naturally: its green shoots, turning upwards, will grow towards the light and if free from the flower pot its roots will grow downwards due to gravity! Another type of movement occurs when, for example, dandelion seeds are blown on the wind. They can be transported across long distances and are widespread in Britain, throughout Europe, and most of Asia.

> Watch a film of plant movement including tropisms at the following website:
>
> http://plantsinmotion.bio.indiana.edu/plantmotion/earlygrowth/photomorph/photomorph.html

Plants obtain energy from the Sun

Plants obtain energy from the Sun (in the form of light) and use it to make sugars. This is called *photosynthesis*. The word equation for photosynthesis is as follows:

$$\text{carbon dioxide} + \text{water} \xrightarrow[\text{chlorophyll}]{\text{sunlight}} \text{glucose (sugar)} + \text{oxygen}$$

Thus during the daylight hours, plants consume water, light energy, and carbon dioxide so as to produce sugar and oxygen. This only occurs in the parts of the plant that contain chlorophyll. Like animals, plants also require cellular respiration, which means that they use some of the sugar they make plus oxygen to undertake the work of each cell so that the plant can grow and reproduce. This cellular respiration in animals and plants is the opposite of photosynthesis, as it uses sugar and oxygen to release energy, producing carbon dioxide and water as by-products.

Other plant requirements

Plants draw water from the soil, transporting it to their leaves through thin tube-like vessels and leaf veins, where some is used in photosynthesis and some returns to the atmosphere through the stomata on the underside of the leaves. This process is called *transpiration*. You can demonstrate this by tying a plastic bag (remember: keep plastic bags away from young children) over a small branch of about ten leaves on a potted or garden plant. Leave the bag in place for 12–14 hours and you should observe condensation on the inside of the bag as a result of the plant transpiring.

Plants require mineral nutrients from the soil, including compounds of nitrogen, phosphorus, and potassium (gardeners know these by their elemental symbols – N, P, and K respectively). These enter the plant dissolved in the water taken in by the roots. They are essential for the healthy functioning of the plant, including as ingredients of plant proteins (nitrogen). Plants that lack nutrients often become stunted.

Gardeners buy products labelled 'plant food' but this term is not scientifically correct because plants make their own food in the process of photosynthesis. The so-called 'plant food' bought in garden centres would be better labelled as 'plant health supplements', as it does a similar job as the supplements that we may take in the form of vitamins and minerals. It is important to note that plants do *not* get their food from the soil, but that they manufacture it themselves using the process of photosynthesis.

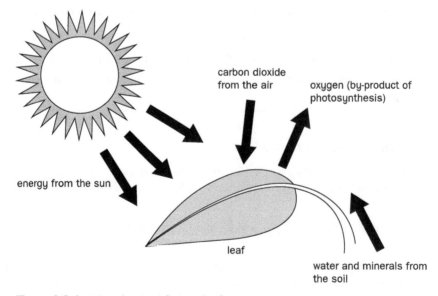

Figure 4.3 Input and output from a leaf

The health of plants can be adversely affected if they are short of any of their basic needs. Plants also suffer from viral, bacterial, and fungal diseases. They can be damaged by the weather and by being eaten by insects, birds and other animals, and can be badly affected by parasitic plants. Some plants are adapted with defences such as stinging leaves, spikes, and chemicals that can make the plant unpalatable or poisonous. Herbs that we use to cook with have chemicals to deter insects from eating them (we like them in small quantities though!) and yew trees have berries that are extremely poisonous to humans, but not to some birds.

Plant cells

A plant cell is easily distinguished from an animal cell by the presence of a vacuole, cell wall, and chloroplasts. The cell vacuole contains cell sap and helps to maintain pressure within the cell so that it keeps its shape. The chlorophyll, essential for photosynthesis, is found in the – often numerous – chloroplasts. The whole cell is protected by a thick wall whose functions include preventing loss of water, providing protection, and maintaining shape. The cell wall is made of cellulose, which is made from glucose. In common with animal cells, the nucleus is the home of the genetic material and this is the control centre for the cell's activity.

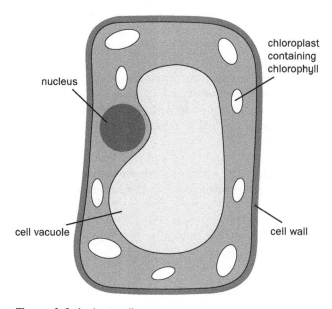

Figure 4.4 A plant cell

The structure of a leaf

Figure 4.5 shows a section through a leaf, illustrating numerous plant cells forming several tissues, each of which performs a specific function.

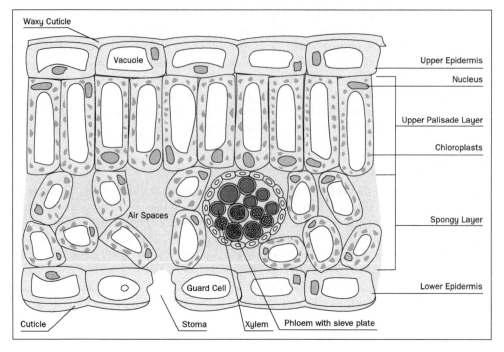

Waxy Cuticle

Vacuole

Air Spaces

Guard Cell

Cuticle   Stoma   Xylem   Phloem with sieve plate

Upper Epidermis

Nucleus

Upper Palisade Layer

Chloroplasts

Spongy Layer

Lower Epidermis

Figure 4.5 A section through a leaf

Similar cells are grouped together in tissues. The cells in different tissues have different functions – we say they are specialised. For example, the cells near the top surface of the leaf are arranged to maximise light uptake and contain many more chloroplasts. The central spine of the leaf is made up of bundles of cells called the mid-rib, part of the transportation system for water and nutrients into, and sugars out of, the leaf. This mid-rib divides and sub-divides into leaf veins. Each leaf has a waxy outer layer (cuticle) on its outside. The waxiness reduces water loss from the leaf. There are tiny holes (stomata) along the bottom of the leaf which can open and close to allow air in and out of the leaf.

If possible, take a few minutes to observe leaves from above and below; see if you can identify the structures above. Is the leaf of a darker green on its upper side? If so, you are observing the concentration of chloroplasts in the upper tissue of the leaf.

The basic structure of a flower

Can you describe the function of the flower parts shown in Figure 4.6?

- petal
- stigma (the top of the carpel)
- stamen (made up of anther and filament) (male part of the flower)
- ovary (bulbous female part of a flower found below the style)

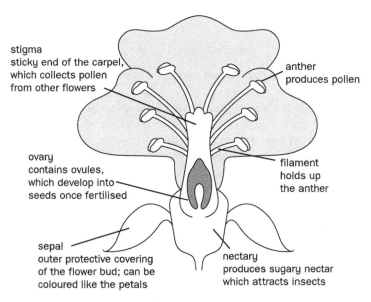

stigma
sticky end of the carpel,
which collects pollen
from other flowers

anther
produces pollen

ovary
contains ovules,
which develop into
seeds once fertilised

filament
holds up
the anther

sepal
outer protective covering
of the flower bud; can be
coloured like the petals

nectary
produces sugary nectar
which attracts insects

Figure 4.6 Structure of a flower

Take a few minutes to find and examine a flower (take care if you have an adverse reaction to pollen). As there is great variety in flowering plants, you may have difficulty identifying the parts in some. If possible, examine a few examples (especially useful are buttercups, lilies, roses, and tulips).

Pollination and fertilisation (sexual reproduction in plants)

The anthers produce minute pollen grains. These are released and are transported (by wind or on the body of an insect) to another flower. When the pollen grain reaches another flower of the same species and lands on the stigma, pollination has occurred. The pollen grain then grows a short tube into the ovary and its nucleus (containing the male genetic material) passes from the pollen into the egg cell (ovule). The following fusion of the nucleus from the male pollen grain and the nucleus of the female ovule (containing the female genetic material) forms one complete cell with a full and unique set of genetic material (this process is called fertilisation). This zygote, consisting of one cell, then divides rapidly to produce a plant embryo. The ovule becomes a seed, with the embryo inside. Food is laid down in seeds in structures called cotyledons. The outer wall of the seed hardens and thickens to form a protective coat.

Plants have developed structures to promote pollination. For flowering plants this is the flower, the purpose of which is to attract flying insects (bees, moths, butterflies, and flies). Some flowers have brightly coloured petals, which insects recognise as a signal that nectar is available. There is great variety here, for example white flowers are often attractive to moths flying at night. In addition, some flowering plants produce scent that some insects find attractive.

Not all plants are pollinated by flying insects, for example grasses are wind-pollinated. These plants produce green flowers with no petals and no nectar. Pollen is

Figure 4.7 The life cycle of a flowering plant

literally blown through the air to another plant. Some trees are also wind-pollinated, including the oak. Many people have never noticed its tiny flowers in the spring. Plants that are wind-pollinated have to produce massive amounts of pollen (so that at least some will hit the right target), as those who suffer from hay fever know to their cost!

The life cycle of a flowering plant includes a number of specific terms, such as *germination*, which you should teach to pupils.

The structure of seeds

Each seed's outer surface dries and hardens as the seed becomes ripe. The seeds of flowering plants contain an embryo plant and a large store of starch to supply the energy for growth (Figure 4.8). In some plants the cotyledon is one single unit, whereas in others it is split into two halves. All flowering plants are divided into one of two groups, depending on whether their seed contains one cotyledon (monocotyledons – usually smaller seeds like grasses, onions, wheat) or two cotyledons (dicotyledons – broad beans, peas).

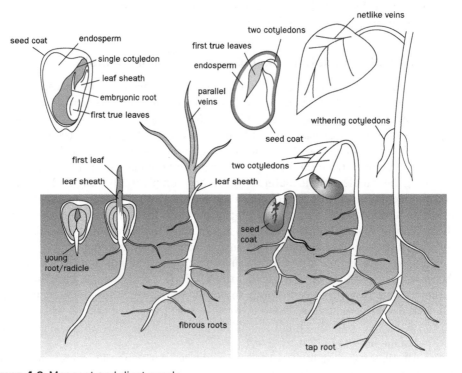

Figure 4.8 Monocot and dicot seeds

Dispersal of plant seeds

The seed will germinate and grow well if somehow it can move away from its parents so that it will not suffer from competition for light and water. Seeds do this in different ways; some fall to the earth and bounce or roll away, others hitch a ride!

Link up the dispersal mechanisms with the examples:

blown by wind   gorse or broom

mechanical flicking   tomato

eaten and later deposited   coconut

carried by water   dandelion

Germination of seeds

Seeds usually undergo a dormant period (often coinciding with winter), after which they respond to changes in temperature, day length, and availability of moisture. The seed coats split and the young root grows towards the pull of gravity and the young shoot towards the light. Energy at this stage comes from the cotyledon. As the shoot reaches the light, it turns green and begins to photosythesise.

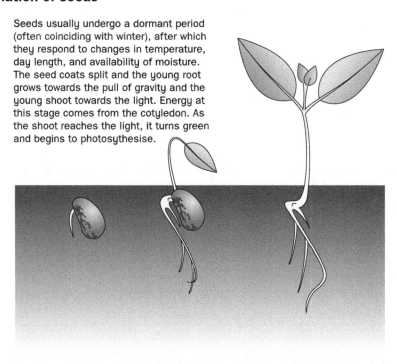

Figure 4.9 Germinating seeds

Some plants make clones (asexual reproduction)

Sometimes, plants produce new plants as 'clones' of themselves. The young produced by this method are genetically identical to the parent plant. Examples of asexual reproduction in plants include:

Variation and Diversity

- strawberry plants produce runners
- willow trees send up shoots from their roots
- daffodil bulbs form more bulbs
- crocus corms form more corms
- spider plants produce shoots supporting baby plants which will easily root
- potato plants produce tubers (potatoes)

Each of these structures – corms, bulbs, runners – has the capability to become a new plant that is identical to the parent. This means that the species will continue. However, only sexual reproduction can lead to young that vary from their parents.

What pupils need to know at Key Stage 1

(ST) denotes Statutory requirements.

(ST) Explore and compare the differences between things that are living, dead, and things that have never been alive

Suggestions for working scientifically:

Sort and classify things according to whether they are living, dead or were never alive and record the information onto charts.

Describe how they decided where to place things on their charts, exploring questions for example: 'Is a flame alive? Is a deciduous tree dead in winter?' and talk about ways of answering their questions.

Raise and answer questions that help them to become familiar with the life processes that are common to all living things.

Find out how living things keep alive and healthy. NB this objective is also dealt with in Chapter 5.

(ST) Identify and name a variety of common wild and garden plants, including deciduous and evergreen trees

Suggestions for working scientifically:

Using the local environment, keep records of how plants have changed over time, for example the leaves falling off trees and buds opening.

Observe the growth of flowers and vegetables that they have planted.

Identify and group plants.

Draw diagrams showing the parts of different plants including trees.

(ST) Identify and describe the basic structure of a variety of common flowering plants, including trees

Suggestions for working scientifically:

Observe closely, perhaps using magnifying glasses, and comparing and contrasting familiar plants; examine their leaves, flowers (including blossom and individual petals), fruits, roots, bulbs, seeds, stem, trunks and branches.

Draw diagrams showing the parts of different plants.

Group similar plants together.

(ST) Observe and describe how seeds and bulbs grow into mature plants

Suggestions for working scientifically:

Observe and record, with some accuracy, the growth of a variety of plants as they change over time from a seed or bulb.

Observe similar plants at different stages of growth.

(ST) Find out and describe how plants need water, light and a suitable temperature to grow and stay healthy

Suggestions for working scientifically:

Set up a comparative test to show that plants need light and water to stay healthy.

What pupils need to know at Key Stage 2

(ST) denotes Statutory requirements.

Lower Key Stage 2

(ST) Identify and describe the functions of different parts of flowering plants: roots, stem/trunk, leaves and flowers

Suggestions for working scientifically:

Explore questions that focus on the role of the roots and stem in nutrition and support, leaves for nutrition and flowers for reproduction.

(ST) Explore the requirements of plants for life and growth (air, light, water, nutrients from soil, and room to grow) and how they vary from plant to plant

Suggestions for working scientifically:

> Compare the effect of different factors on plant growth, for example, the amount of light, or the amount of fertiliser.

(ST) Investigate the way in which water is transported within plants

Suggestions for working scientifically:

> Observe how water is transported in plants, for example, by putting cut, white carnations into coloured water and observing how water travels up the stem to the flowers.

(ST) Explore the part that flowers play in the life cycle of flowering plants, including pollination, seed formation and seed dispersal

Suggestions for working scientifically:

> Discover how seeds are formed by observing the different stages of plant life cycles over a period of time.
>
> Look for patterns in the structure of fruits that relate to how the seeds are dispersed.

Upper Key Stage 2

In Upper Key Stage 2 there is no requirement to teach about plants. However teachers may wish to recap on the features of plants when teaching about the classification of animals and plants.

Ways to teach 'plants' at Key Stage 1

When planning activities for this topic, be mindful that some activities will fit into forty- to fifty-minute lesson blocks quite easily; however, because plants require time to grow, thought and flexibility will be required in the setting up and monitoring of the experiments.

Pupil activity 4.1

Living things, dead things and things that have never been alive

Learning objective: Learn that some things are alive and some things never have been.

Resources required: a living plant, dead leaves, a piece of wood, dried foodstuffs, examples of materials that have never been alive, such as rock, brick, metal, and ceramics

Ask pupils to compare living things and things that have never been alive and ask the question, 'How do we know the living things are alive?' Look at the plant and a pupil as examples of living things. Pupils will talk about breathing, moving, eating, making noises, etc. Move now to things that have never been alive, such as glass, brick, rock, plastics, metals, ceramics, and water, and ask why we are so sure they have never been alive. This is harder, but these have never eaten, breathed, and never had babies, and so on.

Extend this if you feel appropriate by taking the same approach with things that were once alive like a dried flower or dead leaves. For most pupils, it is clear that these were once alive but are now dead. Take this further with examples such as wood, wool, and bread. Now you will have to assist some pupils to be clear about these examples, what they are and where they came from, and that they were once either part of an animal or a plant.

Pupil activity 4.2

Observing and identifying plants

Learning objective: To make careful observations of plants and begin to make identifications.

Resources required: plant material, books of wild flowers, hand lenses

If possible take the pupils outside to an area of the school site with plants and bushes, and ask them to observe leaves, shoots, branches, and flowers (be aware of pupils who may suffer from hay fever). Ask them to speculate about parts of the plants that are hidden underground. Before collecting samples, explain that this is not allowed outside private gardens, that you cannot do this in the wild or in the park. Ask selected pupils to remove a small number of leaves, shoots, etc., to take back to the classroom. Alternatively, if the area needs weeding, involve pupils in digging up a selection of weeds (a weed is a wild flower growing in a garden where it is not wanted by humans), explaining what you are doing.

Pupil activity 4.3

What do plants need?

Learning objective: Learn that plants need water and light to be able to grow (extend with soil, warmth, air, space).

Resources required: Compost, seeds (mung beans, broad beans, peas are easy to grow), plant pots or trays, plants, magnifying glasses

Literacy

Before pupils start this activity show them the equipment and materials, ask them what things are called and what they are for. Explain that they are going to plant seeds and demonstrate the method suggested on the seed packet (depending on the pupils' achievement in reading they could read some of the text on the packet) (make the text bigger with a photocopier or classroom visualiser).

Ask pupils how we might observe and record the growth of the seedlings. Make hand lenses available and record height with life-sized drawing or pieces of string or paper cut to length. Ask the pupils what it is plants need to grow. They may know about light and water, but what about heat (warmth) and soil? Ask them if a plant could grow without light. Could one grow without water? How could they find out?

This could easily be turned into an investigation by growing seedlings in different conditions. One group could try a plant or seedling with no light compared with one with light. This can simply be done by putting the plant or seedling in a cupboard. Another group could compare a watered plant to one that is not watered. When the plants fail to thrive in the darkness or from not being watered, you may want to rescue them once the experiment is done, as the pupils may think we have been cruel to the plants! Soil can be a bit more confusing. Seeds don't need it to germinate, they just need something damp. Young seedlings grow well on damp towels. However, once the seed nutrients have been used up by the seedling, it will require a fresh supply of nutrients, which it will need to get from soil. If it does not get them, it will fail to thrive.

Additionally, you might use games and simulations from the internet to introduce, summarise or as a homework activity. For example:
http://www.bbc.co.uk/schools/scienceclips/ages/7_8/plants_grow_fs.shtml

Pupil activity 4.4

The perfect hotel for plants

Learning objective: Learn about the life processes of plants.

Resources required: potted plants or seedlings, paper, pencils and crayons, audio recorder

Ask pupils to design a table top for the classroom that will act as a perfect indoor garden for plants. Remind them that plants need water, room to move a little and grow, they need air, light to make food and they need warmth. Ideas might include heating, a fan, ventilation, lights, a water supply (watering can), soil or compost, a compost bin, a thermometer, and an indoor greenhouse. Ask pupils to discuss ideas with another pupil before they start.

Ask them to draw clearly because some of the best designs will be used to make a plant growing area in class. They should include the tools and materials needed and label parts so that it is clear that the plants' needs will be provided for.

Review pupils' ideas, checking that these relate to the needs of plants. Ask pupils to describe the features they have drawn and record their voices to make a commentary about the plant growing area. Encourage them to talk about the needs of plants, for example 'Plants need room to grow'.

Pupil activity 4.5

Observing plants and plant material

Learning objective: To make careful observations of plants and name leaf, flower, stem, and roots.

Resources required: plant material, hand trowel, books of wild flowers, hand lenses

If possible take the pupils outside to an area of the school site with plants and bushes, and ask them to observe leaves, shoots, branches, and flowers (be aware of pupils who may suffer from hay fever). Ask them to speculate about parts of the plants that are hidden underground. Before collecting samples, explain that this is not allowed outside private gardens, that you cannot do this in the wild or in the park. Ask selected pupils to remove a small number of leaves, shoots, etc., to take back to the classroom. Alternatively, if the area needs weeding, involve pupils in digging up a selection of weeds (a weed is a wild flower growing in a garden where it is not wanted by humans), explaining what you are doing.

In the classroom, spread out plant material on white paper or trays and ask pupils to observe it initially without any magnifiers. Explain that they will be instructed to wash their hands thoroughly after this activity and that the plant material and dirty fingers must not go near their mouth, eyes or food. Again be aware of pupils with allergies. Explain that we are now going to observe the plant material. Ask them what we mean by careful observation. Then ask them to look at the leaves and ask open questions, such as: 'What shapes can we observe? What colours can we see? Can you describe any lines on the leaf? What does the edge of the leaf look like?'

This is a great opportunity to introduce magnifying glasses; give these out and explain that the object must be still and in a well-lit place. They should then hold their head still and move the lens to and fro to focus the object. Younger pupils should be asked to talk about what they see. Ask them to examine the two sides of a leaf and to talk about similarities and differences. If you have access to a visualiser or computer microscope and data projector, use this equipment to show magnified images to the whole class.

Discuss what has been observed, the detail, the variety, reuse all the vocabulary, talk about how these plant parts fit on the plant and into the life of the plant. For young pupils this can be very general, for older ones you can expect more detail and more prior knowledge. This pattern of observation can then be applied to other plant parts, including flowers, shoots, buds, stems, and roots.

Common misconception

'It's just a plant!'

Some pupils will treat plants and plant material as if they have no value. They will have seen others damage and destroy plants and may not have experience of people who value plants. This is an important role for you as teacher to show that plants are wonderful, a miracle of nature and vital to all of us on Earth. Try to show that every plant should be cared for by each one of us. Amazing facts about plants can help – for example, an oak tree can support thousands of insects, many trees can live for hundreds of years, plants can survive in Death Valley and in the frozen Arctic. Go for awe and wonder in as big a way as possible. In addition, try to grow at least a couple of potted plants in the classroom, with designated pupils in charge of their care.

As lessons progress, younger pupils should be introduced to observation using a range of magnifying lenses, including small and larger hand lenses (glass lenses where possible), larger lenses on a stand, plastic pots with lenses in the lids, and ideally binocular microscopes and microscopes linked to computers and large screens. In each case, teach pupils to use the equipment.

Figure 4.10 Stereo microscope

Pupil activity 4.6

Seeds grow into seedlings

Learning objective: That a seed can grow into a seedling and be able to identify the growing leaves, stems, and roots of a plant. Learn to recognise growth as a life process that plants do (MRS NERG: movement, respiration, sensitivity, nutrition, excretion, reproduction, and growth).

Resources required: plates, damp paper towels, seeds (for easy suggestions, see below)

One of the best seedlings (young plants) to grow is mung beans (often called bean sprouts). These can be sprouted easily from seeds on damp paper towels. They grow rapidly and produce two large leaves and large roots. These are both easily observed. The seedlings are very easy to handle (tell the pupils to pick them up by the leaves). In contrast, many teachers are familiar with cress. Mung beans are as easy as cress to grow, but cress is not as easy to handle by the pupils, and is very readily damaged. Nevertheless, growing both of these plants could make for interesting comparisons.

Ask the pupils to identify the three main parts of the plant; the leaves, stem, and roots. Can they draw and label them? Can they say what each part is for?

They may know that roots suck up water, but do they know that they anchor the plant? They are probably familiar with leaves, but do they know that they collect light from the Sun to make food inside the plant? The stem is often overlooked, but you can tell them this carries water from the roots to the leaves, holds the plant above the soil, and helps it grow above things that may be in the way so that it can reach up towards the light.

Which aspects of MRS NERG (see p. 54) can you get the pupils to focus on?

Pupil activity 4.7

Which parts of plants do we eat?

Learning objective: That we eat different parts of different plants, including their fruits, leaves, stems, and roots.

Resources required: a range of fruits and vegetables. These should include edible fruits, leaves, stems, roots, flowers, and seeds (for details see below)

Infants in school now receive a piece of fruit or vegetable every day but do they know what part of a plant they are eating? Remind them of the parts of a typical plant, such as root, leaf, stalk, flower, and fruit. Start with a discussion about the ones the school has delivered.

They may know that they eat fruits such as apples, tomatoes, tangerines, and cucumber (actually a fruit!). Ask them if they have ever seen the seeds (pips) inside. Ask them what the seeds are for. If they eat carrots, ask them which part of the plant they are eating; they may be surprised to find out it is the root! Have they noticed in the school salad bar that there is lettuce to eat? What part of the plant do they think that is? They may be surprised to find that these are leaves.

Ask them to sort a range of edible parts of plants into the parts we eat. Give them a mix of different plant parts, but don't tell them what fruit or vegetable they are or what part of the plant they are. Tell them that nothing must be eaten in the lesson. Can they identify which part of the plant each item is from? Do they know its name?

- For leaves use lettuce, cabbage, leek, and spinach
- For stalks try celery, rhubarb, and beansprouts
- For flowers try broccoli, cauliflower, and nasturtiums
- For fruits use apples, pears, and bananas
- For seeds use cut tomatoes, strawberries (they'll have to look closely), peas, and beans
- For roots try parsnips, carrots, and turnips

Once the pupils are confident in naming the plant parts and the fruits and vegetables, give them photographs of more exotic ones they are unfamiliar with to see if they can figure out what part of the plant it came from. Photos can easily be downloaded from the internet.

Ways to teach 'plants' at Key Stage 2

Pupil discussion 4.8

Literacy – speaking and listening

Concept cartoons as a stimulus for discussion

Learning objective: Thinking about what we already know about plants.

Resources required: concept cartoon

Both at the start and at the end of a topic such as this, it is useful to elicit from the pupils what they know about aspects of plant life. Use a question or a *concept cartoon* (Naylor and Keogh, 2000) to stimulate discussion.

Figure 4.11 Concept cartoon

Reproduced with permission from Naylor and Keogh (2000).

Pupil activity 4.9

Writing a better account than existing books/sources about plants

Learning objective: Learn about plants by researching in secondary sources.

Resources required: a set of suitable books and internet access

Pupils might examine secondary sources such as reference books and the internet to find out about the functions of parts of the plant. Using the grid in Table 4.3, they should note the titles of books and websites they will examine and in each row identify an aspect they are interested in. They should then examine each source, making notes about the aspect chosen. Notes are made in the table so that after this period of research pupils can write their own account combining a number of sources.

Literacy – non-chronological writing

Table 4.3 Parts of plants

Plant part	Eyewitness Visual Dictionary: Plants by D. Brown	www.saps.org.uk/primary	Find Out about Plants by S. Pollock	Growing Plants by Peter Riley	BBC science clips: growing plants
	Book or website				
Stem					
Root					
Flower					
Leaf					

Pupil activity 4.10

A 'space capsule' providing for the life processes of plants

Learning objective: Learn about the life processes of plants.

Resources required: potted plants, paper, pencils, and crayons

Recap with pupils the life processes of plants (movement, respiration, sensitivity, nutrition, excretion, reproduction, growth) and ask them to design a space capsule that will have placed within it all the things that plants would need if being taken to another planet. Pupils might work on their own design; more challenging and interactive would be to have groups working together on A1 size sheets of paper.

Encourage creativity and detail in terms of what things would be on the space craft and their appearance. You can allow windows for sunlight but this will weaken as you fly away from the Sun. You might challenge them to explain how things will work and where all the energy is going to come from. Other challenging points would relate to the soil and air. They might realise that plants can make their own food, but that it would be necessary, for example, to have animals on board to respire and provide carbon dioxide.

Conclude the lesson with the news that this arc or spaceship exists and they have been passengers all their lives, can they name Planet Earth? You might point out that such a spaceship is probably far too expensive to build and that we don't yet know of another planet worth going to, so we really should look after the one we have got!

Environment

Pupil investigation skills 4.11

Seeds germinating and seedling growth

Learning objectives: Learn from observation that seeds germinate and that roots and shoots grow from the seed. Recognise growth as a life process in plants (MRS NERG).

Resources required: egg boxes or plant pots, compost, seeds

This activity builds on the simpler one done previously in the Key Stage 1 section.

Observation of plants should include growing seeds in the classroom. Each pupil can grow cress or other safe seedlings (any salad seeds, such as mung beans; for advice, see ASE, 2010) in one-sixth of an egg box. Get them to grow a variety of different seeds. Seeds will germinate on damp compost or cotton wool. This can be done as part of a fair test but is also worth doing for pleasure and observation. Find time for daily observations using hand lenses, measuring, and recording. Young pupils can use non-standard measures such as cutting a strip of paper to the same length as the height of the seedling. Alternatively, pupils might make life-sized models of the seedlings from Plasticine™.

Figure 4.12 Bean seeds growing in a transparent jar

An introductory observation can include the observation of sprouting seeds bought at a local supermarket. Larger bean seeds can be grown inside glass jars, or more safely, in transparent, plastic cups. Plant the seed against the side so that its germination and growth can be observed. Wrap the cup in opaque paper or card when you are not observing. Pupils will be able to observe the emergence first of the root and later the leaf shoot, and that the former always grows downwards and that the latter always grows upwards.

The pupils could carry out an investigation into whether larger seeds grow larger roots and shoots. They could compare cress, mung beans, peas, and beans. Ask them to think about why a bigger seed might produce a larger-growing seedling. They may work out that the larger seeds contain larger stores of food that the seedling needs, before it starts to make enough of its own food by photosynthesising using its newly grown leaves.

Watch web-based time-lapse films such as the following:

http://www.haworth-village.org.uk/nature/time-lapse/time-lapse.asp?pic=26

Extend this work by moving on to seed dispersal, perhaps using an interactive whiteboard game, such as:

http://www2.bgfl.org/bgfl2/custom/resources_ftp/client_ftp/ks2/science/plants_pt2/dispersal.htm

Pupil activity 4.12

Exploring the role of the leaf, root, stem, and flower

Learning objective: Learn about the functions of the leaf, root, stem and flower of flowering plants.

Resources required: plant material, potted plants, magnifiers

If you take so-called weeds from the school garden or wild area, pupils will be able observe a whole plant. An alternative is to take potted plants out of their pot for short periods; the root ball can be left bare or put inside a see-through bag. This will allow pupils to observe the roots and then to discuss their function. They might draw and press plant parts to create a poster or class book. Try to find a range of different plants for pupils to examine, so that they can recognise the similarities and differences between leaves from different species, or roots from different species. Even stems vary, although this is not often appreciated.

In addition to learning to recognise and name the major parts of plants, older pupils should learn about the function or role of the parts in the life of a plant. Having examined plants and their parts, pupils should be asked to discuss the functions of these parts. Pupils might be asked to draw a cartoon or comic strip to articulate their understanding of the role of plant parts. For example, the leaves can be seen as little sugar factories, the stem as a motorway with water tankers, and the roots as pipes sucking up water. The flowers are like huge, colourful advertising boards to draw the insects in.

Discuss with them how plants carry out similar living processes to those of animals, and what differences there are (recap on MRS NERG).

Common misconception

'Plant material comes from the soil'

It is a common misconception that most of the material in the tissues of a plant comes from the soil via the roots. This is far from the truth, as most plant material is made of carbon from carbon dioxide in the air. The idea that pupils may have is that the plant is somehow 'eating' the soil, which would be eventually used up. The misconception may arise because plants are made of solid stuff and soil is made of solid stuff, and so in the pupils' minds the two are related. They do not see how gaseous carbon dioxide could become incorporated into the solid plant structure. But it is. Plants use carbon dioxide in photosynthesis to make glucose, which also contains carbon. These glucose molecules can be combined by the plant to make cellulose. Green stems and the trunks of trees are both made of cellulose. The main component of paper and card is also cellulose.

Teacher demonstration 4.13

Demonstrating how the vessels carry water up the stem

Learning objective: To understand that the stem has a role in transporting vital water around the plant.

Resources required: carnation flower, red or blue food colouring, bottle of water

Mix some food colouring with the water, making a very concentrated mixture, the darker the better. Place the carnation in the water and leave overnight. Pupils may be surprised to see that the food colouring will even reach the petals, showing the water is transported up the stem to all parts of the plant.

A similar demonstration can be done with a cut stick of celery left in food colouring overnight. In this case, the colour cannot reach the tip of the plant, but if you cut the stem into sections you will clearly see the vessels stained by the food colouring.

Pupil activity 4.14

Grouping and classifying plants

Learning objective: Learn to group leaves (or flowers) according to the features we can observe.

Resources required: a set of potted plants or a set of plant materials, leaves or flowers (otherwise pictures may be used to make the set bigger)

Ask the pupils to conduct observations of the plant material answering the following questions: 'What can we see? What shapes, colours, and textures can we observe?'

Now ask them to suggest ways to group the material; for example, green and non-green leaves; hairy and non-hairy leaves; smooth edged and non-smooth edged leaves; leaves all green and leaves that are green with other colours. Now demonstrate how questions can help us identify a plant. Pupils could use and construct simple keys as illustrated in the activity in the Chapter 6, 'Variation and diversity'.

The observation of plants leads on to classification, initially into groups decided by pupils. Don't worry if you cannot identify a plant that you find, and even if you know the name, you may hold back the information and ask the pupils to use a poster or pocket guide. Pupils should learn the names of common plants but can construct descriptive names including their own ones just as the early botanists did (e.g. Joel's Yellow Spike Leaf).

Pupil activity 4.15

Classifying plants – a moss plant I know

Learning objective: To recognise that plants can be classified and to know some of the commonly occurring plants in local habitats.

Resources required: access to the school site

Ask pupils about different plants they know, explain that most of these are flowering plants, and that this lesson is about these and the non-flowering plants. Introduce the simple classification of the plant kingdom – that is, the flowering plants, the conifers, ferns, mosses and liverworts. Ask them to suggest where we might find one of each, ideally on the school site.

Use the internet or pocket guides to illustrate the different groups and explain that they are going with you on a plant safari around the school site to identify, draw, and/or photograph examples from as many groups as possible. There are a range of common plants that grow on school sites. In grassy areas, daisies, buttercups, dandelions, and mosses can often be found. In flowerbeds you will often find daffodils and roses. In unkempt areas or even through cracks in the pavement, you might observe thistles, nettles, and docks.

Common misconception

'I have found a plant Miss, this mushroom'

It is a very common error to assume that fungi are plants. They are not, they do not photosynthesise, and the children will never see a green one.

Pupils should be introduced to the idea that plants can be organised into groups. Several pocket guides to plants are organised in colour sections according to the colour of the plant's flower. The disadvantage here is that not all the plants will be flowering when you observe them. Ideal for the identification of plants are the 'Clue Books' published by Oxford University Press, which ask questions of the reader about a plant. The book then guides the reader to other clues and thus ultimately to the name of the plant. More ideas for observation, grouping and classifying along with these identification keys are given in the Chapter 6, 'Variation and diversity'.

Pupils might make drawings, take rubbings, save media representations of specimens (not from the wild), take photographs, and construct diagrams, flow charts, posters, audio commentaries, and multi-media presentations to illustrate plant groupings. They should learn sufficient scientific terms to describe plants and plant material but also participate in more creative, descriptive speaking and writing about, for example, the grandeur and power of trees.

Pupil activity 4.16

Observing flowers

Learning objective: Learn to recognise the parts of a flower and their arrangement.

Resources required: flowers, hand lenses, binocular microscope, computer microscope or visualiser

This should begin in the earliest years, observing the general form and some detail of colour, form, etc. Attention should be drawn to familiar flowers as well as less familiar ones. Key words such as petal and stem should be used and attention should be drawn to the beauty and diversity in the plant kingdom. After a check on the pupils' sensitivity to pollen, ask them to observe the flowers looking for the parts of the flower in the centre. Later use a poster to direct more observation so that everyone has observed each of the parts concerned.

In the later primary years, it is necessary for pupils to become familiar with flower structure and to be able to name and describe the function of the main parts of a flower. The best way to do this is a combination of real plant material and high-quality illustrations on posters, in books, and on the internet. For this you will need to quickly survey the school site, perhaps collect potted plants or access a garden where you have permission to collect flowers, or maybe a local florist will give you bruised and slightly damaged flowers they would otherwise throw away. Good flowers for this are roses, buttercups, daffodils, tulips and lilies, in fact any open flower of reasonable size where the main parts can be seen.

Smaller flowers are useful as they can reveal detail under magnification – this can lead to a 'wow!' from pupils. Very useful observations can be made using an electronic microscope or visualiser connected to a projector. That way you can be sure that all members of the class can see a high-quality picture of plant specimens magnified $\times 10$ or more.

> Observe time-lapse photography of flowers opening at:
>
> http://www.haworth-village.org.uk/nature/time-lapse/time-lapse.asp?pic=28

Common misconception

'All flowers look the same'

Flowers illustrated in this and other books often resemble a buttercup or other common flower. There is enormous variety in the plant world. We often use particular plants in the classroom because they illustrate our teaching objectives well. Pupils may enjoy doing research to find unusual looking flowers on the internet.

Pupil activity 4.17

Making 3D models of a flower

Learning objectives: Learn to recognise and name the internal parts of a flower. Recognise that reproduction is a life process.

Resources required: coloured paper and card, pipe cleaners, Plasticine™

A very powerful way to learn about the structure of a flower is to model one in Plasticine™. Modelling in card and coloured paper is another alternative, as are pipe cleaners and materials from a fabric box. These models require time to construct but can assist in making the science memorable. They force the children to pay attention to the individual parts, and think about what they are for. Pupils may suggest making the different parts with different colours of Plasticine™ to emphasise the differences, or to go for a more natural look and copy the colours that occur in nature (e.g. brightly coloured petals, contrasting stamens, etc.). Photographs of real plants as well as idealised drawings from books will help.

Alternatively, fabric plants and flowers with detachable plant parts and labels can be purchased from educational suppliers. A very useful extension activity is to ask pupils to prepare a talk for younger pupils based on their own models or a bought example.

Literacy

Common misconception

'Flowers look nice, for us'

Plants produce flowers to pass on genetic material – that is, to make seeds and thus more plants. Our appreciation of them is very subjective. For example, the flowers of the common privet are not sold by florists because they judge people would not buy them. Flowers have evolved to attract insects, not humans. However, humans have selectively bred many plants so that they do look attractive to us, often making them bigger, brighter, and more colourful than their wild relations.

Pupil activity 4.18

Role-play flower, pollination, and fertilisation

Learning objective: Learn the function of the parts of a flower in pollination and fertilisation.

Resources required: none

Ask the pupils to demonstrate flower structure physically. Have one child stand erect representing the stigma, with four or six others around him or her, with one arm stretched up, representing the stamen. Around them kneeling with elbows out will be a further four or six pupils as petals. Now ask the class about the function of each. You might mention that often nectar is available for the insects at the base of the stigma. This means that the insect has to push against all the central parts of the flower to get to the nectar. You might set up another 'flower' nearby. Ask the pupils where it will get pollen from. Stress that while some flowers can get pollen from themselves, it is better to get it from another flower. Finally, ask another pupil to play the role of an insect – a moth or a bee. From time to time stop the bee and ask others to explain what the bee is doing and how this is helping both bee and plant. Can the pupils think of ways to further improve this activity, perhaps adding something to represent pollen?

Common misconceptions

'Bees go to flowers to pollinate them, don't they?'

Children will often talk about the role of the bee as if its purpose in visiting the plant is to pollinate it. The insect visiting the plant is searching for nectar, a sugar which the insect needs as food. Its role in pollination is accidental as far as the insect is concerned, it is unaware of it. The plant has been shaped by evolution to be attractive to the insect, to signal by sight and smell that this is a nectar source. To the bee it is free food, to the plant it is an exchange deal! The role-play above will help pupils to understand this.

'Bees fertilise flowers'

Many adults and children confuse pollination and fertilisation. This may be because they sound similar but is more likely to result from a lack of understanding of the reproductive process. *Pollination* is about genetic material (pollen) arriving at a flower from another plant; *fertilisation* is the fusing of the male and female genetic material. Flying insects are responsible for pollination in some species of plants. This is best taught through visual and practical illustration with very clear use of the new language by pupils and teacher.

Pupil activity 4.19

Researching plants using secondary material

Learning objective: Learn about the variety of plant life.

Resources required: a selection of children's biology books and/or internet access

In addition to handling plants and plant material, there is much to learn about plants in field guides, children's books of biology, and from the internet. It may help to research specific questions. With the class, try generating ten investigable questions, such as:

- Do plants live in lakes?
- Is coral a plant?
- What is the biggest plant in the world?

- What is the smallest plant in the world?
- What is the oldest plant in the world?
- Where is the oldest tree in Britain?
- What were the first plants on the planet like?
- What is the most widespread group of plants?

Remember that internet search engines like Google often respond well to questions such as the above typed into them. As well as questions about the biggest, strongest, most long-lived, etc., try to encourage 'why' and 'how' questions, including:

- How do plants in hot deserts survive without much water?
- Why do insects visit flowers?
- Why does the Venus flytrap trap insects?
- How can plants survive the cold in Arctic regions?
- Why don't trees in Britain grow in the winter?

These will lead you and the pupils to seek explanations. You may go way beyond the requirements of the National Curriculum (DfE, 2013a) here, but you may realise an even greater objective if you manage to give the pupil a lifelong interest in the natural world!

Some of the pupils' questions may have the potential to be investigated, for example 'Do plants turn to face the Sun?' These pupil questions should be considered very seriously, perhaps to replace or complement planned investigations to follow. Pupil-initiated investigations often have more power as they have come from the children. However, their questions sometimes need to be reframed to make them investigable.

Questions that could be addressed include:

- Do some plants open and close their petals during the day and at night? What about during the day when the light is low? (Daisies, buttercups and celandine may be found on the school premises and show responses to light.)
- Will a potted plant turn its leaves towards the light? This is very easy to set up and answer over a period of days. Pupils might take photographs each day (from exactly the same place, as movement can be subtle). Note that potted supermarket herbs, such as basil, do this.

The following investigations would illustrate the life processes of 'sensitivity' and 'movement' in plants (MRS NERG).

Pupil discussion 4.20

How can we investigate the best conditions for plant growth?

Learning objective: To recognise that growth is one of the life processes in plants, and it can be influenced.

Resources required: seeds, containers, compost

This remains a focus of interest for research scientists who, for example, hope to find plants that will provide food in areas of low rainfall. After some discussion of the pupils' understanding of the needs of plants, you should ask the pupils to devise a fair test to show the real effects of different conditions on plants. Investigations of light intensity, warmth, moisture, and soil are conducted most commonly in primary classrooms.

These tests can be conducted on seeds to determine the effects on germination, on seedlings, and on more mature plants. Seeds and seedlings are often used because they are available, cheap, and plentiful. Seeds are often preferred because they do not require transplanting. Pupils transplanting seedlings can kill a high proportion through rough handling. A seedling should be lifted by its seed (first) leaves; no other part should be touched, as the stem is easily squashed. Make sure the pupils understand the difference between a seed and seedling (the latter being the young, just sprouted plant). Stress to them that although seeds do not need light to germinate, once a seedling starts to grow it will need light.

One problem with such experiments is that they require days or even weeks to be completed, so that lessons have to be planned to allow time for setting up the experiments, measuring the plants (perhaps at a given time each day), and dealing with the results and conclusions.

Pupils can investigate the conditions that suit plants. As plants need warmth, light, water, and nutrients, all can be investigated to explore the effects of different conditions. The three investigations that follow enable pupils to develop their investigative skills by, for example, asking them to concentrate on predicting/planning in one, recording/measuring in a second, and displaying results in graphic form in a third.

After they have carried out their investigations, you might ask pupils to reflect on the question, 'Is what plants need different from what animals need to grow?'

Pupil investigation skills 4.21

Growth conditions – light

Learning objective: To investigate the light conditions required for healthy plant growth. Learn that plants make their own food using energy from light – the life process of 'nutrition' (MRS NERG).

Resources required: pots, compost, seedlings, boxes, light meter

A classic experiment is to investigate the effects of light intensity on plants. Plants can be grown in different intensities of light. This can be done simply in a qualitative way by growing one plant in the dark, another in normal light, and a third in shaded conditions. This can be achieved in shoe boxes with different sized windows cut into the sides and lid. Time can be measured by young pupils in terms of the days the plants are grown in this way.

If you have a light meter or data logger, you might create environments for the plants that are identical except for the available light.

ICT

Figure 4.13 Five plants grown in different light conditions

Figure 4.14 Hand-held data logger (Vu available from Data Harvest Group)

Pupil investigation skills 4.22

Growth conditions – water

Learning objective: To investigate the effect of water on healthy plant growth.

Resources required: containers, seeds or seedlings, syringe to measure water, cotton wool or tissue paper

Seedlings can be grown from seeds in a range of containers in an identical medium such as cotton wool or tissue paper soaked with different amounts of water, perhaps 0–50 ml per day or every 2–3 days. The containers might be placed in plastic bags to control evaporation. Ask the pupils what might happen if the seedlings get too much water (they can rot, or get a condition that makes them all fall over and die called 'damping off'). Ask them what will happen if the plants get too little. Stress that this is the kind of test scientists do, so they know just the right amount of water a plant might need.

In an emergency, if your seeds fail, you can buy bags of germinating or sprouting seeds from many supermarkets.

Pupil investigation skills 4.23

Growth conditions – transport of water

Learning objective: To investigate how water travels through a plant.

Resources required: containers, water, food dyes, celery sticks, magnifying glasses, visualiser (optional)

When celery stems are placed in containers of water mixed with food colouring, the colour can be seen, over a day or so, to move up the stem as water is drawn into and up the stem. Learners can investigate a number of variables including different coloured food dyes, different lengths of stem, different amounts of dye, stem with and without leaves and different temperatures. These experiments take a day or so which means you need to plan in time for observation and recording of results. If you can leave the celery leaves on the stems then learners can observe closely how the water and dye travel through the leaf veins.

Pupil investigation skills 4.24

Growth conditions – temperature

Learning objective: To investigate the effect of temperature on healthy plant growth.

Resources required: containers, seeds (to sprout) or seedlings, syringe to measure water, cotton wool or tissue paper, cool and warm environments

To investigate how warmth affects seeds or seedling, compare some grown indoors with some grown outdoors. Ask the children to predict which will grow the best. The indoors ones should certainly be warmer and grow more. An extension activity would be to grow some outdoors in a propagator and some indoors in a propagator. A propagator is simply a seed tray with a clear plastic lid, which acts like a mini greenhouse. The clear lid is able to trap the heat from the Sun inside it effectively, raising the temperature of the air inside. It also stops the seedlings from getting a draught, which would reduce the temperature. Can the pupils predict which of the following will be best and worst places for the potted seedlings to grow: (1) indoors on a windowsill, (2) indoors on a windowsill in a propagator, (3) outdoors, and (4) outdoors in a propagator?

Pupil investigation skills 4.25

Growth conditions – soil

Learning objective: To investigate the effect of soil conditions on healthy plant growth.

Resources required: containers, seeds (to sprout) or seedlings, syringe to measure water, growing mediums such as cotton wool, tissue paper, sandy soil, clay soil, sand, gravel, compost

Here the pupils control all the variables but vary the soil or medium in which the plants are grown. Ask them to discuss the relative merits of cotton wool versus soil, compost versus sand, etc. They may know that plant compost from the garden centre contains lots of things added to help plants grow, while sand contains virtually nothing. Ask them if they see a lot of plants growing on a beach. Is plant compost better than soil, and if it is should we fill our gardens with it?

Stress that it is the growing plant (seedling) that you are interested in, as seeds will sprout on virtually any wet medium and so are not the object of this investigation. Pupils often find it confusing to see seeds and very young seedlings growing quite happily without soil. Remind them that soil is needed to provide nutrients for healthy growth, once all those in the seed have been used up. Nutrients are needed by plants like we need vitamins and minerals.

Remember that the objective is for the pupils to plan and carry out the investigation themselves. You will, as teacher, need to be sensitive to past achievement and the need to challenge them to work more independently in groups and alone.

Summary of key learning points:

- the structure of the plant kingdom;
- the names and functions of the main parts of flowering plants;
- the parts of a flower;
- the life cycle of flowering plants;
- basic life processes of plants, including the word equation for photosynthesis;
- that tissues and organs of a multi-cellular organism carry out specialised functions;
- that most organisms are made up of cells and almost all cells have a nucleus which controls their activities;
- that the health of an organism can be affected by a range of factors.

Self-test

Question 1

Green plants (a) respire at night only, (b) use energy from the Sun to produce food, (c) carry out some of the life processes seen in animals, (d) do not move

Question 2

Plant tissues (a) perform specialised functions, (b) require nutrients from the soil, (c) are all green, (d) can photosynthesise if they contain chlorophyll

Question 3

Healthy plants (a) can suffer without essential nutrients, (b) require water and light to photosynthesise, (c) can be killed by vertebrate action, (d) require space, air, and warmth

Question 4

Flowers (a) are pollinated by many flying insects, (b) are fertilised before pollination, (c) can be pollinated more than once, (d) cannot self-fertilise

Self-test answers

Q1: (b) and (c) are correct; (a) is wrong since plants respire during the day and night; and (d) is wrong, though movement in plants is limited and quite different to movement in animals.

Q2: (a), (b), and (d) are correct; (c) is wrong, since not all plant tissues are green; root tissue is never green, as it does not contain chlorophyll.

Q3: All of these statements are correct. Vertebrates cause damage when they eat plants or by excreting waste products that can build up to toxic quantities. It should be added that invertebrates have the potential to cause plants a great deal of harm, for example by eating the plant or growing on or in the plant tissue.

Q4: (a) and (c) are correct; (b) is wrong because fertilisation follows pollination; and (d) is wrong because many plants can self-fertilise, although this tends to be a last-ditch emergency measure if normal pollination and fertilisation has not occurred.

Misconceptions

'It's just a plant'

'Plant material comes from the soil'

'I found a plant Miss, this mushroom'

'All flowers look the same'

'Flowers look nice for us'

'Bees go to flowers to pollinate them don't they?'

'Bees fertilise flowers'

Web resources

http://apps.kew.org/trees/?page_id=17
    (Kew gardens tree identifier)

http://plantsinmotion.bio.indiana.edu/plantmotion/earlygrowth/photomorph/photomorph.html
    (video of plants responding to light)

http://wildflowerfinder.org.uk
    (allows you to search by flower colour, number of petals and other features)

http://www.bbc.co.uk/nature
    (full of video clips and information on British wildlife)

http://www.discoverwildlife.com/
    (BBC wildlife magazine website, lots of free resources and information)

http://www.bbc.co.uk/schools/scienceclips/ages/7_8/plants_grow_fs.shtml
    (science games and simulations)

http://www.haworth-village.org.uk/nature/time-lapse/time-lapse.asp?pic=26
    (time-lapse video of germination)

http://www.nhm.ac.uk/nature-online/british-natural-history/urban-tree-survey/identify-
    trees/tree-key/index.html#tree-s1
    (Natural History Museum Tree identifier)

http://www.opalexplorenature.org/Identification
    (downloadable British species guides)

http://www.ukwildflowers.com/Web_pages_intros_indexes/english_index.htm
    (index of wild flowers)

http://www2.bgfl.org/bgfl2/custom/resources_ftp/client_ftp/ks2/science/plants_pt2/
    dispersal.htm
    (seed dispersal simulation)

5

Life processes – animals

About this chapter

This chapter deals with the science you need to know and understand about life processes in animals. It contains aspects about the Animal Kingdom and provides a focus on human biology, including the main parts of the human body, conditions for life, animal cells, and the basic life processes. It will inform you about the functioning of the major organs and organ systems in the body. Several references are made to health, how to look after different parts of the human body, and major causes of harm such as drugs. The second part of the chapter refers to what the pupils need to learn. This section is followed by one that suggests effective ways to teach life processes in animals, including examples of common misconceptions.

What the teacher needs to know and understand

Resources required: a mirror

Since primary aged pupils are required to learn principally about human biology, it will be our focus here. This therefore means that your teaching of human biology will be able to contribute to Personal, Social, and Health Education (https://www.pshe-association.org.uk/) as well as important aspects of the Every Child Matters agenda renamed Helping Children Achieve More (http://www.elc-gel.org/learning-modules/every-child-matters/), such as keeping healthy.

What is an animal?

Animals do not photosynthesise; for nutrition they eat other living things. They usually move freely, have bodies made of many cells, and reproduce sexually. They include large organisms such as the blue whale and smaller ones invisible to our eyes (e.g. dust mites). The Animal Kingdom is divided into groups or phyla, which includes all the animals with backbones (vertebrates) and those without backbones (invertebrates).

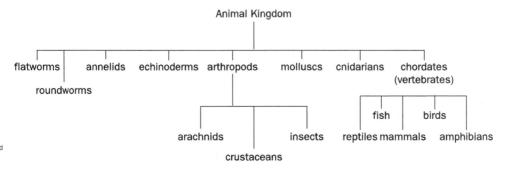

Variation and diversity

Figure 5.1 The main groups within the Animal Kingdom

Some of the above words are familiar to us, others need some explanation and examples often help: annelids are types of worms, echinoderms include starfish and sea urchins, arachnids include spiders, crustaceans include woodlice, molluscs include snails, cnidarians include jellyfish. Animals are adapted to their environment in all sorts of ways: a stick insect's body and movement are adapted so that it will blend in with twigs and branches on a tree; tortoises on some Galapagos Islands have shells shaped like a riding saddle, which allows their neck to reach up higher on bushes for the leaves they eat.

This topic is another opportunity to teach about things that are alive, things that are dead and things that have never been alive. Here you should be confident about examples including harder examples, such as oil. Crude oil is made from parts of the bodies of living things but has never occurred as a living organism itself. Therefore we can call it a material which has never been alive.

Observing and identifying common animals

You will need to be able to make careful observations of animals using your eyes and perhaps at times your ears and sense of touch. Care should be taken with animals to ensure the safety of the observers and the safety of the animals. You will need to learn to use magnifying glasses, other lenses, computer microscopes and visualisers. For all of these you need a little practice and to use them in a well-lit environment against a light coloured background.

You are not expected to identify and name all the animals which may be encountered but you should know examples of the main groups of animals including common animals in your locality. Examples might include the following:

Mammals:

    common pets: cat, dog, hamster, rabbit, gerbil, guinea pig

    farm animals: pig, cattle, sheep, goat, horse

    wild animals: fox, deer, squirrel, field mouse, hedgehog, bat

Birds: sparrow, pigeon, robin, blue tit, chaffinch, blackbird, rook, kestrel

Amphibians: newt, frog, toad

Reptiles: snake, lizard

Fish:

    seafish: cod, plaice, sea bass, mackerel

    freshwater fish: trout, stickleback, tench

Insects: wasp, bee, greenfly, ladybird; butterflies (including red admiral, peacock, tortoiseshell, cabbage white)

Arachnids: spider, harvestman

As a teacher you should work to increase the knowledge you have of these and other animals, remembering that your role will be to enable this knowledge in others rather than be a font of all knowledge. Periodically you might look at our representation above of the animal kingdom and you might check that you can identify and name animals from most sections, for example, in some cases you might know a little about these animals including the body shape, body parts, habits, and food. You would need to give examples of herbivores (eat plant material only, e.g. sheep), carnivores (eat other animals only, e.g. cat) and omnivores (eat plants and animals, e.g. humans).

Conditions required for life

The life processes for animals can be remembered by the mnemonic MRS NERG: movement, reproduction, sensitivity, nutrition, excretion, respiration, and growth.
    Animals require similar conditions to those required by plants:

- food – animals cannot photosynthesise and so must eat plants or other animals;
- air – to breathe;
- water – to drink;
- warmth – animals can only survive at certain temperatures (warm-blooded animals require greater quantities of food than cold-blooded animals, which is used to keep their internal body temperature constant);
- light – in humans vitamin D is made in the skin when exposed to sunlight, and this is one of the main sources of it;
- shelter – animals require shelter to rest, avoid predators, breed, and raise young.

Animals are often physically adapted as a result of natural selection to live in particular habitats; for example, the Arctic fox lives where other foxes could not live because it has extremely thick fur. Animals can also adapt their behaviour to suit different environments; for example penguins in South Africa spread their flippers to lose heat, whereas those in Antarctica huddle together to keep warm.

Animal cells

Animal cells form the various tissues such as nerve, heart, and muscle. As a primary teacher you need to be able to distinguish between animal and plant cells. Animal cells are different to plant cells, which have chloroplasts, cell vacuoles, and cell walls. Each animal cell includes the main constituents illustrated in Figure 5.2. The form and detail of cells of the body vary, as they are specialised within body tissues that perform different functions, including muscle, lung, and brain tissues.

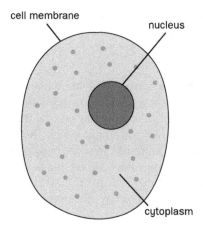

Figure 5.2 An animal cell

Growth and the human life cycle

The life cycles of different animals vary: some are born live, others as eggs, some have dormant periods, others undergo metamorphosis (butterfly, frog), and some spend part of their life cycle inside another animal (such as parasitic worms). The human life cycle below is very familiar. From birth until late adolescence, rapid growth is stimulated by growth hormones released by glands in the body. Healthy growth requires energy and that an individual eats a balanced diet. Towards the end of life some cells die, only a proportion of which are repaired or replaced; at this stage there is no growth.

Primary pupils are not taught about sexual reproduction in primary school science. In science, we teach about the human life cycle and changes that occur at the

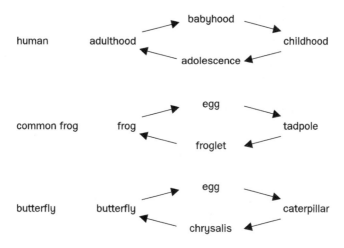

Figure 5.3 Life cycles

different stages. Thus it overlaps greatly with Personal, Social, and Health Education (PSHE). You may be asked to teach aspects of the PSHE programme that deal with, for example, changes that occur in the bodies of boys and girls as they approach the teenage years. For girls, this includes mention of the menstrual cycle. This part of the curriculum is often taught by a visiting nurse. As sex education is a sensitive subject for some parents, they are often consulted in a meeting immediately before the period of teaching.

Sexual reproduction occurs when sexually mature adults have sexual intercourse, coinciding with the female's monthly ovulation or production of a fertile egg. Fertilisation occurs when the male and female gametes, the egg and the sperm (each containing half of the required genetic material), fuse. The resulting zygote, initially a single cell, multiplies into a bundle of cells that continue to grow into an embryo and later a foetus. Non-identical twins result when the female produces two separate fertile eggs at the same time and these are fertilised separately by two different sperm. Thus the two individuals have quite different genetic material. Identical twins result from the fertilisation of one fertile egg and the resulting cell or bundle of cells splitting and separating to form two genetically identical individuals.

Movement and the human skeleton

Humans like many other animals have an internal skeleton that grows as we grow. Some animals such as insects have an external skeleton (exoskeleton) that does not grow. This means that as they grow they have to periodically shed the exoskeleton and form a new one.

The functions of our skeleton are threefold. First, to provide support and shape to our body; second, to allow movement through the skeleton's joints, and third, to protect our internal organs (for example, the skull protects the brain). Our skeleton is an organ made of living tissue, and has a blood supply as well as nerves. You should know the

Can you label these?
You should know these bones:
skull
ribs
pelvis
backbone

How about these?
femur
humerus
radius
ulna
patella
metatarsal
fibula
tibia
scapula
clavicle

In order, the last group are:
long upper leg bone
long upper arm bone
lower arm bone
lower arm bone
knee bone
bone in the foot close to ankle
lower leg bone
lower leg bone
shoulder blade
top of shoulder bone

Figure 5.4 The human skeleton

name and location of major bones in Figure 5.4, as well as how the different joints move and about how to care for bones.

The joints of the human body move in different ways; some move in one plane, such as your knee joint, whereas others move in numerous planes, such as your ankle, hip, shoulder and neck joints. Take a minute or two to examine your joints. Very slowly (take care) turn your head from side to side and slowly look up at the ceiling and back down at this text. Muscles all over your chest and back have pulled and relaxed in a coordinated way to move your skull, resting as it does on top of your backbone. Now put your elbow on the desk and slowly raise your hand. As it rises your biceps muscles in your upper arm are contracting (and pulling) while your triceps behind your upper arm are relaxing. Now lower your hand and the muscles so that the biceps relax and the triceps contract. The muscles act in opposition, relaxing and contracting. Repeat this and feel the contraction and relaxation with your other hand. Your knee joint is similar, allowing movement in one plane only. Your hip joint, a ball and socket joint, can be observed if you stand up, steady yourself by holding on to a solid object, and carefully lift one foot and move that leg first slightly forward, then slightly back, then outwards and back. Are muscles pulling and relaxing? Several sets of muscles are involved here as the movement is complex. It involves several muscle sets in your lower back, buttocks, and leg. You can probably feel them moving a little. There is not time here to examine all your muscles but try turning the palm of your hand up to the ceiling and as you wriggle your fingers can you see movement in your lower arm? This is because the muscles that move your fingers are in your lower arm and connected to your finger bones by tendons. Tendons are strong non-muscular fibrous strands that transfer the movement of your muscles to the bones. Each joint is lubricated by synovial fluid to avoid bones rubbing and grinding on one another. The joint is surrounded by strong fibrous tissue that protects the joint and holds it together; these components are illustrated in Figure 5.5.

All movement in your body results from the movement of muscles. These include heart muscle, muscle attached to bones, and smooth muscle, which creates movement of internal organs such as your intestine through which food is gently squeezed.

You should be able to explain how we look after our skeleton. This would include eating a balanced diet including sources of calcium, taking weight-bearing exercise (particularly important in females to prevent osteoporosis) and avoiding damage to the skeleton (for example, wearing protective clothing, such as a cycle helmet, for the skull).

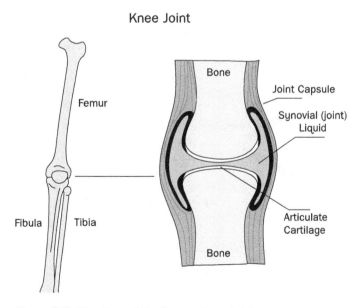

Figure 5.5 Structure of the human knee joint

Circulation of the blood

Figure 5.6 The human heart

The circulatory system is rather like a figure of eight. The heart is composed of two sets of chambers for pumping blood first to the lungs (pulmonary circuit) and on its return pumping blood to the whole body (systemic circuit).

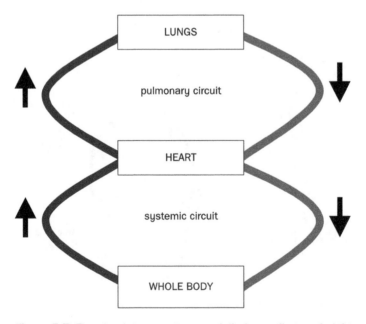

Figure 5.7 The circulatory system modelled as a figure of eight

The four chambers of the heart act as two pairs with the right atrium and right ventricle receiving blood from the whole body and pumping it to the lungs. Here the blood picks up oxygen and disposes of carbon dioxide. The oxygenated blood then returns to the heart and is pumped by the left atrium and left ventricle around the body. The aorta (artery) transports blood from the heart to the whole body where it divides and the resulting blood vessels subdivide repeatedly to the point they become very fine capillaries. Here they are in close proximity to the cells that make up the body tissue. The blood arriving in the capillaries provides cells with oxygen and sugars as well as taking away carbon dioxide and other waste materials. The blood, now deoxygenated, returns to the heart via the veins from where it is pumped back to the lungs to start the cycle again. Backflow of blood is prevented by small valves in the blood vessels and by the constant beating of the heart.

People are often confused that blood vessels seen in the skin look blue or grey rather than the red they expect. In fact, the blue/grey colour is observed because we are seeing the tissue of the blood vessels rather than the blood. Blood is bright red when it leaves the lungs and darker red as it returns to the lungs. On diagrams it is marked red when oxygenated and blue when it is deoxygenated. In reality it is a brighter red when oxygenated and darker red when deoxygenated.

Look at an internet simulation, for example:

http://library.med.utah.edu/kw/pharm/hyper_heart1.html

Pause the heart to observe movement and watch the bright red blood from the lungs flow through the heart to the body.

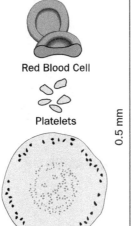

Red Blood Cell

Platelets

0.5 mm

White Blood Cell

Figure 5.8 Components of human blood

Blood is made up of different components. The main liquid component is called plasma. Red blood cells carry oxygen; these are very numerous and give blood its colour. White blood cells are less numerous but have an important role attacking and destroying invading bacteria. The last component to mention here are platelets, which are responsible for clotting the blood when wounds occur (without which most of us would have bled to death by now).

Breathing

There are two things you need to know about mammalian lungs. First, they have air going in and out constantly and, second, blood is constantly flowing through them. Inside the lungs the air and blood are brought into close proximity so that gases can be exchanged (gaseous exchange).

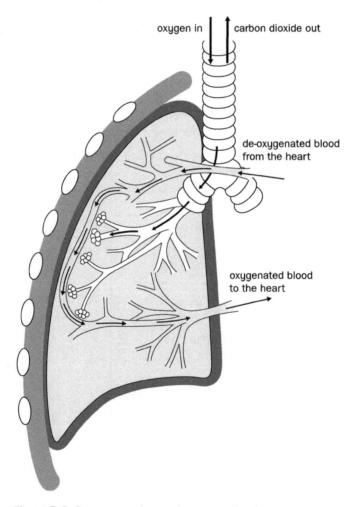

Figure 5.9 Gaseous exchange in mammalian lungs

Blood flowing to the lungs (often coloured blue in diagrams) is laden with carbon dioxide (CO_2) and low in oxygen (O_2). The blood vessels branch down to fine capillaries and come into contact with the alveoli (small air sacs). Here O_2 enters the blood and CO_2 leaves the bloodstream and is exhaled. The blood becomes oxygenated and returns to the heart.

Lung tissue appears spongy as it contains no skeleton or muscles, so how you might ask do the lungs constantly move to inflate and deflate? When we breathe in it appears that the air going in is inflating the lungs, rather like a balloon when we blow it up. The truth is that air is sucked in, the question is how?

The lungs fill most of the cavity created by the rib cage, which is a sealed unit. You can feel your ribs but not so easily the muscle between them. This muscle is able to expand the rib cage, pushing the ribs apart and increasing the volume inside the rib cage. Put your hands on your chest as you breathe in, can you feel the expansion? As the lungs are attached to the rib cage, this increases their internal volume and lowers the air pressure inside the lungs (see Figure 5.10). In addition, the base of the chest cavity is a sheet of muscular tissue known as the diaphragm. This also moves downwards, further increasing the volume of the chest cavity. As long as the airway is open, air will now rush in for a breath. Almost immediately the muscles of the rib cage contract, reducing the volume of the chest cavity and thus the lungs push the air out again. This constant inflow and exhaling provides a constantly changing supply of air.

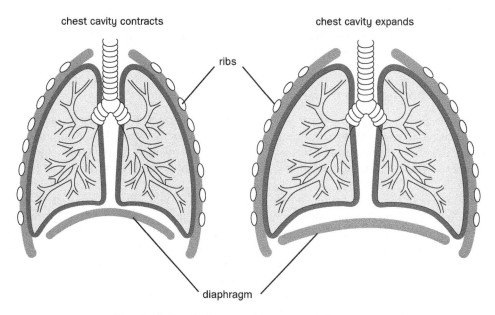

chest cavity contracts   chest cavity expands

ribs

diaphragm

Muscles in the diaphragm and between the ribs
successively increase and decrease the volume of the chest cavity

Figure 5.10 Expansion and contraction of the chest cavity in breathing

Health

Your lungs are important to you and so caring for them is essential; regular exercise is required (avoiding over-exertion) to keep them functioning well, as is the avoidance of dusty or smoky environments or environments containing dangerous gases. Smokers inhale a noxious mix of harmful gases and chemicals, which, even over a short period, adversely affect the efficiency of their lungs. Smoking over a short or a longer period can lead to diseases that adversely affect the individual's health and contribute to the death of a large number of smokers.

Respiration

Energy

It is important to grasp the distinction between breathing and respiration. Breathing is largely a mechanical process of moving gases in and out of the body. Cellular respiration is principally a chemical process that produces energy for the cells and thus the body to use (this also occurs in plant cells).

Oxygen is transported through blood vessels of smaller and smaller diameter, until they become fine capillaries, in which it is in close proximity to living cells. Oxygen passes into the cells and carbon dioxide passes out into the bloodstream. Within each cell the oxygen is used in cellular respiration to release energy from sugars and the waste products are water and carbon dioxide.

$$\text{glucose} + \text{oxygen} \longrightarrow \text{carbon dioxide} + \text{water and energy}$$

Sensitivity

This section deals with the different ways in which your body is sensitive to, and can then react to, your environment.

Structure and function of the ear

Sound

Compressions of air or sound waves enter the ear canal and hit the ear drum, which vibrates as a result. This vibration is passed to the small bones in the middle ear, which pass the vibrations onto the oval window of the cochlea. Inside the cochlea the sound travels as vibrations through a liquid to the auditory nerve and then on to the brain.

A sense of balance is achieved by the semicircular canals in the inner ear, which are filled with fluid. If you move your head with your eyes closed or in a dark room you should be able to feel your head moving. Tiny hairs in the canals sense the movement of the fluid and signal via nerves to the brain that movement has occurred, side to side, forward and backward, and up and down! When you spin around repeatedly, the fluid starts to move and continues to move for a while after you stop. Hence when you stop spinning, you feel as if you are still moving (if you try this, do so with great care).

Our two ears provide a stereo effect which we experience, for example, as a car drives past. Even with our eyes shut we are aware of the movement as the sound of the car travels from one side of our head to another. Those who suffer deafness in one ear are unable to perceive this 'depth' to sound.

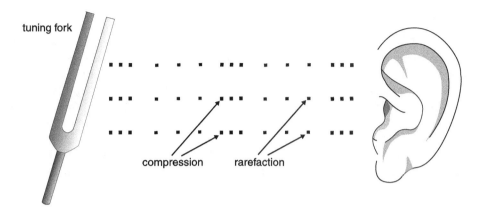

Figure 5.11 Sound waves are compressions in the air

Sound is caused by materials vibrating and is passed through the air by tiny compressions of air molecules. When we hear sound we are responding to the tiny compressions of air that spread out in all directions from an object vibrating in air.

For further explanation and simple graphics, try:

http://www.childrensuniversity.manchester.ac.uk/interactives/science/
brainandsenses/ear/

Structure and function of the eye

Light

When you look into someone's eyes, you are looking into a hole! Use a mirror to examine your own eye. The pupil is a hole and so it appears black because almost no light is reflected out of the eye as the retina absorbs it all, converting the information into nerve impulses, which then travel to the brain along the optic nerve. You will notice the iris as the coloured ring around the pupil. The iris is muscular so that it can vary the size of the pupil 'hole' according to the brightness of the environment. The white of the eye is the sclera, which is the strong fibrous outer coating of the eye. You don't notice the cornea, which refracts light onto the lens as it enters the eye, or the lens, which also refracts the light focusing the light onto the retina. The muscles surrounding the lens change its shape so that it will focus light from objects at different distances from the eye. Also transparent is the conjunctiva, which is protective. People suffering conjunctivitis have an infection of the conjunctiva. The pink spot of tissue on the nose side of each eye is the tear duct and is responsible for keeping the surface of the eye moist. Its other function is to help signal emotions in the form of tears.

Light & lenses

Our two eyes give us a perception of depth so that we can 'see' how far things are away from us. This helps us when using our hands to manipulate small objects. We see in colour; this gives us an advantage when, for example, selecting food, as we can spot a fruit that is slightly 'off colour'. In shades of grey the rotten food might not be so obvious.

Taste

Our sense of taste comes principally from nerve receptors (taste buds) in our tongue. Different parts of the tongue are sensitive to different chemicals in food, which we perceive as the tastes of salt, sweet, bitter, and sour. Try tiny amounts of sweet and salt on different parts of your tongue. Tongues evolved to help us detect foodstuffs that would help us survive, sugar and salt not being freely available in large amounts in the natural world. The other main survival purpose is to allow us to identify foods that might be hazardous, such as bad food or a poison. Toxic plants often have a bitter taste. Several plants and animals have evolved to defend their bodies by including deadly toxins in their body tissue, such as deadly nightshade, deathcap fungi, and several tropical tree frogs.

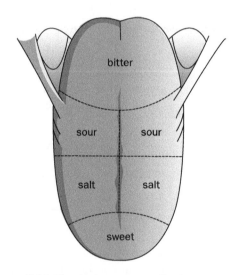

Figure 5.12 The taste areas on the human tongue

Touch

Your skin has touch receptors that react to pressure and heat. This allows you to handle objects and to feel surfaces and degrees of heat. Some parts of the body have many touch receptors (fingertips) and others less.

The nervous system

This is a network of specialised nerve cells (neurons). It includes the central nervous system (CNS), comprising your brain and spinal cord. Messages are sent and received very quickly. Nerve cells known as receptors receive information about the environment (including that inside the body); your CNS then sends messages to muscles and glands to initiate a reaction. Other cells, known as effectors, link to muscles that move part of your body in response to electrical messages, or to glands that release hormones into the bloodstream. The response of nerve signals to the effectors can be involuntary, such as those controlling movement of food through the digestive system; or the reaction can be voluntary, involving the brain in making a decision, for example to flee in the case of danger to life.

The endocrine system

The endocrine system controls several aspects of the body's functions. This system of chemical messages is slower but the effects tend to last longer. Glands release hormones into the bloodstream that can affect more than one organ in the body. Most people have heard of adrenaline, which is released at times of threat or excitement. Adrenaline prepares the body for so-called 'fight or flight' by speeding up the heart and the breathing rate. Another example is the sex hormones of oestrogen (female) and testosterone (male), which initiate the onset of the secondary sex characteristics (hair growth, muscle development, development of breasts) at puberty and regulate the production of sex cells (sperm in males and eggs in females) as well as the menstrual cycle in females.

Nutrition

Structure and function of teeth

The teeth and mouth act as the first step in the way our bodies deal with food. The front eight incisors can nip and cut pieces of food (bites from an apple), whereas the four canines provide a more powerful cutting and gripping action.

Figure 5.13 Adult teeth

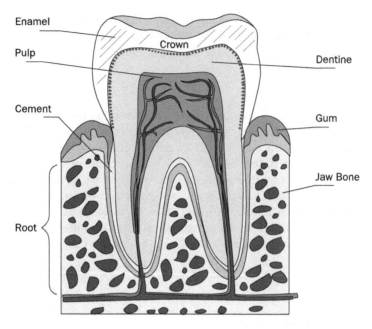

Enamel

Crown

Pulp

Dentine

Cement

Gum

Jaw Bone

Root

Figure 5.14 A human tooth

The eight premolars and twelve molars chew food into much smaller pieces, thus increasing the surface area of the food. This allows digestive juices to be much more effective.

Pupils will know about 'first' or 'milk' teeth, which are lost and are replaced by the set of 32 'adult' teeth. Each tooth has an outer enamel that is hard and brittle (the hardest material in your body). This is supported by the bone-like dentine within which is the spongy pulp, which carries the blood supply to the tooth and the nerve endings.

Tooth decay occurs when a diet containing too much sugar leads to growth of dental plaque, a sticky film that accumulates on the teeth from food debris and bacteria. The bacteria themselves cause little problem; it is their excreted waste materials that are acidic and which destroy tooth enamel. For healthy teeth, food and drink that is high in sugar should be avoided, good dental hygiene should be followed, and regular check-ups at the dentist booked up.

Human digestive system

This begins in the mouth with the mastication (chewing) of the food by the teeth. As this occurs, saliva is mixed with the food and special chemicals in the saliva known as enzymes begin to break up the food. When the food is physically broken into swallow-able portions, it is pushed down the oesophagus by muscles that act in a wave to squeeze the food down to the stomach.

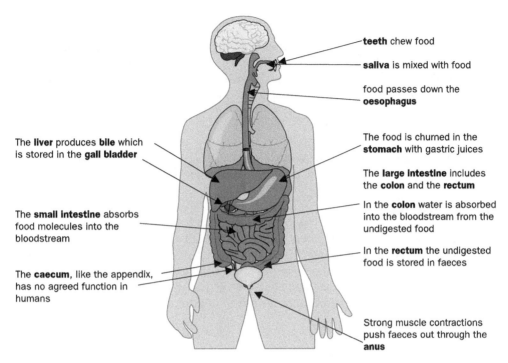

teeth chew food

saliva is mixed with food

food passes down the oesophagus

The food is churned in the stomach with gastric juices

The large intestine includes the colon and the rectum

In the colon water is absorbed into the bloodstream from the undigested food

In the rectum the undigested food is stored in faeces

Strong muscle contractions push faeces out through the anus

The liver produces bile which is stored in the gall bladder

The small intestine absorbs food molecules into the bloodstream

The caecum, like the appendix, has no agreed function in humans

Figure 5.15 The digestive system

In the stomach, the food is churned by muscles so that gastric juices are mixed well with it. A ring of muscle around the exit to the stomach holds it there until it is released into the small intestine where the digestible foods, including sugars, are absorbed into the bloodstream. From the small intestine, food moves to the large intestine, where water is absorbed into the bloodstream from the undigested food.

Table 5.1 Summary of food types and contribution to life processes

Type of food	Example	Broken down to	Examples of use
Carbohydrate	bread, potatoes, rice	sugars, e.g. glucose	energy in cellular respiration
Proteins	meat, milk, beans	amino acids	to make new protein for growth
Fats and lipids	butter, margarine, nuts, fish oil	glycerol and fatty acids	storing energy, insulation
Vitamins	vegetables, fruit, liver	not broken down	support growth, healing and repair
Minerals	salt, milk, cheese	not broken down	assist nerves and muscles, bones, teeth, and red blood cells
Water	drinks and food	not broken down	prevents dehydration
Fibre	fresh fruit and vegetables	largely unchanged	keeps the digestive system healthy and helps movement of bowels

Egestion

The food minus the elements that have been digested finally arrives in the rectum where muscles form it into stools or faeces. Faeces are composed of the materials that could never be absorbed (e.g. plant matter such as cellulose). It is stored until you go to the toilet, when strong muscular contractions push the faeces out.

Excretion

The body excretes carbon dioxide and water vapour in exhalation from the lungs, water and salts in sweat and urea, produced in the liver, via the urine.

Keeping healthy

Personal social and health education

As a teacher you should know about the principles and science behind healthy living, including diet, exercise, rest, and avoidance of harmful habits or factors. As a teacher you will be in a very powerful position to give positive messages. Do remember that your pupils need to learn these things but that they do not buy the food in their home and may themselves be worried about the health of parents who smoke.

Diet

Like other animals, we humans cannot make our own food as the plants do, we must eat plants and other animals. It is important to realise that our digestive system evolved in the distant past when humans had (as some humans do now) less reliable food sources. In our modern world, we can suffer as individuals from overabundance. We often opt for foods that are high in salt, sugars, and saturated fats (which would be rare in most ancient human habitats and so we have evolved to find them highly desirable), avoiding the essential green and whole foods. While fads and diets come and go, there are basic principles to live and eat by that we can pass on to pupils.

> **Ten top tips for healthy eating**
> Food is important and fun
> Food rules apply in some religions and cultures and to some individuals
> Basic food hygiene rules must be learned and followed
> Beware of faddy diets
> Only accept food from reliable sources
> It is good to try new safe foods
> Avoid excessive salt, sugar, and saturated fat
> Ensure that you eat several portions of fruit and vegetables each day
> (5 a day campaign)
> If you eat meat, eat a mix of protein each week (e.g. red meat, chicken, fish, cheese) and avoid excess
> Sugary foods and drinks are OK only as a treat

These principles do not cover all foods, but provide guidance for adults and children. Healthy balanced diets tend to lead to healthy, more active individuals. A useful guide is provided by the healthy eating pyramid in Figure 5.16. The food pyramid gives a visual representation of the proportions of different food that make up a healthy diet.

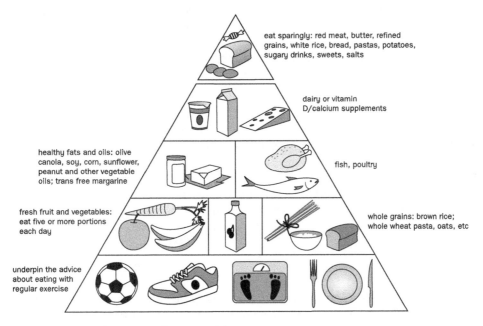

Figure 5.16 The healthy eating pyramid

Sunlight

Sunlight can harm the eyes if a person looks, even for a second, directly at the Sun. Over-exposure to sunlight can also damage the skin in both the short and long terms. We have all seen redness and even blistered skin on those who have been over-exposed to radiation from the Sun. In the longer term, sunlight can cause skin cancer. Pupils should learn to cover up, avoid the strongest midday sunlight, and use high-factor sun creams.

Drugs

Pupils should learn that drugs can harm you but that some are medicines that can make you better if taken in the correct dosage. You will need to explain that medicines should be obtained from a qualified professional employed in a recognised and accountable setting (e.g. a doctor, a dentist, a nurse, a pharmacist). Children should only take medicines under the supervision of a parent or carer and never from a stranger or someone they do not trust.

Exercise

Exercise is important for all but ill human beings. This may include walking each day and at least weekly sessions of exercises, such as jogging, cycling, running or dancing. Exercise can be cardiovascular – that is, active enough to raise your heart rate. Exercise can also focus on suppleness and on stress release. Also important is avoidance of long periods (other than sleep) of complete inactivity and of course over-exertion. Children should be involved in around one hour of physical activity every day. Schools often provide two hours of physical activity each week as part of the curriculum (e.g. games, gymnastics, dance, swimming).

Mental health and rest

The mental health of young people is not always regarded as an issue that teachers should consider. One's mental state influences and is influenced by other aspects of our health. It is important for young people to feel loved, valued, and cared for, and for them to learn to provide these things for others including, for example, pets. You should be able to talk about the need for rest as part of science lessons on health and growth. The other aspects may occur in science lessons or lessons on physical, social, and health education.

PSHE

Pupils' questions

Finally, when teaching animal biology, pupils may become very interested and may ask you all sorts of questions. You cannot possibly know all of the answers so you will have to be prepared to say, 'That's a very good question', 'What do you think?', 'How do you think we could find out?', 'We may find the answer in a book/on the web', or 'We could ask the visiting nurse about that'. Rarely will a child ask an inappropriate question about, for example, an aspect of sexual behaviour. In these cases of natural curiosity, you should follow the school policy on sex education, consult with a colleague, and perhaps refer them to their parents or carers. However, if you have *any* suspicions about abuse, you should inform the school's child protection officer (often the headteacher).

What pupils need to know at Key Stage 1

(ST) denotes Statutory requirements.

(ST) Explore and compare the differences between things that are living, dead, and things that have never been alive

Suggestions for working scientifically:

Sorting and classifying things according to whether they are living, dead or were never alive and record the information onto charts.

Describe how they decided where to place things on their charts, exploring questions, for example., 'Is a flame alive?', 'Is a deciduous tree dead in winter?', and talk about ways of answering their questions.

Raise and answer questions that help them to become familiar with the life processes that are common to all living things.

Find out how living things keep alive and healthy. NB This objective is also dealt with in Chapter 4.

(ST) Identify and name a variety of common animals including amphibians, reptiles, birds, fish, mammals and invertebrates

Suggestions for working scientifically:

Use the local environment throughout the year to explore and answer questions about animals in their habitats. Include pets in any discussion work.

Research how to take care of animals taken from their local environment and the need to return them safely after study.

Use observations to compare and contrast animals at first hand or through videos and photographs, describe how they identify and group them.

(ST) Identify and name a variety of common animals that are carnivores, herbivores and omnivores

Suggestions for working scientifically:

Research how to group animals according to what they eat.

Describe and compare the structure of a variety of common animals (fish, amphibians, reptiles, birds and mammals, including humans and pets).

Identify, name, draw and label the basic parts of the human body (head, neck, arms, elbows, legs, knees, face, eyes, hair, mouth, teeth) through games, actions, songs and rhymes.

Identify which part of the body is associated with each sense and use senses to compare different textures, sounds and smells.

(ST) Notice that animals, including humans, have offspring which grow into adults

Suggestions for working scientifically:

Observe, through video or first-hand observation and measurement, how different animals, including humans, grow. Examples could be egg, chick, chicken; egg, caterpillar, pupa, butterfly; spawn, tadpole, frog; lamb, sheep; baby, toddler, child, teenager, adult.

(ST) Find out about and describe the basic needs of animals, including humans, for survival (water, food and air)

Suggestions for working scientifically:

Pupils should ask questions about what things animals need for survival and what humans need to stay healthy; and suggest ways to find answers to their questions.

(ST) Describe the importance for humans of exercise, eating the right amounts of different types of food, and hygiene

Suggestions for working scientifically:

Design and trial a range of healthy balanced snacks for a 1-year-old, a 5-year-old, a 10-year-old and an adult.

What pupils need to know at Lower Key Stage 2

(ST) denotes Statutory requirements.

(ST) Identify that animals, including humans, need the right types and amount of nutrition, and that they cannot make their own food; they get nutrition from what they eat

Suggestions for working scientifically:

Compare and contrast the diets of different animals (including pets) and decide ways of grouping them according to what they eat.

Research different food groups and how they keep us healthy and design meals based on what they find out.

(ST) Identify that humans and some other animals have skeletons and muscles for support, protection and movement

Suggestions for working scientifically:

Identify and group animals with and without skeletons and observe and compare their movement.

Explore ideas about what would happen if humans did not have skeletons.

(ST) Describe the simple functions of the basic parts of the digestive system in humans

Suggestions for working scientifically:

> Draw and discuss ideas about the digestive system and compare them with models or images.
>
> Research the special functions of the mouth, tongue, teeth, oesophagus, stomach and small and large intestine.

(ST) Identify the different types of teeth in humans and their simple functions

Suggestions for working scientifically:

> Compare the teeth of carnivores and herbivores, and suggest reasons for differences.
>
> Find out what damages teeth and how to look after them.

What pupils need to know at Upper Key Stage 2

(ST) denotes Statutory requirements.

(ST) Describe the changes as humans develop to old age

Suggestions for working scientifically:

> Construct a timeline to indicate stages in the growth and development of humans.
>
> Research the gestation periods of other animals and compare them with humans.
>
> Find out and record the length and mass of a baby as it grows.

(ST) Identify and name the main parts of the human circulatory system, and describe the functions of the heart, blood vessels and blood

Suggestions for working scientifically:

> Learn to sense the human pulse in the wrist and record changes to the pulse rate after different forms of gentle exercise.
>
> Conduct research using secondary sources into the parts of the circulatory system.

(ST) Recognise the impact of diet, exercise, drugs and lifestyle on the way their bodies function

Suggestions for working scientifically:

Explore the work of scientists and scientific research about the relationship between diet, exercise, drugs, lifestyle and health.

(ST) Describe the ways in which nutrients and water are transported within animals, including humans

Conduct research using secondary sources into the transport of water and nutrients in the human body.

Ways to teach life processes – animals at Key Stage 1

Learning about humans and other animals

Pupil activity 5.1

Alive, dead or never alive?

Learning objective: Learn that some animals are alive and others are dead but some have never been alive.

Resources required: illustrations of the materials and animals below

Ask learners to categorise the examples below. You can create circles as sets or a table with the three columns. Ask them to consider these examples: a bee, a dog, a stuffed bird, honey, a fish, the Sun, a frozen fish, a toy animal.

You might try this simple game
http://thinkcans.net/games-centre/alive-or-not-alive

Pupil activity 5.2

Observing pets in the classroom

Learning objective: Learn to name the main external body parts of pets. Learn that animals need food and water to stay alive.

Resources required: pets, pictures of pets, the pet's cage or tank as required

Any animals that live in school (e.g. gerbils, fish) will help greatly as pupils can make longer, regular observations. Pets and other animals can be brought into school for short visits as long as they are safe (see ASE, 2010). Ask pupils to observe the animal, perhaps make drawings and take photographs. Ask them to describe the animals. Pupils should be taught how to provide for the needs of these animals and to deal with all animals with caution and with care and respect, both for the creature and for themselves. This also applies to so-called 'mini-beasts' (common invertebrates such as earthworms and woodlice) we might bring into the classroom; these should be cared for and always returned safely to their habitat. Be aware of pupils who may have allergies to animals, for example their fur.

Take this a stage further by asking pupils about the things that animals do and need. Ask questions about whether they grow, move, eat, and respond to what is going on around them? Do they all eat the same thing, or move the same way? Are some better at seeing or listening than others? How do we know?

Common misconception

'Humans are not animals'

Many pupils will deny that we are animals. Some see us as a special case, a creature that is neither plant nor animal. Ask them what they think we are? Explain that planet Earth has many living things that are either plants or animals, point to different living things and ask them to say 'plant' or 'animal'. Include ourselves in this, are we plants? So we are . . .? Encourage discussion on matters such as these, as we want pupils to question, think, and explore the world. Ask them to identify similarities between us and other animals, including mammals and of course the higher primates. It is likely that many pupils will retain their original ideas, so you will have to return to this topic to reinforce our place in the Animal Kingdom.

Pupil activity 5.3

Naming body parts

Learning objective: To name the main parts of the body we can see.

Resources required: the pupils

Young pupils should be able to name the main external parts of the body: head, eyes, ears, nose, mouth, neck and shoulders, chest, arms, hands, fingers, body, legs, knees, feet, toes. You might extend this list to include lips, wrist, hips, ankle, eyelid, knuckles, elbows, palms. They should also be able to identify and compare these on other

Literacy

animals. This will lead to a great deal of interest from pupils and hopefully lots of questions.

First, find pictures of familiar mammals (cats, dogs, rabbits, etc.) for comparison; always ask about similarities and differences. Then move to less familiar mammals (elephant, cow, kangaroo, etc.). Ask closed questions: Does this animal have a head? Where would we find its ears? Does it have hands? Always establish the special names sometimes given to body parts, for example a lion's mane. What do we call its hands, its feet? Ask open questions such as, why do all these animals have hair/fur? Encourage questions and model question-asking yourself: Why don't we have a tail? Why are the hands and feet of animals the shape that they are? You may not be able to answer them all, so model the behaviour of looking in books, etc. Pupils need to see science as an exploration of the exciting world. Stress that animals' bodies are shaped to assist them in their habitat to do what they need in their lives, just like ours. Ask pupils to draw or cut out pictures of animals or move pictures on a screen to group animals or label their body parts.

After mammals, move on to examples of familiar birds, fish, reptiles, amphibians, and insects. You cannot cover the whole Animal Kingdom but give examples to show the range in the animal world, stressing that these animals are as they are to enable them to live and raise young. For example, the body of a fish is smooth so that it can swim quickly; a bee has wings so that it can travel quickly from flower to flower, escape from birds, and fly back to the nest or hive. Try to use the correct scientific words when you can as long as you do not cause confusion.

> Internet games are available to support the naming of body parts:
> http://www.crickweb.co.uk/ks1science.html

Pupil activity 5.4

Exploration of the human senses

Learning objective: Learn through observation about the five human senses.

Resources required: plastic mirrors, hand lenses, fresh food samples, recordings of sounds

This topic should involve reference to and use of the senses throughout when, for example, observing and talking. Specific reference to the human senses will make the pupils more aware of them. By giving pupils a plastic mirror, they can observe and draw their own eyes and nose. They can examine their own skin and then observe and draw the ears, eyes, and the nose of another. Smelling safe things such as food or drinks can be treated as a game or as a fair test. Pupils should be warned against smelling mysterious substances. Simple hearing games can help focus pupils' attention.

A recording of different sounds can be made by the pupils and played to them. Such recordings can be found at:

http://www.crickweb.co.uk/ks1science.html

Being sensitive to what is around us is one of our life processes. Ask the pupils how our senses help us throughout the day.

Pupil investigation skills 5.5

Comparing and testing the senses

Learning objective: Learn to measure human senses in different ways.

Resources required: paper and pens, sound-making objects, blindfold

Simple investigations can be conducted by pupils to compare and measure the senses, including: eye tests – reading text at various distances; hearing tests – asking blindfolded pupils to point to the source of a sound; touch tests – asking pupils to identify materials held against their skin; taste testing – to identify flavours; smell test – to identify flavoured sweets at different distances from the nose. Whichever is selected, make sure you encourage independence in constructing a simple test.

Remember, some pupils may be unhappy about wearing a blindfold, so ask them to simply close their eyes. Also be aware that you may stumble across a genuine problem with a pupil's sight or hearing; if you do, alert colleagues and parents that a medical opinion should be sought.

Pupil activity 5.6

We need food and water

Learning objective: Learn that humans and other animals need food and water to remain alive.

Resources required: a pet or video of pets and/or pet cages/hutches, pet foods

Pupils know about their own need for food and drink, although they may claim to dislike water. Most schools now make water available for pupils throughout the day. You can illustrate their own needs and those of pets and animals. A visiting pet can be used to illustrate drinking and feeding. Video, including web-based video, is widely available and can extend the examples you can illustrate. If you illustrate animals like fish, children may ask if they drink; the answer is that like us they do require water.

Smaller creatures will help to illustrate eating but observation can be difficult, and often invertebrates collected in a garden will eat each other or die if kept indoors for more than a day or two.

Look in more detail with pupils at the foods and drinks consumed by the pupils and identify exactly what they are and perhaps where they come from and which foods are healthy and which should be avoided or are treats. If you have time, you might do some simple food preparation, visit a shop or invite someone in from the food industry to talk and demonstrate, say, cooking to the class. Larger bakeries and supermarkets will often assist. It is your job to ensure that pupils get messages about caring for animals and healthy diets.

Extend this by asking the pupils why they think that animals need food. What happens if animals (including us) don't get enough food, or the right kind of food? Nutrition is one of our life processes and something that all living things do to keep alive.

Pupil activity 5.7

Getting your food and exercise right

Learning objective: Learn that we must choose healthy foods and take regular exercise.

Resources required: examples of healthy and less healthy foods

The best way to teach this will be to involve exercise and food preparation and/or consumption. For the latter, you will need to be aware of allergies and any foods pupils are unable to eat.

PE/DT

Young pupils almost all love physical activity and will often explain the need for it in terms of making 'you strong'. They can, however, be made aware of the range of activity we call exercise and the amount of exercise that is useful. You should link this in with PE and perhaps ask them to monitor their own breathing, before exercise, after different spells and types of exercise, and after exercise. You should warn against over-vigorous exercise.

Common misconception

'You have to do a lot of exercise'

For general health and fitness, primary aged pupils should participate in a minimum of around sixty minutes physical exercise per day. It helps for pupils to understand that regular activities such as walking, playing a physical game, etc., can be counted as exercise.

Try collecting examples of food eaten by pupils (including healthy and less healthy items) or at least the wrappings of these foods. Ask pupils to collect data, then construct a database (tally chart, pictogram, bar chart, pie chart) of the foods that they eat and if possible the amounts (i.e. number of servings per week). Make a playground pie chart based on a giant circle and draw in sections with examples of boxes and cartons and pictures to illustrate the food. If you have access to puppets, use these to act out good habits of choosing the right foods. Construct a play supermarket/shop in the classroom. This can be very modest but can have a dramatic effect.

Common misconception

'If you eat fat, you are fat'

Take care with the word 'fat', as for some children it is only about body size. All children need to know that it is also the word for a set of foods, some of which should be eaten in moderation (e.g. fats containing saturated fatty acids) and others that are good for you as part of a balanced diet (e.g. olive oil). If you have overweight pupils in your class, be sensitive to them and their self-image but you need to get the messages across.

The concept of a balanced diet should be discussed with young pupils but they may struggle with the term, so explain to them about having some of the healthiest foods each day and two or three treats each week. Create a wall chart or display of healthy foods and ask your class to draw and write captions for different sections. Plan a class assembly or special edition of the school newsletter on pupils' health.

This work can be extended to an investigation of diet, which can be conducted in several ways. Young children might collect information on favourite foods from other pupils and information from food containers. Ensure that you constantly remind them about the healthy foods (e.g. fruit and vegetables) and foods that should be eaten in moderation (e.g. sugary foods and fats).

Pupil activity 5.8

Taking care with medicines

Learning objective: Learn about drugs as medicines.

Resources required: empty, clean medicine boxes

Many adults are cautious about talking about drugs, but it is better that pupils learn about them from informed adults than elsewhere. Lots of substances are drugs and all of them can be harmful: medicinal drugs (drugs from the doctor) are good for you in the right dose only. These are terms that pupils need to know, so use them but be mindful that some pupils may misunderstand.

Explain that nurses, dentists, doctors, and people we know well and who love us are the people from whom we should accept medicines. Emphasise that the pupils should never play with medicines or take them without a trusted adult supervising them. If the pupils find anything that looks like a medicine, they should not touch it but instead tell a trusted adult immediately. If a stranger offers them a sweet, they should not take it – it could hurt them.

Ask the pupils to examine a set of medicine packets. Explain that they should never take medicines unless from a parent or trusted carer. Ask them to look at the features of packets and point out that instructions are written for adults to follow carefully. You might talk about doses and how they are given and their importance. Pupils will be able to tell you about their experiences of medicines when they have been poorly.

A visit to school from a nurse or doctor will add greatly to these messages.

Pupil activity 5.9

We care for animals

Learning objective: Learn to treat animals with great care and sensitivity.

Resources required: modelling bricks, pets or pictures

Check if any pupils are allergic or sensitive to animal hair, etc. The best way to do this is to model it yourself or ask a visitor to do the same. You should teach caution that pupils should exercise when presented with a new or unfamiliar animal. Ideally, the pupils should get close to animals requiring care. Fish and gerbils are easy to care for, can be left over the weekend, and present great opportunities for observation. So-called 'mini-beasts' can be brought in from the school grounds and a perfect home set up for them. What do they need? Dark, cool, damp conditions with leaf litter including dead leaves. (These creatures need shelter to hide, food, and moisture.)

Pupils should consider the needs of different animals. What is the name of its home? You should model the care and sensitivity we expect from pupils. Ask them to design in modelling bricks or on paper an ideal home for the creature, or even better create a real home.

Pupil activity 5.10

Humans and other animals can produce offspring and these offspring grow into adults

Learning objective: Learn that adults produce offspring and about the growth of baby animals including humans.

Resources required: pictures, handprints or footprints of babies, toddlers, etc.

PSHE

This will tie in with the PSHE programme and sex education. The National Curriculum (DfE, 2013a) at Key Stage 1 only makes a reference to life cycles and that is as far as it goes in science. Animals produce offspring that are similar to their parents. Human babies grow from babies to toddlers, through childhood and the teenage years to adulthood and later to old age. Pictures of the different stages can be arranged by pupils into the correct order. Establish a collection of footprints and handprints from different aged pupils that can be put in order and measured. Ask pupils to talk about the differences and similarities between one stage and the others, perhaps their stage – childhood – and the others. Ask them to illustrate pictures with the correct clothing and belongings you might expect of the ages and stages; for example, a baby might have a rattle, a teenager a mobile phone, and an adult a house.

You can further enhance this learning by asking a parent to bring in a baby or toddler into class for the pupils to meet and talk to both parent and child.

Ways to teach life processes – animals at Key Stage 2

Pupil activity 5.11

Stop the plaque attack!

Learning objective: Learn about the function and care of our teeth.

Resources required: toothbrush, toothpaste, flossing materials, mouthwash, hand lens

PSHE

Before teaching this topic, write to a toothpaste manufacturer who will normally supply you with a pack of toothbrushes, toothpaste, dental mirrors, and posters to assist your teaching of this topic. As part of this science, pupils could observe teeth; options include looking in a mirror at their own teeth or examining those of another pupil. Magnification will help using a simple hand lens or perhaps a microscope linked to a computer.

Can pupils create a dramatic poster, a set of simple rules to guide younger pupils or a radio broadcast? Explain that bacteria live on their teeth but that the bacteria themselves do no harm – it is their acidic waste that destroys tooth enamel. Good dental hygiene keeps the numbers of bacteria down and removes the acidic waste materials. It prevents the build-up of plaque that can lead to gum disease. Plaque is a combination of bacteria and old food particles, which build up into layers.

If possible, arrange for a dentist or dental hygienist to visit the class to emphasise these messages about dental care. Such a visit could become a focus of several science and Literacy lessons, for example researching about teeth and their care, preparing questions, listening, and writing. It may be possible to obtain X-rays of teeth. These are

Literacy

usually of enormous interest to pupils who will examine them carefully and be interested in orienting them to their own mouth.

Extend this work by asking the pupils to research/review the amount of sugar in drinks and learn how sugar leads to an increase in plaque and how this destroys tooth enamel.

Common misconception

'It does not matter if my first teeth rot!'

Pupils might feel that their first teeth are expendable as they will be replaced. They should realise that poor dental hygiene can lead to other problems such as gum disease and also to damage of the adult teeth, which are dormant under their 'first' teeth.

Teacher demonstration 5.12

Why do we have different types of teeth?

Learning objective: Learn the different names and functions of human teeth.

Resources required: apple, bread, scissors, card, two cheese graters

Pupils should learn the names and functions of the teeth. If they have examined their own or those of others in the last activity, they may be wondering why there is such variety.

The teeth at the front of our mouths are the incisors. These are for biting lumps out of food. You could demonstrate their action with a pair of scissors, cutting a piece of card. Pupils could bite an apple, or a piece of bread; the food left behind will show a clean cut.

The canines are often familiar to pupils, particularly if they have dogs and cats. They are pointed for tearing and ripping food, which we cannot normally do with the incisors. Ask them to think about eating a tough piece of meat, or even a toffee bar. We automatically use canines for such food.

Finally, the premolars and molars grind and crush food. Ask them to observe someone eating something that takes some chewing (with their mouths closed!). They will see the jaw rhythmically grinding away. You can simulate this action by putting a piece of bread between two cheese graters and rubbing them together, making the bread break up into small pieces. Many pupils think that the back teeth just move up and down, but it is the grinding backwards, forwards, and sideways that does a lot of the work.

To extend these activities, perhaps compare the pupils' teeth with the teeth of animals like sheep and carnivores such as a tiger. Can they explain why these animals have different teeth from each other, in terms of their diets? Nutrition is one of the life processes for all living things (MRS NERG) and for many animals the finding and eating of food takes up a huge amount of their time. The pupils might like to compare a cow's diet and how long it spends eating to that of a lion and how it hunts and feeds.

Pupil activity 5.13

My varied diet

Learning objective: Learn about foods and how different foods contribute to a varied diet.

Resources required: examples of food and/or pictures/adverts

Pupils need to be clear about why our bodies need food and the effects of a well-balanced diet. They might detail their own diets over a number of days and compare these with fictitious examples of unhealthy diets you might provide. You might talk about good foods, others which are good in moderation, and those that should be consumed sparingly. Discuss these words 'moderation', 'treat', and 'sparingly'. Remember most primary aged pupils are not in control of the food bought for the family meals and are very much influenced by adverts. Ask the pupils to talk about decisions they have made to improve their diet. Get them to examine adverts for food, food cartons, and the information presented. Ask them to interview a selection of pupils and adults about the food they eat. You could model hot seating where the pupils ask you questions about your diet. If you do this, you should model positive actions.

Common misconception

'My sister's on a diet, not me'

We all hear about different diets, slimming diets, hi-carb diets, etc. Children often associate the word diet with these special diets, not realising that what they eat is their own diet. You might point this out and make sure you use the term correctly when you focus in lessons on their diet and whether they feel they can improve it. Perhaps the simplest thing to put to them is the effect of sugary drinks on their teeth.

Pupil activity 5.14

Walking around the circulatory system!

Learning objective: Learn through a dance drama about the way the heart pumps blood around the body, including the lungs.

Resources required: stethoscope, chalk/masking tape, labels, poster showing a simplified circulatory system

Earlier in this chapter the circulatory system was illustrated as a figure of eight. Draw a giant figure of eight on the floor of the classroom or on the playground using chalk or masking tape. After you have labelled the figure as below, ask three or four pupils to walk around it slowly as red blood cells. Ensure that they follow the arrows and explain what happens where and confirm this by calling 'freeze frame' to stop them. Then ask them and other pupils to explain where they are in the circulatory system, where they have just been, and where they are going next and what will happen. Then set them off adding a few more pupils. Repeat the freeze-frame and questions section. Use the example of the dance drama to illustrate what is occurring on the poster.

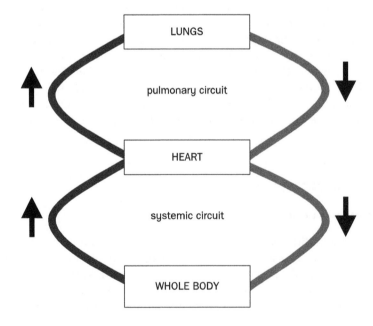

Add to the above by giving the 'red blood cell pupils' sheets of red and blue paper stuck back to back. They can flip these over at the lungs to show red, that they have picked up oxygen, and again in the whole body to show blue, that they have now given up oxygen.

Common misconception

'Blood is sometimes blue and sometimes red'

Having seen diagrams of the heart and circulatory system, pupils may think that at times blood is blue. You need to point out that this is just the way that scientists try to make diagrams clear. Oxygenated blood is sometimes described as bright or cherry red and deoxygenated as a darker red.

Film, photograph or record an audio commentary of the pupils involved and post this perhaps on the school website.

In addition, pupils can observe their own blood vessels in, for example, their forearms and hands. Ask them to describe what they see and explain why they can see what they see. The vessels do not appear red because they are observing the wall of the vessel not the blood inside. They may be willing to talk about bleeding (but take care, some pupils may find this difficult and may be excused) about nose bleeds and cuts. You might tell them that adults have about five litres of blood. To help them visualise this amount of blood, you could show them two full two-litre bottles (pop bottles) plus one half full. Blood donation and blood types could also be discussed. Keep the focus on the main function of the cardiovascular system so that everyone in the class is gaining that basic knowledge.

Extend this lesson further using internet-based simulations, such as those at:

http://www.bbc.co.uk/schools/scienceclips/ages/9_10/keeping_healthy.shtml and http://library.med.utah.edu/kw/pharm/hyper_heart1.html

These simulations often run quickly and so are best if they can be slowed, paused, and show different colours. If possible, obtain a wall poster and a plastic model heart.

Pupil investigation skills 5.15

How does the speed of the heart rate change with exercise?

Learning objective: To understand how the heart can speed up or slow down, depending on what the body is doing.

Resources required: none

Ask the children to work in pairs and count their pulse rates. You will have to teach them to find their pulse in their wrist or neck and the pulse of others. They should learn to ask and wait for permission before they touch other people. If they cannot find pulse points, they can often hear another person's heart by putting their ear against that other person's chest. This works well even through clothing. Pupils can record and then check their prediction. Then ask them to predict how many heart beats in a minute their heart will do after three minutes of vigorous exercise (say, running on the spot). They can take it in turns to exercise and then measure. Were their predictions close? Can they explain the difference between the rates at rest and after exercise? The data can be gathered in to create a graph of the children's heart rates at rest and after exercise.

Remember, discourage over-vigorous exercise and competition.

Pupil activity 5.16

The effect of exercise and rest on the heart rate

Learning objective: Learn about the effect of exercise on the heart rate.

Resources required: optional – electronic pulse meter

You might lead or suggest an investigation into pulse rates. Elements of this might include:

* taking the pulse (you will have to teach this) while at rest;
* repeating this after gentle exercise;
* repeating this after moderate exercise;
* taking the pulse rate every minute for five minutes to demonstrate recovery rate (the time it takes for heart rate to return to a normal resting rate); this is best done with an electronic pulse meter.

Figure 5.18 An electronic pulse sensor

Pupils need to understand there has to be a direct link from physical activity to heart rate. Your body needs more oxygen to 'burn' sugar so the heart rate (and breathing rate) increases. The best illustration available uses a heart monitor linked to an inter-active whiteboard. Here pupils can be asked to do a little exercise, or not, and then have their heart rate displayed to the class. Stress that rates will vary for different people so a range of results will be seen. Much of your emphasis should be on encouraging pupils to look after their heart and have a healthy heart.

The following website demonstrates different activities and their associated heart rates:

http://www.bbc.co.uk/schools/scienceclips/ages/9_10/keeping_healthy.shtml

Pupils might construct a poster or webpage outlining the essential care of their heart (regular exercise, the need for periods of rest, a balanced diet low in saturated fats, avoidance of over-exercise/strain on the heart).

Extend or conclude this learning by relating it back to the real world and ask why it is that an animal might need a raised heart rate so as to be able to move quickly. Catching food and running away are examples they might come up with. Are there times when humans have to move quickly? Finally, remind them that animal movement is one of the seven life processes (MRS NERG).

Pupil activity 5.17

Our skeletons are not scary!

Learning objective: Learn about the appearance, arrangement, and function of bones in the skeleton.

Resources required: X-ray pictures, posters, and/or models of skeletons

Pupils will be aware of their skeletons and will be able to name bones such as the ribs and skull. They may have heard of sports injuries, including famous footballers breaking their metatarsals (small bones in the foot). They should observe books, models, posters, X-rays, and screens illustrating the human skeleton and skeletons of other animals. They should learn the names of the main bones (skull, backbone, ribs, pelvis). Beyond these we might be happy with foot bones, leg bone, and so on. You can provide more of a challenge by presenting biological names of bones, including: femur, fibula, and tibia (leg bones); humerus, radius, and ulna (arm bones). Others may be learned but this is not essential.

What is important is that the pupils learn a little about the structure of bones and the purpose of bones. They ought to know that bone is living tissue with a blood supply and nerves, which is how bones grow. You might include the production of red blood cells in the tissue within the bone. The purpose of the bony skeleton should be learned.

Purpose of bones:	support	protection	movement
Example:	backbone	skull protects brain	hip joints

Literacy

Groups of pupils might investigate different bones, preparing a short talk on those bones and their function. Older pupils might prepare resources about bones to share with younger pupils. This could centre on a book such as *Funnybones* by Ahlberg and Ahlberg (1993). They might read all or part of the story with extra information added in the form of posters and or text.

An alternative is to ask them to copy the style of the Horrible Science (http://www.horrible-science.co.uk/books) series and present the gory side of the human body! Internet-based games related to the human body may be useful, including 'Annie – Put me back together', which can be accessed at:

http://www.bbc.co.uk/schools/podsmission/bones/annie02.shtml

Common misconception

'Bones are dead'

This may be a product of the bones pupils see on the kitchen table and others used in art and science lessons. These bones were once alive but now are dead. Their appearance when dead is like a form of stone, which reinforces the view that they are inert and lifeless. They may have seen bones before cooking oozing blood and all will have heard about the pain of broken bones. This is all clear evidence that bones are living tissue, albeit harder but living nonetheless.

Bones cannot move or even maintain their position without muscles. Your head is a good example: whatever position you are in, muscles in your upper body are relaxing or pulling your head into position. Pupils can observe skin movements as muscles move below the skin. Arm and leg muscles can be seen moving as arms, hands, and feet move. Other muscles such as heart muscles contract and relax all day and night with little awareness by us, other than we can take our pulse or feel our heart pounding after exercise.

Pupils might make a model of the elbow joint and try attaching string to simulate muscles; this is not easy and provides some appreciation of the complexity of the elbow joint and others like the pelvis, which give even greater movement.

Can you pull on the strings to simulate the
action of muscles on the forearm?

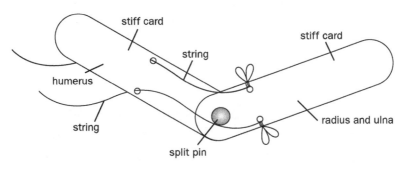

Figure 5.19 A model elbow joint

Pupil activity 5.18

Our circle of life

Learning objective: Learn about changes and stages in the human life
cycle.

Resources required: pictures of the stages of growth, access to other
pupils

The main stages of the human life cycle include baby, toddler, child, teenager, adult,
and older adult and should refer to birth and death. You should review the different
stages and expect detailed observations from pupils who you might ask to interview
people of different ages either at home or in school. The best way to teach this is to
involve people. Younger pupils can be interviewed, as might older members of staff
you have briefed in advance.

Your class might construct a life story of a fictitious boy and girl, predicting a fit
and healthy future for them, or perhaps a less healthy one if bad choices are made. Be
sensitive to pupils who, for example, may have poor health or be overweight. They
might look at average life spans for humans and the duration of the stages of the
human life cycle. You could point out that due to better health care, diet, etc., Europeans
live much longer lives nowadays (average around 70+ years), whereas in other parts
of the world life expectancy is still around 45 years.

You might extend this work by asking pupils to collect data around school about
height and perhaps hand span size of the different age ranges of pupils. They could, for
example, record the mean, mode, and median height of pupils of different ages. The
result might be a series of graphs summarising all sorts of growth data based on quite
a large population.

Maths

Personal social
and health
education

Death is an important topic but rarely mentioned; sensitivity is required as pupils might get upset if they have recently experienced bereavement. Having class pets can assist, as when a pet dies pupils have an opportunity to discuss what it means. Birth provides an immediate link to sex education but the primary science curriculum does not require that you teach this. Each school will have a sex education policy that should be consulted before embarking on this topic.

Pupil activity 5.19

Choices that can harm you

Learning objective: Learn about the effects of tobacco, alcohol and other drugs, and how these relate to personal health.

Resources required: books, pamphlets, and posters that provide information about the effects of tobacco and alcohol, as well as access to the internet

Ask pupils to research and make a presentation about the effects of smoking and drinking alcohol. Use Table 5.2 as a starting point; challenge the pupils to find out more from books, other materials, and websites.

Pupils need very strong messages about behaviour that is bad for their health. Talk to them about how people have cared for them to date and how this will continue,

Table 5.2 Effects of smoking and alcohol use

Drug	Short-term effects	Longer-term effects
Tobacco	• decreased appetite • loss of taste • shortness of breath • smelly breath, hair, and clothes • hands yellowed • difficulty sleeping	• lung disease • bronchitis • emphysema • heart disease • lung, mouth, and throat cancer • aged skin • it can have the same effects on those you live with, i.e. children • death
Alcohol	• addiction/craving • loss of control and accidents • mood swings/anger • unconsciousness • death	• liver damage • kidney failure • heart disease • cancer • stroke • increased weight • mental health problems • diabetes • death

but that as they get older they will have more and more responsibility to make choices for themselves. You might suggest that the human body is a gift and we only get one; doctors and nurses cannot always cure a problem you have made for yourself. Pupils should see all drugs as potentially harmful. Some special drugs – medicines – are carefully made and given out by qualified medical staff or people who love us. These medicines must be taken as we are told to take them, in the correct dosage. If you take more or less than you should, the drug can be useless or harmful. Other drugs must be taken very seriously; adults who drink excessive amounts of alcohol or who smoke must do so knowing the likely effects of these drugs. Pupils might learn the above principles and prepare campaign material to discourage, for example, smoking.

> Useful websites include 'Smoking Stinks' at:
>
> http://www.kidshealth.org/kid/stay_healthy/body/smoking.html

The school PSHE policy and related teaching will focus on helping pupils to say 'no' to drugs; the science programme should at a minimum inform them about the negative effects, including the fact that smoking is responsible for 114,000 deaths a year in the UK.

Pupil activity 5.20

Why is exercise so important?

Learning objective: Learn about the importance of exercise for good health.

Resources required: books, pamphlets, posters, and websites containing information on exercising

Primary pupils should be aware of the need for exercise but need to learn about why we need to exercise and the amount of exercise that is suitable. They should look at

Figure 5.20 Positive effects of exercise

different exercise regimes, perhaps those of footballers, swimmers, and other athletes. Remember to point out that top athletes devote their lives to exercise but that for them one hour a day of physical activity is enough. They should aim for a minimum of one hour a day and take a variety of exercises, including walking, running, jogging, skipping, swimming, and dancing. Emphasise that a number of sports and games the pupils play count as exercise.

Ask the pupils to research exercises and then put together a plan for a given person (e.g. a 10-year-old girl, a 30-year-old teacher). They could write a letter explaining the benefits of exercising and the consequences of not exercising. You should explain that exercising does not guarantee good health but it increases the chances of a longer and better-quality life (as do avoidance of smoking and ensuring a balanced healthy diet). One spin-off of good health is that if you are ever ill, you have a much better chance of recovery.

> Information about exercise is available on the internet at sites such as:
>
> http://www.healthykids.nsw.gov.au/kids-teens/get-active-each-day-kids.aspx

In all such investigations, you should avoid pupils competing and perhaps straining themselves and be sensitive at all times to pupils' circumstances; for example, we would not recommend collecting data on pupils' weight.

Pupil investigation skills 5.21

How quickly do we react?

Learning objective: Learn through investigation about reaction time.

Resources required: rulers

Reaction times can be tested by dropping a ruler through the open hand of an individual and measuring their response time by marking where they catch the ruler. Demonstrate this simple test to the class. Ask pupils to predict what will happen. Make sure you discuss how this will be made a fair test. Perhaps extend this work by comparing left and right hands.

You might extend this to talk about why humans have fast reaction times. When can a fast reaction time be useful? What dangers do humans need to spot and move quickly to avoid? Relate this to life processes (MRS NERG) and how our senses help us to understand what is good for us and dangerous for us in a given environment. Do animals use their senses in a similar way?

Pupil investigation skills 5.22

Investigations about range of size of body parts

Learning objective: Learn through investigation about growth and the range of body size of humans.

Resources required: equipment for measuring length, including tape measures

Investigate growth in a population of children. Gather data from a class or even better a sample across the whole school. You might look at one or more features, such as: overall height, hand span, foot length, shoe size, arm length, head circumference. The pupils could pose a question to be investigated such as 'Do people with long arms have long legs?' or 'Do people with small feet have small hands?' They may be able to correlate links between body part sizes, but do be sensitive about how the children collect and present this material. Many pupils do not like to be reminded that they are small for their age.

Link this activity to the life processes (MRS NERG). Growth is a life process common to all living things. The pupils could compare the growth pattern of human children to those of other mammal groups such as cattle. Why do they think humans take so long to grow to become adults? This is a fascinating question they may like to research, but there are no easy answers.

Pioneering animal scientist: Jane Goodall

Jane Goodall has spent over four decades studying chimps in Tanzania. When she started in 1960, little was known of the social behaviour of these animals in the wild. She recorded carefully their very different personalities and the alliances and friendships they formed with each other, some of which could last for tens of years. She witnessed the use of tools – chimps would pull termites from a mound using stalks of vegetation. They would also modify twigs to use as tools by stripping off the parts they did not want. At the time this was a surprising revelation as it was thought that humans were the only tool users. In 1977 the Jane Goodall Institute was set up to promote conservation within Africa. Today she continues to be a tireless campaigner for animal rights, and for the protection of animal habitats.

http://www.janegoodall.org.uk/home (website dedicated to Jane Goodall)

Summary of key learning points:

- a simplified structure of the Animal Kingdom;

- the names and functions of the main parts of the human body;

- the life cycles of familiar animals;

- basic life processes of animals, including movement, growth, reproduction, respiration, sensitivity, digestion, and excretion;

- that the tissues and organs of multi-cellular organisms perform specialised functions;

- that most organisms are made up of cells and almost all cells have a nucleus which controls their activities;

- the health of an organism can be affected by a range of factors – for example, in humans, drugs, exercise and other physical, mental and environmental factors.

Self-test

Question 1

Breathing (a) is achieved by the lungs alone, (b) gets oxygen into the blood and carbon dioxide out, (c) gets carbon dioxide into the blood and oxygen out, (d) is the same as respiration

Question 2

A balanced diet (a) is just for slimmers, (b) contains no fat, (c) is made up of different proportions of different food types, (d) contributes to a healthy lifestyle

Question 3

Animal cells (a) contain chloroplasts, (b) have no cell walls, (c) are each controlled by a nucleus, (d) have a cell membrane

Question 4

Blood (a) is sometimes blue and sometimes red, (b) flows in one direction only around the body, (c) is plasma, (d) is present in all organs

Self-test answers

Q1: (b) is correct. Although air goes in and out of the lungs, it is the rib muscles and diaphragm that do all the work in breathing. Respiration is a chemical reaction, taking place in body cells to release energy from sugar. Breathing is getting air into and out of the body.

Q2: (c) and (d) are correct. Small amounts of healthy fats are needed for efficient functioning of the body and diets are simply what we eat.

Q3: (b), (c), and (d) are correct (there is an exception to (c) as mature red blood cells have no nucleus). Chloroplasts and cell walls are features of plant cells.

Q4: (b) and (d) are correct. Blood is never blue and is not just plasma, as it contains other elements such as red and white blood cells.

Misconceptions

'Humans are not animals'

'You have to do a lot of exercise'

'If you eat fat, you are fat'

'It does not matter if my first teeth rot'

'My sister's on a diet, not me'

'Blood is sometimes blue and sometimes red'

'Bones are dead'

Web resources

http://kidshealth.org/kid/stay_healthy/body/smoking.html
    (kid's health website, section on smoking)

http://library.med.utah.edu/kw/pharm/hyper_heart1.html
    (heart simulation)

http://www.bbc.co.uk/nature
    (full of video clips and information on British wildlife)

http://www.bbc.co.uk/schools/scienceclips/ages/9_10/keeping_healthy.shtml
    (exercise/heart rate simulation)

http://www.discoverwildlife.com/british-wildlife
    (BBC wildlife magazine website, lots of free resources and information)

http://www.horrible-science.co.uk/books
    (the famous Horrible Science books)

http://www.janegoodall.org.uk/home
    (website dedicated to Jane Goodall)

http://www.pshe-association.org.uk
    (resources for PSHE)

6

Variation and diversity

About this chapter

This chapter deals with what you need to learn about variation and diversity. It includes the role of DNA in inheritance and how the characteristics of individuals are determined by genetic material. It also covers sexual repro-duction, during which genetic material is copied, recombined, and passed on. It will explain how this leads to variation in the population and that, under pressure from the organism's environment, the resulting natural selection leads to evolution. Sexual reproduction will be compared with asexual repro-duction. The second part of the chapter will refer to what the pupils need to learn, and the third part deals with effective ways to teach it, including common misconceptions.

What the teacher needs to know and understand

Resources required: access to a garden, park or potted plants

Similarity and difference

This part of science is about similarity and difference in individuals and populations, leading to variation and change over time. It is important that you begin to understand some of the mechanisms that allow change to happen, and that you realise that change occurs slowly.

You are a member of a species, *Homo sapiens*. A species is a group of organisms that can inter-breed to produce fertile young. Within any species there will be variation in body size and in features such as the shape of eyes, hair colour, skin tone, and so on. The mechanism that leads to variation is sexual reproduction, which relies on the inheritance of genetic material from *two* parents. These inherited genes combine to provide slightly different instructions to the offspring's cells, about the way they will grow and thus their ultimate appearance. Darwin (1872) explained how environmental factors may favour variations that provide a slight advantage; for example, an individual with slightly longer legs might be able to run faster, so avoid being eaten, and pass their genes on.

Some species (almost exclusively plants) reproduce asexually as well as sexually. Asexual reproduction produces clones – that is, new individuals that are exact genetic copies of their parent. An example is strawberry plants, which produce shoots or runners on the end of which are small plantlets. These will root and form new plants identical to the parent plant. Many trees have roots close to the surface, and in many species these will readily sprout and form a new tree identical to the parent. This phenomenon is much less common in the animal world so in most cases, like you, offspring are similar to their parents but not identical.

Just pause for a moment and consider which of your features are inherited from your mother and which from your father. You undoubtedly share features with both your parents but you are not identical to either of them. You are a unique individual.

DNA, genes, and chromosomes

The general size, shape, and make-up of your body is determined by genetic material, the basic building block of which is deoxyribonucleic acid (DNA). DNA forms the basis of genes, which themselves form the chromosomes found in the nuclei of body cells. Genes contain chemical codes that provide the body with instructions for particular body features (e.g. eye colour, size, etc.). A recent scientific triumph was the mapping of the human genome in 2000. Essentially, this is a very long list of the genes on the 46 human chromosomes.

Sex cells (sperm and egg) are made in the gonads (female ovaries, male testes). They are unlike other body cells in that they only contain half the full complement of chromosomes – 23. During fertilisation, a sperm and egg fuse to form the first cell of a new individual. This cell now has a combined set of 46 chromosomes containing genes from both parents. This new combination of genes provides the instructions for the characteristics of the new individual. One genetic combination controls gender. The sperm carries either an X or a Y chromosome, whereas the egg carries only X chromosomes, thus when sperm and egg fuse, around half the combinations will be XX (female) and half XY (male). This results in a human population of roughly equal proportions.

Identical twins are formed when the first cell, formed from the fusion of the sex cells, divides into two and these two cells become separated. They can then develop into two individuals with identical genes. Non-identical twins are formed when two separate ovum are fertilised by two separate sperm. Thus they will develop together but be genetically different.

Sometimes a mistake occurs when genetic material is copied, for example some of the sequence may be lost, moved, or added to. This can result in genes that do not work or work differently. A sudden change in a gene is called a mutation. Most mutations are not advantageous and so the change is not passed on to future generations. However, some mutations provide an advantage to the individual carrying them, making them more successful and so more likely to pass the change on to the next generation.

Evolution

Evolution by natural selection was first explained by Charles Darwin in his book *The Origin of Species* (1872). In it he described numerous examples to support his theory, including, for example, isolated populations on islands, where over thousands of years slight differences had become apparent. He saw that in each generation offspring varied slightly from their parents and that numerous slight changes could add up to produce more significant change so that offspring are more suited, or adapted to, their environment. The key thing he introduced was the influence of the environment and the pressure it applies to populations. For example, if food was scarce and the only food available was in high bushes, only the tortoises with the longest necks would thrive and have offspring. Hence their genes for long necks would be passed on and future generations would have the slightly longer neck. Natural extinction (not caused by humankind) is a natural part of evolution; organisms that are not successful eventually die out and become extinct.

Put simply, the theory of evolution is based on the fact that life has been on Earth for many millions of years, that offspring are not identical to their parents, and that tiny changes accumulate in populations because of the environment in which they live. You may hear about the so-called 'theory' of intelligent design; this suggests a superior being who has 'designed' living things. This is *not* a scientific theory, it has no scientific evidence to support it and should not be taught in science lessons.

Genetics

Darwin's work caused great controversy at the time and is still not accepted by some religious groups, despite the overwhelming evidence in its favour. When a later edition of *The Origin of Species* (Darwin, 1872) was being published in London, an Austrian monk, Gregor Mendel, was growing peas and carefully noting the characteristics of parents and offspring. He noticed that some characteristics were passed on and that the proportion of young with the characteristic varied but that these proportions were predictable. In some cases, half the young inherited the characteristic, whereas in others the proportion was 3:1. Unfortunately, the value of Mendel's work was not appreciated in his lifetime. It led to the science of genetics and in the twentieth century many of his ideas were used, together with those of others, by scientists such as Watson and Crick who in the 1950s were credited with the discovery of the structure of DNA. They and others unlocked the mechanisms which enable evolution to occur. We now see this area of biology moving rapidly and presenting ethical challenges; for example, genetically enhanced varieties of crops offer great benefits in terms of crop yields but some fear they could lead to 'unnatural or harmful offspring'. Not all of these fears are supported by science.

There are internet simulations that illustrate how populations can change over time, including the following:

http://www.channel4.com/science/microsites/G/genetics/activities/buglab.html

Differences in groups (diversity in a population)

As a teacher you will need to be able to identify differences and similarities in a group of individuals. It is important that we observe different animals and plants but the biggest population of living things available to us in a school is human beings, so think about the characteristics you could study. Examples include height, eye colour, ability to roll the tongue, handedness, hair colour, arm length, stride length, and hand span. Height and weight are controlled partially by genes but also by the environment, including diet and exercise. Weight is, of course, a sensitive subject and a pupil could be devastated if they appeared on a table or graph as the heaviest pupil in class or school! Skin tone is another area to treat with sensitivity.

Plants can also contribute to this work, perhaps the best example being the height of seedlings. Peas, beans or common garden flowers (e.g. nasturtiums) are usually adequate for these tests. Seedlings grown in similar conditions will show some variation, and the taller, stronger seedlings will thrive while the weaker, smaller seedlings may not. The longer you grow them the more marked the differences may be, but there is of course a limit to available space and time. Note that seedlings often look quite different to the adult plant. The first leaves are different to those that will follow and are called 'seed leaves'. The second set and subsequent leaves are usually the same shape as those found on the parent plant.

Grouping and classifying

You should be confident yourself in identifying similarities and differences between different animals and plants. This includes similarities and differences from species to species and, within a species, from individual to individual. If you have a garden or live near a park, you may be able to observe grassland (a 'wild' area would be more useful than a lawn). From a distance, this looks as if it is made up of identical blades of grass but, if you get close, kneel down, and observe, you will see a range of plants, grasses, wild flowers, and mosses. Taking one group of these, such as the grasses, you may notice colour variation as well as differences in leaf width, stem length, and so on. You should begin to notice that there are different varieties of grass; for example, taller, faster growing varieties and varieties that are eaten by animals and others that must be less palatable. Thus we can classify living things according to these characteristics. Biologists have spent centuries developing a classification system that is accepted around the world. Some of the terms and the main groupings identified are presented in Chapters 4 and 5 on plant and animal biology respectively.

What pupils need to know at Key Stage 1

(ST) denotes Statutory requirements.

(ST) Notice that animals, including humans, have offspring which grow into adults

Suggestions for working scientifically:

> Examine baby photographs from the class, can they see similarities between then and now?
>
> Survey height of children in school from youngest to oldest. NB also see that this objective is mentioned in Chapter 2.

What pupils need to know at Lower Key Stage 2

(ST) denotes Statutory requirements.

(ST) Recognise that living things can be grouped in a variety of ways

Suggestions for working scientifically:

> Sort vertebrate animals into groups such as fish, amphibians, reptiles, birds, and mammals; and invertebrates into snails and slugs, worms, spiders, and insects.
>
> Sort plants into categories such as flowering plants (including grasses) and non-flowering plants, such as ferns and mosses.
>
> Raise and answer questions based on their observations of animals and what they have found out about other animals that they have researched.

(ST) Explore and use classification keys to help group, identify and name a variety of living things in their local and wider environment

Suggestions for working scientifically:

> Use and make simple guides or keys to explore and identify local plants and animals.

What pupils need to know at Upper Key Stage 2

(ST) denotes Statutory requirements.

(ST) Describe the life process of reproduction in some plants and animals

Suggestions for working scientifically:

Research different types of reproduction, including sexual and asexual reproduction in plants, and sexual reproduction in animals.

Grow new plants from different parts of the parent plant, for example, seeds, stem and root cuttings, tubers, bulbs.

Observe changes in an animal over a period of time (for example, by hatching and rearing chicks), comparing how different animals reproduce and grow.

(ST) Describe how living things are classified into broad groups according to common observable characteristics and based on similarities and differences, including micro-organisms, plants, and animals

Suggestions for working scientifically:

Use more detailed keys and classification systems.

Examine classification system in more detail, including broad groupings such as micro-organisms and how these can be subdivided.

(ST) Give reasons for classifying plants and animals based on specific characteristics

Suggestions for working scientifically:

Classify animals into commonly found invertebrates (such as insects, spiders, snails, worms) and vertebrates (fish, amphibians, reptiles, birds and mammals).

Discuss reasons why living things are placed in one group and not another.

Use classification systems and keys to identify some animals and plants in the immediate environment.

Research unfamiliar animals and plants from a broad range of other habitats and decide where they belong in the classification system.

Research the significance of the work of scientists such as Carl Linnaeus, a pioneer of classification.

(ST) Recognise that living things have changed over time and that fossils provide information about living things that inhabited the Earth millions of years ago

Suggestions for working scientifically:

> Research how creatures have evolved over time, for example the horse or the elephant.

(ST) Recognise that living things produce offspring of the same kind, but normally offspring vary and are not identical to their parents

Suggestions for working scientifically:

> Research different breeds of dogs, and what happens when, for example, labradors are crossed with poodles.

(ST) Identify how animals and plants are adapted to suit their environment in different ways and that adaptation may lead to evolution

Suggestions for working scientifically:

> Observe and raise questions about local animals and how they are adapted to their environment.

> Compare how some living things are adapted to survive in extreme conditions, for example, cactuses, penguins and camels.

> Research about how giraffes' necks got longer, or the development of insulating fur on the arctic fox.

> Analyse the advantages and disadvantages of specific adaptations, such as being on two feet rather than four, having a long or a short beak, having gills or lungs, tendrils on climbing plants, brightly coloured and scented flowers.

> Research about the work of palaeontologists such as Mary Anning, and about how Charles Darwin and Alfred Wallace developed their ideas on evolution.

Ways to teach 'variation and diversity' at Key Stage 1

Pupil activity 6.1

Me, what I am like

Learning objective: Describe my own appearance and body.

Resources required: paper, mirrors

Let the pupils spend time looking at themselves and aspects of their body. This could include a self-portrait, perhaps based on the use of a mirror and/or a digital photograph. They might focus on the features of their head or include all aspects of their body, including measurements of height, arm length, foot size, and so on. They might record their observations using descriptive writing, or construct a card file detailing eye and hair colour, height, etc. One way to do this is to produce a 'pupil passport' containing all this information.

Links to other subjects can be made by using the data in mathematics and by spending time on more accurate drawing and other pictures of ourselves in art and design.

Maths

Art and design

Common misconception

'We're not animals'

Many young children will be reluctant to group themselves with animals. They appear to see three groups of creatures on the planet: plants, animals, and humans. By looking at the similarities between us and the higher primates (apes), they may accept the truth.

Pupil activity 6.2

Me and other people

Learning objective: To use information gathered to look for similarities and differences between classmates.

Resources required: class data on, for example, hair colour, eye colour, height, hand span, and stride length

Maths

After compiling information and a description of themselves, pupils can use this information to develop a database about a group or the whole class. This database could be paper based in the form of a book or a wall display. It could be stored electronically and be displayed as electronic cards or as pictograms or block graphs. Pupils should then be asked to look at the information and talk to classmates as they answer simple questions, such as 'How many people have blue eyes?' and 'What is the most common hair colour?' Make sure you stress similarity, as well as identifying differences.

Pupil activity 6.3

Observing other living things

Learning objective: Describe and compare living things.

Resources required: living things – animals or plants

For this activity, there is an advantage if you are able to observe animals, as pupils can compare them more readily to themselves. Ask pupils to observe pets or a set of invertebrates or plants in suitable trays or aquaria. First, you should ask them to describe what they see in as much detail as possible. Can they describe and name body parts, textures, colours? Can they describe how bodies appear to be assembled? Then move to ways to group the creatures, which can include many body segments versus no body segments, shiny looking versus dull looking, legs versus no legs, and so on. Finally, ask pupils to describe comparisons they make between different organisms and between those organisms and others including themselves. Differences should be easy to spot but pupils may need support in recognising and talking about similarities, such as 'we have legs and so do they' and 'they eat, and so do we'.

You can extend this work by utilising good-quality field guides that provide detailed illustrations.

Pupil activity 6.4

Grouping animals

Learning objective: Learn to group animals according to their observable features.

Resources required: a set of pictures of known animals, including some that occur locally and some from other countries; model animals are an alternative

Remind pupils about the great variety of living things and that these can be assigned to two groups we call animals and plants. Ask them to name animals they know. They are likely to refer to mammals and may need encouragement to include other groups such as fish and reptiles. When you have about seven examples, ask the pupils why they are animals and not plants.

Give pairs of pupils a set of animal pictures which they will later group. Ask the pupils to help you with a list of words that might help to describe the animals (e.g. legs, fur, feathers, fins, paws, can swim, can fly, eats meat, eats plants, etc.). Begin by modelling ways of grouping a set of animals on the whiteboard, for example hairy and not hairy, legs and no legs, lives on land versus lives in water. Ask the pupils to look at their set of animals and to think about ways they are the same and ways they are different. They should then work with their partner and arrange the pictures into two smaller groups. They should then add labels as, for example, in Figure 6.1. Ask the pupils to phrase a question that would lead to our splitting them in this way, for example 'Which animals are hairy?'

Figure 6.1 Sorting animals

A challenge for higher-achieving pupils would be to ask them to come up with a different way of making two groups or take it a stage further and begin to think of a way to subdivide one of the new groups – for example, legs and no legs, eats animals versus eats plants.

Pupil activity 6.5

Grouping plants

Learning objective: Learn to group plants according to their observable features.

Resources required: a set of leaves, a set of edible fruit, flowers or colour pictures of fruit, leaves or flowers of common local plants printed and/or on the electronic whiteboard

Repeat the format of the activity above introducing the plant material or images, the examples you have, the describing words, and then the grouping activity. This may be harder with plant material, as pupils may be less familiar with plants and the language of plants.

Pupils may immediately subdivide a group. If so, use this or another example to demonstrate this to the class. Make sure that that they record their original grouping and then move them on to talking about and then subdividing groups.

Alternative ways to record these grouping activities include using photographs on an interactive whiteboard or on a poster on the floor as in Figure 6.2.

Figure 6.2 Grouping flowers according to colour

Ways to teach 'variation and diversity' at Key Stage 2

The need to group animals and plants

Spiritual

Pupils should be becoming aware of the great variety of living things in the world. They are unlikely to be fully aware of the vast numbers of animals and plants here on Earth. The numbers are too hard to grasp; no person on the planet knows the names of all these plants and animals and nobody could. Try to think of a million residents of a big town or city all having different names and trying to learn them all! Explain to the pupils that we need to be able to talk about the characteristics and lives of such groups as fish, birds, trees, and flowers without knowing all the names. Scientists talk to each other like everyone else, so if they are going to do science on living things, they need to be able to talk about groups just the same. At some point, you should encourage the pupils to consider our wonderful world with this amazing diversity of different animals and plants living together.

Pupil activity 6.6

What have I inherited?

Learning objective: To recognise features inherited from my parents.

Resources required: the pupils, an older or younger brother or sister

Given that most pupils live with at least one biological parent, you can discuss characteristics they have inherited. Be sensitive to pupils who may not know their parents. Challenge all pupils to consider which of the following are inherited: height, weight, eye colour, hair colour, tongue rolling, handedness. If pupils have siblings, ask them to talk about their features and establish that there is variation between parents and children and among brothers and sisters.

You can make this lesson more challenging by asking pupils to consider features that are wholly inherited (e.g. you either have one eye colour or another), others that are partially influenced by parents (e.g. height, handedness), and ones that are not inherited (e.g. preference for different foods, love of sport).

Arrange for an older brother or sister of a pupil to join the lesson for a few minutes. Be aware that they may not share both parents. Ask pupils to talk with a partner about any similarities and later about differences. Complete this by asking the siblings to talk about what they see as similar or different about each other. The class might prepare and ask questions about likes and dislikes, skills, and so on.

If you have twins in the class or if pupils know twins, you might discuss their similarities and differences. This can be made even more challenging by referring to twins who are identical and twins who are not.

Pupil activity 6.7

Differences in groups

Learning objective: Learn that there is always a range of features within a group.

Resources required: access to data about a group of pupils

To get a real sense of the diversity and proportion of characteristics in a population, scientists require a large sample. Ask the class to gather data from a larger sample, such as the eye colour of children from every age (or selected) range in school.

Challenge them to construct a database including 50 or more pupils. Once they have the data they can construct tables and graphs to present the information in a form that can be interpreted. Ask them to use the data to answer certain questions, such as 'What is the most/least common eye colour in different age ranges, in the whole school?' Characteristics such as height are affected by age but hair colour and eye colour are not.

Maths

Larger numbers can be hard to come across, although one example is seedlings, which can be grown in their hundreds, but measuring can become laborious.

Pupil investigative skills 6.8

Grouping living things

Learning objective: Use our observation of features to group living things.

Resources required: pictures of familiar animals, PE hoops

Ask pupils to assemble a set of pictures of known mammals and to discuss with partners the mammals' features, such as number of legs, type of feet (claws, hooves, etc.), hair/fur coverage. In discussion, ask the pupils to describe the range they have observed and to consider similarities and differences.

Common misconception

'One similarity is that we have different hair colour'

Often pupils find differences easier to identify than similarities. You may need to provide examples and encourage pupils to describe similarities, as they are often too obvious. Start with similarities they spot and then point to others – both have hair, both have a mouth, both have eyes, both have spotted fur. Share this issue with the class and challenge them to be as good at observing similarity as difference.

Provide named labels of familiar animals or plants, including those living on the school site. Check out the less familiar names and ask pupils in pairs to sort them into two groups. Challenge them to do this more than once; give them the opportunity to hear about other pupils' ideas and to generate more.

They should then organise animals or plants into groups. Splitting a set into two groups is the first step.

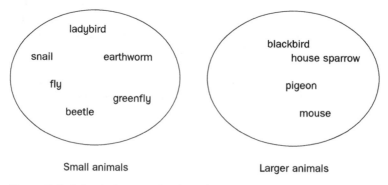

Small animals   Larger animals

Figure 6.3 Animals in our school garden

There will be many more small animals (invertebrates) on the school site, particularly if you have 'wild' areas. So you might then subdivide these smaller creatures into other groups, including legs and legless, colour groups, animals found on a plant, animals found on the ground. Similar groups can be made with plants, including leaf shape, leaf colour, overall plant height, colour of flowers, and where the plant is growing (habitat).

Beware of two things when working with plant material. First, it is illegal to collect any living plant tissue from the wild (the school site is fine). Second, only take minimum quantities for classroom work, as the loss of leaves and flowers will affect the plant adversely. Photographs and rubbings are a great alternative.

When observing animals, model a scientific approach and try to be confident when handling them. Where possible, refer to the wonder of nature and the amazing way these creatures are suited to their environment. Pupils may espouse such sentiments as 'Slugs are disgusting!' This can be a genuine phobia, but in the main it is often a learned response from adults. With slugs, ask them to look closely at their different features. Ask them why they think a slug is slimy (to make birds not want to eat it). As long as you emphasise hygiene and make sure the creatures are contained in a tray or aquarium, pupils can become confident and observe the amazing creatures on their doorstep.

Spiritual

Pupil activity 6.9

Making and using keys

Learning objective: Use observable features of living things to use and construct simple keys for grouping and classifying them.

Resources required: poster paper, a branching database programme (optional), and identification key

Explain that the previous activity of grouping living things leads on to the use of keys, which can be very straightforward and fun. For example, a set of leaves can be split into two by posing the following questions: 'Is it green?', or 'Are the edges smooth?', or 'Is it hairy?' Pupils can then add other questions so that a dichotomous or branching tree is created. Show the key in Figure 6.4 to them: test it, check it works, improve it if

Literacy

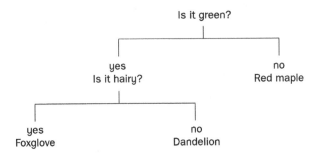

Figure 6.4 A key dealing with three different leaves

you can, and then ask a pupil or pupils to suggest a familiar plant to be added (e.g. rose). With the rose in mind, follow the key to the dandelion and ask for a question that will divide dandelion and rose.

Although children are unlikely to know the names of plants, this should not get in the way; leaves can be drawn or even stuck onto the paper, or leaf rubbings can be used. Flowers can be dealt with in a similar way. Begin with a very simple one as above and then add more examples; this will require new questions and editing of existing ones. The example in Figure 6.5 can be used in the same way.

Numeracy

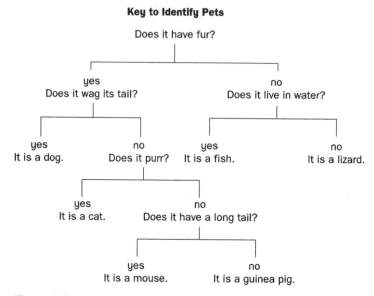

Figure 6.5 An example of a dichotomous key

Branching keys

This key should be tested. Can the pupils use it? Does it work? Are the questions good enough? You can then challenge the pupils by adding, for example, a gerbil. (A picture would be very helpful. Internet search engines offer image searches that are a good source of animal pictures, and these can be printed out.) Thus the pupils will have to devise a question to distinguish between a mouse and a gerbil.

> There are a number of computer programs that will construct these simple keys for you on screen. One of the best examples is called Flexitree3, available from:
>
> http://www.flexible.co.uk/
>
> A very simple online game called Animal Game is available at:
>
> http://www.rogerfrost.com/start.htm
>
> It will help pupils think about the questions they can ask.

Literacy

You can further extend this work or reinforce the idea by showing pupils the format in Figure 6.6.

Key to Identify Pets

1) Does it have fur?	if yes go to 2 if no go to 3
2) Does it wag its tail?	if yes it is a dog if no go to 4
3) Does it live in water?	if yes it is a fish if no it is a lizard
4) Does it purr?	if yes it is a cat if no go to 5
5) Does it have a long tail?	if yes it is a mouse if no it is a guinea pig

Figure 6.6 Example of a key presented as a list of clues (a 'sequential key')

maths

Pupils could then progress to using published versions of these keys or lists of clues. The Oxford University Press 'Clue Books' are excellent examples, as they include a set of clues, are comprehensive, and use correct botanical terms such as petal and sepal.

Pupil activity 6.10

Literacy

Using keys to identify local plants

Learning objective: Learn to use identification keys to identify plants.

Resources required: identification key for locally occurring wild flowers and/or trees

This activity should follow on from those above on grouping and classifying plants and animals. It must take place when plants are in leaf and at least some in flower. Be aware of pupils who may suffer from hay fever. Introduce them to simple published identification keys by illustrating the process of identification with some examples. Take the class outdoors and, in a well-defined area, following a summary of the process ask them to work with another pupil to identify one or more trees or wild flowers. Photographs, sketches, and notes should be taken as field notes to be reviewed back in class along with the identification.

This can be done in the winter with trees using keys that utilise the twigs only. This is quite challenging, as the detail to be observed is smaller and less familiar.

Pupil activity 6.11

Conditions for cuttings

Learning objective: Learn that plants can reproduce from seeds and from cuttings.

Resources required: a geranium plant, a sharp knife, plant pot, sandy compost, plastic bag and elastic band

Explain that this is a flowering plant which normally reproduces after the flowers are pollinated, the ovum fertilised, and seeds produced and then dispersed. Explain that if a part is broken off in the right conditions it will root and become a new plant. Pupils should know that gardeners use this feature when they take cuttings. You might use a sharp knife to remove 8–10 cm sections of stems as cuttings which learners can then plant in a sandy or 'sharp' soil or compost. These cuttings should be watered and have a plastic bag placed over them before they are placed in a bright but not sunny spot in the classroom. After a week or two the cuttings may begin to root. It might be useful to have some at hand that you started several weeks ago.

Other suitable plants are busy lizzie, rosemary, fuchsia, and honeysuckle.

Explain that as cuttings are part of the 'parent' plant, there has been no change in the genetic material. This means the genes of the new plant are the same as the parent so the new plant will not vary in its characteristics if grown in the same conditions. This is a form of asexual reproduction, producing a clone of the parent.

Figure 6.7 A cutting is taken

Pupil activity 6.12

Modelling evolution

Learning objective: Learn that we can suggest an evolutionary sequence.

Resources required: a range of biscuits or sweets

On different tables arrange a selection of biscuits including very simple biscuits and others with layers and others with obvious bits and toppings. Explain that in this activity the pupils should suggest how biscuits might have evolved from simple through to more complex types (e.g. which came first, Digestives™ or Chocolate Digestives™?). Encourage discussion which will be assisted if there is not complete agreement over the sequence the children place the biscuits into. Explain that this is a model and is in some ways like the work scientists do when they look at sequences of plant remains or animal remains such as shells.

The simplest biscuits can be seen as the most primitive (e.g. Digestives™, Rich Tea™ or Morning Coffee™). Biscuits with bits in them (e.g. currants) or on them (sugar granules) are more complex, because they have more differing parts. Biscuits with layers of chocolate or cream are also more complex (e.g. Chocolate HobNobs™). Some have layers of biscuit, with chocolate, cream or jam sandwiched in between (e.g. Bourbon™, Custard Creams™, Jammy Dodgers™). The most complex biscuits consist of more varied layers and/or parts (e.g. Club™, Wagon Wheels™). By challenging the pupils to arrange the biscuits in order of simplest to most complex, they can start to appreciate the pattern of evolutionary change. In evolutionary time, the simplest organisms evolved first and then more complex ones evolved from these. However, this doesn't mean that all simple organisms will die out. Many simple organisms still exist because they are good at survival and reproduction, just like 'plain' biscuits still exist because people still buy them.

Pupil activity 6.13

Young vary from their parents

Learning objective: Learn that offspring vary from their parents.

Resources required: pictures of different dog breeds and their puppies

Ask pupils to research or cut out from suitable magazines pictures of dogs and if possible their puppies. They might look at the parents and draw their puppies. This can be completed with parents of the same dog breed (e.g. collie dogs) and developed by considering the offspring of, say, a Dalmation and a collie or a bulldog and a poodle. Any combination should allow discussion of features which might be inherited and how these vary. Begin with obvious features like colour and fur, then move to characteristics such as speed of running, learning commands, and so on. Can pupils draw the offspring and describe its features?

Pupil activity 6.14

Adapted to an environment

Learning objective: Learn that animals can change over time to become adapted to an environment.

Resources required: paper and pencils

Describe the environment on a new planet, for example, warm but wet and marshy with streams, dangerous giant eagles circle overhead, food is plentiful in the form of well-camouflaged, very fast-swimming fish.

Explain that pupils should design an animal which would be successful in this environment. You might suggest that they consider: type of feet, number of legs and arms, hands, claws, beaks, wings, skin or skin covering (fur, feathers), mouth, beak, teeth, eye size, ears, and nose.

Extend this task by suggesting a change to the environment, for example, it gets much colder or much drier. Ask them to show how their animals might change after many generations in the new environment.

Evolutionary scientists Charles Darwin and Alfred Russel Wallace

Charles Darwin first hit on the idea of evolution through natural selection in 1838, but spent 20 years building up the evidence. His studies in geology indicated that the Earth was very ancient, leaving plenty of time for a whole range of plants and animals to evolve from simpler, common ancestors. Darwin's work on the HMS *Beagle* voyage, during which he observed and collected a multitude of animal and plant species, led him to see how adaptations could arise. He was cautious in amassing the data and meticulous in sifting the evidence, and perhaps was reluctant to rush to publish his ideas before he was fully ready.

Alfred Russel Wallace was a similarly experienced naturalist. He had done a huge amount of fieldwork in the Amazon basin and Malay archipelago, and was interested in how geographical barriers could perhaps explain how new species could arise. In 1858 Wallace sent Darwin an essay, describing the theory of evolution through natural selection. Darwin realised that the time had come to publish and promote his theory within the scientific community, and to the wider public. Accordingly, Darwin and Wallace published together a joint scientific paper explaining their ideas. Because Darwin had spent so long compiling the evidence for evolution, he tends to get more credit. The following year Darwin published a full length book *On the Origin of Species*, which explained his thoughts at length, and became a bestseller.

http://www.english-heritage.org.uk/daysout/properties/home-of-charles-darwin-down-house/ (Charles Darwin's house, English Heritage – includes panoramic tours of his vegetable garden and notebooks)

http://www.wallacefund.info/ (website dedicated to Alfred Russel Wallace)

For more websites about evolution, see the web resources section at the end of this chapter.

Summary of key learning points:

- a species is a group of organisms that can inter-breed to produce fertile offspring;
- there is variation within all species;
- the principal agent controlling the characteristics and working of cells and organisms is their genetic material, DNA;
- reproduction results in DNA from the parent or parents being passed on to future generations;
- before reproduction, the genetic material of an organism is replicated;
- mutations may occur during the process of DNA replication and during sexual reproduction, and genetic material will inevitably be re-combined, both of which will cause variation in the offspring;
- in asexual reproduction (cloning), there is no variation, the offspring look exactly like the parent;
- scientists know that variation caused by genetic mutation and recombination, coupled with interaction between organisms and their environment, leads to natural selection and evolutionary change.

Self-test

Question 1

Each species (a) can breed with another species to produce fertile offspring, (b) is unique, (c) is a group of organisms that can breed to produce offspring, (d) will evolve into a new species

Question 2

Genes (a) are found on chromosomes, (b) cannot mutate, (c) are the basic unit of inheritance, (d) are only found in animal cells

Question 3

Sexual reproduction (a) is basically the same as asexual reproduction, (b) produces offspring that are non-identical to the parents, (c) is preceded by replication of genetic material, (d) requires more than one parent

Question 4

Evolution by natural selection (a) is accepted by all scientists, (b) results from mutations and re-combinations and rearrangements of genetic material and the influence of the organism's environment, (c) was first described by Gregor Mendel, (d) naturally involves extinctions

Self-test answers

Q1: (b) and (c) are correct. Different species cannot breed with one another to produce fertile offspring; this is a feature within a species not between species. Species may evolve, may become extinct, but may remain unchanged for many thousands of years.

Q2: (a) and (c) are correct. Genes do mutate. Plant cells contain genes too.

Q3: (b), (c), and (d) are correct. Sexual and asexual reproduction both result in young but are quite different, as asexual reproduction results in identical genetic copies (clones).

Q4: (a), (b), and (d) are correct. Charles Darwin developed the theory of evolution by means of natural selection.

Misconceptions

'We're not animals!'

'One similarity is that we have different hair colour!'

Web resources

http://darwin-online.org.uk/content/frameset?itemID=F391&viewtype=text&pageseq=1
    (complete works of Charles Darwin online)

http://darwin200.christs.cam.ac.uk/pages/index.php?page_id=j
    (Darwin for children)

http://www.africanfossils.org
    (fossils of human ancestors, from a research lab in East Africa)

http://www.english-heritage.org.uk/daysout/properties/
        home-of-charles-darwin-down-house/
    (Charles Darwin's house English heritage – includes panoramic tours of his vegetable garden and notebooks)

http://www.evolution-of-life.com/en/observe/video/fiche/darwin-on-the-evolution-trail.html
(10 minute cartoon illustrating Darwin's travels – suitable for teachers)

http://www.wallacefund.info/
(website dedicated to Alfred Russel Wallace)

7

The environment

About this chapter

This chapter deals with organisms on planet Earth, where and how they live, interact, depend on one another and how one species, humankind, has a significant effect on the environment. It explains terms such as ecosystem and habitat and describes such phenomena as acid rain and global warming. The water and carbon cycles are included as they are significant to the interaction between living things and the planet. The second part of the chapter deals with what pupils need to learn about the environment, and the final part suggests some of the best ways to teach pupils about the environment, including common misconceptions.

What the teacher needs to know and understand

Resources required: access to different environments

This section includes aspects of ecology, which is the science of the environment. Because of changes in the environment caused by the activity of humankind, we have included reference to such issues as global warming which we feel are important. You are not expected to develop an encyclopaedic knowledge of animals and plants. It is useful, however, to be able to name a range of animals and plants, maybe one or two from each order (see Chapters 4 and 5 on the plant and animal kingdoms). Do not worry too much about remembering the names of plants and animals, as much of the science here is about the relationship of the organism with its environment, including other organisms. Most importantly you should develop your:

- skills of observation, including the identification of similarities and differences in plants and animals;
- appreciation of the variety in the living world;
- appreciation of the way these organisms survive;
- understanding of the impact of humankind.

Take opportunities to observe different habitats in parks, along the seashore, in mountainous regions, hedgerows, ponds (take care), and the ground below the canopies of trees. Observe the plants you can see; animals will be harder to observe as they tend to hide or leave as you approach (you could be a predator). Do the plants provide shelter for other organisms, food, a place to raise young? Do plants suffer from the presence of animals? Are there ways they benefit from one another? If one plant is eaten does another benefit? As one organism thrives, do others benefit or suffer from competition? Consider the ideas of a food web or a food chain; can you see possible links? Can you identify plants as producers and the different consumers?

The planet as a biosphere

The organisms on planet Earth developed together and so have become dependent on the planet, its habitats, and in very many cases on one another. In the chapters on plant and animal life processes, you will see that animal respiration (how animals release energy from sugars in each cell of their body) can be viewed as the 'reverse' of photosynthesis (how plants make sugars from water and carbon dioxide, in the presence of sunlight). This is one of biology's numerous examples of interdependence. Another is the way so many animals and plants are dependent on micro-organisms and fungi to decompose excreta and the bodies of dead organisms. Knowledge and understanding such as this will provide a firm scientific basis for the promotion of environmentally sensitive behaviour in pupils as young citizens of the world.

Earth in Space

Citizenship

Ecosystems

Ecosystems range greatly in size but usually include a space large enough to sustain a community of organisms. An example might be an extensive forest area in Scotland, where a plethora of plants and invertebrates live together with reptiles, birds, and mammals. While each population might fluctuate from season to season and from year to year, each species remains, some feeding on others, others living side by side for many years. Can you think of other ecosystems around the world? Perhaps ones you have visited or have seen on television? You might suggest a shallow sea, a rainforest, an area of savannah, a large area of mixed farmland or woodland in England, or a desert region.

Habitats

A habitat is a place in which an organism lives. A shore crab's habitat might be a bay on the coast, whereas that of a golden eagle is many square miles of Scottish upland.

Could you describe your habitat? Most habitats are home to a range of diverse organisms. A tree may be habitat to other organisms such as algae and lichen and to numerous invertebrates such as caterpillars.

Food chains, food webs, and pyramids of numbers

Scientists can represent the inter-dependence of organisms in different ways, one of which is to chart how energy moves from one organism to another in an environment. A food chain is a simple version of this and represents a linear path of energy as one organism feeds on another. The exception to this is the primary producer, a plant, which gets its energy from the Sun.

Of course, this is over-simplified. For example, not all sparrows are eaten by sparrow hawks; some are eaten by domestic cats and others just die of old age. A more realistic model is a food web (Figure 7.1).

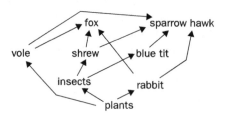

Figure 7.1 A food web

A food web is still unlikely to be a comprehensive picture of the feeding relationships and energy flows but it does give a better idea of inter-relationships. Can you identify the producers (the plants) and the consumers (the animals)? It usefully illustrates the fact that all the animals depend on plants for energy and that some animals feed on a range of foods while others are more limited. As you begin to appreciate these relationships, you can see what will happen when, for example, a late spring will reduce the insect population and so perhaps reduce the number of young shrews and blue tits. This will then affect the number of young raised by sparrow hawks. In a good year, populations are affected positively.

A pyramid of numbers also informs us about these relationships. The example in Figure 7.2 illustrates that a population of, say, 50 killer whales depends on healthy populations of seal and fish whose numbers far exceed those of the whales. A pyramid of numbers also demonstrates the devastating effect of pollution. Plankton may take in a

Maths

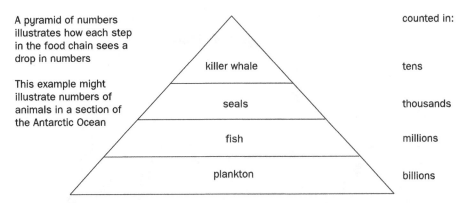

Figure 7.2 A pyramid of numbers – Antarctic Ocean

toxic chemical in small amounts and be unaffected. As fish eat many millions of plankton, the chemical accumulates in the bodies of the fish. This effect is repeated up each level so more and more poison is concentrated in fewer and fewer individuals. Thus it is often the top feeder that suffers most. As you, a human, are a top feeder (nothing eats you!), you ought to be concerned about any toxic materials in the food chain.

You will find that pupils become very engaged with feeding relationships. Predator–prey feeding relationships can be illustrated by graphs that show how the population of the predator is affected by the population of the prey.

Maths

Various internet simulations and paper-based games are available. A suitable one is available at the following website:

http://home.messiah.edu/~deroos/CSC171/PredPrey/PRED.htm

You will see interesting results if you make adjustments. For example, reducing the starting numbers of rabbits leads to a massive increase in the rabbit population before the fox population catches up.

The water cycle

Water on planet Earth is constantly cycling from oceans, lakes, and rivers to the atmosphere, to the land, and back to the oceans. We depend on the water the cycle provides at different stages of the cycle.

Water evaporates from oceans, rivers, and lakes. The resulting water vapour is carried upwards by convection to form clouds in the atmosphere. Many of these are blown by wind towards the land where they are forced to rise and, as a result, cool and begin to condense. The resulting drops of water fall to the ground as rain, hail or snow and begin in streams, rivers, and underground water courses to travel back towards the ocean. Can you think of places on the planet where there is little rain/snowfall? Your list might include very small islands or cold or hot deserts such as Death Valley in Nevada in the USA.

Figure 7.3 The water cycle

How many stages can you identify that are directly exploited by humankind? You may have included every stage apart from the evaporation from the sea and lakes.

An animated version of the water cycle is available at:

http://www.bbc.co.uk/schools/riversandcoasts/water_cycle/rivers/index.shtml

Games based on labelling a diagram are available at:

http://apps.southeastwater.com.au/games/education_kidsroom_wcactivity.asp and http://www.turtlediary.com/grade-1-games/science-games/the-water-cycle.html

The carbon cycle

Although you will not teach pupils about the carbon cycle, it is very useful background knowledge and is linked to arguments about climate change. Carbon can be found in most environments on Earth, in the plants and animals of the oceans, in rocks such as limestone, in oil and coal deposits, in land plants, animals, and soil. Carbon moves between these stores naturally. As plants and animals die and are decomposed, the carbon from their bodies moves into the soil. When forest fires occur, carbon is released into the atmosphere. Take a moment to look at Figure 7.4 and consider what is meant by each arrow. Some processes are short-lived, such as a tree growing 1 metre. As it does so, it traps atmospheric carbon dioxide in its tissues. Other process take much longer. For example, the skeletons of dead sea creatures create a deposit of carbon on the ocean floor; after millions of years, this can become limestone and be pushed upwards to become part of the land.

Humans exploit these stores to provide food, building materials, and fuels. Just consider for a moment, looking at Figure 7.4 and around your home, which of the carbon stores you exploit either directly or indirectly. If you breathe, eat plant tissue, animal tissue, burn fuel for transport or to keep warm, and live in a human-made wooden, rock or brick dwelling, you are exploiting all the major carbon stores.

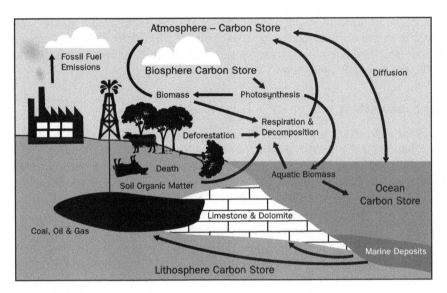

Figure 7.4 The carbon cycle

Almost every time we exploit a carbon-based resource such as coal or food, carbon is released into the atmosphere, usually in the form of carbon dioxide. When our population was small (10,000 years BCE, it may have been around 1 million worldwide), our use of carbon was of course limited and the Earth's carbon stores were able to soak up what we released. Now the massive and growing human population – 6.5 billion now, 7.5 billion by 2020, and 9.4 billion by 2050 (source: US census bureau at http:// en.wikipedia.org/wiki/World_population) – is exploiting these carbon-rich resources at a much higher rate. This increase is further magnified as the human population becomes financially richer, as each person consumes more food, more gas, more limestone, more steel, and so on.

There are other cycles (e.g. nitrogen cycle, oxygen cycle) including, most likely, ones we don't even know about! Which parts of the water or carbon cycles occur within a mile of your home? Within 200 miles?

Acid rain

Acid rain has the effect of making rain, groundwater, lakes, and rivers slightly acid, which is enough to kill plants and animals in those habitats. Acid rain occurs when sulphur dioxide and nitrogen oxide are released into the atmosphere. The resulting chemical reactions mean that rain becomes slightly acidic. British industry and power plants have released these gases in the past. These have been blown on prevailing winds to the north east and so parts of Scotland and Scandinavia have suffered very badly. Whole forests and lakes have been devastated.

Ozone depletion

We release all sorts of particles and gases into the air. Some chemicals destroy the protective layer of ozone in the upper atmosphere (e.g. CFCs found in some refrigerators). As the ozone layer helps to keep out harmful ultraviolet radiation from the Sun, its thinning has become a serious problem. Scientists have detected a 'hole' that appears over the Antarctic every summer.

Greenhouse effect

The greenhouse effect is a natural phenomenon that keeps the surface of the Earth warm. Without it the Earth's surface would be too cold for life as we know it. It is caused by greenhouse gases (e.g. methane, carbon dioxide, and water vapour) trapping heat and making the lower atmosphere warmer. Put simply, this happens when radiation from the Sun warms the surface of the Earth and the warmed surface then itself emits heat in the form of infra-red radiation. This heat is absorbed by the greenhouse gases in the atmosphere. The warmed greenhouse gases themselves emit infra-red radiation, which has the effect of further warming the atmosphere and the surface of the Earth. Without humankind's use of fossil fuels and land use, the greenhouse effect maintained a balance.

The Greenhouse Effect

Figure 7.5 Increased greenhouse gases result in a changed greenhouse effect

The following animation will assist your understanding:

http://news.bbc.co.uk/1/shared/spl/hi/sci_nat/04/climate_change/html/greenhouse.stm

Climate change caused by humankind

Climate change is still treated with scepticism by some people. However, most scientists now accept it, or are sufficiently concerned to accept that action should be taken to mitigate it. It is humankind's activity (e.g. transport, farming, waste materials, fossil fuels) that is causing an excessive build-up of carbon dioxide, which is not being removed by the Earth's natural systems, and this is causing climate change.

What pupils need to know at Key Stage 1

(ST) denotes Statutory requirements.

(ST) Observe changes across the four seasons

Suggestions for working scientifically:

Observe and talk about changes in the seasons.

(ST) Observe and describe weather associated with the seasons and how day length varies

Suggestions for working scientifically:

Make tables and charts about the weather.

Make displays of what happens in the world around them, including day length, as the seasons change.

(ST) Identify that most living things live in habitats to which they are suited and describe how different habitats provide for the basic needs of different kinds of animals and plants, and how they depend on each other

Suggestions for working scientifically:

Identify different habitats (a natural environment or home for a variety of plants and animals, e.g. field, lake, woodland).

Identify different microhabitats (very small habitat, for example woodlice under stones, logs or leaf litter).

(ST) Identify and name a variety of plants and animals in their habitats, including micro-habitats

Suggestions for working scientifically:

> Describe the conditions in different habitats and micro-habitats (under log, on stony path, under bushes) and find out how the conditions affect the number and type(s) of plants and animals that live there.
>
> Compare animals in familiar habitats with animals found in less familiar habitats, for example, on the seashore, in woodland, in the ocean, in the rainforest.

(ST) Describe how animals obtain their food from plants and other animals, using the idea of a simple food chain, and identify and name different sources of food

Suggestions for working scientifically:

> Raise and answer questions about the local environment that help them to identify and study a variety of plants and animals within their habitat and observe how living things depend on each other, for example, plants serving as a source of food and shelter for animals.
>
> Construct a simple food chain that includes humans (e.g. grass, cow, human).

What pupils need to know at Key Stage 2

Lower Key Stage 2

(ST) denotes Statutory requirements.

(ST) Construct and interpret a variety of food chains, identifying producers, predators and prey

Suggestions for working scientifically:

> Make observations of living things and their food sources.
>
> Use secondary sources to conduct research into animals, their food and feeding relationships.

(ST) Recognise that environments can change and that this can sometimes pose dangers to living things

Suggestions for working scientifically:

Identify how the habitat changes throughout the year and the effect this has on plants and animals.

Upper Key Stage 2

(ST) denotes Statutory requirements.

(ST) Describe the differences in the life cycles of a mammal, an amphibian, an insect and a bird

Suggestions for working scientifically:

> Observe life cycle changes in a variety of living things, for example, plants in the vegetable garden or flower border, and animals in the local environment throughout the year.

> Compare the life cycles of plants and animals in their local environment with other plants and animals around the world (in the rainforest, in the oceans, in desert areas and in prehistoric times).

> Ask pertinent questions and suggest reasons for similarities and differences in life cycles.

> Research the work of naturalists and animal behaviourists, for example, David Attenborough and Jane Goodall.

Ways to teach 'environment' at Key Stage 1

Find out about different plants and animals in the local environment

Young pupils should spend significant periods of time in science lessons outside in the school grounds and at times further afield in parks and nature reserves. One of the key objectives is to kindle an interest, a love, and an appreciation of the living world. This will be affected by the pupils' interest in exotic creatures such as dolphins and elephants but can also be developed through observations of local plants and animals. They need to get beyond the 'yuk' factor and learn to look carefully at the small animals all around us.

Pupil activity 7.1

The Weather

Learning objective: Learn about the weather and how it is associated with the season.

Resources required: access to outdoors

Take the learners outside on a series of consecutive days, ask them to make simple drawings to record the weather they observe and get them to talk about what they see, feel and hear. In the classroom talk about the current season. Can they remember another time of year, another season when it was colder or warmer? Wetter or drier? Windier or calmer?

Can they suggest how they would dress a doll or a teddy bear for this weather, in this season? Can they say what the weather might be like in the coming days? Over the weekend?

Take them outside one morning to observe the weather, repeat this in the afternoon and ask if the weather appears to be changing. Ask them to make a prediction/weather forecast for tomorrow, and see if it turns out to be right.

Pupil activity 7.2

Observing changes between seasons

Learning objective: Learn about the changes which occur from season to season.

Resources required: thermometer (optional), paper

Ask learners to describe the weather today (for the best results take a short walk outside). If you have a thermometer then measure the temperature outside. Ask the class to talk about the recent weather and how it represents the season at present. Ask them to consider and talk about the animals and plants at present. Are animals active and abundant? Are plants growing (look for new young-looking leaves), flowering or bearing fruit?

Give the learners a sheet of paper folded into three parts. Ask them to name the middle section after the present season and to draw some typical weather. The picture might include animals and plants which are present in this season. Ask them then to talk about the preceding season and the season which will follow. Ask them to talk about the differences from season to season and to reflect these in the drawings they make of the preceding and following seasons.

An excellent selection of films showing how the weather of the changing seasons affects British wildlife can be viewed at:

http://www.bbc.co.uk/programmes/b03hj893/clips

Pupil activity 7.3

Changes in day length

Learning objective: Learn that day length changes each day and varies widely from season to season.

Resources required: access to outdoors

Ask learners to talk about times when they have noticed the day (daylight) is short and times when the day length is longer. Do they associate this with the seasons? Have a look at http://www.childrensuniversity.manchester.ac.uk/interactives/science/earthandbeyond/sunrisesunset/ (This webpage was designed for older children but if you take care it is useful with Year 2 pupils.)

This will tell you the length of the day in Manchester, which is similar to the rest of the United Kingdom. Can they read the hours and minutes of day length (daylight)? Can they talk about when it gets light (dawn)? When it goes dark (dusk)? Ask a child to click forward a day to see what difference the day makes. How much difference do they see? (About 4 minutes.) So can they say what a difference this makes from day to day? From this week to next week? Do they think this will continue forever?

Ask them to describe day length in the middle of winter and the middle of summer.

NB the explanation for day length is to do with the tilt of the Earth as it takes its annual journey around the Sun. This explanation is normally too advanced for this age range. (See full explanation in teacher's section in Chapter 11, 'The Earth in space').

Pupil activity 7.4

Observing a local environment

Learning objective: Learn about a local environment and the animals and plants that live there.

Resources required: access to an environment, sketching and drawing materials, books that identify common wild plants, computer microscope or visualiser

After selecting a local environment such as the corner of a school field, an area of trees or a garden area, take the class to examine the area and to sketch plants they find. Ask them to observe carefully, such as looking for signs of plants being eaten. They may have to search for animals which can be drawn in the same way. Larger animals such as birds are harder to observe and so the class may have to discuss birds seen in the vicinity.

Ask the pupils to make a profile of each living thing, finding its name or giving its name, its location, and its appearance. They could find out about how it lives, for example that it needs light, water and warmth, that it flowers and makes seed, that it is visited by flying insects and eaten by some. View plants and perhaps invertebrates through a computer microscope or visualiser. Some plants will be unfamiliar and so pupils may be uncertain about whether they flower – this is where pocket guides to wild plants will assist. Most of the plants you find will flower in some way; grasses flower but as they are wind pollinated the flowers are not coloured to attract insects. Most of the animals you find will be invertebrates and will be small and unfamiliar. Again simple pocket guide books to insects and other invertebrates will assist.

Pupil activity 7.5

Listening to earthworms!

Learning objective: Learn by observing how the body of the earthworm is adapted to its habitat.

Resources required: deep trays, leaf litter, earthworms, hand lenses, paper, computer microscope or visualiser

Earthworms like damp conditions, so by providing them with moist (not wet) leaf litter they can spend a few hours in the classroom (ensure that they are returned to the habitat at the end of the day; point this out to pupils). Remind pupils that earthworms live by eating soil close to the surface and so spend their lives moving through this environment. Ask the pupils whether they can see the many segments of the earthworm's body. What colours can they see? Can pupils describe how they move?

Try carefully placing earthworms onto dry paper for a few minutes and listening; you may be able to hear a scraping, rasping sound because their bodies are covered in tiny bristles. Can pupils say how an earthworm's body is adapted to the environment in which it lives? A computer microscope may assist. How might the bristles help? Pupils should wash their hands after this activity.

Common misconception

'If you cut an earthworm in half, two earthworms will be made'

This is not true! It is a popular fallacy. Only one end of the earthworm can feed (the head end with its brain in) and this end *may* survive. The other end cannot grow a new head!

Pupil investigation skills 7.6

Do earthworms like dry or damp conditions?

Learning objective: Learn that animals will select a habitat that suits them.

Resources required: deep tray, moist leaf litter, earthworms (or other invertebrates such as snails, slugs or woodlice)

Arrange a deep tray or aquarium with dry leaves at one end and with moist leaves at the other. Ask pupils to predict what will happen, perhaps working in pairs before the class shares the predictions. Place a few earthworms (or other invertebrates) in the middle section and then return to observe them after fifteen and then thirty minutes. By this time they ought to be congregating at the damp end. Pupils might record where they are at 5-minute intervals. Do all invertebrates react in this way? Make sure it is moisture they are reacting to, not light or temperature.

Extend this activity by keeping the earthworms in a wormery, which can be made from a giant transparent drinks bottle (with the top removed). Add successive layers of sand and soil with leaf litter on the top, add a little water for moisture, several worms, and cover between viewings. The worms should slowly mix up the layers and draw the leaves down. Ensure that the earthworms never dry out and are returned to a suitable habitat.

Pupil activity 7.7

We care for our environment

Learning objective: Learn about how we can care for the environment.

Resources required: initially, you require access to the school site

Identify – or, even better, identify with the class – one of a number of options for pupils to plan to carry out care for the environment. An ideal example is reduction of litter on the school site. Pupils can see how their behaviour and that of others can have an immediate and positive effect. This activity can include, for example, production of posters, carrying out surveys of litter and/or of pupils, taking photographs, and conducting an analysis of the problem. Is it caused by people? Pupils? Others? Are there insufficient bins? How could things be improved?

Citizenship

Enrich this work by involving staff from the local authority who have responsibility for reducing littering; they are usually delighted to help.

Pupil activity 7.8

Animals and plants in two different habitats

Learning objective: Learn about the features of two different habitats and the animals and plants found there.

Resources required: access to two habitats, paper, camera, Plasticine™

This work is best done in the late spring, summer or early autumn months and may require two or more lessons. It is worth starting with a sunny, dry, quiet area if possible. Young children should initially focus on one environment, describing it and the plants and animals they find there. Is it dry or wet? Is it in full sun, part shade or shade? Is it visited by dozens of children every day? Ask them to record what they see; options include drawings, writing, photographs, and models. Now repeat this in another environment that differs in some ways: drier/damper, more overgrown, more/less light. Ask pupils about the many similarities as well as the differences.

You may need to return for more detailed observation of plants. Ask the pupils to describe the plants, draw them, photograph them, and/or make models out of Plasticine™. Draw their attention to plants that are many times their own height (e.g. trees) and plants that are tiny (e.g. mosses). Focus on size, shape, colour, and introduce the key vocabulary of plants – roots, shoot, stem, leaf, flower, and seed. Point out that many plant parts are poisonous to humans. Can pupils keep a diary/make a class book/make a display about our 'Mini Wildlife Park'? Take a similar approach with animals, although these may be harder to find; some animals such as birds are visitors, whereas smaller invertebrates may spend all of their lives in the area.

Pupils can observe and explore environments further afield such as might be encountered on school visits or viewed on television, DVD or internet sites. There is little doubt that physically visiting an environment is the best way to appreciate the conditions. A good film or TV programme can introduce pupils to environments and organisms that would not otherwise be seen, for example ants building an underground nest.

Pupil activity 7.9

A food chain

Learning objective: Learn how food chains show where each plant or animal gets its energy. Learn that each food chain begins with a plant, a producer.

Resources required: examples, pictures or perhaps an invertebrate (e.g. snails)

Start with familiar animals and plants such as:

rose → greenfly → sparrow

daffodil → snail → thrush

grass seeds → mouse → hawk

Pupils may well think of examples from wildlife films involving predators such as sharks:

plankton → fish → seal → shark

Use the familiar for the main part of the lesson and the less familiar to challenge and intrigue pupils. If possible, introduce animals into the classroom to observe them feeding (e.g. slugs or snails feeding on lettuce). Emphasise that the food provides energy. When talking about plants as primary producers, emphasise their energy source is the Sun. The hardest part of this lesson for pupils is drawing arrows in the correct direction when drawing food chains and webs. The arrow points in the direction in which the energy moves.

lettuce → slug

A very good way to reinforce this learning is illustrative role-play. Use large card arrows and pupil badges representing animals and plants. Give these out and ask pupils to stand in line, placing the arrows to represent different food chains and later food webs. Ask pupils to describe how each organism gets its energy. The step to food webs is more challenging and so you can expect discussion of feeding relationships.

Pupil activity 7.10

A desirable habitat?

Learning objective: Learn that we can measure and describe the main features of a habitat.

Resources required: metre rulers, tape measures, safe thermometers, anemometer, rainfall gauge, data-logging equipment

Introduce pupils to at least two habitats and ask them how we might describe them to plants and animals looking for a home? Recap the living conditions required for living things (light, air, warmth, shelter, water, food), and ask pupils to consider shelter and food sources as they tackle this activity. Ask them about words to describe the habitat and then ways we might measure features of the habitat, such as temperature, light, and rainfall. Ask pupils to plan how to measure and record and to begin to conduct measurements of these aspects (this may require daily measurements over a week or two).

A website like this might assist:
http://www.switcheroozoo.com/games/habitatgame.htm

Pupil activity 7.11

A microhabitat?

Learning objective: Learn that the habitats of some living things are very small.

Resources required: magnifying glasses, access to woodland area, examples or pictures of small invertebrates

Remind learners about the idea of a habitat. Can they describe the habitat of a rabbit? A local song bird? Can they say how big these habitats are? The size of a football pitch? A little smaller or bigger?

Introduce an invertebrate or a picture of one. Where does it live? Can it get all its food, water, air and shelter there? Some animals live in a very small area which is a microhabitat. Examples of microhabitats include shellfish in a rock pool, woodlice on a rotting log, earthworms living in a compost heap.

Ways to teach 'environment' at Key Stage 2

Pupil activity 7.12

Describe and identify plants and animals

Learning objective: Learn to describe and identify plants and animals.

Resources required: hand lenses, field guides, digital camera, drawing materials, access to the internet

Utilising two (ideally contrasting) habitats on the school site, ask pupils in groups to observe, describe, and identify either plants or animals on those sites (fewer pupils will need to observe animals as they will probably be less numerous). Pupils will need to spend time outside and record what they see (take photographs, draw pictures, take rubbings, measure). Pupils should be able to discuss in pairs and then select a method for presenting the information (book, poster, blog, spreadsheet, etc.). Challenge higher achieving pupils by expecting them to make more accurate observations and measurements. Ask the groups to report back to the class with some emphasis on how they went about the task.

This activity can be extended by counting or estimating the numbers of such plants and animals. This is easy with larger plants but as you move to smaller plants and animals, you will have to estimate a number or a range based on your observations; for example, we estimate that in the lawn, which is 10×10 m, there are 100–200 earthworms or count the number in one square metre and multiply.

Pupil activity 7.13

Show how plants and animals are adapted to their habitat

Learning objective: Learn about the features of plants and animals and how these help them adapt to their habitat.

Resources required: records from the previous activity and access to the habitat

Ask pupils to observe plants and ask questions to describe how they are adapted to their environment:

- Do they have roots? How do these help them live here?
- Do they have colourful flowers? If so, why? If not, why not?
- Are the leaves high off the ground? If so, why?
- Are the leaves making a mat on the floor? If so, why does this assist the plant?
- Does the plant lose its leaves in the winter? If so, why? If not, why not?

Apply similar questions to the animals:

- Does the shape of the animal assist the way it lives?
- Does its colour help it survive?
- Can it move around? How does it move? How does this help it?
- Is its body covered in hair or feathers? If so, why?
- An additional feature of animals is behaviour. How does this help them? Do they hide when alarmed? How does this help them? Can they flee from a threat? Why do they do this? Can they search for food? How do they do this? How does this help?

You may not be able to answer all of these questions, but asking them and other questions and seeking answers is modelling good scientific practice.

Common misconception

'I get energy asleep'

Many pupils do not have a clear idea of energy and where animals like humans get their energy. Some associate lack of energy with tiredness. They hear people say things like 'I need a rest, I have no energy'. Ask the pupils to think of the times they eat as times they take energy into their bodies.

Pupil activity 7.14

Role-play a food chain

> **Learning objective:** Learn about feeding relationships in an environment.
>
> **Resources required:** Post-it® notes

After writing the letter 'f' on numerous Post-it® notes, scatter these around the walls and furniture of the classroom. This may cause interest as pupils arrive. When you are ready, explain that you are going to model a food chain and the example you have chosen is an area of the Antarctic Ocean. First, ask six pupils to stand and to represent seals; all around them is food. Each Post-it® note represents a fish. Ask them what the fish eat (plants), and explain that the plants are the producers. Producers make food from sunlight. After about 30 seconds, tell them to stop or 'freeze frame' and ask three others to stand and introduce them as killer whales. Ask what killer whales eat (seals). Introduce the terms 'predator' and 'prey'. Then, insist on no running but allow the killer whales to move around the room hunting and eating seals! Stop the role-play when a seal or two are surviving; the whales never catch all the seals, or what would happen? Challenge the pupils to identify the predator and prey, the consumers, the top consumer, and the producer (plankton on which fish feed).

Try this approach with other food chains, for example:

oak leaves → caterpillar → sparrow → sparrow hawk

grass → rabbits → foxes

Pupil activity 7.15

Use an ICT-based simulation for predator–prey populations

Learning objective: Learn that animal populations fluctuate and are influenced by prey populations.

Resources required: a predator–prey game or simulation

The relationship between a predator and prey population can be represented by the graph in Figure 7.6. Pupils can see that as the population of the prey increases, there is a delay and then an increase in the predator population. Ask pupils to explain this delay.

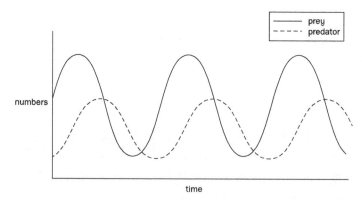

Figure 7.6 Graphical representation of relative predator–prey populations over time

Predator–prey games are available on the internet. Simple ones that are suitable for primary classes include:

http://www.snh.org.uk/teachingspace/whattodo/peatlands/predator_and_prey_game.asp

Pupil activity 7.16

An environmental campaign

Learning objective: Learn about ways we can care for the environment.

Resources required: newspapers, periodicals, news websites, etc.

Newspapers and news websites are a good starting point for looking at an issue such as global warming or acid rain (now threatening stonework in the City of Venice), a threat to local woodland or the need to promote recycling. Either you can select an issue for the pupils to address or they can select one for themselves. Initially, you might look at a local issue such as litter, a new road or limited local recycling. It could even be a fictitious example, perhaps a new roadway through the local park. They might consider some of the following questions:

- What is the issue?
- Do pupils understand what is going on?
- What is the effect?
- What is the science behind it?
- What different proposals have been made?
- What are the advantages and disadvantages?
- Can they suggest proposals to improve the situation?
- Can they make a case for an action or actions?
- Could they communicate their ideas to decision makers involved? Others?

Literacy

Pupil activity 7.17

Citizenship and care for the environment

Learning objective: Learn about ways in which our behaviour can damage or improve the environment.

Resources required: access to parts of the school site, access to the internet

Ask the pupils about the school site and the different places animals and plants live. Take them on a short walk to see several areas and ask them to think of ways these areas could be home to a greater variety of plants and animals. If you have time ask the pupils to research ways of caring for such habitats on the internet. Alternatively, ask a local park ranger to speak to the class about such approaches.

Citizenship

After discussion in pairs, ask the pupils to suggest ways that these habitats, together with the animals and plants, could be looked after, so that the animals and plants will grow and not be hurt. They might suggest planting more plants, excluding people, writing a sign, not dropping litter; all sorts of things may come up. Try to accept all ideas and select several to explore, trial, and put into place. Pupils may want to visit the site regularly, so you might suggest rules; for example, not removing leaves, not moving rocks, putting stones they have turned over back in their original place the right way up, and so on.

An alternative or additional approach is to ask pupils to consider ways to reduce, reuse, and recycle resources. This work can extend to their home and the local, national, and global communities. If your school is registered as an Eco School (see http://www.eco-schools.org.uk), it will have a pupil-led Eco-Committee, the members of which should be delighted to hear about your work and may be able to assist. If not, you might consider taking on some ideas of the scheme and perhaps promoting it in school. This would contribute to your school's plan to become a sustainable school.

Pupil activity 7.18

Research and discussion about micro-organisms
Learning objective: To understand the harmful and beneficial roles of micro-organisms.
Resources required: books on micro-organisms, access to the internet

We tend to be unaware of micro-organisms but are aware of the negative consequences of their lives on us. If they make us unwell, we experience discomfort and even serious illness; however, when we eat bread and other foodstuffs, we often forget the role they played. As the positive examples of the lives of micro-organisms are perhaps less familiar, consider emphasising these. Ask pupils to do some research (book or web based) to identify foods and products in which micro-organisms have been used in production, for example, breads, yoghurt, beer, wine, and medicines. This could be extended to other ways we benefit from micro-organisms, such as composting, removal of dead animal and plant materials, and their/our waste products. Negative effects of micro-organisms include bacterial and viral illness, the rotting of food, and damage to materials such as clothing that can rot.

Pupil Activity 7.19

Comparison of Life cycles

Learning objective: To understand differences between the life cycles of different animals.

Resources required: access to secondary sources of information

Ask learners to research the stages in the life cycle of a mammal (e.g. sheep, rabbit), an insect (e.g. butterfly, wasp), a bird (e.g. blackbird, robin), a reptile (snake, lizard), and an amphibian (e.g. newt, frog). Ask them to draw and label a simple diagram which they can present to the class. Ask learners to note differences and similarities between the different life cycles, for example, are all the young born as live births or some as eggs?

Pupil discussion 7.20

Micro-organisms recycle nutrients

Learning objective: Learn about the abundance and role of micro-organisms in recycling nutrients.

Resources required: none

Recap with examples of a food chain. Remind pupils about micro-organisms, that they live in the environment, often in the soil, and briefly how they live. Ask them to talk to others and then contribute to a discussion about where micro-organisms fit into a food chain. Share ideas but establish that they are abundant in the environment and deal with death and waste materials at each stage of a life cycle.

Figure 7.7 Micro-organisms and their role in the food chain

Pupil investigation skills 7.21

Observation of rotting food

Learning objective: To understand that micro-organisms can break down food and how this is a necessary process, but can be a problem for humans.

Resources required: food to grow mould on, securely sealed bags (see Safety Point below)

For these investigations, food should be sealed in containers because observation of moulds can be dangerous. The pupils could use a sealed bag within another sealed bag. Ask them to plan an investigation of the conditions that speed up the rotting of food, such as temperature, light, and moisture. The latter is perhaps the easiest to set up. Challenge them to design a fair test and to vary one variable (e.g. amount of moisture). Sliced bread is very good for growing mould on. The bags must not be re-opened at any point and at the end of the investigation place them all in a strong bin bag and dispose of appropriately.

David Attenborough: broadcaster and naturalist

David Attenborough would best be described as a naturalist – someone who knows a huge amount about animals, plants, and geology from habitats all over the world. He is perhaps best known for his 'Life' series, beginning with 'Life on Earth', which outlines how life evolved and became increasingly complex. Filming all around the planet with the BBC Natural History Unit, Attenborough has brought many and varied animals and plants into the viewer's home, in stunning detail. Later series have focused on mammals, reptiles, birds, invertebrates, amphibians, and plants, as well as broader themes of ecology. Many of the series used pioneering camera work; for example, stunning time lapse photography of plants enabled them to be seen as very dynamic organisms. Attenborough has done much to encourage people to appreciate the wonder of nature, in all of its forms. Our understanding of nature's beauty and complexity helps foster our desire to conserve valuable habitats, wherever they are found.

http://www.bbc.co.uk/nature/collections/p0048522

(David Attenborough's favourite moments from the last 30 years as a naturalist – video clips)

Summary of key learning points:

- a diversity of organisms exists, which includes bacteria, fungi, plants, and animals;

- a diversity of organisms is found in most habitats;

- the organisms, including humans, in an ecosystem interact with each other and with the physical aspects of the environment;

- micro-organisms are widely distributed;

- planet Earth can be seen as a single biosphere with all animals and plants living together and inter-dependent;

- the weather varies from season to season in a predictable way;

- resources such as water move through a cycle that is essential to life on Earth;

- most scientists believe that much human activity is raising average temperatures and that this climate change has the potential to adversely affect populations of animals and plants;

- many aspects of human activity have known and unknown consequences on the planet, its atmosphere, and populations of plants and animals (e.g. ozone depletion);

- people – including pupils – can alter their behaviour and choices to reduce the negative affects of human activity on the planet (e.g. reducing energy consumption, measuring and reducing one's carbon footprint).

Self-test

Question 1

Humankind's effect on the planet (a) is to warm it up, (b) can have positive and negative consequences, (c) is the fault of scientists, (d) is undesirable

Question 2

Animals and plants (a) exist for the benefit of humankind, (b) will always recover from the impact of humankind, (c) are inter-dependent, (d) are themselves stores of carbon

Question 3

Food chains (a) always start with a producer, (b) represent 'what eats what', (c) show how pollutants can move into other organisms and become concentrated, (d) all rely on the Sun for energy

Question 4

We can reduce humankind's negative effect by (a) consuming less fossil fuels, (b) waiting for other people to take action, (c) reducing our consumption of raw materials, for example, by recycling, (d) composting waste organic material

Self-test answers

Q1: (b) is correct as not all our activities warm up the planet. Humans are responsible for discoveries and inventions that have led to some of the environmental problems. However, it is how these inventions and discoveries have been used that has caused the problems. Often the potential damage was not known in advance. Fossil fuels have been burned for a long time, but humans have only recently found out about the greenhouse effect. It is only through science that we have been able to quantify the problem and offer potential solutions. Humankind's effect on the planet is not all undesirable – for example, we have protected some creatures from natural disasters.

Q2: (c) and (d) are correct. Living organisms do not exist for our benefit and do not always recover from the impact of humankind.

Q3: (a) and (d) are correct. At a simple level, food chains show 'what eats what' (b) but it is better to think of them as showing energy flow from organism to organism. (c) is partly correct but pyramids illustrate the impact of pollution more effectively.

Q4: (a), (c), and (d) are correct. Waiting for others to take action would be less effective.

Misconceptions

'If you cut an earthworm in half, two earthworms will be made'
'I get energy asleep'

Web resources

http://home.messiah.edu/~deroos/CSC171/PredPrey/PRED.htm
    (predator–prey simulation)
http://news.bbc.co.uk/1/shared/spl/hi/sci_nat/04/climate_change/html/greenhouse.
        stm
    (animated simulation of the greenhouse effect)
http://earthguide.ucsd.edu/earthguide/diagrams/watercycle
    (animated diagram of the water cycle)
http://www.bbc.co.uk/programmes/b03hj893/clips
    (An excellent selection of films showing how the weather of the changing seasons
    affects British wildlife)

http://www.turtlediary.com/grade-1-games/science-games/the-water-cycle.html
     (animated water cycle with interactive labelling)
http://www.eco-schools.org.uk
     (for the Eco Schools site)
www.keepbritaintidy.org/home/481
     (keep Britain tidy campaigns)
http://www.snh.org.uk/teachingspace/whattodo/peatlands/predator_and_prey_game.asp
     (a whole-class predator–prey game)

8

Materials

About this chapter

This chapter provides an explanation of what all materials are made of, discussing atoms and their constituent parts. It distinguishes between the various configurations of atoms and how these affect the behaviour of materials. It addresses properties of materials and the ways that materials can be changed. Solids, liquids, gases, mixtures, and separating techniques are also covered. Reversible and irreversible changes are discussed. The second part of the chapter addresses what the pupils need to learn and the final part suggests effective ways to teach about materials, including how to address common misconceptions.

What the teacher needs to know and understand

Materials are selected for purposes because of their properties

Younger pupils often find it hard to explain why a particular object is made from a particular material. Indeed, they often find it difficult to separate the object from the property of the material (e.g. they might say 'the key is hard' rather than 'the metal is hard'). To break down this knowledge into easily understandable concepts, we can start by naming everyday materials we see around us. For example, wood, stone, metal, glass, card, paper, and so on. We can classify them as 'natural' or 'made by humans'. Wood and stone are naturally occurring, but other materials such as plastic are made by humans. Humans take a natural resource and turn it into the material we see before us. Metal was once metal rock ore which had lots of impurities that needed removing, glass was once sand, plastic was once oil, and paper is made from wood.

Once we have correctly named materials and understood where they have come from, we can turn to their properties. Many of the properties will be obvious to pupils: hard, strong, shiny, opaque, and so on. These properties can often be grouped into opposites as follows: hard versus soft, weak versus strong, shiny versus dull, opaque versus transparent, bendy versus rigid, stretchy versus stiff. This grouping into opposites allows pupils to sort materials based on their similarities and differences (see Pupil activity 8.3), a very powerful evidence-based teaching technique (Marzano *et al.*, 2003) that really helps them get to grips with the properties of individual materials. Note that materials have more than one obvious property – for example wood is hard (you don't want to bang into it), strong (it can bear a large load – that's why it's used for shelving), and rigid (it doesn't bend that much under weight) and opaque (you cannot see through it).

Once the pupils have learnt the most obvious property of a material, we can challenge them to search for more properties (again see Pupil activity 8.3). This last part of the discussion has touched on the fact that materials are selected for a certain job because of their properties and this fact is often hard for pupils to grasp. To help them do this we can challenge them to design objects that use inappropriate materials (see Pupil activity 8.10). They could draw a picture of a shoe made of paper, with liquorice laces. They can then say why the material properties they selected are not good for the job. This forces them to look at why the right materials are selected for everyday objects – leather for shoes is mostly waterproof, it's flexible, and so on.

Finally, pupils often find it hard to grasp that different materials can have similar properties. A key must be hard and strong, so it's made of metal. But a spoon can be made of wood, plastic, or metal. All of these are hard, tough (they don't scratch too easily) and strong. But some are better than others: metal cooking spoons can get too hot as they are very good conductors of heat; plastic spoons don't conduct heat, but they can easily melt if left in the pan for too long. This final section of getting pupils to understand the advantages and disadvantages of certain materials for the same jobs can be the most tricky. But if we have started with naming materials, naming properties, and sorting on the basis of properties, then they will be equipped to deal with this knowledge.

For younger pupils, an understanding of the ways that materials can undergo simple changes is required. The simplest of changes involves using forces to push or pull a material. The examples they should know are that some materials can be squashed (by pushing on them), stretched (by pulling on them), twisted (a twist is a push and a pull at the same time), bent (by pulling down at either end of a material), or folded (if a material is thin).

The more complex changes that younger pupils should know about are mixing, heating, and cooling. By mixing materials together we can change them (e.g. to make a 'magic potion' in a story, or a bubble mixture in the classroom). They should also know about heating materials to melt them (e.g., holding a piece of chocolate in a closed hand). A combination of mixing and then heating would be the familiar processes of baking bread or a cake. Cooling a material can make it go harder; an example would be butter or chocolate placed in a fridge.

The following section delves into the building blocks of all materials. This section on atoms, elements, molecules, and concepts is quite in-depth, but is useful for teacher background knowledge. Some sections can be tricky, particularly if it is a while since you studied these concepts at school, so take it slowly and re-read sections that don't immediately make sense.

The final section on solids, liquids, gases (including changes of state), and reversible/irreversible changes is directly applicable to your knowledge required to teach Key Stage 2 Materials.

Atoms

All materials are constructed from atoms. The easiest way to think of an atom is as a simple sphere and when we talk later of solids, liquids, and gases, this is the model we shall use. An atom is not really a simple ball shape, however, as it contains different parts inside it. In the centre of each atom is the nucleus, which itself is made of two different particles: the proton and the neutron. Different types of atoms have differing numbers of protons and neutrons. The proton has a positive electrical charge and the neutron has no charge. Orbiting this central nucleus region is an electron, which is negatively charged. Opposites attract, so the negative charge of the electron is attracted by the positive charge of the proton, and this keeps the orbiting electron in place. The electron is the thing that electricity is 'made of', while the proton and neutron are much bigger and can be thought of as the 'hard stuff' in an atom.

The simplest atom is hydrogen, which unusually does not even contain a neutron; it simply has one single proton being orbited by one single electron. Other atoms are bigger, and contain more protons, neutrons, and electrons. Figure 8.1 shows a helium atom, which contains two protons (marked with a '+' sign) and two neutrons, all of

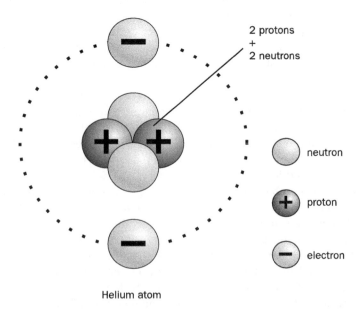

Helium atom

Figure 8.1 An atom of helium showing protons, neutrons, and electrons which are being orbited by two electrons (marked with a '–' sign). Other familiar atoms are oxygen, which has eight protons, eight neutrons, and eight electrons, and carbon, which has six protons, six neutrons, and six electrons (see Figure 8.2).

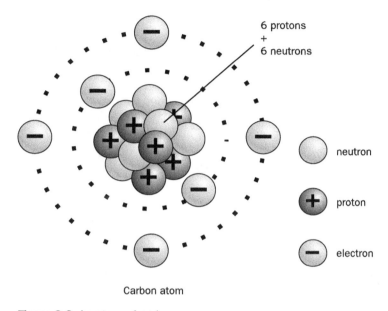

Carbon atom

Figure 8.2 An atom of carbon

An atom of gold is more massive and has 79 protons, 118 neutrons, and 79 electrons. As already stated, there are different types of atoms and they differ because they have different numbers of 'subatomic' particles in them, namely, differing numbers of protons, neutrons, and electrons. It is as simple as that. To address how many different types of atoms there are, we will look at what scientists call 'elements'.

Elements

Familiar atoms such as oxygen, carbon, and gold are called 'elements' and form the building blocks of the materials around us. An element is a 'pure' substance that only contains atoms of that same element. There are about 90 naturally occurring elements, and the common ones include silver, iron, oxygen, nitrogen, calcium, titanium, copper, aluminium, zinc, sulphur, phosphorus, magnesium, neon, potassium, sodium, and lead. The reason that they differ from one another is that each of them has different numbers of protons, neutrons, and electrons inside them, which gives them their unique properties. Elements cannot be changed into each other – for example, lead cannot be turned into gold.

One atom is the smallest amount of an element that can be found in nature (e.g. one atom of gold). If we were to put one atom of gold alongside another, they would be identical in every way, having the same numbers of protons, neutrons, and electrons.

After this brief discussion of the pure substances we call elements, you may be wondering how 90 or so such elements are enough to make everything else we see in the world. There are no elements of wood or elephants, so where do these things come from? To answer that question, we must look at how elements are arranged and bonded together to produce all of the materials that we come across.

Arranging the elements: molecules, compounds, and mixtures

Molecules

When atoms bond together they form what is called a molecule. The atoms can be the same type (e.g. two hydrogen atoms) or they can be different types (e.g. a carbon atom and an oxygen atom). When two atoms of hydrogen bond together they form a molecule of hydrogen (H_2). When a carbon atom and an oxygen atom bond together they form a molecule of carbon monoxide (CO).

Compounds

When atoms of certain different elements meet they react together to form a compound. Water is the most familiar compound, made from the elements hydrogen and oxygen. Compounds do not have properties the same as their elemental parts. For example, water is H_2O, which means that each molecule has two hydrogen gas atoms bonded to one oxygen gas atom. This is unexpected, two gases combining to make a liquid! Salt is sodium chloride, which is sodium metal atoms bonded with poisonous chlorine gas atoms to make common table salt, not at all obvious! Plastic is made from long chains of carbon and hydrogen atoms.

It is these arrangements of atoms that provide different materials with their properties and it is a complex business. As primary school teachers we can leave it to chemists to worry about how different arrangements of the atoms achieve the properties that they do. What we need to know about is which materials have which properties and we do not have to worry about their underlying chemical structure and arrangement.

Mixtures

Mixtures occur when different substances are mixed together, but *do not react* with each other. This means that the particles do not interact with each other to make new substances with new properties. Everyday examples include the air, which is a mixture of nitrogen, oxygen, carbon dioxide, and water vapour. Mixtures can often be separated easily (e.g. sand can be separated from water by filtering).

Solids, liquids, and gases

To explain the behaviour of solids, liquids, and gases, we need to understand particle theory. Particle theory treats a single atom or molecule as a single, spherical particle. This simplification allows us to understand how something like water can be a solid (as ice), liquid, or gas (as water vapour).

In its solid ice form, all the particles of water do not move appreciably. This means that a block of ice in a cold room retains its shape. As heat is added, the particles gain energy, and can move around more. This means that the ice starts to melt. Eventually, it will all become a liquid, which means it can change its shape and flow. Over time, the particles of water at the surface of the liquid can gain enough energy to leave the liquid and go up into the air. This is evaporation. The hotter the surroundings, the more easily the particles on the surface can gain energy to evaporate and become a gas.

As illustrated in Figure 8.3, the opposite can also happen. In a warm room, the water vapour particles may hit a cold window, lose energy, and turn back into liquid form. This process is condensation. Water placed in a freezer soon becomes ice. As the liquid loses energy, the particles lose their ability to move around so freely and so solid ice forms.

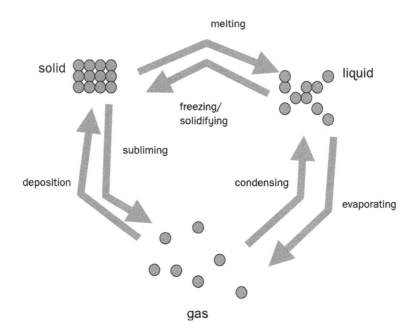

Figure 8.3 Particle theory showing how a substance can exist as a solid, liquid, or gas

Subliming is much less common. This is where a solid turns directly to a gas. Some snow lying on the ground will often sublime rather than simply melt. The opposite process is called deposition, where, for example, water vapour changes directly into ice, e.g. frost formation.

Reversible and irreversible changes

The above processes are referred to as reversible changes, since water can change easily from one state to another. Another kind of reversible change is dissolving. If salt is added to water and stirred in slowly, the large grains of salt begin to break down into smaller pieces. These smaller pieces bond weakly with the water, forming salty water. The salty water is what is termed a 'solution', which simply means a liquid with a solid dissolved in it. The process can easily be reversed by boiling off the water (or letting it slowly evaporate), leaving the salt grains behind. However, not all solids dissolve in water. When solids that do not dissolve are stirred into water, they form what is called a 'suspension' (e.g. talcum powder in water). If left, the solid will eventually settle at the bottom.

Other changes are not reversible. These irreversible or permanent changes produce new substances. Irreversible changes happen during chemical changes, for example, burning. When wood is burnt it produces smoke and ash. The smoke and ash can never be recombined to form wood. Another example of irreversible change is when two substances react together, for example vinegar and bicarbonate of soda. In this case, the bonds inside the vinegar and bicarbonate of soda molecules are broken and the atoms released form new bonds in new combinations to make a new substance, which is carbon dioxide gas.

Polymers

Polymers are materials made from very long chains of repeating molecules, usually carbon and hydrogen. Plastic would be a polymer that pupils are most familiar with. Polymers tend to be both flexible and strong. Some can be stretchy too. As well as the more familiar plastics, the pupils will know about polystyrene (or Styrofoam), chewing gum and rubber – all examples of polymers. Rubber is natural latex, made from the sap of the rubber tree. Human-made polymers are made from oil.

What pupils need to know at Key Stage 1

(ST) denotes statutory requirements.

Everyday materials

(ST) Identify and name a variety of everyday materials, including wood, plastic, glass, metal, water, and rock

Suggestions for working scientifically:

> Pupils should explore and experiment with a wide variety of materials, not only those listed in the programme of study, but including for example: brick, paper, fabrics, elastic, foil.

(ST) Describe the simple physical properties of a variety of everyday materials

(ST) Distinguish between an object and the material from which it is made

(ST) Compare and group together a variety of everyday materials on the basis of their simple physical properties

Suggestions for working scientifically:

> Pupils could classify materials as hard/soft; stretchy/stiff; shiny/dull; rough/smooth; bendy/rigid; waterproof/ absorbent; opaque/transparent.

> Pupils could perform simple tests to explore questions, for example: 'What is the best material for an umbrella? (i.e. most waterproof); ... for lining a dog basket? (i.e. softest); ... for curtains? (i.e. most opaque); ... for a bookshelf? (i.e. strongest).

Uses of everyday materials

(ST) Identify and compare the suitability of a variety of everyday materials, including wood, metal, plastic, glass, brick, rock, paper, and cardboard for particular uses

Suggestions for working scientifically:

> Compare the uses of everyday materials in and around the school with materials found in other places (at home, the journey to school, on visits, and in stories, rhymes and songs).

> Observe closely, identifying and classifying the uses of different materials, and recording their observations.

> Think about the properties of materials that make them suitable or unsuitable for particular purposes.

> Become familiar with *how some materials are used for more than one thing* (metal can be used for coins, cans, cars and table legs; wood can be used for matches, floors, and telegraph poles).

> Understand that *different materials are used for the same thing* (spoons can be made from plastic, wood, or metal, but not normally from glass).

> Think about unusual and creative uses for everyday materials.

> Find out about people who have developed useful new materials, for example John Dunlop, Charles Macintosh, or John McAdam.

(ST) find out how the shapes of solid objects made from some materials can be changed by squashing, bending, twisting and stretching

What pupils need to know at Key Stage 2

(ST) denotes statutory requirements.

Lower Key Stage 2

States of matter

(ST) Compare and group materials together, according to whether they are solids, liquids or gases

Suggestions for working scientifically:

> Explore a variety of everyday materials and develop simple descriptions of the states of matter (e.g. solids hold their shape; liquids form a pool, not a pile; gases escape from an unsealed container).

(ST) Observe that some materials change state when they are heated or cooled, and measure or research the temperature at which this happens in degrees Celsius (°C)

Suggestions for working scientifically:

> Pupils should observe water as a solid, a liquid and a gas and should note the changes to water when it is heated or cooled.
>
> Explore the effect of temperature on substances such as chocolate, butter, and cream.
>
> Research using the internet or library books the temperature at which materials change state, for example, when iron melts or when oxygen condenses into a liquid.

(ST) Identify the part played by evaporation and condensation in the water cycle and associate the rate of evaporation with temperature

Suggestions for working scientifically:

> Observe and record evaporation over a period of time, for example, a puddle in the playground or washing on a line.
>
> Investigate the effect of temperature on washing drying or snowmen melting.

Upper Key Stage 2

Properties and changes to materials

(ST) Give reasons, based on evidence from comparative and fair tests, for the particular uses of everyday materials, including metals, wood, and plastic

(ST) Compare and group together everyday materials on the basis of their properties, including their hardness, solubility, transparency, conductivity (electrical and thermal), and response to magnets

Suggestions for working scientifically:

> Carry out tests to answer questions, for example, 'Which materials would be the most effective for making a warm jacket, for wrapping ice cream to stop it melting, or for making blackout curtains?'
>
> Compare materials in order to make a switch in a circuit.

(ST) Know that some materials will dissolve in liquid to form a solution, and describe how to recover a substance from a solution

Suggestions for working scientifically:

> Explore reversible changes such as dissolving and melting, recognising that melting and dissolving are different processes.

(ST) Use knowledge of solids, liquids and gases to decide how mixtures might be separated, including through filtering, sieving and evaporating

Suggestions for working scientifically:

> Explore reversible change, including evaporating, filtering, and sieving.

(ST) Demonstrate that dissolving, mixing and changes of state are reversible changes

(ST) Explain that some changes result in the formation of new materials, and that this kind of change is not usually reversible, including changes associated with burning and the action of acid on bicarbonate of soda

Suggestions for working scientifically:

> Explore changes that are difficult to reverse, for example, burning, rusting and other reactions, for example, vinegar with bicarbonate of soda.

Observe and compare the changes that take place, for example, when burning different materials or baking bread or cakes.

Find out about how chemists create new materials, for example, Spencer Silver, who invented the glue for sticky notes or Ruth Benerito, who invented wrinkle-free cotton.

Research and discuss how chemical changes have an impact on our lives, for example cooking.

Discuss the creative use of new materials such as polymers, super-sticky and super-thin materials.

Ways to teach 'materials' at Key Stage 1

Naming materials and identifying their properties

Pupil activity 8.1

What is the classroom made of?

Learning objective: To identify common materials in everyday use.

Resources required: everyday classroom objects

Discuss with your pupils the materials that things are made of in the classroom. They should be able to spot things made of wood, metal, hard plastic, glass, and soft fabric (often cotton). For some familiar objects, it is much harder to work out what they are made of. Many pupils don't know that cups are made of pot or fired clay; they often think they are made of glass (because they smash when dropped!).

Ask the pupils to draw or photograph the metal objects, the wooden objects, and so on, in the room. Different groups might be assigned different materials. Can they explain why certain materials are used in terms of their properties, such as why metal and wood are so common in the classroom? (Because they are strong and hard). Glass is transparent, letting light through, whereas curtains and blinds are opaque, so block the light to stop sunlight shining in people's eyes. Ask pupils to label their drawings with the properties of the materials.

Art and design

Table 8.1 A record of materials and useful properties

Object	made of . . .	useful property . . .
window	glass	strong and transparent

Pupil activity 8.2

Science songs

Learning objective: Learn why some materials are used to make particular objects.

Resources required: none

Try making up some songs with the pupils to name a material and describe its useful properties. It is easy to insert the words into a simple 'template song' such as 'Frere Jacques'. Here are two verses to start you off:

Music

Song (to the tune of *'Frere Jacques'*)

Glass for windows,
Glass for windows,
It is clear,
It is clear
So it lets the light through!
So it lets the light through!
That's why its here,
That's why its here.

Wood for doors,
Wood for doors,
Not too heavy,
Not too heavy,
It's very strong and hard,
It's very strong and hard,
That's why its here,
That's why its here.

A search on http://www.youtube.com for 'materials songs for kids' will give some simple songs for the pupils to sing along with (take great care using YouTube in class as inappropriate material can be accidently displayed).

Common misconception

'Aren't materials just fabrics?'

In everyday speech, we often use the word 'material' to refer to a fabric. Many classrooms may have what is called a 'materials box', which is a box full of different fabrics. The sense of the word we want to convey to the pupils is the scientific one of each object being made from one or more substances.

Pupil activity 8.3

Sorting materials based on simple characteristics

Learning objective: Learn to identify the different properties a material may have.

Resources required: sorting hoops labelled with different properties (see below), a range of everyday objects that are easily handled (e.g. cups, balls, pencils, rulers, books, simple toys, pencil cases, cards)

Prepare a range of objects that can easily be handled by the pupils. Include numerous wooden, metal, and plastic items as well as different fabrics. Challenge them to see how many different ways they can sort or group the materials. Start off simply with two categories like 'hard' or 'soft', 'rigid' (like wood) or 'bendy' (like foam), 'dull' or 'shiny'. Encourage the pupils to handle the materials and place them in hoops marked with the correct description (e.g. hard, rough, smooth). They should rapidly see that some objects can be placed in more than one hoop, as some materials have more than one property.

Extend this task by asking how many different properties the pupils can identify for each material. This can lead on to a discussion of why certain objects can be made from different materials (e.g. a spoon to stir sauces can be made from wood, metal or hard plastic). This is because each of these materials is rigid (keeps its shape), strong, and waterproof. Some objects tend always to be made from the same material. Keys are nearly always made of metal, as wood and plastic are too likely to break or lose their shape to be effective keys.

Common misconception

'Is it the spoon that's hard or the material?'

In your discussion with the pupils, you may find that they frequently focus on the object itself rather than the material. To the question 'Which material is hard?' they will often reply 'the spoon'. Ask them then to say what the spoon is made of and stress that it is the material that makes the spoon hard. Another approach is to use a 'materials kit' bought from an educational supplier. These have discs and blocks of materials that are not shaped into usable objects, so the pupils are more likely to focus on the material itself.

Common misconception

'Wood is heavy, so it sinks doesn't it?'

If pupils compare materials that float to those that sink, they may be surprised that wood floats, as many will expect it to sink. Pupils often think that 'light things float' and 'heavy things sink'. What we are really talking about here is density. Density can be thought of in terms of how closely particles are packed together in a material. Dense materials have particles packed closely together, whereas less dense materials have their particles packed further apart. Materials that are denser than water sink in water, and those that are less dense than water float in water. For younger pupils, the concept of density is too difficult, but perhaps an alternative term could be used and they could think of materials as being either 'heavy for their size' or 'light for their size' and sort them accordingly. Wood being 'light for its size' can float and even a big log can float down a river.

Another way to think about floating and sinking is through the concept of 'upthrust'. Upthrust is a force in water that directly counteracts the weight of an object. This concept is introduced in upper Key Stage 2 (see teacher's section in Chapter 10 on forces).

Natural, manufactured, and modified materials

Pupil activity 8.4

Is it natural or man-made?

Learning objective: Learn to identify and discuss whether materials are natural or man-made.

Resources required: a range of example materials, including wood, plastic, glass, steel, chalk, soil, and fabric. Include materials that have a natural and a processed state – for example, a polished and unpolished pebble, a twig and a wooden spoon, clay and pot, sand and glass marbles, twig and paper, twig and card, vegetable oil and plastic spoon (some plastics are made from vegetable oil rather than other types of oil)

A more tricky way for the pupils to sort materials is into those that occur naturally (e.g. wood and sand) and those that are made or manufactured (e.g. plastic and glass). It is not always apparent to pupils which of these categories these materials fit into. To further complicate matters, many natural materials are changed before they are used. For example, wool and cotton are washed and dyed, wood is often planed and polished, while stone can be ground and polished. Offer the pupils a range of materials in their natural and processed state to see if they can link them together. Encourage discussion and explain that it is not always easy to categorise a material.

Common misconception

'It's from the supermarket!'

Some pupils will have difficulty saying where a material has come from. Many will give the source of foodstuffs as the local supermarket. Try this activity with the class to challenge this idea:

object ...	comes from ...	comes from...	comes from ...
magazine is made of ... paper	printing factory giant rolls of paper are printed, cut, and stapled	paper factory wood pulp is made into paper	trees raw material is wood

---

Pupil activity 8.5

What's in the bag?

Learning objective: Learn to recognise the differing properties of a material.

Resources required: feely bag (any small bag that cannot be seen through), range of easily handleable everyday items made from a single material (e.g. ruler, rubber, coin, etc.)

Feely bags are a great way to get the pupils to focus on the different textures of materials. Out of view of the class, place a mystery object in the bag. One pupil feels the object while the others ask that child questions about it. Check that he or she knows the answer. Give the other children some questions to start off with, such as 'Is it hard or soft?', 'Smooth or rough?', or 'Bendy or rigid?'

The child with their hand in the bag must resist the temptation of telling the others what the object is, and should only respond to direct questions from the others, not spontaneously giving clues away. The questioners must name the material correctly, not the object. Only then can the object be revealed to see if they were correct.

Pupil activity 8.6

The right material for the job

Learning objective: To learn why certain materials are selected for particular jobs.

Resources required: writing materials

Ask the pupils to draw a ship, house, car or anything that has lots of different materials in it. They should draw the exterior and interior of the object and label the different materials. Then get them to write down why those materials have been chosen for each part. For example, the metal on the outside of cars is extremely strong and waterproof, while the seats on the inside are made from leather and foam to make them soft and comfortable. Challenge them to draw and label as many parts as they can, and put the reason for each material choice on their picture as well.

Testing materials

Pupil investigation skills 8.7

The best waterproof material?

Learning objective: Through investigation be able to distinguish between waterproof and absorbent materials.

Resources required: some disposable foam or paper cups with a large hole cut in the bottom (prepare beforehand), paper towel, kitchen roll, plastic sandwich bag, pieces of cotton, and so on. Cut these different materials into a square shape, so that they easily cover the hole in the cup, and reach to about halfway up the cup when placed inside

Tell the pupils you want to repair some broken picnic cups and so have to find a waterproof material. Ask them to predict the best materials for the job. They can easily test their material by placing it in the cup and pouring a little water in, taking care to pour the water onto the material and not down the sides of the cup. Does the water stay in the cup or drain through the material? A discussion might follow as to the best material for an umbrella, coat or cover.

Common misconception

'It soaks up water so isn't it waterproof?'

Many pupils think that absorbent materials such as paper towels, tissue paper, and kitchen roll are waterproof. Here they are confusing absorbent (soaks the water up) with waterproof (keeps the water out). It is worth demonstrating the difference to all the pupils after the investigation above.

Pupil investigation skills 8.8

The best cat litter!

Learning objective: To be able to compare materials to identify the best one for a particular job.

Resources required: paper towels, tissue paper, J-cloth®, A4 paper, plastic trays or plates, measuring cylinders (the smaller the better) or plastic syringes (calibrated in millilitres)

Challenge the pupils to find the most absorbent material. You could say it was to make a new cat litter for your pet that is not house trained! Don't compare a range of kitchen towels, as they are pretty similar. Instead, offer squares of material that includes printer paper, tissue paper from tissue handkerchiefs, tissue paper from kitchen roll, a blue J-cloth®.

The procedure is to pour a small amount of water onto the sheet, wait for a short time, and then pour it back again into a measuring cylinder and see how much has been absorbed. Fair testing involves the amount of water used, the amount of time given, and the size of each sheet.

The pupils may find it tricky initially to decide on the amount of water to pour on and how long to wait. The less water the better if you are only using single sheets. They could try 10–15 ml of water and wait for it to soak in for about 15 seconds, so let them do a few trial runs before doing the investigation.

Pupil investigation skills 8.9

How hard, how soft?

Learning objective: To be able to test materials for a particular property.

Resources required: small rubber bouncy balls, squares of materials of similar thickness, such as foam, carpet tile, cotton sheet, wood, and paper (some materials can be folded to increase the thickness, for example, paper and cotton sheet; an ideal thickness is about half a centimetre), sticky labels with the name of each material on, metre stick

Tell the pupils you want to make the softest cushions in the world, and so need to test some materials. Materials can easily be ranked from hardest to softest by how high a ball bounces when dropped on them. The hardest materials give the ball the biggest bounce; the softest give the smallest bounce. It is worth you taking the time to demonstrate this and discussing it with the pupils to ensure they understand the concept.

Challenge the pupils to design a fair test. They need to drop the ball from the same height each time (a ruler could help here) and use the same thickness of material. Measuring the height of the first and highest bounce on each material can be tricky, but using a metre ruler and placing stickers on it for each separate material is useful. The pupils will need to test each material more than once to check their results are accurate.

Pupil activity 8.10

Draw it like it is!

Learning objective: To identify the key properties of common materials.

Resources required: materials for drawing

Ask the pupils to illustrate materials in terms of their properties by drawing the name of the material in the style of its property; for example, the word 'steel' could be drawn and coloured as shiny, silver grey riveted letters, 'glass' could be drawn as three-dimensional block letters that can be seen through, 'rubber' could have bendy letters, and so on.

Pupil activity 8.11

The wrong material for the job

Learning objective: To identify the key properties of materials and then imagine their opposites.

Resources required: materials for drawing

Challenge your pupils to draw an everyday object (e.g. a shoe, table, fridge) and label the materials and their properties, and why those properties are suitable. Then ask them to draw the same object but using the most unsuitable materials (e.g. paper for the upper part of a shoe, sponge for its sole, wet spaghetti for the shoelaces). They again should label what the properties are and why they are not suitable.

Heating and cooling materials

Pupil activity 8.12

Melting, solidifying, and freezing everyday things

Learning objective: Learn about the ways that heat can affect solids.

Resources required: butter, margarine, chocolate, plastic sandwich bags

Place the foods in separate sandwich bags. These can be held in the hand and the heat from the hand will start to melt them. Chocolate melts within moments, whereas margarine takes a few minutes to melt. Ask your pupils how the substances can be changed back to solids. They may suggest putting them in a cool place, perhaps even the fridge. Ask them what will happen if the substances are put in the freezer.

 Stress that the food should not be eaten after it has been used in science investigations.

Pupil investigation skills 8.13

Where are the hottest and coldest parts of the school?

Learning objective: Learn through investigation that some places are warmer than others and how this can be proved.

Resources required: balloons or rubber gloves, bowls to place them in, measuring jugs and cylinders

Fill the balloons or rubber gloves with water and seal up. Freeze overnight. Ask the pupils to select places around the school to leave frozen gloves in bowls. Ask them where the ice will melt quickest and where it will last longest.

 Cool places might include cupboards; hot places might be a sunny windowsill or near a radiator. Care needs to be taken not to leave them near any electrical appliances that could be affected by leakage. The amount of water produced from the melting ice can be measured after cutting the balloons or untying the gloves and using the measuring jugs. A simple graph can be drawn to show the results.

Ways to teach 'materials' at Key Stage 2

More complex properties of materials

Thermal conductors, insulators, strength, and hardness

Your pupils should have done some testing of materials in Key Stage 1. Some of the investigations outlined in the Key Stage 1 section above would be suitable for younger Key Stage 2 pupils – testing waterproof materials, absorbency, hard and soft materials – if they have not done them previously. By upper Key Stage 2, pupils are expected to look at and test more complex properties of materials. For example, thermal insulators and conductors are investigated, as are strength and hardness and how these could be tested. This section could also include looking at magnetic and non-magnetic materials, building on their experiences of using magnets at lower Key Stage 2.

Pupil investigation skills 8.14

Keeping ice from melting

Learning objective: To be able to identify thermal insulators as materials that can keep things cool.

Resources required: ice cubes or ice pops (keep the wrappers on – this makes them easy to handle during the experiment), syringes to measure the amount of water produced from melting ice, small bowls to put the ice in, a range of materials to wrap the ice in (e.g. woollen fabric, cotton fabric, foil, plastic sandwich bags)

Challenge the pupils to find the best material to stop an ice cube from melting. Ask the pupils to discuss how they will make it a fair test by using the same thickness of material, the same number of layers, the same sized pieces of ice, and so on. They are looking for good thermal insulators that will stop heat from the surroundings flowing into the ice cube and making it melt.

Which materials were poor at stopping the ice from melting? Could we class these as thermal conductors? Challenge pupils to think of examples where such insulation would be used (e.g. refrigerated lorries, ice rinks, ski domes). Then ask them how this is similar to keeping things warm. It is about something being at a higher or lower temperature than its surroundings and trying to keep it that way for as long as possible.

Common misconception

'But won't wool and other fabrics make them hotter?'

Pupils might think that materials such as wool, which are good thermal insulators, will be no good because they 'warm us up'. Here we have confusion – we generate heat and the wool jumper keeps us warm by stopping the heat from flowing away from our body, it does not generate heat itself. Pupils often think that materials 'keep the cold in the ice' rather than keeping the heat out.

Pupil investigation skills 8.15

Keeping liquids hot

Learning objective: Learn to identify thermal insulators as materials that keep things hot.

Resources required: thermometers, plastic cups, range of materials to wrap around the cups, warm water to act as the 'soup'

The water used in this experiment should only be 'hand hot'. Hand hot is just warm enough to wash the dishes with (about 45 °C) (it is worth your pupils knowing this figure).

Can the pupils make a cup that would keep soup hot for as long as possible? Ensure they consider fair testing. Ask them to think about thickness of material and number of layers of material. Discuss with the pupils the need to measure the temperature at regular intervals. Can they predict the ones that are poor at keeping the water warm (good conductors)? If you can acquire lids for the cups (or simply place a piece of the test material over the top of the cup), you will achieve better results because the water will stay warm for longer. The pupils may want to set up a cup that has no material wrapped around it, to see if it becomes cold more quickly (it does, and this is worth them observing).

These last two investigations should demonstrate that thermal insulators can keep cold things cold and hot things hot, which pupils often find hard to understand. The cold things are kept cold by the insulator preventing heat from the surroundings from flowing into the cold thing. The hot things are kept hot by the thermal insulator stopping heat flowing out of the hot object.

Pupil investigation skills 8.16

Insulators and conductors – thermal or electrical?

Learning objective: Learn that thermal insulators are also electrical insulators and thermal conductors are also electrical conductors.

Resources required: thermal insulators and conductors (for more detail, see above section), simple electrical testing circuit (see Figure 12.9 in Chapter 12)

If the pupils have done one or both of the above preceding investigations, they should be in a position to address the following two questions. Are good thermal conductors good electrical conductors? Or are good thermal insulators good electrical insulators? By setting up a simple electrical testing circuit for conductors and insulators (see Chapter 12), they can test their ideas.

Teacher explanation: metals are good conductors of heat and electricity because they contain a lot of 'free' electrons and it is these that can move easily and carry the heat or electricity. (See the teacher's section in Chapter 12.) Non-metals don't have these 'free electrons' – all their electrons are tightly held by the atoms and cannot be easily moved. This means that they cannot transmit heat or electricity that easily. With non-metals, the way that heat can be transmitted is by the heat energy being transferred into the material. This causes all the particles to vibrate, and so to pass on the heat energy. Basically, this is what heat is – the more a particle vibrates, the more energy it has, and this energy can be passed from one particle to the next. Heat energy is just a way of thinking about how much particles are vibrating or moving. So any material can transmit heat by its particles vibrating, but metals have the added advantage of freely moving electrons as well that can move through a material, transmitting heat as they go.

Pupil investigation skills 8.17

Strength of paper

Learning objective: To test a range of similar materials fairly and identify the strongest.

Resources required: different kinds of paper (kitchen roll, toilet paper, computer paper, tissue, filter paper, etc.) made into loops by taping or stapling, force meters (with a range of scales, e.g. 0–5 N, 0–20 N)

The strength of a material is the measure of how hard it is to break it. Paper is often used for bags because it is lightweight, yet surprisingly strong. Challenge the pupils to find which paper is the strongest. For a fair test they will need to cut small strips of paper of the same width and length and make them into loops by stapling or gluing the ends together.

loop of paper

Figure 8.4 A force meter used to measure the strength of paper

The paper can be tested by placing each loop on the desk, putting the hook of a force meter at one end, and securing the other end (this end could be clamped to the edge of a table for stronger paper, or when testing weaker papers just held down on the table by a child). Then the force meter can be pulled and a measure given for how many Newtons of force are required to break the paper. It won't require a lot of force and the pupils will need to ensure that they have accurate results by performing repeat measurements.

Pupil investigation skills 8.18

How hard is it?

Learning objective: To understand the property of hardness and how it can be measured.

Resources required: a range of different objects to test, made from different materials (e.g. metal drinks can, block of wood, plastic bottle, play dough or play clay, metal spoon, stone, wax crayon, pasta, metal coin, glass bottle, 'pot' cup, stone), a metal nail to scratch with

Hardness is a measure of how scratch-resistant a material is. Ask the pupils to arrange the objects or materials in order of hardness, from softest to hardest. Then get them to test their predictions by carefully scratching the materials with a steel nail. The softer they are, the easier they are to scratch.

Ask pupils to justify why we use hard materials for some objects and soft materials for others. Note that hardness is not the same as strength, although these two properties often go hand in hand. Many food preparation surfaces are hard because we do not want them to scratch. Similarly, cutlery and pans should not scratch easily, but be 'hard wearing'. Your pupils may be surprised to find that the glass bottle and pot cup do not scratch, whereas many stones do.

Pupil investigation skills 8.19

Which material is the best one for the job?

Learning objective: Learn that alternative materials can be selected to make the same object.

Resources required: you may wish to show a range of bottles (e.g. glass, plastic, metal, ceramic) or pictures of these bottles to stimulate the start of the discussion

Over the years, bottles have been made from pottery or ceramic, glass, and more recently plastic. Ask your pupils to think of good and bad points for each of the three materials. For instance, in the past, glass bottles used to be taken back to the shop and sent back to the factory where they were washed out and refilled. This was common practice 30 years ago. Today, they are sometimes recycled, which involves sorting, crushing, and making new bottles. This probably uses more energy overall than the collecting, washing, and refilling method of the past. Reusing something is usually more efficient than recycling it.

Plastic bottles are cheap to make, light, and much safer than glass or ceramic. They are, however, difficult to recycle as there are so many kinds of plastic in use which have to be separated. You can try doing this by reading the code for each plastic, which is stamped on or near the base of most plastic containers (e.g. 1 = polyethylene terephthalate used to make many fizzy drinks bottles).

More information can be found at:

http://dl.dropboxusercontent.com/u/21130258/resources/InformationSheets/Packaging.htm

Other objects that might make interesting discussion points include:

- teapots – made from pottery, glass, and metal (metal ones are common, but being a thermal conductor is it really a good idea?)
- stirring spoons – made from metal, plastic or wood
- camping mugs – made from plastic or metal

This could lead to a discussion of why many objects are made from more than one material; for example, pans are made of metal but have plastic handles, kettles are plastic but have metal heating elements, a computer mouse has metal parts inside but plastic on the outside, plugs have plastic or rubber on the outside and metal on the prongs.

Solids and liquids

Pupil investigation skills 8.20

Sort the solids from the liquids

Learning objective: Learn how the properties of solids and liquids differ.

Resources required: a range of solids and liquids (see below), a range of containers

Discuss with pupils the properties of typical solids and liquids, such as solids keep their shape and don't easily change their shape, whereas liquids can be poured, will take the shape of the container they are put in, and so on. Give pupils a range of materials to sort into solids and liquids. Some they will easily be able to name as solids (e.g. wood and metal), but others may prove more difficult (e.g. sand and cloth). Not very runny liquids like honey and syrup are also interesting to examine (although messy!). Try wood, metal, plastic, sugar, salt, and bicarbonate of soda for solids. For liquids try water, washing-up liquid, milk, honey, syrup, colourless vinegar, and brown vinegar. For interesting discussion points, try jelly, hair gel, and shaving foam. These last three show that some materials are hard to classify and may have both solid and liquid properties. In science, we often create simple categories such as solids and liquids and then find things that don't quite fit in.

Common misconceptions

'Sand can be poured, so does that make it a liquid?'

Sand causes problems because it can be poured, and pupils often think that if something can be poured it must be a liquid. The reason sand can be poured is that a pile of sand consists of many small grains. A single grain can't be poured, just like a single brick can't be. But a heap of sand can be poured, just like a skip load of bricks can be tipped. You may also point out to pupils that when liquids are poured they always have a flat top when allowed to settle, but when grainy solids are poured they will often make a mound with a pointy top.

'Cloth is soft, so does that mean it's not a solid?'

Pupils often think that solids must be hard as so many solids they encounter in their life are hard, but paper and cloth are solids and are soft. Paper and cloth are very thin so can be easily folded. If left alone, they keep the shape that has been given them, as we would expect a solid to do.

Gases

Pupil activity 8.21

What gases are there?

Learning objective: To understand that there are many different gases that have different properties.

Resources required: fizzy drink in a bottle, packet of crisps

Gases are often introduced to Key Stage 2 pupils, but younger pupils will know something about them. Pupils will have heard of 'air' and may know some of the gases that make up the air. Air is a mixture of gases that include oxygen, carbon dioxide, water vapour, and nitrogen. Oxygen is the gas that humans need to live and fires need to burn. There is a very small amount of carbon dioxide in the air, which is the same gas that makes the bubbles in all fizzy drinks. Carbon dioxide is also used by plants together with water to make sugar. Water vapour is less familiar and often forgotten by pupils. Evidence for water vapour is less direct (see the section on 'Condensing' below). The main gas in the air is nitrogen. It does not easily react with anything and for this reason it is put inside crisp packets to keep the crisps fresh. If the bags were full of oxygen, the crisps would be stale by the time the bag was first opened!

From their discussion, ask pupils to draw a number of pictures where gases are of use or their presence can be inferred. For example, scuba divers carry air in their tanks, food can be cooked on a gas stove (usually propane or butane gas), and many houses are heated with gas central heating. Party balloons that 'float' contain helium gas. The properties of gases are less obvious than those of solids and liquids because usually they cannot be seen. Gases can flow, they fill any container they are introduced into, and will disperse to fill a room as can be demonstrated by spraying some perfume into the air in the next activity.

Teacher demonstration 8.22

How gases move

Learning objective: To be able to describe how gases move by themselves.

Resources required: perfume bottle, can of air freshener

Perfume can be poured onto a plate and left. Soon the perfume will evaporate and particles will end up all round the room. The pupils should be able to smell them. An air freshener works more quickly, spraying a liquid out in tiny droplets that immediately evaporate in the air to become a gas. Ensure that it is sprayed away from pupils. Challenge the pupils to say exactly what happened in each of the cases, using the correct scientific terms where possible.

Pupil activity 8.23

How do we know gases are there?

Learning objective: To be able to demonstrate the evidence for gases.

Resources required: sponges, washing-up bowls containing water, beakers, marbles, jugs of water, and squashy plastic drink bottles with lids on

The pupils can try the following demonstrations:

- Squeeze a sponge under water. Where do the bubbles come from? (Answer: from the spaces or gaps within the sponge.)
- Fill a beaker half full with marbles and another half full with sand. When the pupils pour water in, where do the bubbles come from? (Answer: from the gaps between the solids.)
- Show the pupils an 'empty' plastic drinks bottle with a lid on. Try and squash it flat between the hands – why won't it flatten? (Answer: the air inside pushes back to prevent you squashing it.)

Owing to their often invisible nature, there are many more misconceptions about gases than there are for solids and liquids. The following are some.

Common misconceptions

'Gases don't weigh anything do they?'

This comes from the idea that because gases are invisible they have no weight. A related idea is that because they are invisible they are not 'really there'. For example, we say a cup drained of liquid is 'empty'. It is empty of liquid, but it would now be full of gas (air). To get the pupils to see the difference, try getting them to squeeze a bottle full of air, with the lid on. It can only be compressed so much before it pushes back and resists any further force.

'Air is the only gas there is'

Pupils often say 'air' when they mean 'gas'. This is probably because their main experience with gases is the air. The above discussion, where different component gases of the air are distinguished and discussed together with their uses, should help.

'Oxygen and air is the same thing'

This may have arisen from younger pupils being told that 'we need air to live' and later being told that 'we need oxygen to live'. Oxygen is the vital component and as before a discussion will help to clarify. Oxygen is approximately 20% (or one-fifth) of the air.

'Air is good, gases are bad'

Pupils may have been told to go outside and get some 'fresh air' in their lungs. They may also have been warned of the dangers of cooker gas, because it is poisonous and can cause explosions. Aerosol cans also contain poisonous gases and pupils may be aware of that. Some have heard of carbon monoxide, a deadly gas given off by car exhausts. Stress that gases have to be used with caution, especially flammable or poisonous ones.

'Air makes things lighter'

Hot air floats above cold air because it is less dense and so is lighter. Hot air balloons are launched on cold mornings, the hot air kept warm by a burner underneath.

A related belief is that party balloons, inflated by blowing them up with air from our lungs, will float away. They won't, as the air in our bodies is of similar temperature to the surroundings. Balloons that do float are filled with helium, a gas that is lighter than air.

Changing state: melting, solidifying, evaporating, and condensing

Once pupils are familiar with the properties of solids, liquids, and gases, we can introduce the idea of how they can change from one to the other. This is commonly termed 'changing state'. The pupils need to know the key terms of melting, solidifying, evaporating, and condensing, and when these occur.

On the face of it, solids, liquids, and gases are so dissimilar it is hard for pupils to see how one can turn into the other. Many teachers use 'particle theory' to explain this, and although this is not required until Key Stage 3, without some grasp of it, it is hard for pupils to see how such changes take place.

Common misconception

'Particles are the same size as grains aren't they?'

When we talk about particles, pupils often think about grains, such as sand or powder. We need to get across the idea that particles are much, much smaller than that. If you use the idea of particle theory with the pupils, explain that particles are very small, much too small to see. For an idea of their size, get the pupils to look at the rubber on the end of a pencil. The distance across the rubber (its diameter) would be about 70 million atoms lined up end to end – considerably smaller than grains of salt! It is hard to imagine such large numbers, but you could remind the pupils that the population of the UK is around 60 million.

Pupil activity 8.24

Being solids, liquids, and gases

Learning objective: To understand a simple model of how a substance can change state.

Resources required: a large space, such as the hall or playground

Each child is to represent a particle. To represent a solid, the pupils should clump together and stay as still as possible. Then tell them that the solid is melting, and they should slowly move apart, into smaller groups, moving fairly freely to be a liquid. Then tell them the liquid is evaporating. For a gas they should move into their own space and continue to move around more quickly. For condensation they should return to the more clumped, more slow-moving state of a liquid. Finally, for solidifying (or freezing) they should return to their solid state, which is stationary and close together.

The experience could be enhanced with different types of music for the pupils to respond to. Try silence for a solid, slow classical music for a liquid, and high-energy dance music for a gas. Alternatively, a tambourine or drum could be used. Beat a slow

Music

beat for a solid, quicker beats as heat is added and the solid melts, and even faster beats as the liquid becomes gas. Make sure you use the science words frequently during the activity.

Melting and solidifying

If the pupils have not already tried doing the hand-held melting activity in Key Stage 1, then do this (see Pupil activity 8.12). 'Freezing' is the term we use for water when it solidifies and is usually reserved just for water, not for other substances. However, many everyday things have a very high water content and can be frozen (e.g. milk and meat).

Common misconception

'Do things solidify because they lose water?'

This is a common misconception. In reality, when a liquid turns to a solid, the particles in it slow and get closer together and then remain in one place. The confusion arises from things like mud. Mud is a mixture of solid clay and liquid water. As the water evaporates, the mud becomes less sloppy and eventually when the water is gone all that is left is the solid clay particles. Contrast this with wax. When wax is melted it becomes a liquid and when cooled it returns back to being a solid. In this case, water plays no part.

Teacher demonstration 8.25

Freezing milk

Learning objective: To learn that things containing water (such as food and drinks) can be frozen and thawed.

Resources required: one pint of full-fat milk in its sealed plastic carton, access to ice box in a fridge

You could place the plastic carton in the ice box freezer in the staffroom and leave it overnight. It can be removed the next day and the pupils can observe the difference. Ask them to predict what will happen if the milk is left at room temperature for the rest of the day. Do they think the milk would be safe to drink when it has fully thawed out? What other things can they think of that can be frozen in this way? How does freezing these things change their properties? Can they think of any food that does not freeze and thaw well?

Milk is a colloid. A colloid is halfway between a solution, where a substance has dissolved in a liquid, and a suspension, where a substance has not dissolved. Milk is a colloid of fatty oils in water. It is the yellow fat that can be seen when the milk is frozen. When thawed, the milk becomes white again as the fat mixes back in with the rest of the milk's constituents.

Evaporating

Pupil activity 8.26

Drawing around puddles

Learning objective: Learn how evaporation occurs in an everyday context.

Resources required: containers to carry water to the playground, chalk

Ask the pupils to make their own puddles on a dry playground, and draw around their edge with chalk. Ask them what will happen to their puddles. They should be able to redraw their puddle boundaries during the day and observe them getting smaller. What differences do they think a particularly hot day would make to the speed the water evaporates? What about in different seasons? Would a windy day make a difference? To help them answer this, ask them if they have ever noticed that the school dinner staff may leave windows and doors open in the hall after mopping the hall floor, to speed up the rate at which the water evaporates.

Common misconception

'Puddles just dry up don't they?'

This is the everyday term we use for what happens to puddles. We use the same term to describe how we get the dishes dry after washing them, using a cloth to remove the liquid from the dishes, we say we have 'dried them up'. Pupils often take the phrase 'dry up' to mean that the liquid is soaked away into the ground, but we need them to focus on the idea that the water has evaporated.

Pupil investigation skills 8.27

Evaporating water – does the size of the container matter?

Learning objective: Learn about the role surface area plays in the rate at which water can evaporate.

Resources required: measuring cylinders, plastic containers of different sizes

Show the pupils a range of different-sized plastic containers and ask them which (if any) water would evaporate more quickly from, and to give their reasons. The pupils may be able to plan their own investigation. Ask the pupils about fair testing. They may suggest keeping the amount of water constant and to place the containers in the same place. They will need to measure the amount of water remaining each day, and return it to the container afterwards. It can take some time, so be prepared to do this activity over a number of days.

The containers that provide the largest surface area of water will give the fastest rates of evaporation. This is because the water can only evaporate from the surface of the liquid to the air, not from the lower depths of the liquid. The difference between the rate of evaporation of 50 ml in a jug and 50 ml in a measuring cylinder is quite dramatic, but do tell the pupils they may have to be patient!

Pupil investigation skills 8.28

How can we speed up the rate of evaporation?

Learning objective: Learn about the role of heat in evaporation.

Resources required: measuring cylinders, plastic containers that are of the same size

This could be a follow-up to the above investigation. The main way to speed up evaporation is to expose the containers of water to more heat in their surroundings. Moving air can also speed up the rate of evaporation. This time the pupils will need to think about fair testing in terms of the containers being of the same size and will need to think of different places where they can be left safely (i.e. away from electrical equipment in case they are overturned accidentally) and monitored from time to time. They may choose places outside, such as shady areas or sunlit areas.

Common misconceptions

'Soft dough "just goes" hard'

Pupils rapidly grasp the idea of water evaporating from a plate or a dish, but they may have problems applying the idea to other contexts. For example, a mixture of flour and water will harden if left alone, because the water will evaporate, but this is not immediately obvious to some pupils.

'Is it evaporating or boiling?'

Pupils frequently mix these two up. Evaporating occurs at pretty much any temperature, it's just slower the colder the surroundings are. Talk about puddles evaporating on the playground. Boiling only occurs in water around 100 °C. Here bubbles of water vapour form within the water and the water vapour is released as they burst when they reach the surface. It is NOT recommended to do boiling water demonstrations in the classroom, because of the risk of scalding.

Condensing

Pupils need to know that condensation is the opposite process to evaporation. They may be familiar with 'steamed-up' windows in a kitchen or classroom on a cold day, or with their breath forming 'little clouds' on a cold day.

Pupil activity 8.29

Why do cold cans from the fridge become wet?

Learning objective: Learn to recognise why condensation occurs in everyday contexts.

Resources required: drinks cans stored in the fridge (leave for a few hours, so that they are fully chilled), paper towels

Place cold cans on the pupils' tables with a paper towel underneath. After a few minutes they should notice that water droplets have started to appear on the can. Given time, the droplets get bigger and run down the can onto the table. Some pupils may think that the liquid may be seeping through the can from the inside. When you tell them that the liquid is water that used to be water vapour gas in the air, can they work out what is going on? They may be able to work out that the water vapour from the air in the classroom is cooling down on hitting the cold can and turning into liquid water. Can the pupils explain what has happened? Can they suggest other examples in the world? For example, water condensing on the glass of a cold drink, clouds in the sky or mist on a cold morning. Challenge pupils by asking them why water does not condense on a hot surface.

Pupil activity 8.30

Why does condensation happen around the house?

Learning objective: Learn to recognise when evaporation and condensation have occurred.

Resources required: one bowl quarter-filled with water, cling film

Cover the top of the bowl with cling film, making sure there are no gaps. Given enough time water will evaporate from the bowl and condense on the cling film, particularly in warmer weather. Place near a warm windowsill or radiator for best effect. Ask the pupils where they think the water has come from. Can they say how the rate of evaporation or condensation could be speeded up? When have they seen the process of condensation in their own homes? They may mention the kitchen window when it is cold outside but hot in the kitchen on a day in winter. Alternatively, they may mention a cold mirror in the bathroom after a hot bath or shower.

Common misconceptions

'Condensation and evaporation are the same'

Pupils frequently muddle up these terms, saying one when they mean the other, or even thinking that they are the same thing.

'Is it steam or condensation?'

Adults often refer to windows with water droplets on as 'steamed up'. Pupils say on a cold day that 'steam' is coming out of their mouths. What they actually see is a cloud of water droplets. Pupils need to know that the process that turns water vapour to water liquid is condensation and it is nothing to do with steam.

Steam only occurs when water is at boiling point. We cannot actually see steam, as it is very hot water vapour and being water vapour it is invisible. When a kettle boils the invisible steam coming out of the spout rapidly cools, forming droplet clouds a little way from the spout. These droplets clouds are what people commonly call 'steam', and from this the above confusions arise.

Water cycle

The water cycle involves water evaporating from the sea as it is warmed by the Sun. As the rising water vapour cools, it condenses into water droplets and forms clouds. Once the drops become big enough they may fall as rain, which goes into the ground. Ground water joins streams and rivers, which flow into the sea.

Evaporation and condensation, the main parts of the water cycle, are covered in the above section, but here is a misconception that pupils may have about the water cycle.

Common misconception

'Is salt too heavy or do the clouds get rid of it?'

Pupils often know that the sea is salty, but rain is not. They may believe that the salt from the sea is 'too heavy' to evaporate, but the reality is that only liquids can evaporate, not dissolved solids. Another belief is that the clouds 'filter out' the salt from the rain before it falls.

For further detail on the water cycle, see Chapter 7, 'The environment'.

Making mixtures

Pupil investigation skills 8.31

Which things dissolve?

Learning objective: Be able to distinguish between solids that dissolve and those that do not.

Resources required: plastic cups, spoons, and a range of dissolvable and non-dissolvable solids. Try sugar, salt, coffee, talc, flour, stones, sand, glass marbles, pasta, rice, powder paint

Dissolving is a reversible reaction. The pupils should be able to sort common solids into those that dissolve and those that do not. Challenge the pupils to do this and then ask them to test their predictions. The pupils may think that coffee is more unusual than sugar or salt because when it dissolves it changes the colour of the water, unlike salt and sugar. An undissolved solid such as talc will form a suspension, temporarily making the water look cloudy, but if left it will 'settle out' forming a layer at the bottom.

Common misconceptions

'It's disappeared!'

Pupils often think that when a substance has dissolved it has disappeared. Certainly, many are invisible, but there are ways to prove that the dissolved solid is still there. For example, pupils should know that salt water tastes salty, and sugar water tastes sugary.

'Dissolved solids make the water look "cloudy" '

If the pupils put too much salt or sugar in water, it won't all dissolve and the water will look cloudy. Explain that it is undissolved solid that makes the liquid look cloudy. Get them to dissolve very small amounts of solid while stirring vigorously, to show that a dissolved solid cannot be seen.

'Sugar melts in water'

Pupils often confuse the terms 'melt' and 'dissolve'. The correct term is dissolve in this case. The confusion of melting may be caused when pupils see foods such as sugar cubes put into hot water and appear to 'melt' like an ice cube would if put in hot water.

'Filter salt water to get the salt back'

This is a common misconception. Pupils should observe salt dissolving in water and then use a filter to recover it if they believe it will work. It won't, because the dissolved salt is small enough to fit through the holes of the filter. Beware though if the filter is left to dry, as the water will evaporate, leaving some salt behind on the filter and the pupils will believe that filtering works! The way to retrieve the salt from the salty water is to evaporate the water. Ask pupils if they can work out the quickest ways to evaporate the water. (See Pupil investigation skills 8.27 and 8.28 in this chapter.)

Pupil activity 8.32

How much salt or sugar can the water hold?

Learning objective: Learn that a small volume of water cannot dissolve an infinite amount of a solid.

Resources required: cup or beaker, sugar or salt, spoon, lukewarm water

Half-fill the cup with the water and tell pupils you are going to make a solution. Ask the pupils how many spoonfuls could be dissolved before no more will dissolve. When the water is saturated and no more sugar will dissolve, ask them what will happen when more sugar is added. They may be able to predict that this sugar won't dissolve and will settle to the bottom of the cup.

Pupil investigation skills 8.33

What could be changed to speed up the rate of dissolving?

Learning objective: Learn about the factors which influence how quickly a solid can dissolve.

Resources required: sugar or salt, beakers, thermometers, spoons, sugar cubes (optional)

Ask pupils to suggest ways to speed up the rate at which a solid dissolves. There are a range of factors that can speed up the rate at which a soluble solid will dissolve. Pupils could investigate:

- temperature of water (fridge cold, room temperature, and hand-hot water)
- number of stirs (none, 5, 10, 15, etc.)
- size of grains of solid or surface area

Whichever factor pupils choose to investigate, they must keep the other factors constant.

A typical investigation might seek to answer the question 'does surface area matter?' The pupils could compare how fast a sugar cube dissolves compared with one that has been crushed up (giving a larger surface area). The pupils should know that to do a fair test the following need to be constant: temperature of water, amount of stirs, amount of water, container size and shape, amount of sugar.

Separating mixtures

Challenge the pupils to separate a number of mixtures. They may use filtering, sieving, magnets or other methods such as evaporating. The following four activities could be given to the pupils to do with a full explanation of how to go about it. Older pupils with experience of separating materials may like the challenge of working out for themselves what equipment and which techniques to use in each case. The last two examples (Pupil activities 8.37 'A polluted pond' and 8.38 'kitchen disaster') combine a range of techniques.

Pupil activity 8.34

Sieving

Learning objective: Learn how to separate solids of different sizes using sieves with appropriately sized holes.

Resources required: dry peas, pasta, rice, flour; colanders, mesh sieves or home-made sieves (foam plates with holes in) can be used to separate mixtures

Sieving is a simple way to separate solids of different sizes. Can the pupils create mixtures and then separate them completely? Could they challenge each other as to who can do it with the least mess? Or, the fastest way in which to do it?

Pupil activity 8.35

Filtering

Learning objective: To learn that a filter is needed to separate an insoluble solid from a liquid.

Resources required: beakers, spoons, jugs of water. For filters, try filter paper, blue J-cloth®, paper towels, and wide bandages. Funnels can be useful to put the filter in, but with a bit of careful work they may not be needed. The insoluble solid could be sand, clean soil, small pieces of gravel or glitter

Filtering is the way to separate a solid that does not dissolve from a liquid. Sand and water can easily be separated this way. You may want to tell the pupils that filters are used by many factories to separate polluting solids from their waste pipes, before the pipes pump the liquid out into rivers. The filters used in industrial processes are often made from a woven cloth, not from paper.

Pupil activity 8.36

Separating magnetic and non-magnetic metals

Learning objective: Learn how to separate metals on the basis of their magnetic properties.

Resources required: magnets, any small metal items (e.g. paper clips, metal split pins, metal clips, pencil sharpeners, coins, keys)

Paper clips and metal split pins can be separated with a magnet as the paper clips contain steel whereas the split pins are made from brass. Can the pupils think of a real-world application of this? At recycling plants, steel cans are separated from aluminium ones using powerful magnets.

Pupil activity 8.37

A 'polluted' pond

Learning objective: Learn that some separation may require more than one technique.

Resources required: bowls, jugs, paper clips, and marbles. The pupils will need sieves and magnets, but let them ask for these when they have worked out the puzzle

Pupils may be able to choose methods to separate out a range of different materials. Stress that they may need to use more than one method. For example, try mixing together paper clips, glass marbles, and water. Tell the pupils it is a pond that people have thrown metal and glass into. Can they separate out the solids for recycling? They should be able to attract the metal with magnets and sieve the glass marbles from the water.

Pupil activity 8.38

A kitchen disaster

Learning objective: To understand that separation techniques may need to be done in a certain order.

Resources required: sugar, raisins, flour. Let them ask for sieves, filters, beakers, and jugs when they have worked out a plan to solve the puzzle

Someone has accidentally mixed together three ingredients in one of the big storage jars. Challenge the pupils to separate sugar, raisins and flour. (Answer: when added to water the sugar will dissolve. The sugar water can be filtered off, and left for the water to evaporate. Allow the flour and raisin mixture – left behind after filtering – to dry, and then this can be easily sieved to separate.)

The last two activities show how separation problems may require more than one technique and may need to be done in a certain order. Discuss with the pupils the problems that collecting recycled waste presents. Some councils collect waste in a single 'green' bin. Could the pupils work out a way to separate metals, glass, and plastic with the minimum use of people doing it 'by hand'? For example, metals are separated from each other using magnets and councils sometimes have machines that can tell the difference between transparent plastic bottles and translucent ones by analysing them first using light beams! Many councils now have waste collection lorries containing many compartments, so that the householder and refuse workers never allow the waste to mix in the first place. This is obviously a good approach for the council but can the pupils spot the problems for the householder? This approach means more work for the householder and a proliferation of different bins in the house. The pupils could have a thinking session and list the pros and cons of the different recycling approaches.

Irreversible changes

Irreversible changes are also termed 'non-reversible', 'permanent', or 'chemical' changes. The most common irreversible changes that the pupils will come across are (1) burning and (2) mixing substances together that react to make something new.

When substances are burned, new substances are produced. Wood, paper, and card all burn to produce ash and smoke. Wax and oil burn and produce gases. There is no way to reassemble the products of the burning reaction to reproduce the original ones. Baking and cooking are irreversible processes too. Discuss with the pupils the difference in appearance of an uncooked pizza compared with a cooked one, and a fresh egg to a fried one.

Common misconceptions

'Burning wax is reversible, isn't it?'

Candles can cause a lot of confusion. When a wick is lit, the wax around it melts. The liquid wax turns to vapour and the wax vapour then burns. If left, all the wax will burn and there will be no candle left. Pupils are often confused by the fact that when the flame of a burning candle is blown out, some melted wax around the wick will solidify. This leads them to think that a candle works by the wax melting, and the wax is never really lost to burning. Nightlights are very confusing, because the whole candle becomes liquid wax, and the solid wax reforms when they are blown out (although there will be less).

Get them to think about the difference between wax melting and burning. A candle left on a hot windowsill or in a conservatory may melt and change its shape, but no wax is lost. When a candle flame is lit the wax burns to produce gas and smoke. The burnt wax is gone forever and cannot be reclaimed. Only a tiny bit of liquid wax around the wick turns back to solid wax when the candle is blown out.

'You can turn toast back to bread'

Some pupils think that by scraping the burnt bit off they are turning toast back to bread! Explain that the outside layer has been burnt, but the bread underneath is untouched.

'Everything melts'

Many pupils think all solid materials can melt, but this is not the case. Materials that do not melt, but burn instead, are usually ones made from plant or animal matter (e.g. paper, wood, card).

Mixing substances that react together differs considerably from burning, but it is similar in that new substances are produced. One of the easiest reactions to do is to mix things together that react to make a gas.

Vinegar and bicarbonate of soda produce carbon dioxide gas. Water, bicarbonate of soda, and cream of tartar mixed together also produce carbon dioxide. Ask the pupils if they think the gas can be changed back to the initial substances. It cannot.

Pupil investigation skills 8.39

Does it burn or does it melt?

Learning objective: to know which materials will burn and which ones will melt when heat is applied.

Resources required: Tealight candles, candle and burner holder (see Figure 8.5), foil dishes and trays, range of materials (e.g. paper, wood, bread, ice cube, butter, margarine, chocolate). Prepare the materials by breaking them into small pieces – for example broken matches (with the head removed) for wood, small pieces of paper, little cuts of butter, etc.

Ask the pupils to predict which materials will burn (or smoulder in this case) and which will melt. Then they can place the materials in the foil dish and place it on the holder over the candle. The candle does not produce a lot of heat, so they will have to be patient in their observations. They should find that the following melt: butter, margarine, ice cube, chocolate. They should find that the following will smoulder: wood, paper, bread. The teacher could later show that these will burn by doing a demonstration and holding them in a flame.

Challenge the pupils to classify melting and burning as reversible or irreversible reactions. Ask them how they could revert the melted substance back to a solid. It should be obvious that it should be just allowed to cool down again. The burnt object cannot be changed back – some of it has been turned into ash and smoke (smoke is just airborne ash) and again they should be able to see this for themselves.

Figure 8.5 Heating apparatus

With a naked flame, ensure that pupils know how to work safely with the lit candle. The candle can be placed in a larger foil tray, with sand if required. Remind pupils that the small tray the material is placed in will become hot.

The candle does not put out a lot of heat, so they may have to wait half an hour before seeing an effect!

Pupil investigation skills 8.40

What can react to make a gas?

Learning objective: Learn to recognise which substances when mixed together create a fizzing reaction and make a gas.

Resources required: a range of solids and liquids including bicarbonate of soda, limestone, cream of tartar, vinegar, lemon juice, water, baking powder, talc, sugar, salt, and coffee, together with a spoon and plastic cups

Challenge the pupils to discover which substances when mixed together produce a gas. If they see fizzing and bubbles being produced, this is evidence of gas formation. The gas in each case will be carbon dioxide and this is safe for the children to make. Ask the pupils if they think there is any way in which the gas can be changed back into the solid and liquid. They may know that there is no way that this can be done, as the process is irreversible.

Pupil investigation skills 8.41

What makes metal rust?

Learning objective: Learn to recognise that rusting is an irreversible process and what factors produce it.

Resources required: small (500 ml) plastic bottles, bottle lids, salt, water, wire wool or wire wool pan scrubbing pads (the cheaper the better!). Prepare the wire wool beforehand by cutting it into small strips. Warn the pupils to handle it carefully (avoid sharp edges and keep away from the face)

Iron rusts readily in the presence of water, but some things speed up the process. Ask the pupils to set up an investigation to find out which substances speed up the rate of rusting, and which do not. They could prepare separate bottles, each containing a piece of wire wool – one with water, another with salt water, another with salt only, and the final one left empty, i.e. just air inside.

As the iron starts to rust, it removes oxygen from the air to form iron oxide, which is what we call iron rust. This reduces the amount of air in the bottle and therefore the air pressure inside the bottle. Over a few days, in the bottles in which rust is forming, you may see the sides of the bottle start to collapse as the air in the surrounding room presses in on the bottle.

From their results, can the pupils work out the worst (or best!) combination of rust factors? Salt water should speed up the rate of rust formation compared with tap water. To stop things from rusting, paint is often used to cover the metal, to stop liquid and oxygen reaching the surface. Can they think of things that must be repainted to stop them rusting? They may think of road bridges, which have to be continually painted, as the weather strips off the paint to reveal the bare metal underneath. Similarly, cars that have a bad scratch on them may start to rust. Piers at the seaside can easily rust because of the salt water of the sea pounding the pier legs and the sea spray hitting the sides.

For more ideas for irreversible changes (including a video of a candle burning at both ends!) try:

https://sites.google.com/site/jbprimaryscience/irreversible-changes

Making a polymer

Polymers are made of very long chains of molecules (see explanation in 'What the teacher needs to know' section). The pupils can make a polymer from PVA glue and a weak borax solution. The borax reacts with the PVA glue and makes huge long chains, thereby creating a polymer. The polymer is able to absorb water and makes the putty-like substance the pupils end up with.

Pupil Activity 8.42

Make a bouncy blob polymer

Learning objective: To understand how materials can be combined to make a polymer and to recognise some of the properties of a polymer.

Resources required: borax solution, PVA glue, teaspoons, plastic cups, food colouring, disposable gloves

Borax is a mild irritant, but can be used safely in the classroom if you follow these instructions. Before the lesson prepare a weak borax solution by dissolving one teaspoon of borax in a plastic cup of water. This solution is safe for the pupils to work with. Borax can be obtained from most pharmacies.

Pupils need to add two teaspoons of PVA glue to a beaker, and a drop of food colouring. They then take one teaspoonful of the borax solution and add this to the mix. They must stir the mixture immediately, and keep stirring vigorously for 3–4 minutes. In the next stage the pupils will handle the blob, so have them put on their disposable gloves. When the mixture forms a definite blob, it can be taken out and kneaded between the hands for 5 minutes. The blob is now ready – like many polymers it can be stretched. It can also bounce.

To keep the blob in a good condition after use, place in a re-sealable plastic sandwich bag. The blob is safe for the pupils to play with in the classroom, but don't allow them to take it home, and dispose of it with non-recyclable refuse after two days.

Ask the pupils what would happen if we added 2–4 teaspoons of water to the PVA glue, before adding the borax solution? How would this affect the blob? (The answer is that the blob becomes much slimier.)

Researching new materials

Chemists are keen to make new materials that the world has never seen before, but can make our lives better. An internet search on 'super sticky', 'super strong', or 'super thin' materials by the pupils will reveal what scientists are working on. If the pupils put in the epithet 'for kids' in their internet search (e.g. 'super sticky materials for kids') the websites are usually pupil friendly. Two promising new materials are outlined below.

A super sticky material called 'geckel' that even stays sticky under water, using ideas inspired by the feet of geckos. This could be used to make waterproof bandages and to stick wounds back together, instead of stitching them up. (See https://student. societyforscience.org/article/super-sticky-power)

A super thin and super strong material is graphene, invented at the University of Manchester by Andre Geim and Kostya Novoselov. The video at http://luratia.com/ graphene/category/kids-students shows how they made it and how it could be used in a huge range of products, including the repair of human bodies!

Materials scientists John Dunlop, Charles Macintosh, and John Macadam

John Dunlop invented the inflatable bicycle inner tube, making bike riding a much more comfortable experience!

Charles Macintosh took naptha (a liquid made from natural tar) and used it to dissolve India rubber (from a rubber tree). This new material could be used to make clothes completely waterproof, for the first time.

John Macadam invented a system for constructing hard-wearing roads, but did *not* use tar to do this. The use of tar was a later invention that built on his ideas (hence we have 'tarmac' covering our roads). Macadam's original idea was that roads did not need big rocks as foundations, which was the usual method. Instead they could be built on soil, providing the underlying soil was protected from rain turning it into mud. This could be done by cambering the road (the middle is the highest part, and then either side of the middle is a gradual slope), so that rain runs off it to the side. He then used graded gravel, that is, different sized pieces of gravel. A large piece of gravel would be a stone of around 7 cm in size, a smaller one around 2 cm. The larger pieces of gravel were laid down first to make the bottom layer of the road, then the smaller ones poured on top. The smaller pieces bind with the bigger ones to give a smooth, water resistant surface that water cannot penetrate. Macadam's ideas were being used from the 1820s onwards. It was only much later in the early 1900s when tar was added to his method, to make the roads even more robust, and this was called 'tar Macadam'.

Ruth Benerito invented wrinkle-free cotton. In the 1930–40s artificial nylon clothes became popular as they needed little ironing and care. The downside of nylon is that it can be uncomfortable and causes sweating. Cotton has neither of these drawbacks, but its wrinkling was seen as a time-consuming disadvantage. Cotton fibres are made from the plant material cellulose. Benerito discovered how to chemically alter the cotton, by allowing the cellulose molecules to link together many more times. This meant much less wrinkling, and much less ironing. Later she added chemicals to the cotton to make it more stain resistant, and more flame resistant.

Spencer Silver was trying to create a 'super strong' glue, when he accidently created the opposite, a 'not very sticky' glue. For five years no one in his company 3M could imagine what such a glue would be useful for. Then, his colleague Art Fry came up with the idea of using it to make a sticky bookmark for his choir hymnbook. He was fed up with his ordinary bookmarks falling out when the hymnbook was held open as he sung. The glue was strong enough to hold the bookmark to the page, but could then be taken off the page and put on another one. The glue did not cause any damage to the pages of the hymnbook, nor did it come off the bookmark, so the bookmark was permanently sticky and could be reused. They thought about other pieces of paper that could use a non-sticky glue so that they could be stuck on paper, moved around and reused. This was the basis of their Post-it® note, a brand that has made millions of dollars for 3M.

http://www.ulsterhistory.co.uk/johndunlop.htm
    (for John Dunlop)

http://www.lookandlearn.com/blog/26532/scotlands-other-charles-macintosh-invented-the-eponymous-waterproof-fabric/
    (for Charles Macintosh)

http://www.undiscoveredscotland.co.uk/usbiography/mac/johnloudonmacadam.html
    (for John Macadam)

http://www.chemheritage.org/discover/online-resources/chemistry-in-history/
themes/petrochemistry-and-synthetic-polymers/synthetic-polymers/
benerito.aspx

(for Ruth Benerito)

http://web.mit.edu/invent/iow/frysilver.html

(for Art Fry and Spencer Silver)

Summary of key learning points:

- materials can be classed as natural or made by humans ('man-made'). Their properties can be tested and classified (e.g. hard versus soft, opaque versus transparent). An object will be made of a material because of the suitability of the material's properties (e.g. a spoon can be made of plastic, metal or wood because they are all hard and don't melt or burn too easily);

- materials are made from different atoms. There are around 90 naturally occurring different types of atoms and these are called elements. Many elements are familiar to us, such as gold and oxygen;

- elements can react and combine with each other to make compounds. The most familiar compound is water. Compounds are very different from the elements that make them (e.g. water is nothing like its constituent elements of hydrogen and oxygen);

- mixtures occur when substances are mixed together but don't react with each other, essentially remaining separate. This means that they are easy to separate (e.g. sand from water);

- some things can exist as solids, liquids or gases. Water commonly is found in all three states and its state depends on the amount of heat in its surroundings;

- the processes of change include melting and evaporation when heated and condensing and solidifying (or freezing) when heat is taken away. These types of changes are called reversible changes;

- dissolving a solid in a liquid is also a reversible change;

- some changes are irreversible. These are chemical changes. These include baking, burning, and the reaction of certain chemicals when they are combined (e.g. vinegar and bicarbonate).

Self-test

Question 1

Which of the following are irreversible or permanent changes? (a) burning toast, (b) baking bread, (c) mixing water with salt and sand, (d) mixing vinegar and bicarbonate of soda

Question 2

Which of the following are elements? (a) water, (b) silver, (c) iron, (d) steel

Question 3

Which part of an atom carries a charge? (a) the electron, (b) the neutron, (c) the proton, (d) all parts

Question 4

Which of the following statements about air is true? (a) it contains mostly oxygen, (b) it is a mixture of gases, (c) it contains mostly carbon dioxide, (d) the gas found in the highest quantities is nitrogen

Self-test answers

Q1: (a), (b), and (d) are all correct. Burning and baking food cannot be reversed. Vinegar and bicarbonate mixed together produce a new substance, carbon dioxide. (c) is incorrect as sand can be separated by filtering and evaporation will separate the water from the salt. Although it is tricky to turn the water vapour back into liquid water, it can be done by condensing the water on a cool lid for example.

Q2: The correct answers are (b) and (c). Silver and iron are pure substances and so we class these as elements. Water is not an element, it is a compound made up of oxygen gas and hydrogen gas that have reacted and bonded together to form water. Steel is made from iron and carbon.

Q3: (a) and (c) are correct. The electron is negatively charged and is attracted to the positively charged proton. The neutron has no charge; it is neutral as its name suggests.

Q4: (b) and (d) are correct. Air is a mixture of nitrogen (its main component by far), oxygen, and carbon dioxide. At times it will contain traces of pollutant gases such as carbon monoxide, the poisonous gas from car exhausts.

Misconceptions

'Aren't materials just fabrics?'

'Is it the spoon that's hard or the material?'

'Wood is heavy, so it sinks doesn't it?'

'It's from the supermarket!'

'It soaks up water so isn't it waterproof?'

'But won't wool and other fabrics make them hotter?

'Sand can be poured, so does that make it a liquid?'

'Cloth is soft, so does that mean it's not a solid?'

'Gases don't weigh anything do they?'

'Air is the only gas there is'

'Oxygen and air is the same thing'

'Air is good, gases are bad'

'Air makes things lighter'

'Particles are the same size as grains aren't they?'

'Do things solidify because they lose water?'

'Puddles just dry up don't they?'

'Soft dough "just goes" hard'

'Is it evaporating or boiling?'

'Condensation and evaporation are the same'

'Is it steam or condensation?'

'Is salt too heavy or do the clouds get rid of it?'

'It's disappeared!'

'Dissolved solids make the water look "cloudy" '

'Sugar melts in water'

'Filter it to get the salt back'

'Burning wax is reversible isn't it?'

'You can turn toast back to bread'

'Everything melts'

Web resources

http://dl.dropboxusercontent.com/u/21130258/resources/InformationSheets/
    Packaging.htm
    (this useful website includes the symbols used to categorise containers so that they
    can be recycled correctly, including the numbers found on plastic bottles)

http://web.mit.edu/invent/iow/frysilver.html
    (Spencer Silver and Art Fry)

http://www.chemheritage.org/discover/online-resources/chemistry-in-history/themes/
    petrochemistry-and-synthetic-polymers/synthetic-polymers/benerito.aspx
    (Ruth Benerito)

http://www.lookandlearn.com/blog/26532/scotlands-other-charles-macintosh-invented-the-
    eponymous-waterproof-fabric/
    (Charles Macintosh)

http://www.ulsterhistory.co.uk/johndunlop.htm-
    (page about John Dunlop)

http://www.undiscoveredscotland.co.uk/usbiography/mac/johnloudonmacadam.html
    (John Macadam)

https://sites.google.com/site/jbprimaryscience/irreversible-changes
    (for irreversible changes demonstrations)

9

Rocks and soils

About this chapter

This chapter is about the different groups of rock found on the surface of planet Earth, fossils (both their formation and different types), and the composition and value of soil. The second part of the chapter addresses what the pupils need to learn and the final part suggests ways to teach about rocks, fossils and soils, including misconceptions.

What the teacher needs to know and understand

Three different groups of rock

Igneous

Igneous rocks are made when molten magma cools. Pupils may have seen pictures of molten magma coming out of volcanoes. As the magma cools, crystals form in the rock. Granite and basalt are both igneous rocks. They are strong and hard-wearing. Granite is used for gravestones (as they last a long time and so does the inscription), for building (e.g. steps of a prestigious building), and the food preparation surface in a kitchen. Granite has large crystals, which were formed when the rock cooled and solidified very slowly underneath the ground. Basalt, however, cooled above the ground as it formed and so cooled quickly, producing smaller crystals.

Sedimentary

Some sedimentary rocks are formed from layers of sediment produced by the weathering of other rocks. The grains that are produced are then compressed (over millions of years) and become stuck together to form sedimentary rocks. Sandstone and mudstones are formed this way. Other sedimentary rocks form from the deposition of the remains of animals and plants that are compressed to form rocks such as limestone and chalk. Sandstone and limestone are used for building, as they are easily shaped but can weather badly over the years as many very old buildings show.

Metamorphic

These are sedimentary or igneous rocks that have been later squeezed under high pressure and baked at high temperature. Examples of metamorphic rock are slate (formed from mudstone) and marble (formed from limestone). Metamorphic rocks tend to be harder than other rock types. Marble is used for decoration because of its attractive appearance; slate is used for roofing tiles as it can easily be split along one axis to make thin (but tough) tiles.

A simple introduction to the three types of rocks should include some common examples of each (e.g. granite, limestone, slate), how they were formed, and their distinctive appearances. This will help the pupils group and understand similarities between different rocks that have been made in similar processes. The terms are also used on most rock websites the pupils may visit.

The characteristics of rocks include:

- how rough or smooth they are;
- whether they have grains, and if so, the grain size;
- whether or not they have crystals in them;
- how permeable they are to water;
- how easily the rocks are worn down;
- how strong the rocks are;
- the colour (although this can vary quite a lot).

By considering the characteristics and properties of rocks, we can select them for different uses, some of which have been outlined above.

Fossils

Most fossils are formed when a plant or animal dies and the body is quickly covered up by clay or mud and buried. This would normally occur in a river, or in the sea. This quick covering means that the normal decay processes are halted. A dead animal or plant would usually be eaten by an animal scavenger, but the rapid burial prevents this. Burial also prevents the normal erosion that would occur on the surface to bones, and also stops speedy decay from bacteria, particularly in low oxygen conditions. Even with all that taken into account, the softer tissue of skin, feathers, and internal organs on an animal do not usually survive. It is the much tougher bones and teeth that will become the fossil. Similarly in a plant, it is usually the tough woody part that will become the fossil, not the leaves. In exceptionally favourable circumstances, soft delicate parts of plants and animals can, and do, survive.

After burial, further layers of clay or sand get piled on top of the organism, and under pressure this starts to form sedimentary rocks of mudstone or sandstone. Groundwater rich in minerals can still get through the small grains of the newly forming rock, and this may react with the hard bones, shell, teeth or wood, preserving the form of the organisms through the process of remineralisation. The organism is being transformed into rock or crystal. Years later the fossil may come to the surface, when the overlying rock has been eroded away by a river or quarried away for stone.

Fossils can form in other ways. Sometimes an imprint of the organism is left in the surrounding rock, as the original fossil minerals have been dissolved away. Shellfish imprints are quite common, for example. Other fossils are literally just 'traces' of activity, for example, footprints of a dinosaur, even wave ripples lapping on a shore. While it might seem incredible that such delicate imprints could be preserved, we know that this process is still going on today. On Formby beach in England, preserved in the mud are delicate footprints of humans and extinct auroch cattle from around 6000 years ago. These are not fully fossilised, and what is revealed in one tide can be destroyed by the next.

Perhaps one of the most famous fossil types are flies trapped in amber. Amber is fossilised tree sap. Some trees produce this sticky substance to gum up holes in their bark when they have been damaged. Small creatures can get stuck in them, and their soft delicate parts are preserved for millions of years.

Soils

Soil is formed when rock is weathered and broken down into small grains. Two other constituents are essential: decaying organic material and a population of micro-organisms.

The size of grain the soil is made of determines the soil's drainage properties. The three grain types are sand, silt, and clay. The largest grains are those of a sandy soil and this drains water quickly because it has the largest air space between grains. An intermediate size grain is found in a silt soil and a clay soil has the smallest grain. Clay soils often become waterlogged because they have very small air spaces, so draining water cannot move through them quickly. Soils may have one of these three types as the main constituent, or contain a mixture of them. For example, a loam soil contains a mixture of all three types.

The second essential ingredient is decaying organic material – that is, parts of the bodies and waste material of plants and animals which are being broken down by micro-organisms. The micro-organisms themselves are an essential part of the soil as they break down the organic material, releasing nutrients for the plants growing in the soil.

A soil has recognisable layers as we move from the surface to the underlying bedrock. Above the soil is a layer of leaf litter composed of recently discarded or dead organic material. The top layers tend to contain the recognisable remnants of dead plants and animals and a vast number of living micro-organisms. This layer is called 'humus'. As we move down towards the bedrock, there is less humus and more rock grains. The rock grains become larger as we reach the bedrock.

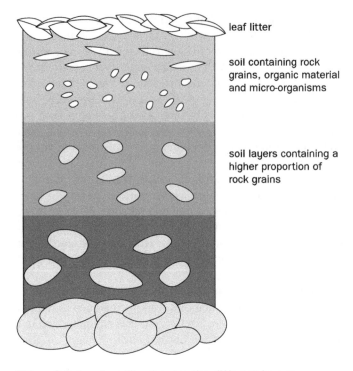

leaf litter

soil containing rock grains, organic material and micro-organisms

soil layers containing a higher proportion of rock grains

Figure 9.1 A soil profile showing the different layers

What pupils need to know at Key Stage 1

Teachers are not required to teach about rocks and fossils at Key Stage 1. Soil and its importance should be referred to in the context of growing plants in science.

What pupils need to know at Key Stage 2

(ST) denotes statutory requirements.

Lower Key Stage 2

(ST) Compare and group together different kinds of rocks on the basis of their appearance and simple physical properties

Suggestions for working scientifically:

Explore different kinds of rocks, including those in the local environment.

Observe rocks, including those used in buildings and gravestones, and explore how and why they might have changed over time.

Use a hand lens or microscope to help them to identify and classify rocks according to whether they have grains or crystals, and whether they have fossils in them.

(ST) Describe in simple terms how fossils are formed when things that have lived are trapped within rock

Suggestions for working scientifically:

Research and discuss the different kinds of living things whose fossils are found in sedimentary rock and explore how fossils are formed.

(ST) Recognise that soils are made from rocks and organic matter

Suggestions for working scientifically:

Linked with work in geography, pupils should explore different kinds of soils, including those in the local environment.

Explore different soils and identify similarities and differences between them.

Investigate what happens when rocks are rubbed together or what changes occur when they are in water.

Raise and answer questions about the way soils are formed.

Ways to teach 'rocks and soils' at Key Stage 2

Rocks

Resources required: Rock samples can be bought in sets from educational supply companies. You can also find them at garden centres, as they are used for driveways and ornamental gardening. The following are available as 'chips' (pebbles) from most garden centres: granite (black to pink with crystals in), sandstone (light brown in colour), limestone (white to grey in colour), slate (blue to dark green in colour), and flint (translucent surrounded by white or orange colour) (found in 'Golden Gravel'). They need to be washed before being handled. Photographs of all of these common rocks can be seen on the websites detailed below.

Pupil activity 9.1

Chocolate and sweet rocks

Learning objective: To recognise the features that different rocks have.

Resources required: magnifying glasses, paper plates to place the 'rocks' on, shrink wrap film, description cards of rocks (see below), a range of chocolates and sweets to represent rocks. We suggest the following (but you may think of more apt examples):

- Fudge – sandstone. When the fudge is broken apart by hand, it shows a brown grainy structure. Leave it in the fridge beforehand to make it harder.
- Mints – chalk. If crushed, these show a very bright white crumbly structure.
- Chocolate buttons – slate. Place in the fridge to harden, these can be stacked in layers (slate is a layered rock). Unfortunately slate tends to be a bit more blue in colour, but it can also come in a very dark grey which is closer in appearance to chocolate buttons.
- Cola cubes – pink granite. These are very hard sweets (like granite!) and the sugar coating resembles the crystals of the rock.
- White chocolate – limestone. Limestone is often an off-white colour, and this crumbly chocolate can give good grains. For a deeper yellow limestone you could use digestive biscuits.

Getting the pupils to focus on the different appearance of rocks and learning a few simple types of rocks can be tricky. Try this activity with chocolates and sweets, which show exaggerated properties of rocks that are easier for the pupils to focus on, before they tackle the real thing.

Place the 'rocks' on separate paper plates and cover with shrink wrap film to begin with. The pupils can write down their observations about the colour and texture of the 'rocks'. At this stage, don't reveal which one represents chalk, granite, and so on.

Next, allow the pupils to remove the shrink wrap film to handle the rocks, breaking them apart with their hands if they can. They should then write about how the rock feels, how strong or weak it is, and what it is like inside (if it can be broken). Tell them the 'rocks' must not be eaten! Present the pupils with a range of cards to see if they can match the name and description to each rock. You may wish to mention the colour when it is appropriate. We suggest the following:

- Sandstone – brown rock with grains inside
- Chalk – brilliant white and can be crushed to make very small grains
- Slate – feels hard, but easily snapped in half, thin layers

- Granite – very tough and strong, containing different coloured crystals
- Limestone – crumbly with visible grains

Finally, if you are feeling generous, the pupils could ask for the rock of their choice by name to eat, from the untouched packets. Will they correctly name the right one though?

Pupil activity 9.2

Handling real rocks

Learning objective: Learn to identify rocks by their features.

Resources required: a range of rocks, stones or pebbles (see below), magnifying glasses, paper plates, description cards of rocks (see above activity)

If the pupils have carried out the sweet and chocolate 'rock' activity, they will now be well prepared to tackle the real things. The most common rocks they will come across are slate, granite, chalk, limestone, sandstone, and flint. The rocks will need washing beforehand. If you have a computer microscope, you should use this to show enlarged views of the rocks to the pupils. Once again, ask the pupils to examine the rocks visually and then by handling them. They cannot split the rocks in half and see the sections inside but if they are fresh, unweathered samples, the grains or crystals should easily be seen on the surface. Can they match the rocks to the description cards you have prepared and successfully name the rock?

An extension activity for this would be for them to describe and identify less commonly known rocks. Examples might include basalt, gneiss, and chert. Pupils can take digital photographs of rocks which they might use to make a rock family album on paper or in electronic form.

A simple document with clear pictures of rocks is available at:

www.oum.ox.ac.uk/educate/resource/rocks.pdf

A comprehensive and pupil friendly site for rocks (especially those smaller ones found in driveways) is

http://www.saltthesandbox.org/rocks/namesrocks.htm

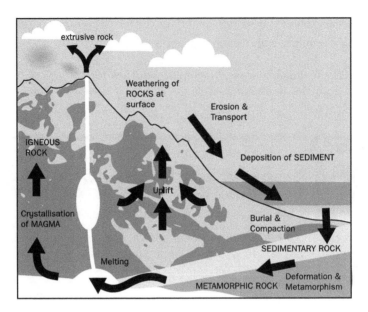

Figure 9.2 Rock cycle

Common misconception

'Rocks have always been there'

Pupils often have no conception of geological time. Rocks appear permanent and so they assume that they have always been there. Seeing examples of local stone buildings that have weathered will help them to understand that rocks do change over time. Pupils have usually heard about dinosaurs and know they lived a long time ago. You might tell them that most rocks are much older than this. Some igneous rock is very young, having erupted just this year, but most are many hundreds of millions of years old. Igneous rock in the Lake District is an example of this type of ancient rock.

Pupil investigation skills 9.3

Scratch test for hardness

Learning objective: Learn to test the hardness of rocks.

Resources required: rock samples and materials to try scratching the rocks with, such as plastic, cork, paper, metal nail, card, chalk

After protecting the tables, ask the pupils to examine rock samples, predict how hard they are, and then try scratching them with different materials. They might keep a written note about the success of the different materials. Ask pupils to report back and see if everyone's results point to the same material. Point out that when you have several test results that are in agreement, this is a reliable result.

Pupil activity 9.4

Acid test for limestone and chalk

Learning objective: Learn to use a test to identify limestone or chalk.

Resources required: rock samples of limestone and/or chalk, vinegar, hand lenses, dropper or teaspoon, newspaper

After protecting the tables with newspaper and warning the pupils about keeping vinegar away from their eyes, ask them to observe the effect of putting tiny drops of vinegar onto samples of chalk or limestone rock. This can be done individually by pupils, in pairs or as a demonstration in class, ideally using a digital microscope and projector. Check that they observe using eyes and ears. Does a magnifying glass help or improve observation? The fizzing occurs because the rock has a high content of calcium carbonate, which reacts with the acidic vinegar to produce carbon dioxide. (This is similar to the bicarbonate of soda and vinegar reaction producing carbon dioxide gas that pupils may be familiar with.) Establish what they observe and what it tells them and ask them to devise a fair test with other samples, not forgetting to ask for predictions at the start.

Add another challenge by trying other safe acids such as lime or lemon juice.

Pupil investigation skills 9.5

Testing how easily rocks can be broken down

Learning objective: Learn that some rocks are 'harder wearing' than others.

Resources required: a range or rocks, small squares of sandpaper (the rougher the better), white paper plates to collect the grains

Some rocks wear down easily, while others do not. Ask the pupils to predict which will be the hardest wearing and which will be the least so, and list the rocks in order. They need to devise fair tests – for example, rubbing each rock for the same amount of time (or same number of strokes), with the same amount of pressure. After they have recorded their predictions, they can carry out their investigation. They may be surprised how easily some of the harder feeling rocks can be eroded. A lot of grains can be collected for each rock, which can be compared visually to identify which rocks are most and least easily eroded.

The pupils should find that granite and flint produce virtually no flakes, whereas limestone, sandstone, and slate make quite a lot. Ask the pupils what could cause this erosion in real life. They may come up with ideas such as wear from feet, wear from vehicles, and wear from rivers. This can lead to a discussion of which rocks they would select for which jobs (see later section).

Pupil investigation skills 9.6

Testing rocks for water permeability

Learning objective: Learn that some rocks allow water to pass through, whereas others do not.

Resources required: a range of rocks both permeable and impermeable, pipettes or droppers, cups of water

Permeable rocks include pumice (pumice stone used in the bathroom will do!), chalk, sandstone and limestone. Impermeable rocks include slate, flint, and granite.

Ask the pupils to predict which rocks will allow water to pass through. Once they have recorded their predictions and designed a fair test (e.g. same amount of water for each rock), they can undertake the experiment. They can place a few spots of water on the rock and see if it remains on the surface or not. They may be surprised to find that limestone and sandstone can be permeable, slate and granite not so. Again this can lead to a discussion of suitability of rocks for various jobs. Slate clearly doesn't let water go through and so is a great roofing material.

An online rock testing simulation is available at:

www.bbc.co.uk/schools/scienceclips/ages/7_8/rocks_soils.shtml

Pupil discussion 9.7

The right rock for the right job

Learning objective: Through discussion, learn that rocks are used for certain jobs because of their features.

Resources required: pictures of buildings, roads, bridges, shops, and so on

Literacy

After all their hands-on practical activity, the pupils are ready to evaluate why certain rocks are used for particular jobs. For visual simulation, pictures of various city scapes could be useful, showing brick buildings, slate roofs, concrete (made partly of limestone), roads (crushed limestone under tarmac), decorative marble, granite, sandstone, and limestone building blocks. It may not be possible to name every rock correctly, but an educated guess can be made. The pupils may find some building materials more difficult to identify the origin of, namely bricks, concrete, and aggregates. Bricks are not rock but usually compressed and baked clay, concrete is made from crushed limestone, and aggregates can be any crushed up rock.

The pupils should look out for signs of damage to building stone in their environment. Processes that damage rocks include wind and rain weathering, frost damage, and frictional wear (e.g. worn steps from years of footfall). Ask them why the strongest rocks are not always chosen (e.g. granite is tough and hard-wearing but expensive).

The following websites offer a good visual guide to building materials and their uses:

The British Geological Survey and English Heritage have produced some excellent reports on the use of building stone. They have done one for each county in England. Follow the link below to the British Geology Survey website, click on the area you want and then click 'atlas':

http://www.bgs.ac.uk/mineralsuk/buildingStones/StrategicStoneStudy/EH_atlases.html

https://sites.google.com/site/jbprimaryscience/rocks includes instructions for making igneous, sedimentary and metamorphic rocks out of chocolate!

http://www.rocksforkids.com is a very comprehensive United States site.

Fossils

Pupil activity 9.8

Internet research

Learning objective: To understand the differing ways fossils can form.

Resources required: access to the internet

Pupils can do a lot of their own research on line into the different ways fossils form and the different types of organisms that form fossils. You could challenge them to find out about:

* how fossils can be made in different ways
* the most common fossils
* the most important fossils

Here are some excellent websites to get them started.

The BBC Nature Prehistoric life website gives a wealth of short video clips showing how animals became fossilised. As well as the more familiar methods, including amber and mud fossilisation, there is also the rarer case where tar pits have preserved huge creatures: http://www.bbc.co.uk/nature/fossils#intro

The Natural History Museum, London has some good photographs and explanations of fossil formation on its website: http://www.nhm.ac.uk/nature-online/earth/fossils/index.html

UK Fossils network site provides a regional and, in some cases, county by county guide to fossil sites, with photos of fossils that have been found there. This website has a clear commercial aspect in that it sells equipment to collect fossils: http://www.ukfossils.co.uk/

The formation of footprints from around 6000 years ago on the Formby shore, Merseyside, gives an insight into how trace fossils form: http://www.formby-footprints. co.uk/index.html

Pupil activity 9.9

Drawing fossils

Learning objective: To understand why certain creatures are preserved; to know why only particular parts of creatures are preserved.

Resources required: books containing fossil photographs, internet access, or real fossils

Using a selection of good photographs from books or the internet, or even real specimens, have the pupils select and draw a range of fossils. By observing very carefully as they draw, they will start to see the underlying structure of the animal or plant preserved. Ask them why this part is preserved, but the rest is gone, that is, why the surviving part is usually the shell, the bones, the teeth, the insect external skeleton (exoskeleton), the plant stem or trunk of the organism. (*Teacher hint*: these are the hardest parts, the softer parts usually rot away before they can be fossilised.) The commonest fossils are often things that lived in the sea, where preservation is easier than for things that lived on land.

Some of the commonest fossils include:

*   ammonites (molluscs with spiral shells)
*   brachiopods (marine animals with overlapping double shells)

- crinoids (these look like plants rooted to the sea bed, but are actually animals related to starfish)
- trilobites (armoured creatures that once dominated the oceans)

A good website for pictures and information on the commoner fossils is the British Geological Survey:

http://www.bgs.ac.uk/discoveringGeology/time/fossilfocus/brachiopod.html

Soils

By examining rocks, stones, and pebbles, pupils will have come to realise that rocks come in different sizes and shapes. This can then lead to a discussion of what soils are made from. Many pupils will be surprised to learn that soils are made from broken down rocks, plus animal and plant material and micro-organisms. Micro-organisms include bacteria and fungi.

Providing different soils for pupils to handle can be tricky. If you collect soil for them to look at, it must be free from contamination and other hazards (e.g. animal waste and broken glass). To make soil safe, either purchase compost in sealed bags as this is heat-treated or microwave soil samples to kill micro-organisms. Alternatively, you might decide to keep samples in containers and you should certainly talk to pupils about the danger of handling soil (e.g. fouling by pets and wild animals). They should be told not to put anything in their mouths while handling soil and to wash their hands thoroughly afterwards. You may prefer to make up your own 'simulated soil'. This can be made with pebbles, potting compost, play sand, dried leaves, and bits of twigs all mixed up and prepared beforehand. This would be safe for the pupils to handle and interesting for them to separate.

Pupil activity 9.10

Separating soil

Learning objective: Learn that soils are made up of various sized components.

Resources required: dry simulated soil (see above) or dry real soil, soil sieves

Challenge the pupils to separate and identify the different components of the soil. Good quality graded sieves are needed for the pupils to be able to separate out the different size components of the soil.

> **Common misconception**
>
> **'Soil is just dirt'**
>
> Pupils often see soil as an accumulation of dirt. They do not appreciate what it is made of and the fantastic value it has for the production of our food and the recycling of waste material.

Pupil investigation skills 9.11

Which is the best soil?

Learning objective: Learn that soils have different drainage properties and consider how this might affect plants.

Resources required: sand, potting compost, small pebbles, funnels, measuring cylinders, stopwatches

You could set up the scenario by telling the pupils they need to find the best soil for a new garden landscape project, where a derelict area is being changed into a wildlife and garden area. There are three major components the pupils should test first: a funnel of pure sand, a funnel of pure stones, and a funnel of pure potting compost.

Ask the pupils to predict which funnel will drain water from the fastest to the slowest, putting them in rank order. For fair testing, they should add the same amount of water to each (e.g. 100 ml). Both the sand and the pebbles increase the air spaces in the soil and so increase drainage. Ask them why a fast draining soil might not be good for plants. (The water doesn't stay in the soil long enough for the plant roots to draw it up.) Why might a slow draining soil be equally bad in a different way? (The soil could get waterlogged and the plants rot.) Remind pupils that many outdoor pot plants have a layer of stones at the bottom, and ask them why this might be.

With the results in mind, the pupils should be able to make up a soil themselves with the best properties – more sand, more stones, or both. They need to measure in small cupfuls or weigh how much sand or stones they will add. They can then measure how fast their soil drains the water, and how waterlogged their soil looks at regular intervals. (*Teacher hint:* a part-sand, part-stone, part-compost soil works best!)

> For a useful animated website about soil, explaining what it is, how it forms, what it is used for, and even the type of soil in every part of England and Wales, try:
>
> www.soil-net.com/cms_test
>
> To help the pupils understand some of the complexity of getting a soil just right for a plant, they can play simulator games at:
>
> http://www.growingthenextgeneration.com/just-for-kids-games.html

Common misconception

'Soil is bought from a shop'

Pupils may see soil as a product made by humankind after buying compost in a shop or garden centre. However, soil is a natural product of active ecosystems.

Scientists of rocks, fossils and soils

James Hutton founded the science of geology. He recognised the natural processes that built up mountains (through volcanic eruption). He also realised that the same mountains could become worn down through the effects of wind and rain over vast periods of time, and the resulting sediment washed into rivers and seas. This sediment could be compacted and turned into new rock, again over long periods of time. (See the diagram of the rock cycle in Figure 9.2). Through his careful observations and research he realised that the Earth was much, much older than anyone had previously thought.

Mary Anning lived in Lyme Regis, Dorset. She was a collector and seller of fossils, making a meagre living from the trade. The coast is rich with fossils from the Jurassic era. In 1811 she discovered the first fossil ichthyosaur, a marine reptile that resembles a dolphin (but is not related, dolphins evolved much later). In 1823 she discovered the first plesiosaur, a long necked marine reptile.

http://www.amnh.org/education/resources/rfl/web/essaybooks/earth/p_hutton.html

http://www.nhm.ac.uk/nature-online/science-of-natural-history/biographies/mary-anning/

Summary of key learning points:

- rocks are grouped into three major types – igneous, sedimentary, and metamorphic;
- rocks move and change following weathering, erosion, heating, and deposition;
- fossils are formed under a range of rare conditions;
- soil is a mixture of three ingredients – mineral, organic, and living components.

Self-test

Question 1

Granite is (a) a metamorphic, hard-wearing rock, (b) an igneous rock that usually contains crystals, (c) a sedimentary rock made from the remnants of animals, (d) an igneous rock that forms above the surface of the Earth

Question 2

Soils are usually made of (a) bacteria, sand, and silt, (b) grains of rock, micro-organisms, and remnants of dead plants and animals, (c) rock and organic matter, (d) a mixture of sand, silt, and clay

Self-test answers

Q1: Only (b) is correct. Granite is an igneous rock that forms below the ground and crystals form as it cools.

Q2: The most complete answer is (b). The grains of rock may be sand, silt or clay (or a mixture of these). Part of the organic content will be decaying animal and plant remains. The micro-organisms such as bacteria and fungi will feed off the decaying remains.

Misconceptions

'Rocks have always been there'

'Soil is just dirt'

'Soil is bought from a shop'

Web resources

http://www.amnh.org/education/resources/rfl/web/essaybooks/earth/p_hutton.html
   (James Hutton biography)

http://www.bbc.co.uk/nature/fossils#intro
   (BBC site showing how animals become fossilised)

http://www.bgs.ac.uk/discoveringGeology/time/fossilfocus/brachiopod.html
   (British Geological Survey guide to the commonest fossils)

http://www.bgs.ac.uk/minerals/uk/buildingStones/StrategicStoneStudy/EH_atlases.html
   (downloadable guides to building stones in each English county)

http://www.formby-footprints.co.uk/index.html
   (intriguing footprints from prehistoric Britain)

http://www.growingthenextgeneration.com/just-for-kids-games.html
   (soil structure simulator games)

http://www.nhm.ac.uk/nature-online/earth/fossils/index.html
   (Natural History Museum London's site on fossils)

http://www.nhm.ac.uk/nature-online/science-of-natural-history/biographies/mary-anning
(short biography of Mary Anning, fossil finder)

http://www.oum.ox.ac.uk/educate/resource/rocks.pdf
(clear pictures of different rocks)

http://www.rocksforkids.com
(comprehensive United States website)

http://www.saltthesandbox.org/rocks/namesrocks.htm
(guide to small rock samples)

www.bbc.co.uk/schools/scienceclips/ages/7_8/rocks_soils.shtml
(simulation of rock testing)

http://www.soil-net.com/cms_test
(animated website about soil in England, very comprehensive)

http://www.ukfossils.co.uk
(includes a regional guide to fossil finds in Britain)

https://sites.google.com/site/jbprimaryscience/rocks
(includes instructions for making igneous, sedimentary and metamorphic rocks out of chocolate)

10
Forces

About this chapter

This chapter is about forces and how they affect the movement and some-times the shape of objects. The forces discussed are simple pushes and pulls, magnetism, friction, air and water resistance, upthrust, and gravity. Simple mechanisms of levers, pulleys, gears, and springs are introduced. The second part of the chapter looks at what pupils need to learn, and suggests activities and ways to tackle common misconceptions.

What the teacher needs to know and understand

Simple contact forces

At its simplest, a force is either a push or a pull. Every time an object moves, a push or a pull has made it move. Sometimes a push and a pull can be done simultaneously to create a twist, for example, when turning the handlebars of a bicycle, one hand pushes while the other one pulls.

Objects can be made to start moving or stop moving by directly applying a force. Think about someone throwing a ball and a second person catching it – one person started the movement and the other one stopped it. Forces can also be made to speed things up or change direction. Think about a footballer kicking a ball that is already moving towards a goal to speed it up, and the goalkeeper deflecting it and changing its direction of travel. Forces can also slow things down. For example, if someone is pushing a trolley in one direction, you could push it gently in the opposite direction, thereby slowing the overall movement of the trolley. Pushes and pulls can also be more subtle and not so obvious. A toy car rolling along a floor slows down as it goes, as the frictional force of the floor rubs against it, causing it to lose energy and eventually stop. All the above examples are contact forces, where we can see a force being directly applied to move an object. Contact forces are the forces that most people are familiar with in their everyday life, for example, pushing a door closed, pulling a drawer open, and so on.

Other kinds of forces are classed as non-contact forces, where the force from one object can act at a distance to move another object. An everyday occurrence of a non-contact force is one magnet making another one move, without the two magnets touching. Gravity from the Earth is also a non-contact force.

Magnetism

A magnet always has a North (N) and South (S) pole, which are sometimes labelled (e.g. bar magnets are coloured red and blue in school) but not always (e.g. a fridge magnet). Two magnets can repel or attract each other. When magnets repel, they push each other away; when they attract, they pull together. Opposite or unlike poles attract each other (so North attracts South); like poles repel (so North repels North and South repels South).

Magnets generate what we call a magnetic force field around them. This field gets weaker the further it gets from the magnet. Because of the field, magnetic force can act at a distance from the magnet. It can attract or repel another magnet, or attract a magnetic material (e.g. a paper clip) that will 'jump' towards the magnet. Typically, the magnetic force field only extends a few centimetres away from the magnet. Magnetic force can act quite easily through thin solid materials such as paper, card, and fabrics. The more a magnet is dropped on the floor, the less effective it becomes, and the weaker the magnetic field it generates. Old school magnets have often been dropped a lot!

Magnets tend to be made of iron or steel that have been magnetised, although this is not always obvious to the children, as modern ones used in the classroom tend to be encased in coloured plastic, with contrasting colours for each pole. If a magnet is not labelled N and S or coloured, it is possible to find its poles by suspending it by a piece of thread. If left for some time it will slowly spin, but should settle with the North pole of the magnet pointing to the North Pole of the Earth. This could be checked with a compass. The needle of a compass is just a thin magnet and it always points North.

Magnetic materials are iron, steel, nickel, and cobalt. Nickel and cobalt are rarely found in everyday objects; most magnetic materials we attract using a magnet are likely to be of iron and steel. In primary school, we often treat iron and steel as separate metals (which is fine), but steel is actually made from iron and carbon, and it is the iron content that makes it magnetic.

While magnets can attract *or* repel each other, magnetic *materials* are only ever attracted to a magnet (i.e. you cannot repel a magnetic material with a magnet). Armed with a magnet, children can use these ideas as a test to determine whether a given object is a magnet, or just a magnetic material.

Friction

Friction is the force that opposes movement. We commonly think of friction as a force between two surfaces in contact with each other. Friction both makes it difficult for something to start to move and for something to continue moving.

Rougher surfaces can give a greater grip, as these have more indentations to mesh with the surface it is in contact with. Heavy objects may experience more friction as they move across a surface, as their weight increases the number of contact points between the object and the surface, and hence increases the friction.

It can be helpful to address the two types of friction that occur between surfaces. These are static friction and sliding friction. With static friction, the two surfaces are in contact with each other and are stationary. The little indentations between them are meshed together, making it hard for them to start to move. Think of a filing cabinet resting on an office carpet. With sliding friction, one surface moves across another. For example, think of a sledge being dragged across a concrete drive. This is the form of friction that children are most familiar with. Things that experience sliding friction can get hot quickly (as anyone who has slid down a climbing rope will know).

Liquids reduce friction because they form a layer between two surfaces, making it harder for the indentations of the surfaces to come into contact with each other. This can be helpful in some cases (think of oiling a bike chain) and hazardous in others (such as a floor that has just been mopped).

Air resistance

Air resistance is a form of friction. When objects move through the air, the air pushes against them and slows them down. A common misconception is that air resistance only occurs on objects falling through the air, but it also occurs when objects are moving along the ground and the air pushes against them (e.g. a car travelling along a motorway). Through your investigations, demonstrations, and discussions you can show a range of experiences to demonstrate air resistance at work in different directions.

Two factors influence air resistance. The first is the size of the object or, more exactly, its surface area. Objects with a larger surface area have more particles of air pushing against them as they move, and so experience more air resistance (think of a falling open parachute compared with a falling closed parachute). The other factor is the speed the object is travelling at. The faster the object is going, the harder the air particles hit it and the greater the air resistance it experiences. People often experience this when riding a bicycle down a steep hill and feeling their hair being blown backwards.

Air resistance is often confused with upthrust in air. Upthrust determines whether something will float or sink in air, owing to the object's weight. Things like helium balloons and hot air balloons experience enough upthrust to float, as their gases weigh less than air. Upthrust on most other objects (e.g. a parachutist) is negligible and should therefore be ignored.

Water resistance

Water resistance occurs when an object moves through water or across the top of water. Someone swimming across the surface of a swimming pool experiences water resistance pushing against them and slowing them down. So does a water skier as they are pulled along. Things moving under water also feel water resistance, including a submarine going up and down or from side to side, and a dolphin chasing fish. Water resistance is very often mixed up with upthrust in water. Upthrust is to do with whether an object floats or sinks and water resistance is to do with water slowing things down, whichever way they are moving. Investigations of water resistance are difficult to perform to get convincing results. A few good demonstrations and discussions may be preferable.

Gravity and weight

Gravitational attraction acts on any object on or near the Earth. Gravity always pulls the object towards the centre of the Earth. Very large objects can exert a great deal of gravitational attraction on smaller objects (e.g. the Earth pulls on an apple and attracts it). Gravity extends into outer space. For instance, the Earth pulls on the Moon and attracts it, keeping it in orbit. In turn, the Sun's gravity pulls on the Earth and attracts it and so the Earth orbits the Sun.

Weight is the force on an object due to gravity, and is measured in Newtons. Gravity pulls on all objects here on Earth, but it does not pull on them all equally. We can think of weight as how *hard* gravity pulls on an object. When scientists talk about weight, they mean this force. Weight is often confused with the word 'mass'. Mass is the amount of 'stuff' in an object (a measure of the amount of material in the object). Mass is measured in grams or kilograms. A cannonball has more mass than a football because it is made of denser material (there is more 'stuff' in it). As a cannonball has more mass, we find it heavier to pick up, because it has more weight and a greater attraction to the Earth. Generally, if an object loses mass, it will lose weight too. It is easier to pick up half an apple than a whole apple because half an apple weighs less, and the Earth's gravity pulls it less hard. There isn't much difference between an apple and half an apple, but a bus has much more mass, so has much greater weight too. This means there is greater attraction between the bus and the Earth and a bus would be much harder for us to pick up!

Confusingly, people talk about 'weighing themselves' or 'weighing out ingredients' and use grams or kilograms to do this. What they are actually doing in these instances is measuring mass, not weight!

The Moon

Gravitational attraction occurs between any object on or near the Moon and the Moon itself. Objects on the Moon weigh less than on Earth because the Moon has less mass, so can exert less gravitational attraction on the object. The Moon's gravity is only one-sixth of that on Earth. If a bag of pasta with a mass of 500 grams is flown from the Earth to the Moon, on the Moon its mass would be the same, 500 grams, because it hasn't lost any 'stuff' on the journey. But the Moon cannot pull it down as hard as the Earth can, so it would weigh less than on Earth (and would be easier for us to pick up). For this reason, in theory a high jump athlete could jump much higher on the Moon than on Earth, because the Moon's gravity is much weaker (it might be difficult in a space suit though!)

Support forces can 'cancel out' the effect of gravity

On Earth, a table can 'cancel out' the force of gravity. Place a cup on the table and it will stay there. This is because gravity pulls it down, but a support force from the table pushes up and keeps the cup in place, balancing the force of gravity. A support force can also be called a 'reactive force' – the idea being that as gravity pulls the object down against the table, the table reacts to this and pushes back with an equal force on the object.

People find this concept very difficult and often believe there is no counteracting force from the table. However, if there was no counteracting or support force from the table, the cup would fall right through it to the floor. When the cup is at rest on the table, we can say the two forces acting on the cup are equal and balanced so the cup will not move.

Balanced and unbalanced forces

The cup on the table experiences balanced forces and does not move. When forces are balanced an object can be stationary, but in some cases balanced forces also allow an object to move at a steady speed. Imagine a car driving down the motorway at a steady rate of 60 miles per hour. The forces acting on the car are friction from the road, air resistance from the air hitting the front of it, and the force from the engine makes the wheels move (we can ignore gravity and the support force from the road). If the car continues at a steady speed, the forces trying to slow it down (friction and air resistance) and the force pushing it forward (from the wheels) are equal, and we can say the forces are balanced.

Unbalanced forces cause a change in the speed of something. Imagine a dragster car racer speeding along a race track. These cars have no brakes, so to slow down they normally use a parachute at the back of the car. When the parachute is deployed, it will experience a huge amount of air resistance. The air resistance of the parachute will cause the car to slow down and as it slows down the car will experience unbalanced forces – that is, the air resistance will be greater than any force propelling the car forward. Whenever anything accelerates or slows down, it is unbalanced forces that are making this happen.

Upthrust in water

Upthrust is a force that acts upwards on objects in water. When an object floats, its weight is equal to the upthrust provided by the water. The object has actually displaced its own weight in water. On the other hand, when an object sinks, it is because its weight is greater than the upthrust that the water can provide. Objects that would normally sink can be made to float by changing their shape. For example, a solid ball of Plasticine™ will normally sink because its weight is greater than the upthrust from the water. However, if we mould it into the shape of a boat, it will now float because it can displace more water, and hence the upthrust force acting on it is greater than before.

If an object floats, the forces acting on it are balanced – the weight is equal to the upthrust force. If an object sinks, the forces are unbalanced – the weight is greater than the upthrust force. See Figure 10.1.

Levers

A lever consists of an *arm*, a *fulcrum*, and a *load*. The arm is also called a *rod* and this is the fixed, unbending part of the lever. The fulcrum is also called a *pivot*, the point at

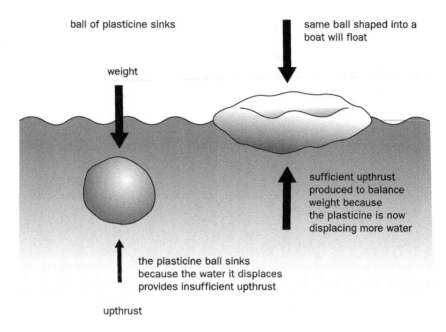

ball of plasticine sinks

same ball shaped into a boat will float

weight

sufficient upthrust produced to balance weight because the plasticine is now displacing more water

the plasticine ball sinks because the water it displaces provides insufficient upthrust

upthrust

Figure 10.1 Shaped Plasticine™ displaces more water, creating greater upthrust

which the lever moves around. The load is the thing that the lever is trying to push and move. The force you put into the lever is called the *effort force*. Levers are effectively force multipliers, whereby you put a small force in, but this force is magnified to act on the load. Levers are classed as types 1, 2 or 3.

In type 1 levers the effort force is applied at one end, the load is at the other end and the fulcrum is somewhere in between. An example of a type 1 lever is a seesaw. A force can be applied to one end, the seesaw turns around the fulcrum in the middle and this makes the load at the other end of the seesaw rise. See Figure 10.2.

Effort force

Load

KG

Fulcrum

Figure 10.2 See-saw as a type 1 lever

In type 2 levers the fulcrum is at one end, and the load is in the middle and the effort force is at the other end. Think about a wheelbarrow. The fulcrum is at the wheel. When an effort force is applied to lift the handles, the load in the middle is lifted easily, as the axle turns within the wheel. See Figure 10.3.

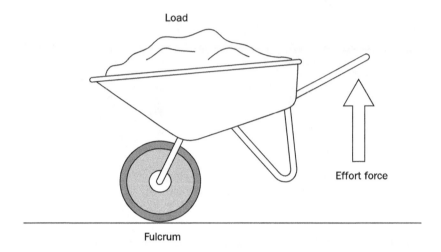

Figure 10.3 Wheelbarrow as a type 2 lever

A third kind of lever is the type 3, which includes tongs and tweezers. Here the fulcrum is at one end, the load at the other end, and the effort force applied in the middle. See Figure 10.4.

Figure 10.4 Tongs as a type 3 lever

Once you understand how levers work, you start to see them in lots of everyday surroundings. A door pivots around a hinge and despite its considerable weight, you can move it easily. With scissors we have two levers that work at the same time. When the effort force is applied on the handles, the blades turn around the fulcrum in the middle to apply a magnified force on the load between the cutting blades. See Figure 10.5.

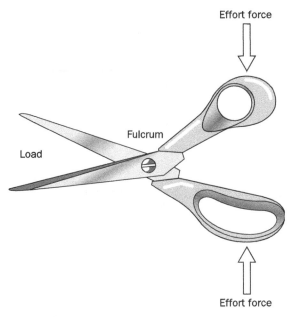

Figure 10.5 Scissors as a pair of levers

By now you may have realised that all the different types of levers are just made by rearranging where the fulcrum, load and effort force are.

An excellent webpage takes you through how all three types of levers work:

http://www.enchantedlearning.com/physics/machines/Levers.shtml

Pulleys

In its simplest form, a pulley consists of a grooved wheel, an axle and a rope. The wheel rotates around a fixed axle, and the wheel is grooved so the rope can fit snugly onto it. There are two types of pulleys: a 'fixed pulley' that is fitted to a frame or a ceiling, and a 'moveable pulley' where the pulley is connected directly onto the load that needs to be lifted.

Imagine having to lift a load up from a table. You could tie a rope to it, and lift it directly upwards. Here you are pulling the rope straight up, to lift the load straight up. See Figure 10.6.

Now imagine having a simple pulley attached to a frame, sitting on the table. The load is still attached to a rope, but this time the rope goes around the pulley wheel and back down to the table. To lift the load up, you have to pull down on the rope. It's easier to pull downwards than upwards, but you still have to put the same amount of force into the job. This type of pulley is called a 'fixed pulley', as it is fixed to the frame. Here we are 're-directing' the force, because although we pull down, the load moves up in the opposite direction. See Figure 10.7.

Figure 10.6 Lifting up a load

Figure 10.7 A fixed pulley

To make it easier to lift the load, we have to generate a *mechanical advantage*. *Mechanical advantage is a way to increase the force acting on the load.* First tie the rope to the top of the frame, and attach a moveable pulley onto the load. (This type of pulley is called a 'movable pulley' because it moves with the load.)

To raise the load, pull up on the rope and both the load and the pulley will travel up the rope to the top of the frame. The load is easier to move – you actually have to

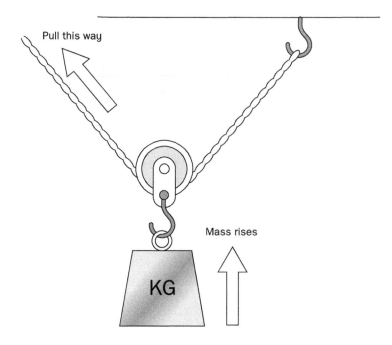

Figure 10.8 A movable pulley

supply *half the force* you did before, but you have to pull the rope *twice as far* this time. See Figure 10.8.

This example could be scaled up, for example to use on a building site. For every metre you want to lift the load up, you have to pull your end of the rope 2 metres (a mechanical advantage of 2:1). Pulling a rope further is easier, if overall the force required is half as much as before!

Now we can gain additional mechanical advantage by adding more pulleys. We may add fixed or moveable pulleys in a systematic way. As we add more pulleys, we will have to use more rope and pull it further, but it will require much less force, even to move a heavy load. See Figure 10.9.

Another way to make things easier to lift is to add *more wheels* on to the existing pulleys. Here the rope passes back up and down between the wheels, but is always held in place by the grooves. The pulleys above only had a single wheel, but look at Figure 10.10 – one pulley has two wheels on it, the other has three.

A good video clip that introduces simple pulleys (and a bit of maths – nothing too scary!) is

http://www.youtube.com/watch?v=yfAdmRJDKIc

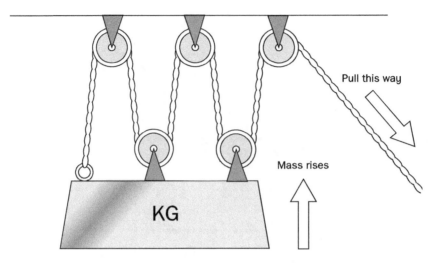

Figure 10.9 Adding more pulleys

Figure 10.10 Pulleys with multiple wheels on them

Gears

A gear is a toothed wheel. Gear teeth from one wheel can fit into those of another wheel. This means that if you turn the first wheel, the second wheel will turn too, but in the opposite direction. If the two gears are the same size, then turning one will make the other one turn at exactly the same speed. See Figure 10.11.

If one gear is bigger than the other, then they will turn at different speeds. For example, imagine a big gear connected to a small gear. If we turn the big gear around once, the smaller gear may have rotated around twice in that time, and it will move at a faster speed to do this – in fact twice as fast.

We can work out how fast two gears will rotate by counting their number of teeth. For example if a big gear has 60 teeth and the small gear has 30 teeth, then we can do it as a ratio: 60:30 or 2:1 – that is, the smaller of the two gears will make two full rotations in the time the larger gear makes one rotation, and the smaller gear will go twice the speed of the bigger gear. See Figure 10.12.

So if a big gear turns a small gear, the small gear rotates faster than the big one. And vice versa – if a small gear turns a big gear, then the big gear rotates more slowly. Gears can be used to create a mechanical advantage, that is, to *increase a force*. To do this a small gear drives a big gear. See Figure 10.13.

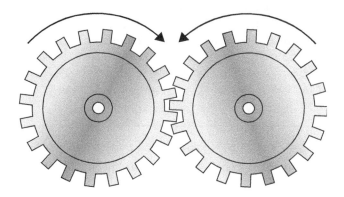

Figure 10.11 Gears turning in opposite directions, at the same speed

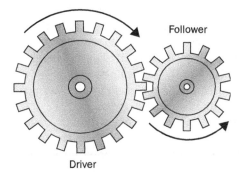

Figure 10.12 Small and large gear, where the small gear turns faster, and the large gear turns more slowly

Figure 10.13 A small gear can be made to turn larger ones, to create mechanical advantage

Gears can be connected together in greater numbers, to move a force across a surface. The gear that you turn (or a motor turns) is called the *drive gear*, and the other gears are called *driven gears*. See Figure 10.14.

Some can be placed at right angles to each other and these are called bevelled gears. Their teeth are set at 45 degrees. With normal gears (all the examples we have seen above) they all sit alongside each other, and the forces all operate on the same horizontal plane. With bevelled gears being at right angles to each other, this means that the force from one gear can be transferred to the other one at 90 degrees. This would allow any shafts connected to them to operate on a different plane. See Figure 10.15.

Worm gears are long and thin. They can be used to slow the speed of a connecting gear and give it increased 'torque'. See Figure 10.16. Torque is a term that means 'turning force' or 'twist'.

An excellent website summarising how levers, pulleys and gears work is http://www.dtonline.org and click through to the 'mechanisms' page.

Pulling and pushing – springs and rubber

Springs can be stretched by pulling them or squashed by pushing on them. Some springs can only be pulled (stretchy springs), some can only be pushed (squashy springs), and some can do both. When a stretchy spring is pulled, it exerts a force in the opposite direction, trying to pull back to its normal shape. When a squashy spring is pushed (compressed), it pushes back in the opposite direction to try to get back to its normal shape. The greater the force pulling or pushing on a spring, the greater the force the spring uses to move back to its normal shape.

Rubber behaves in a spring-like manner. Rubber elastic bands can be stretched and will pull back on the thing stretching them to try to get back to their normal shape. A rubber bouncy ball can be squashed by pressing it and this is essentially how it bounces. When dropped, it is squashed on the side that hits the floor, and then 'springs' back and up in the air to go back to its normal shape, pushing on the floor as it does so.

Figure 10.14 Multiple gears

Figure 10.15 Bevelled gears   **Figure 10.16** Worm gear

What pupils need to know at Key Stage 1

Forces is not a topic at Key Stage 1, being first introduced in Key Stage 2. However, we feel that pupils will benefit from an introduction to forces, with a focus on pushes and pulls. A list of learning objectives is outlined below:

- When something moves, a push or pull has caused it to move.
- A push or pull can make an object start to move, or stop it from moving.
- A push or pull can make an object speed up or slow down.
- A push or pull can make an object change direction.
- A push can squash some materials, and a pull can stretch some materials.

If the above content is not covered at Key Stage 1, then it will need to be covered at the start of lower Key Stage 2. In the above cases, the application of these forces is very visible in everyday life, for example, a pupil pushing a toy car or pulling a door open. The simple language and concepts used here will prepare the pupils for the more difficult ideas of friction, air resistance, magnets, upthrust, and gravity. In these cases the forces acting are invisible and more complex to understand, but they too are pushes or pulls that can make things start, stop, speed up, slow down, and change direction.

What pupils need to know at Key Stage 2

(ST) denotes statutory requirements.

Lower Key Stage 2
Introduction to friction

(ST) Compare how things move on different surfaces

Suggestions for working scientifically:

> Raise questions and carry out tests to find out how far things move on different surfaces. Gather and record data to find answers to their questions.

Everyday forces

(ST) Notice that some forces need contact between two objects, but magnetic forces can act at a distance

Suggestions for working scientifically:

> Compare how different things move and group them (is it a push or pull that moves them?)
>
> Observe that magnetic forces can act without direct contact, unlike most forces, where direct contact is necessary (e.g. opening a door, pushing a swing).

Magnets

(ST) Describe magnets as having two poles

(ST) Predict whether two magnets will attract or repel each other, depending on which poles are facing

Suggestions for working scientifically:

Find out about the way that magnets behave in relation to each other and what might affect this, for example, the strength of the magnet or which pole faces another.

Explore the behaviour and everyday uses of different magnets (e.g., bar, ring, button and horseshoe).

Identify how these properties make magnets useful in everyday items and suggest creative uses for different magnets.

Magnetic materials

(ST) Compare and group together a variety of everyday materials on the basis of whether they are attracted to a magnet, and identify some magnetic materials

Suggestions for working scientifically:

Sort materials into those that are magnetic and those that are not.

Explore the strengths of different magnets and find a fair way to compare them.

Upper Key Stage 2

Everyday forces

Suggestions for working scientifically:

Experience forces that make things begin to move, get faster or slow down.

Gravity

(ST) Explain that unsupported objects fall towards the Earth because of the force of gravity acting between the Earth and the falling object

Suggestions for working scientifically:

Find out how scientists, for example, Galileo Galilei and Isaac Newton helped to develop the theory of gravitation.

Forms of friction: contact between two surfaces (ordinary friction), air resistance, water resistance

(ST) Identify the effects of air resistance, water resistance and friction, that act between moving surfaces

Suggestions for working scientifically:

Explore the effects of friction on movement and find out how it slows or stops moving objects, for example, by observing the effects of a brake on a bicycle wheel.

Explore falling objects and raise questions about the effects of air resistance e.g. sycamore seeds, paper cones or cup cases.

Design and make a variety of parachutes and carry out fair tests to determine which designs are the most effective.

Explore resistance in water by making and testing boats of different shapes.

Simple mechanisms: levers, pulleys, gears and springs

(ST) Recognise that some mechanisms, including levers, pulleys and gears, allow a smaller force to have a greater effect

Suggestions for working scientifically:

Pupils should explore the effects of levers, pulleys and simple machines on movement.

Design and make products that use levers, pulleys, gears and/or springs and explore their effects.

Ways to teach 'forces' at Key Stage 2

Contact forces

The type of forces that pupils will be most familiar with are simple pushes or pulls that they do themselves, to make things move. For example, kicking a ball, opening a door, pedalling a bike. Younger pupils may find the difference between a push and a pull confusing. The phrases 'push away' and 'pull towards' may be helpful, with the children miming these activities while saying the phrases.

Pupil activity 10.1

Drawing and miming contact forces

Learning objective: To understand that we use contact forces every day to move things.

Resources required: paper and pens or pencils

Ask the children to draw three pushes and three pulls they have done that morning. Give a few pointers, such as did they pull a door open or push a drawer closed? Some activities like brushing teeth involve pulls and pushes. An individual child could mime to the class a push or pull they have done that morning with the rest of the class trying to guess it (make sure they tell you first what it is they are miming!) Point out that they need to actually touch the objects to make them move, and that's why we call these contact forces.

Pupil activity 10.2

Pushes and pulls in the classroom

Learning objective: To know how contact forces are used in the classroom.

Resources required: blank stickers, pens

The children write 'push' or 'pull' on stickers and then place these around the class to show the pushes and pulls they do to objects to make them move. Some things will have both push and pull on them (e.g. drawers may have push and pull on them and doors may have push on one side and pull on the other).

Pupil activity 10.3

Songs

Learning objective: To help understand push and pull forces in everyday life.

Resources required: none

Songs that can be sung while doing motions can be helpful when thinking about pushes and pulls. 'Wind the bobbin on' and 'Row, row, row your boat' both feature the use of forces, which children can sing along to while miming the actions.

Music

Find science songs at:

www.kidsinglish.com/ which is Peter Weatherall's website of science songs and simple explanation videos. You can preview the songs on www.youtube.com

Pupil activity 10.4

PE forces

Learning objective: To understand how we use forces when playing sports.

Resources required: see below

Physical education (PE) lessons can allow a range of pushes and pulls to be demonstrated. Kicking and hitting balls both involve giving the ball a push. A bat is usually pulled backwards before being pushed forwards. Jumping involves pushing as hard as possible with the legs on the ground. Tug-of-war is an obvious example of pulling.

Physical education presents a good opportunity to show how contact forces can stop, start or change the direction or speed of things; for example, we might kick a ball (push) to start it moving and someone else might stop it with their leg (a push), then make it change direction. Big kicks or throws (both pushes) can make things go faster. PE equipment can also demonstrate how pupils use pushes and pulls to make their bodies move, such as when pulling themselves up on apparatus when climbing. Make sure you promote lots of talk using scientific language and say that this is part of science.

Common misconception

'Round things just move by themselves'

Young children often think things move because of their intrinsic shape. For example, a ball rolls because it is 'round', wheels move because they are of a circular shape. The shape does help the ball and wheel to move, but a force must provide the push or pull to get the thing moving. Help pupils to identify exactly when a force applied makes an object move.

Pupil activity 10.5

Pushes and pulls with toys

Learning objective: To understand how toys move using forces.

Resources required: see below

Many toys use pushes or pulls to make them start to move, speed up, slow down or change direction. Foundation Stage classes may have a good range of hand-held toys to borrow, as well as larger things such as tricycles and see-saws. These can be used to demonstrate the whole range of what forces do. Collect a range of toys, including pull-along toys, water wheels, cars, in fact anything that demonstrates movement. Challenge the children to work out if pushes or pulls are required to make the toys work. Ask them which ones can be made to change direction easily (e.g. tricycles turning) or can be slowed down. Challenge them to point in the direction of the push or pull.

Pupil activity 10.6

Changing shape using contact forces

Learning objective: To know that a force can change the shape of something.

Resources required: play clay (or Plasticine™)

Play clay can be pushed or pulled into many shapes. Working in small groups, set the children the task of making something simple from a ball of play clay such as a pig. Each child takes it in turn to pull or push the play dough to make one of the features. This might require considerable discussion about how to make each part!

Pupil activity 10.7

Other things that move using pushes and pulls

Learning objective: Using discussion to learn about more things that move.

Resources required: none

So far we have concentrated on the children moving their bodies, or physically manipulating objects to get them to move (e.g. toys and PE lessons). Have a discussion about things that move 'by themselves' – for example, the wind blowing things (a push), a ball rolling down hill (a tricky idea for younger pupils – gravity pulling the ball downwards). We can talk about forces that need to be in contact to make things move, and those that do not. For example gravity and magnetism don't have to be in contact with things to attract them. Note also that forces can be transferred from objects to us, for example if we got in the way of a moving bowling ball, we would certainly feel its force! Can they draw a range of different forces, both contact and non-contact ones, and label them correctly?

Pupil activity 10.8

Starting to measure pushes and pulls

Learning objective: Learn that big and small forces can be measured.

Resources required: force meters, objects that can be moved safely, elastic bands (optional), knicker elastic (optional), balloon (optional)

Force meters can be used to make things move safely in the classroom. The spring inside a force meter can be seen to stretch, so the larger the force needed to move the object, the greater the stretch. A push meter will also show a spring stretching or squashing and the children can feel the force of the object pushing back on them. Care needs to be taken in selecting objects that can be moved safely with force meters (see section below). A great place to start is to use a balloon as a push meter. Push a chair with a balloon and you will see the balloon flatten slightly as a result of the pushing. Do the same by pulling objects with large elastic bands or knicker elastic!

Pupil activity 10.9

Accurate measurement of pushes and pulls

Learning objective: To be able to quantify the size of a force.

Resources required: force meters, a range of objects to move (see Table 10.1)

Before using force meters, ensure the children are familiar with how they work. Draw their attention to the fact that they have two scales (a grams scale for measuring mass and a Newton scale for measuring force). It is Newtons that they will be using (if possible, cover up the grams scale). Get them to note that the bigger the force the more the spring changes shape. Remind them that they will need to make more than one reading, to 'check their results' for each object.

Maths

The most useful force meters have a scale of 0–10 N. Lifting an apple off the table only requires a force of about 1–3 N (depending on the size of the apple). The children can predict and then confirm how much force is required to move things such as water bottles and pencil cases. It can be tricky to measure such small forces, so larger objects can be used, including a school bag (not too heavily laden). Once the pupils have got the idea with a few objects, get them to select and predict some more. Caution against trying to move items that are too heavy.

Table 10.1 Approximate forces (in Newtons) required to move various familiar objects

Object	Approximate force required to lift	Approximate force required to drag or push across a table top
Apple	1 N	0.5 N
Book	4 N	2 N
Stapler	1 N	0.5 N
PE basket	15 N	10 N
Rounders bat	2 N	1 N

Common misconception

'Dragging or lifting something uses the same amount of force'

Children may be surprised that it requires less force to drag an object along a table than it does to lift the same object into the air. When we drag an object across a table, the main force we have to overcome is the friction of the object rubbing on the table. When lifting the object up, we now have to pull against the object's weight (owing to gravity) and this requires greater force. When the object was on the table, its weight was effectively 'cancelled out' by the table, as the table pushed back with equal force (this is called the 'support force' or 'reactive force'). The air cannot provide a corresponding support force like the table, hence the greater stretch of the spring. Explaining this to children is tricky though, as they find it hard to believe that the table pushes back!

Schools can buy force meters with a hook to measure pulling and force meters with a bar or rod to measure pushing. The pushing version can be easier to use with objects that have no obvious hooking point such as an apple. Alternatively, just pop the apple in a lightweight bag so that hooking it is now easy! Care needs to be taken with large, heavy objects.

Learning about forces with springs

Bare springs can be difficult for children to handle effectively and safely. There are two ways around this – the children can make their own springs or they can handle force meters.

Pupil activity 10.10

Making a spring

Learning objective: Learn to make a spring.

Resources required: pencil with 'round' sides, thin gauge garden wire, scissors

Thin gauge garden wire can be cut with scissors and this does not leave a sharp edge.

The children can wrap wire around the pencil in tight coils, and then simply remove the pencil. The children will find they can pull the spring and feel a slight opposing pull in the opposite direction, or push it and feel the spring pushing them back. The springs are not particularly 'strong' but this means they are safe to handle.

Pupil activity 10.11

Using force meters to find out about springs

Learning objective: To understand how a spring reacts to forces.

Resources required: force meters, small masses

This activity could be used as an introduction to teaching how springs work. Children need to observe how a spring changes its length in response to different forces. A simple pull force meter contains a spring that is stretched in response to a pull. If the children pull on the force meter, they can feel the opposing pull of the spring inside it. They can even read the scale in Newtons and see how hard the spring is pulling back.

You might pose the following questions to pupils:

- In which direction is the spring pulling?
- What happens if you pull harder on the spring?
- It takes a larger force to move a heavier object, so what happens to the force meter's spring when you try and move a heavier object?

If they have a range of force meters, ideally push as well as pull ones, get them to look at the size of the springs inside. Can they say which springs are the hardest to pull or push? (The stronger springs are in the force meters with the largest scales. These springs also tend to be thicker, which makes them stronger.) Do the springs in pull meters work in the same way as those in push meters?

Pupil investigation skills 10.12

How does adding extra weight and mass affect springs?

Learning objective: Learn that the weight of something can exert a force and stretch a spring.

Resources required: force meters, objects to stretch the spring (e.g. masses)

A simple investigation can be done to find out what happens to a spring as the weight of objects the children attach increases. The children should be able to spot the simple relationship 'the greater the weight, the more the spring stretches'. They could measure the stretch of the spring and plot against the weight of object added.

Masses in 100 g units would be ideal for this. Each 100 g added would give an extra 1 Newton of force on the spring and stretch it further.

Learning about magnetism

Pupil investigation skills 10.13

How do magnets move each other?

Learning objective: Learn that magnets can attract or repel each other.

Resources required: bar magnets

Many magnets have their poles in contrasting colours. Traditionally, red is North and blue is South, but other combinations are used. Sometimes a magnet will have a small letter N and S inscribed on it to show which pole is which. Set the children the following tasks:

- Which ends of the magnets attract each other and which repel?
- What combinations are there (North attracts South, North repels North, South repels South)? This may take some detective work if the poles are not labelled or colour-coded.
- Can they work out if attracting and repelling are pushes or pulls? Remind them of 'pull towards' and 'push away'.

Discussion: What do magnets look like?

Children are familiar with magnets used in school, which are often brightly coloured and have their opposite poles clearly marked. However, they fail to recognise magnets that do not have their poles marked and are just 'bare' (i.e. no plastic coat on them).

It is worth showing children these magnets and discussing when they are used in everyday circumstances. Such magnets are used on novelties to attach notes to fridges. They are also used on some cupboard doors to keep the cupboards shut firmly. They have recently started to be used in pairs attached to sponges to clean fish tanks or windows.

Pupil investigation skills 10.14

Are bigger magnets more powerful? Two simple investigations

Learning objective: Learn that magnets can have different strengths.

Resources required: paper clips, a range of magnets – the more the better (e.g. bar magnets, ring magnets, wand magnets, fridge magnets, horseshoe magnets, toys with magnets attached to them). Such a range of magnets may take time to collect, although educational suppliers do sell sets. Without such a range, you can still do the investigation, but it will be more limited

Ask the children to make chains of *linked* paper clips. Chains of five, four, three, two are good to compare to each other. Ask them to devise a way to determine which magnets are the most powerful. They can do this by dragging ever longer links of paper clips along a desk with a magnet, or using a magnet to lift up ever longer chains.

Pupil activity 10.15

Testing the strength of magnets

Learning objective: To be able to quantify how strong a magnet is.

Resources required: button or ring magnets, A4 paper, magnetic notice board or steel table leg or PE climbing frame

We have all put leaflets on a fridge and held them in place with a fridge magnet. Sometimes they all end up on the floor because the force cannot penetrate them all and hold them to the fridge door. Accordingly, different strengths of magnets can be tested in this way. Ask the children to guess how many sheets (layers) of paper the magnet can hold. They need to add a sheet at a time to each magnet and see how many it can hold to the steel table leg or climbing frame.

Pupil investigation skills 10.16

Which materials are magnetic?

Learning objective: Learn which metals are magnetic.

Resources required: a range of shiny materials for younger children (see 'Common misconception' below)

A range of metals for older children; try a range of everyday metal things that are easily handled (coins, spoons, split pins, etc.). If you have a set of metal discs with the name of the metal on (often found in 'classifying materials' sets), add these to the mix.

Common misconception

'All metals are magnetic aren't they?'

There are age-related misconceptions about this. Younger children tend to think that any shiny, silver-coloured material is magnetic. Get them to predict and then test a range of materials, including baking foil pieces, pie dishes, 'foil' wrapping paper, silver-coloured card, and paper clips.

Older children often think that *all* metals are magnetic. A more subtle belief is that only silver-coloured metals are magnetic. Eventually, children learn that only some metals are magnetic – but they often can't remember which ones!

Ask the children to record their predictions about which objects are magnetic before they test them. Then, they can simply see if they are attracted to a magnet or not. The only magnetic items they will find will be of iron or steel. They might not know what all the metals are (and you might not be able to identify them either), but they will be confident once they have tested them to state which are magnetic and which are not.

Pupil investigation skills 10.17

Confusing 'copper' coins!

Learning objective: To understand why two-pence and one-pence coins can react differently to magnets.

Resources required: a range of two-pence and one-pence coins with varied dates, including old ones from the 1970s, 1980s, and 1990s; magnets

Ask the children to test the coins to determine which ones are magnetic and which are not. They can separate them into two piles, and make a note of the date for each coin. Ask them why some are magnetic and some are not.

Common misconception

'Copper coins are magnetic'

Older children frequently think copper is magnetic. A confusing fact is that some two-pence and one-pence coins are magnetic and some are not. Children often know that these coins are made of copper, so what is the explanation? Older coins contain a lot of copper, newer ones are merely copper-coated and are made of steel – hence they are magnetic.

Children often think that the newer copper coins are magnetic because they are shiny, and the older ones are not because they are dirty – however, a little experimentation can reveal the dirt layer makes no difference. To prove or disprove this idea, the children can 'clean up' the coins by leaving them in cola drink overnight. The acid in the cola will dissolve the dirt layer. The dirty solution must be thrown away and the coins washed carefully before they are retested. The Royal Mint started putting steel in the coins because copper has become very expensive and steel is cheaper! Since 2011 the Royal Mint has also started putting steel in five-pence and ten-pence coins, so these are magnetic too. Before that date, none of the silver colour coins were magnetic.

Pupil investigation skills 10.18

How can you tell a magnet from a magnetic material?

Learning objective: To understand the difference between a magnetic material and a magnet.

Resources required: magnets (include ones that don't 'look' like magnets – i.e. they don't have the poles marked – such as fridge magnets and button magnets), magnetic materials (iron, steel, new two-pence and one-pence coins, paper clips)

Can the children sort the magnets from the magnetic materials? The idea is that magnets can attract *and* repel each other. A magnet can *only* attract a magnetic material. Magnetic materials *neither* attract nor repel one another.

Pupil investigation skills 10.19

Does magnetic force go through different materials?

Learning objective: To understand that magnetic force can travel through thin solid materials.

Resources required: paper, fabrics, thin plastics, thin card, magnets, and paper clips

Ask the children to predict which materials the magnetic force will or will not go through. They can test their ideas by placing the magnet on one side of the test material and the paper clip on the other side. Can they move it around using the magnet? If they can, then they have shown that magnetic force goes through the material.

They will find that magnetic force goes through all thin materials, except those that contain iron and steel! The iron and steel direct the magnetic force around their structure, whereas other materials just let it go straight through.

Common misconception

'Magnetic forces can only travel through air'

It is a common misconception among children that magnetic force does not go through solid material. A good way to tackle this is to get them to try this out in the above investigation.

Pupil investigation skills 10.20

Does magnetic force go through water?

Learning objective: Learn that magnetic force can travel through liquids.

Resources required: paper clips, magnet tied to a piece of string, bowl of water

This investigation can be conducted as a quick and simple test. Set up magnetic fishing with a bowl of water. Ask the children to go 'fishing' for paper clips. Ask them to predict whether it will work or not. They should be able to 'fish' the clips out of the water.

> **Common misconception**
>
> **'Magnetic forces do not work in liquids'**
>
> A common misconception is that magnetic force does not work under water, but it does! The above is only a quick investigation and could be done as a demonstration.

Friction

For some of the following investigations, you will need to make some simple slopes. These can be simply a short plank of wood or a sheet of stiff card. Blocks or books can be stacked to different heights to raise or lower the slope at one end.

Figure 10.17 Wooden block sliding down a slope

Pupil investigation skills 10.21

Different shoe grips

Learning objective: Learn how shoe grips affect friction.

Resources required: a range of the children's footwear with different grips, a simple slope, some books or blocks to vary the height of the slope

Ask the children to predict which shoe 'grip' provides the most friction and which the least. Try increasing the steepness of the slope by raising one end. The height of the slope can be measured quite easily. As the height increases, the pupils should see how only shoes with the best grip (i.e. the most friction) stay on. A discussion about why different forms of footwear (e.g. hiking boots, school shoes, football boots, trainers, high heels) have different grips could follow.

Pupil investigation skills 10.22

Different slope surfaces

Learning objective: Understand how surfaces affect friction.

Resources required: one shoe, a simple slope, a range of surfaces (try newspaper, sandpaper, overhead projector transparencies)

Ask the pupils to modify a slope using a range of surfaces that are easily taped on to the slope. Ask the children to predict which surface will be the easiest for the shoe to remain on as the steepness of the slope is increased. Ask them about fair testing and why they should use the same shoe each time. This could lead to a discussion about, for example, wheelchair access ramps and what type of surfaces they should have.

Pupil investigation skills 10.23

Friction makes it harder to continue moving (pulling or pushing) an object

Learning objective: Learn how friction works against moving objects.

Resources required: flat surfaces to test (e.g. a table, the carpet, the hall floor, the playground, plus any surfaces you can make yourself such as strips of sandpaper stuck to the table), something to pull (old food tubs are ideal, but these need to be made fairly heavy for you to be able to make a reading on a force meter, so add heavy things such as masses [weights], stones or marbles), force meters, and string to attach to the food tubs

The children can predict which surfaces will experience the most friction (i.e. give the highest reading) before testing. They may notice that the force meter gives a slightly higher reading as the object begins to move, and then the reading is reduced as the object is pulled along. Objects often need a bit of extra force to get them moving (hence the jerk). It is easier for them to take the reading as the object is pulled along the surface. This could lead to a discussion about why we might prefer a surface with more friction. For example, playground surfaces are always rough so that even in wet weather the children won't fall over easily. They might also discuss where we would prefer a smooth surface (e.g. a dance hall or skating rink).

Pupil investigation skills 10.24

Friction makes things slow down: How far can a ball roll?

Learning objective: Learn that friction slows down moving objects.

Resources required: a ramp, cars or small balls, different long surfaces to put at the bottom of the ramp – the longer the better (playground, hall floors, wood floors, and carpeted areas are ideal)

Children can predict which of the flat surfaces will allow the moving object to travel the furthest. Using the same ramp at the same height each time (remind them about fair testing), they can measure how far the ball or car moves along the surface at the bottom of the ramp before stopping. Remind them again that the same ball or car needs to be used in all their experiments, and ask them why.

Pupil discussion 10.25

Which way does friction work?

Children find it hard to visualise that friction opposes the movement of an object, always working in the opposite direction to the object's movement. Discuss with the children which way it is working; use diagrams with arrows to emphasise the point. Ask them if they could feel the friction pulling against them as they dragged the heavy food tubs (in activity 10.23) across different surfaces. If friction worked in the same direction as the object was moving, then it would add to the force on the object and so speed it up; this clearly does not happen.

Pupil discussion 10.26

When is friction useful and when is it a nuisance?

Get the children to list instances when friction can be of use. They should be able to think of lots of ideas after doing the experiments above. Rough surfaces in the wet on the playground and roads, boots with large grips for bad weather, and handlebars of bikes are just a few examples. Children often think that friction is a 'bad' thing. This is because they are familiar with the ideas of things slowing down, but less familiar with the idea that friction is needed to hold on to something. Try the demonstration below for a fun way of showing this. Friction also causes things to wear down. Pupils should be able to think of instances such as brake blocks on bikes and cars and the bottoms of their shoes wearing out.

Teacher demonstration 10.27

Friction demonstration with jelly and chopsticks

Learning objective: Learn how liquids reduce friction.

Resources required: jelly cubes, chopsticks, cooking oil, paper plates

This is a good way of demonstrating how friction is required to move even everyday objects around. If we didn't have friction, the objects would slip out of our hands. Get a volunteer to move blocks of jelly from one plate to another using chopsticks. Then try putting vegetable oil over the jelly and get them to repeat the challenge!

Teacher demonstration 10.28

Does the surface area affect air resistance?

Learning objective: Learn how surface area affects air resistance.

Resources required: A4 paper

Air resistance can be very simply demonstrated with two pieces of A4 paper.

Ask a volunteer to crunch one into a ball and leave the other intact. Holding them at the same height, get the class to guess which one will hit the floor first. Using the same pieces of paper, get the volunteer to see how far he or she can throw each one. They will find it easy to throw the crunched-up one, showing that air resistance not only acts on falling objects.

Pupil activity 10.29

Speed affects air resistance

Learning objective: Learn that greater speeds increase air resistance.

Resources required: large piece of sugar paper or card

In the playground, ask two volunteers to hold a large piece of card or sugar paper, one either side of it, with it facing the direction they are walking in. When they walk with it, do they feel much air resistance? They could try jogging or running. As the speed increases, they should feel more air resistance and observers should see the card 'bow' more as the greater force hits it. Ask pupils how they could reduce the air resistance. Some may suggest cutting holes in the card. Others may think of turning the card so that it is edge-on before they run with it.

Pupil investigation skills 10.30

Parachute canopy size

Learning objective: Learn how surface area and air resistance are related.

Resources required: bin bags, string, paper clips or Plasticine™

Cut different-sized squares of plastic from thin (cheap!) bin bags. Attach a piece of string or cotton to each corner with a small piece of tape, and fasten these together in the middle. Add Plasticine™ or paper clips as weight in the middle. The only problem with this investigation is the dropping of the parachutes, as you will need a bit of height to see any differences. Health and safety requirements dictate that we cannot stand on chairs and desks to launch them. If you do not have a safe high point to launch them, you can try wrapping the string around them and throwing them up, but this takes a bit of practice to get them to open properly.

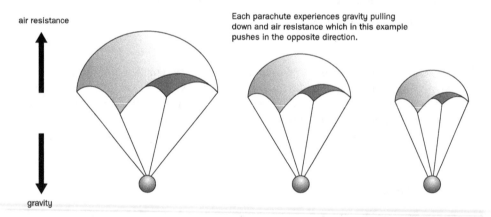

Figure 10.18 Parachutes carrying identical mass but different canopy size

Water resistance

Water resistance occurs whenever an object moves, in any direction, through water. It slows us down when we swim across a pool and when we dive under water. Ships have streamlined hulls to minimise the water resistance. Ask the children to do some research from books or the internet on how water resistance can be reduced. They should be able to find examples of streamlining in different objects and animals that enables water resistance to be minimised. They should be able to come up with adaptations by fish, sharks, and dolphins and comment on the design of boats, submarines, and hovercraft.

Teaching floating and sinking with weight and upthrust

The best way to teach floating and sinking is for pupils to be taught two concepts. First, things that are 'light for size' and 'heavy for size' is a good guide; for instance, things that are less dense than water float (e.g. a block of wood), but things that are more dense than water sink (e.g. a block of steel). If objects contain a lot of air they tend to float, as air is very light (less dense than water).

Second, they should look at the shape of objects. A piece of Plasticine™ can be made to float or sink, depending on its shape. A ball of it will sink, but if it is flattened out into a boat shape it should float (with a bit of patience). Boat shapes displace a lot of water, so creating a lot of upthrust force to counter their weight. It is also worth pointing out to the children that a boat contains a lot of air in its bottom bit, some of which is actually 'under the level of the water'. Ask them what would happen if they filled the boat with water. They might know that that would make it sink.

Common misconception

'Light things float, heavy things sink'

Children tend to think that 'light things float but heavy things sink'. As a rule of thumb, however, this will not explain that an ocean liner floats (which is very heavy) while pennies sink (which are not quite as heavy!).

Pupil activity 10.31

How many marbles are required to sink a boat

Learning objective: Learn that weight and upthrust work in opposite directions.

Resources required: Plasticine™ or foil, marbles, washing-up bowl or trays with water

A great idea is to challenge the children to see how many marbles their boats can hold! Boats can be made from Plasticine™ or from foil. The children need to take care in making their boats, as only certain shapes float. Shallow, flattish ones work well. They need to ensure that their boats are good floaters before they start to add any objects to them. Adding marbles is interesting because as the weight increases the boat will float 'lower down' in the bowl – that is, the water level rises up its hull. It displaces more water as the number of marbles increases (this will slightly increase the force of upthrust). Eventually, the weight of the marbles will be too great and the upthrust will be insufficient to counter it, and the boat will sink.

Common misconception

'Deeper water means better floating!'

Children often think that if an object is placed in deeper water-filled containers, there will be more chance of it floating because there is 'more water pushing on it'. This can be shown to be untrue quite easily. Providing a floating object can displace its own weight in water, it will float just as easily in any container. Similarly, a penny will sink in a cup of water and in a swimming pool – the depth makes no difference.

Upthrust in air

So far we have focused on upthrust in water, but there also is an upthrust force in air, albeit usually negligible on most objects. This could confuse some pupils, so perhaps save this for those who need to be challenged. Things that do use upthrust to float upwards in the air are hot air balloons and helium balloons. Both hot air and helium gas are less dense than cold air and therefore upthrust enables them to float.

Common misconception

'All inflated balloons will float upwards'

Younger children often think that all inflated balloons will float upwards, 'because they are so light'. They also believe the same about soap bubbles blown from a small hoop. Balloons and bubbles with cold air inside are similar to the air around them and so have insufficient upthrust. Gravity will pull them down to the ground!

Teacher demonstration 10.32

Upthrust in air and weight

Learning objective: Learn that upthrust can occur in air.

Resources required: a helium balloon, bread stick, thread

If released, a helium balloon will rise to the ceiling, but if something of a certain weight is tied to it, it can be made to stay still in mid-air. A breadstick (or piece of paper rolled up) can be attached to provide weight and bits taken off until its weight is just equal to the upthrust. The balloon will then remain stationary, 'suspended' in mid-air, as the forces acting on it are balanced.

Gravity and weight

Many children know that gravity is the force that 'pulls things down' here on Earth. Gravity pulls on all objects, but it does not pull all of them equally as hard. This is where the concept of weight as a force comes in. Different objects have different weights, because the gravitational attraction between them and the Earth differs. Generally, the more mass a thing has, the greater the gravitational attraction between it and the Earth, and the harder it is for us to lift up. Weight is a tricky concept for many children to understand and often it is only the older, higher achieving ones that will fully grasp it. If a pupil uses a force meter to lift a rock and notes the reading, they are measuring the rock's weight (in Newtons). Most children will be happy with the concept of gravity and how it works, but there are still plenty of misconceptions about it.

Common misconception

'Things just fall down. There's no force involved'

Young children often believe this, having observed things naturally 'falling down' for years. In contrast, they may accept that to make a ball go up in the air, you have to throw it, using a pushing force. Through discussion we can enable them to see that if something moves in a certain direction, a force must have started it moving in that direction (e.g. a toy car is pushed, a ball is kicked). This means things can't just 'fall down' of their own accord; a force must make them do it – gravity!

Pupil activity 10.33

Which way do things fall down?

Learning objective: Understand how gravity acts towards the centre of the Earth.

Resources required: paper and pencils

Children should be familiar with drawing different arrows to represent the directions forces work in. Ask them to draw a picture of the Earth with a giant standing at the North Pole. Ask them which way his trousers would fall if he was to take off his belt. They should answer that his trousers would fall 'down' towards the centre of the Earth. They should then draw the arrow pointing this way, indicating the direction in which gravity pulls.

Next, get them to draw the giant at the South Pole and draw an arrow to show which way his trousers would fall if he took them off this time. They should get the idea that the trousers again would move towards the centre of the Earth, but some may want to have them fall 'down' over his head towards the bottom of the picture! Children will often explain that gravity 'pulls things down'. The idea of it 'pulling things down towards the centre of the Earth' is more difficult for them to grasp. Often they mangle this sentence into 'gravity *comes* from the centre of the Earth'. It does not; it comes from the whole of the Earth, but always acts towards the centre.

A follow-up activity would be to draw a giant holding a ball at the North and South Poles and east and west along the equator and ask the pupils to draw which way the ball would fall when dropped in each case. Similarly, clouds with rain drawn at these four points can be very revealing. Some children will draw clouds that would appear to people on Earth to be sideways on, raining horizontally!

Teacher demonstration 10.34

Whack a rat! (Catch a falling object)

Learning objective: Learn that gravity can make things move very quickly.

Resources required: pencil or playing card

A popular summer fair attraction used to be 'Whack a rat', whereby a fluffy toy was dropped down a drainpipe and you had to hit it with a wooden bat as it came out the bottom of the pipe – very difficult! By the time you had seen the rat and swung the bat, it was halfway to the floor. This is because gravity pulls objects down very quickly (it actually accelerates them, which means it moves them ever faster moment by moment).

You can recreate this effect with a volunteer. Ask a pupil to hold their hand as if they are holding an invisible plant pot (so there is a good gap between their fingers). Now drop a pencil through the gap (point facing upwards). Don't warn them when you are about to let go. Many won't be able to catch the pencil, as gravity pulls it so fast! If they can catch the pencil as it moves through their fingers, try a playing card. Although our reactions are very fast, gravity can beat them quite easily, and often the pencil or card will not be caught.

Simple mechanisms: levers, gears and pulleys

A full explanation of how levers, gears and pulleys work is included in the 'What the teacher needs to know and understand' section at the beginning of this chapter.

Pupil activity 10.35

Levers make life easier

Learning objective: To know the names of different parts of a lever, and that a lever is a force multiplier.

Resources required: some actual examples of levers (e.g. scissors, tweezers, see-saw [made from a cork and a ruler]) and photographs of levers from an internet search (e.g. wheelbarrow, crowbar lifting a paving stone, screwdriver lifting a paint pot lid, hammer pulling up a nail, see-saw)

The teacher may demonstrate a simple lever to begin with, for example a model of a see-saw, by placing a cork flat on a table and resting a ruler on top. The teacher can point out the fulcrum (where the ruler pivots around the cork), arm (or rod) which is the long part that moves, and load (perhaps put a small block on the end of the ruler). The teacher can also demonstrate the effort force, by pushing on one end of the ruler, and raising the block on the other end.

Can the pupils label their photographs of levers, using the terms fulcrum, arm, load, and effort force? Likewise, can they put sticky notes with these four terms on the real objects? For some objects it is tricky and we have to see them in action, for example, a hammer pulling out a nail. If they spot the fulcrum first, this often reveals how the rest of the lever moves. Scissors are a pair of levers, and work best when the material being cut is closest to the central fulcrum. Challenge pupils to cut card using the ends of the scissors, away from the fulcrum. What do they notice? Ask them what would happen if the hammer, crowbar or screwdriver had smaller arms – would they be as easy to use?

Pupil activity 10.36

Gear wheels construction kit

Learning objective: To understand how gears can make each other move.

Resources required: gear construction kit (available from most school suppliers of science and design technology)

In this activity you can set the pupils a number of tasks, where they have to set up gears in differing states and observe what happens. Show some gears of different sizes, but don't reveal how this affects their speed of movement. Introduce the term 'driver gear' for the gear the pupils will turn and 'follower gears' for any of the rest of the gears used.

Ask the pupils to set up the following:

To find out about the directions in which gears turn,

- Instruct the pupils to put two gears of the same size together. Ask them to observe that if the driver gear turns clockwise, which way does the follower gear turn (they should see it goes anti-clockwise).
- If they add another follower gear connected to the first follower gear (so all three gears are lined up in a row) which way does the new gear turn (it should turn the same way as the driver gear).
- Can they work out a pattern for any number of gears as to which way the individual ones will turn?

To find out about the speed at which gears turn,

- Start with two gears of the same size. When the pupils turn the driver gear, does the follower gear turn at the same speed? (They should see that it does.)
- Introduce a small driver gear and a larger follower gear. If the driver gear rotates one turn, how far does the follower gear turn? (It should turn less than a full turn.)
- If the driver gear is large and the follower gear is small, if the driver gear does one complete turn, how many turns does the follower do? (It should do more than one turn.)
- Can the pupils work out their own 'law of gear speed' saying how fast gears will go, depending on the size of the driver and size of the follower?

Teacher demonstration 10.37

My bicycle has gear wheels

Learning objective: To observe and describe gear wheels connected by a chain.

Resources required: at least one bicycle

Ask pupils to observe the following moving parts of a bicycle: the pedals, pedal gear wheel, cycle wheel, chain and the small gear wheels at the back. Ask them what the chain does. Why is it oiled? Carefully turn the bicycle upside down so that it stands on the seat and handlebars. Point out that this could fall over and so everyone needs to stay at a safe distance. Ask one pupil to turn the pedals and another to describe the resulting movement of the gear wheels, chain, and cycle wheel. Allow others to repeat, ensuring that the pupils are clear about the effort required to turn the pedals, the direction, and speed of rotation of the parts (the larger pedal-driven gear will make the smaller follower gears rotate faster). Note that the back wheel of the cycle turns faster than the pedals. Can they explain why this is a benefit to the cyclist? Can they talk about times they have cycled and the effort required and the resulting movement of wheels and cycle?

If the pupils are examining a bicycle with multiple gear wheels, have them talk about which gears are the best for pedalling uphill, on the flat, and downhill. Can they link this to the size of the gear wheels? If a pupil rides the bicycle on the flat school yard, can they describe how it feels to pedal using the different gears?

Teacher demonstration 10.38

Pulleys and broom sticks

Learning objective: To understand how pulleys can reduce the force required to move a load.

Resources required: two broom handles, a length of rope about 8 metres long

Safety: First instruct the pupils taking part that they must stop pulling immediately if you tell them to. This is just to ensure that if anyone looks like they might fall over, you can stop the demonstration safely.

Ask two pupils to stand facing each other, 1 metre apart. Each pupil should hold a broom handle. The two broom handles should be parallel to each other and parallel with the floor. Tie a piece of rope around the middle of one broom handle, making sure to secure it in place with a good knot. Then pass the rope around the middle of the other broom handle. Have a third pupil hold the free part of the rope, and see if they can pull the other two pupils together (see Figure 10.19). They will not be able to – the two pupils holding the broom handles can easily keep them apart.

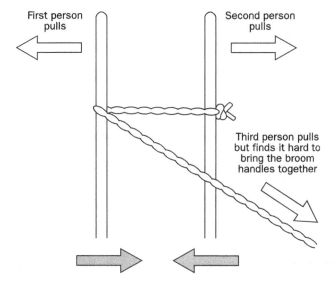

Figure 10.19 Two broom handles can easily be kept apart

Now wrap the rope four times around the broom handles (see Figure 10.20). Once again, the two pupils holding the broom handles need to try to keep them apart, while the person pulling the rope should try to pull them together. It should be much easier to bring the broom handles together this time!

The rope passes over the curved surface of the broom handles. Each wrap of the rope acts like a pulley, so by putting more wraps in we are effectively adding more pulleys. The third pupil can pull the broom handles together as by adding pulleys you are multiplying the effect of any force applied.

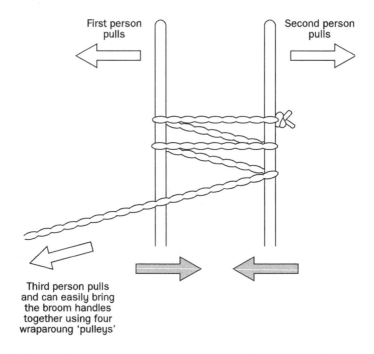

First person pulls

Second person pulls

Third person pulls and can easily bring the broom handles together using four wraparoung 'pulleys'

Figure 10.20 The addition of pulleys (rope wrapped four times around the broom handles)

Scientists and forces – Galileo Galilei and Isaac Newton

Galileo was one of the first true scientists, as he used observations and experiments to test his ideas to see if they were true or not. His most famous experiment involved dropping two balls made from the same material, one large and one small, from the Leaning Tower of Pisa. These would have differing amounts of mass and weight owing to their differing sizes. The idea was to see which one would fall the fastest, or if they would both reach the ground at the same time. Even today, most people believe that the larger ball with the most mass would fall the fastest, but this is not the case. They should both reach the ground at the same time because gravity will accelerate them both to the same extent. This is counter-intuitive, but true. Gravity might pull harder on the larger ball, but it can't pull it any faster downwards than it does the smaller ball.

The problem is that most people have seen something like a feather fall, and concluded that it falls slowly because it is light. However, it falls slowly because it has a large surface area and so has more air resistance. The barbs on the feather also increase the air resistance. This greater air resistance slows the descent of the feather, but fools us into thinking that gravity cannot pull the feather down quickly. If we got rid of all the air, and did an experiment in a vacuum, dropping a hammer and a feather, then they would both hit the ground at the same time. In fact this has been done by Apollo 15 astronaut David Scott on the Moon. The Moon has gravity, but no air and so no air resistance.

The clip for Scott's amazing experiment is on YouTube (just type in 'hammer and feather drop on the moon' or follow this link: http://www.youtube.com/watch?v=4mTsrRZEMwA

The story of Galileo and the Leaning Tower of Pisa comes to us from his pupil Vincenzo Viviani, who wrote a biography of Galileo and describes the experiment. We know that Galileo did similar experiments rolling steel balls of different sizes down slopes, but some historians disagree as to whether he ever dropped them from the Leaning Tower.

Isaac Newton told his friends that he saw an apple fall to the ground and wondered why it did not go 'sideways' or 'up'. He knew it always went downwards, as if pulled towards the centre of the Earth. This led him to develop a theory of gravity – an invisible force that operates over great distances. Small objects are attracted to larger ones by the gravitational force from the larger objects, so an apple is pulled down to the Earth. Just as the Earth's gravity holds the Moon in orbit around it, so the Sun's gravity holds the planets of the solar system in place as they go around it. Newton's mathematical calculations showed how this would work. The apple story comes to us from a long time ago in history, but historians agree that it is probably true.

http://www.bbc.co.uk/history/historic_figures/newton_isaac.shtml   (for   Isaac Newton).

Summary of key learning points:

- the unit in which forces are measured is the Newton (N);

- a force can change the shape or movement of an object;

- the larger the force, the larger the change can be;

- frictional forces can slow down moving objects;

- friction can occur when an object moves over a surface – the rougher the surface, the more friction the object experiences;

- friction can also help an object move, as when something provides a good grip;

- to keep something moving, a driving force is needed to overcome the friction the object is experiencing;

- air resistance and water resistance are both forms of friction;

- the mass of an object is the amount of matter in it – mass is measured in grams or kilograms and is not to be confused with weight, which is a force;

- gravitational attraction exists between very large bodies and smaller objects (e.g. the Earth attracts a dropped cup);

- gravity acts towards the centre of the Earth;

- the weight of an object is a force measured in Newtons, caused by the gravitational attraction between the Earth and the object – different objects have different weights;

- an object will have the same mass on the Earth and on the Moon because it contains the same amount of matter;

- an object will weigh more on the Earth than on the Moon because the Earth is more massive and so can exert a greater gravitational attraction than the Moon;

- balanced forces produce no change in the movement or shape of an object;

- when an object is stationary or moving at a steady speed in a straight line, the forces acting on it are balanced;

- unbalanced forces acting on an object can change its motion or its shape;

- magnets have poles – similar poles repel each other, whereas opposite poles attract each other;

- the pole that points northwards is the north-seeking pole;

- magnetism can act over a short distance, so magnets can exert forces on objects with which they are not in contact;

- pulleys, gears and levers can all be used to move heavy loads, by applying mechanical advantage.

Self-test

Question 1

Examples of friction include (a) a parachute falling through air, (b) a water skier being pulled over the surface of a lake, (c) a submarine moving at the bottom of the sea, (d) rubbing your hands together

Question 2

Gravity (a) does not exist in space, (b) pulls a falling pencil, (c) does not exist on the Moon, (d) does not exist on Venus

Question 3

Magnets (a) always have a North and South pole, (b) can only attract a magnetic material, never repel one, (c) do not work under water, (d) generate a magnetic field that can act through certain materials

Question 4

Unbalanced forces can make objects (a) slow down or speed up, (b) change shape, (c) stay still, (d) move at a steady speed

Self-test answers

Q1: All four are forms of friction. In (a), the air rubs against the parachute, causing air resistance, which is a form of friction. In (b), the friction is between the water skis and the water. There will also be air resistance between the water skier's body and the air as they are dragged along. In (c), a submarine rubs against the water as it moves and this form of friction is again water resistance. The submarine is streamlined to reduce the friction. In (d), the tiny indentations on the two surfaces of the hands catch against each other; the friction here will generate heat if the hands are rubbed fast enough.

Q2: Only (b) is true. The gravitational attraction between the Earth and the pencil will cause the dropped pencil to move downwards towards the centre of the Earth. Example (a) is false because gravity is able to travel through space. The Sun's gravity causes the Earth to orbit the Sun, in effect holding the Earth in place in the Solar System. Example (c) is false because the Moon has less gravity than the Earth, but it is a fairly massive object so it will pull things towards it. If there was no gravity on the Moon, then the astronauts would have floated away from it, instead of walking on it. Example (d) is false, since again Venus is fairly massive and so will pull smaller objects towards itself.

Q3: (a), (b), and (d) are true. Magnets always have a North and South pole, even if these are not coloured or marked. Even if a magnet were snapped in half, the two halves would still both have a North Pole and both have a South Pole. A magnetic material such as iron or steel can only be attracted. It could not repel a magnet, as only another magnet can do that. A magnet is a special kind of iron or steel that has been 'magnetised' – that is, it has undergone a special process to make it a magnet. Magnets are surrounded by a magnetic field, which means magnetic force can travel short distances through the air, and even through several sheets of paper, hence can hold paper onto a fridge door. Example (c) is false because the magnetic force can travel through water quite easily over short distances.

Q4: (a) and (b) are true. Balanced forces can keep an object moving at a steady speed, or prevent an object from moving at all. Whenever something is accelerating or decelerating, some of the forces acting on the object must be larger than others, causing this change to occur.

Misconceptions

'Round things just move by themselves'

'Dragging or lifting something uses the same amount of force'

'All metals are magnetic aren't they?'

'Copper coins are magnetic'

'Magnetic forces can only travel through air'

'Magnetic forces do not work in liquids'

'Light things float, heavy things sink'

'Deeper water means better floating!'

'All inflated balloons will float upwards'

'Things just fall down – there's no force involved'

Web resources

http://www.bbc.co.uk/learningzone/clips/forces-in-action-no-narration/1601.html
(general friction)

http://www.bbc.co.uk/learningzone/clips/how-different-surfaces-affect-the-frictional-force/273.html
(friction)

http://www.dtonline.org
(an excellent website summarising how levers, pulleys and gears work; click through to the 'mechanisms' page)

http://www.enchantedlearning.com/physics/machines/Levers.shtml
(An excellent webpage takes you through how all three types of levers work)

http://www.kidsinglish.com/
(Peter Weatherall's website of science songs and simple explanation videos)

http://www.primaryresources.co.uk/science/science4b.htm
(BBC learning zone)

http://www.youtube.com/watch?v=yfAdmRJDKlc
(A good video clip that introduces simple pulleys, and a bit of maths – nothing too scary)

11

The Earth in space

About this chapter

This chapter deals with the science you need to know and understand about the Earth in space. It includes aspects about the Earth and the Moon such as how they move in relation to one another and how they relate in space to the Sun and other components of the Solar System. It will tell you about our galaxy (the Milky Way) and its place in the universe. You will find clear explanations of the causes of day and night, the length of the year, the seasons, eclipses, and the phases of the Moon. The second part of the chapter addresses what pupils need to learn. The final section will provide you with very effective ways to teach about the Earth in space, including common misconceptions.

What the teacher needs to know and understand

Resources required: a torch, a medium-sized ball, a small ball

Earth is a planet which orbits the Sun as part of our Solar System

As a primary teacher, you will need to know basic facts about the Earth and space and understand how, for example, the Earth and the Moon move in relation to the Sun and the other large bodies (mainly planets and moons) in the Solar System.

Each of the planets is held in orbit around our nearest star, the Sun. They are held in orbit by the Sun's strong gravitational force. We say that their orbits around the Sun trace out a circle, but this is a slight simplification, as the orbits are elliptical (i.e. a slightly squashed circle). In the discussions and models we use in this chapter, we will continue to say that the planets have circular orbits, as this is an acceptable simplification that most other books adopt. The planets vary in composition and size. All are almost spherical in shape. The four inner ones – Mercury, Venus, Earth, and Mars – are relatively small and rocky. The next four – Jupiter, Saturn, Uranus, and Neptune – are gas giants; the last is Pluto, which is very small and icy. They all travel in an anticlockwise direction around the Sun (if viewed from above). However, the durations of their orbits around the Sun are different. As you will see in Figure 11.1, Mercury is closest to the Sun and so completes an orbit of the Sun in just 88 Earth days. Pluto, now designated a dwarf planet by some scientists, but still referred to as a planet by many, is so far from the Sun that one orbit takes around 248 Earth years! New dwarf planets are expected to be discovered over time. In 2005 astronomers discovered Eris, a dwarf planet beyond Pluto. You are of course very familiar with the orbit of the third planet from the Sun – this is our planet, Earth, which takes 365¼ days to orbit the Sun.

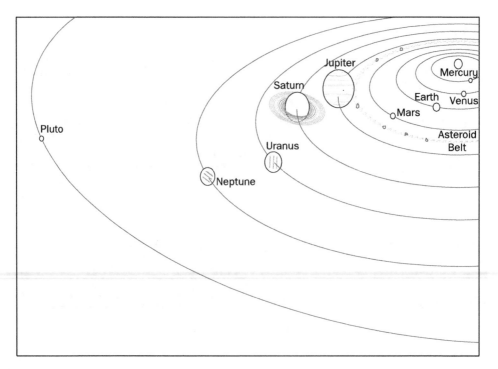

Figure 11.1 Eight planets and Pluto (dwarf planet) orbit our Sun to make up our Solar System

Light

All the planets rotate or spin on their axis but at different speeds. The Earth, like several of the planets, spins anticlockwise (Venus, Uranus, and Pluto spin clockwise) and does so once every 24 hours. We see evidence of planet Earth's spinning in the daily cycle of light and dark, which gives us day and night. As the Earth spins, the Sun appears to travel across our sky.

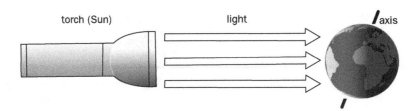

Figure 11.2 Simulating day and night on Earth

The Moon and how it orbits the Earth

Several of the planets are orbited by one or more moons. Jupiter has more than 16 moons (and recently over 20 more were discovered), whereas the Earth has only one. The Earth's Moon orbits the Earth in an anticlockwise direction approximately once every 28 days. The Moon is relatively close to Earth and so is affected by the Earth's gravitational attraction. The Moon only spins once on its axis every time it orbits the Earth, so the same face of the Moon always points towards the Earth. This means that from the Earth we can never see the other side of the Moon. To show that you under-stand the Moon's movement, model it by using a ball as the Earth and a smaller ball as the Moon. Make a small mark on one side of the 'Moon'. Now hold the small ball in orbit (travelling in a circle around the 'Earth') so that the mark always faces the 'Earth'. This means that it takes the same time for the Moon to orbit the Earth as it does for one spin of the Moon. This is tricky so take your time, repeat it so that you can say what is happening at each point of the orbit. Even better, explain it to a friend. The difficulty people have with this is that they don't understand that the Moon has completed one turn on its axis as it completes the orbit, because the spin is so slow. By the time the Moon has gone halfway around the Earth, it will only have completed half a turn on its axis. It only completes the full turn when it has completed a full orbit of the Earth.

The phases of the Moon (or why the Moon appears to change shape!)

The Moon does not always appear as a bright round disc (known as a full Moon as seen at point 5 on Figure 11.4) in the night sky. At different points of its 28-day orbit of the Earth, we see different Moon shapes or 'phases'. This is because we on Earth view the Moon from different angles on different nights as the Moon orbits the Earth. This effect can be simulated with a torch and a ball in a darkened room. If you keep the torch and ball fixed as in Figure 11.3 (the torch is the 'Sun' and the ball the 'Moon'), and imagine your head to be the Earth, by moving your head to different positions you can see a crescent, half, and full Moon.

Read this paragraph keeping one eye on the text and the other on Figure 11.4. The cycle starts on the first night (1) when earthbound observers would not see anything as the side of the Moon facing Earth is not illuminated. Seven nights later we are one-quarter way through the Moon's orbit (3) and so we see half of the Moon illuminated – the Moon is waxing. After about 14 nights (5), viewed from Earth the Moon is full – it appears in the sky as a fully illuminated disc. We then move into the second half of the

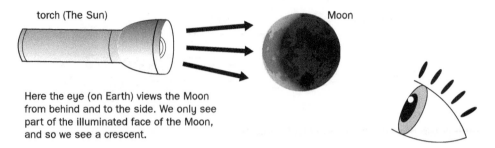

torch (The Sun)   Moon

Here the eye (on Earth) views the Moon
from behind and to the side. We only see
part of the illuminated face of the Moon,
and so we see a crescent.

Figure 11.3 Demonstration of how we view the Moon from Earth

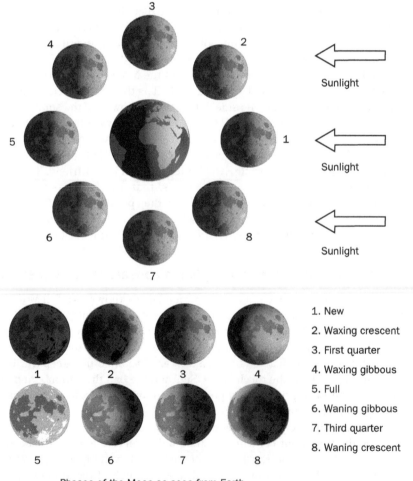

Sunlight

Sunlight

Sunlight

1. New
2. Waxing crescent
3. First quarter
4. Waxing gibbous
5. Full
6. Waning gibbous
7. Third quarter
8. Waning crescent

Phases of the Moon as seen from Earth

Figure 11.4 Eight stages in the phases of the Moon

cycle and the Moon appears to shrink or wane night by night. The Moon wanes through nights 15–20 until it reaches the three-quarter orbit mark at about 21 nights (7) (another half moon) and then progresses to the completion of the orbit and another New Moon.

The presence of the Moon and the turning of the Earth cause the ocean tides

The Earth itself is influenced by the Moon. For example, every 24 hours each of the large oceans on Earth is on the side closest to the Moon. At this point, the middle of the ocean is raised or pulled towards the Moon by the Moon's gravity. There is a corresponding bulge in the waters on the opposite side of the Earth at the same time. This gives us two high tides within a 24-hour period. Without the Moon we would not have high and low tides, and would not therefore see the sea recede on the shoreline as part of the daily rhythm of the tides.

Eclipses are caused by the relative movement of the Earth, the Moon, and the Sun

Most people will not experience a complete solar eclipse; however, these are more common than you think. In Figure 11.5 the Moon reaches a point where it passes between the Sun and the Earth. At this point, the shadow cast by the Moon falls on the Earth's surface. As the shadow is quite small and it often falls on the ocean, it is not often observed by large populations of people. If people were in the shadow, they would not be able to see the Sun as the Moon moves in front of it, creating the solar eclipse. It is merely a coincidence that the Moon is just the right size to cover the Sun so perfectly. On Earth, we would see the dark disc of the Moon and a halo around the Sun at full eclipse. As the Moon moves away, the Sun comes slowly back into view.

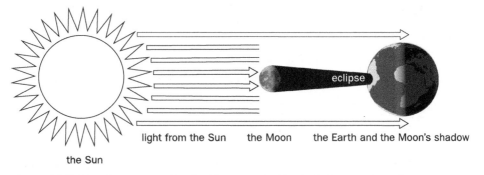

light from the Sun   the Moon   the Earth and the Moon's shadow

the Sun

Figure 11.5 The shadow cast by the Moon on the Earth during a solar eclipse

A useful internet simulation of a solar eclipse is available at:

http://www.pbslearningmedia.org/resource/ess05.sci.ess.eiu.totaleclipse/total-solar-eclipse-animation/

The Earth orbits the Sun every 365¼ days. As is evident by looking at a globe, the Earth spins but is tilted slightly (by 23.45°). This tilting has an important effect as the Earth orbits the Sun, since it is responsible for the seasons on Earth (see Figure 11.6).

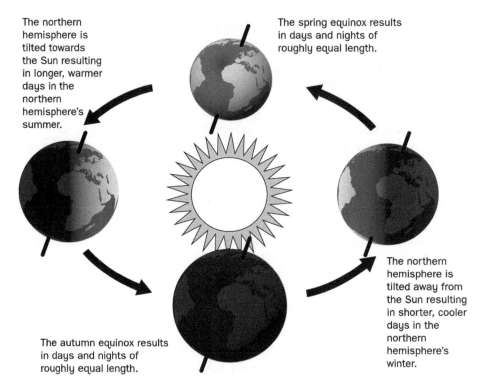

The northern hemisphere is tilted towards the Sun resulting in longer, warmer days in the northern hemisphere's summer.

The spring equinox results in days and nights of roughly equal length.

The northern hemisphere is tilted away from the Sun resulting in shorter, cooler days in the northern hemisphere's winter.

The autumn equinox results in days and nights of roughly equal length.

Figure 11.6 The orientation of the Earth at the four seasons (not drawn to scale)

A number of web-based simulations will assist you, including the following:

http://astro.unl.edu/classaction/animations/coordsmotion/eclipticsimulator.swf

When it is summer in Britain, the northern hemisphere is tilted towards the Sun. (See how much more sunlight falls on the northern hemisphere than on the southern hemisphere in summer in Figure 11.6.) The Sun appears in the sky for longer each day, so Britain has longer days and shorter nights. During summer, the Sun appears higher in the sky and so the rays of sunlight hit the northern hemisphere of Earth more directly and the temperature is therefore higher. Note that in this position the North Pole is in sunlight 24 hours a day. In winter, the northern hemisphere is tilted away from the Sun. In Britain, the Sun appears lower in the sky and for less time each day, giving us colder, shorter days and longer nights. The light rays that hit the northern hemisphere are not as direct as in summer, spreading out over larger areas, and so the light is weaker and produces long winter shadows. The North Pole is in darkness 24 hours a day (again refer to Figure 11.6).

To model this and confirm your understanding, use two balls (one large, one small). The larger 'Sun' ball stays still in this demonstration with the smaller 'Earth' ball orbiting in a circle around it. Hold the Earth to the right of the Sun and tilt it away from the Sun (towards the wall on your right). In this position as the northern hemisphere is tilted away from the Sun, it is winter in this hemisphere, days are shorter, and the Sun appears lower in the sky. Now move the Earth around the Sun tracing out a circular path in an anticlockwise direction, keeping the tilt constant (towards that same wall). After one-quarter of an orbit, three months have gone by and we reach the spring equinox. Continue this anticlockwise orbit so that another three months later the Earth is to the left of the Sun. The northern hemisphere is tilted towards the Sun and it is summer. Trace out a further quarter of an anticlockwise circle in the Earth's orbit and this brings us to the autumn equinox. We have now travelled three-quarters of the way around the Sun in our circular orbit. Another three months pass as we trace the final quarter of our circle to reach the winter position again, where we started from. We have completed one full orbit of the Earth around the Sun, taking a year to do so.

See the web-based simulation mentioned above and other explanations, such as that found at:

http://www.morehead.unc.edu/Shows/EMS/seasons.htm

Asteroids, meteorites, and comets

As a teacher, you ought to know that there are other objects observed in our Solar System. You don't need to know a great deal about them but as pupils might ask or might be intrigued by their existence, you may find this interesting and useful. People often confuse asteroids and meteorites. The asteroids are thousands of rocks orbiting the Sun in a belt between Mars and Jupiter (see Figure 11.1). Some are the size of large boulders, others the size of Mount Everest! One, named Ida, has recently been observed to have its own tiny moon.

Meteorites are rocks from outer space and are usually very small. Most are only the size of a speck of dust, rarer larger ones could be as big as a plum. We see them in the night sky as they very quickly burn up as they enter the Earth's atmosphere. Most never make it to the Earth's surface; some larger ones do and are occasionally found. Meteorites are often incorrectly called shooting stars. There is no such thing as a shooting star. Meteorites flash across the night sky and look as bright as the stars and this is where this inaccurate term comes from. The brightness is caused by frictional effects of the meteorite rubbing against the Earth's atmosphere and burning up. The visible stars in the night sky are mostly massive balls of burning gas and display no apparent movement when observed with the naked eye.

Forces

Comets are made of rock, ice, and gas and survive for many thousands of years. They travel around our Sun in huge elliptical orbits. They can leave the Solar System for many years but as they return and get close to the Sun they warm up, glow, and become visible in the night sky. They appear in the sky for several nights, appearing to move slowly against the background of stars, before they slowly fade. The most famous is Halley's Comet, which appears every 75 years or so and last appeared in 1986.

Find out more about comets at:

http://www.bbc.co.uk/science/space/solarsystem/other_solar_system_bodies/comet

Our Solar System in the Universe

Maths

Finally, as a teacher you need to understand that the Solar System, although large in human terms, is part of something much bigger. Our star, the Sun, is 93 million miles from Earth. The next nearest star is Proxima Centauri and is 4.24 light years away (1 light year is about 5900 billion miles). We are in a region of space that is rather short of stars because we are at the edge of a very large cluster of stars (known as a spiral galaxy). We call our galaxy the Milky Way and it is made up of around 100 billion stars. We can see the Milky Way when we look at the night sky, if we are well away from city lights. It is observed as a milky band across the night sky made up of millions of tiny (very distant) stars. The galaxy appears like this to us because we are looking at it edge-on. Scientists have estimated that in the Universe there are at least 100 billion galaxies. The Universe is everything – all the space, galaxies, and everything within them, including us.

When we view the stars at night from Earth we see constellations such as the Plough and Orion, which are patterns of stars that humans have perceived in the night sky. They are quite artificial but help observers recognise and talk about specific stars. The reason they are artificial is that the stars in a constellation are not actually anywhere near each other in three-dimensional space. When early people looked at the stars they imagined them all at the same distance and so made two-dimensional patterns with ones that appeared to lie near each other.

What pupils need to know at Key Stage 1

This topic is not referred to by the National Curriculum at Key Stage 1.

What pupils need to know at Key Stage 2

(ST) denotes statutory requirements.

Upper Key Stage 2

(ST) Describe the Sun, Earth, and Moon as approximately spherical bodies

(ST) Use the idea of the Earth's rotation to explain day and night and the apparent movement of the sun across the sky

Suggestions for working scientifically:

> Compare the time of day at different places on the Earth through internet links and direct communication.
>
> Construct simple shadow clocks and sundials, calibrated to show midday and the start and end of the school day.
>
> Find out about how structures such as Stonehenge might have been used as astronomical clocks.

(ST) Describe the movement of the Moon relative to the Earth

Suggestons for working scientifically:

> Understand that a Moon is a celestial body that orbits a planet (Earth has one moon; Jupiter has four large moons and numerous smaller ones).

(ST) Describe the movement of the Earth, and other planets, relative to the Sun in the solar system

Suggestions for working scientifically:

> Create simple models of the solar system, featuring the Sun and its eight planets: Mercury, Venus, Earth, Mars, Jupiter, Saturn, Uranus and Neptune (Pluto was reclassified as a 'dwarf planet' in 2006).
>
> Find out about the way that ideas about the solar system have developed, understanding how the geocentric model of the solar system gave way to the heliocentric model by considering the work of scientists such as Ptolemy, Alhazen, and Copernicus.

Ways to teach 'Earth in space' at Key Stage 2

Stellar bodies and movement

'Stellar bodies' is a term that relates to anything out in the universe, be it a comet or a planet. Here we discuss activities to help pupils understand the relative size of the bodies and to distinguish the tricky terms of how they move (e.g. the difference between spin and orbit).

Pupil activity 11.1

Space words

Literacy

Learning objective: Learn to recognise and use the vocabulary of space. Learn about the relative sizes of objects in space.

Resources required: none

Find out what the pupils know and get them talking about and using space words by providing them with the following set of words (or an edited set to suit your class). Ask them to put them in order from the largest to the smallest.

asteroid   moon   galaxy
                          meteorite
star   planet   universe
            comet   solar system

Literacy

The correct order is (though sizes vary!) from biggest to smallest: universe, galaxy, solar system, star, planet, moon, asteroid, comet, meteorite.

Extend this activity by constructing a class glossary of space.

Common misconception

'Is it spinning or orbiting?'

Terms describing the movement of stellar bodies are often confused by children. Terms such as 'spin', 'orbit', and 'rotate' are often used incorrectly. As a teacher, it will be important to use them correctly. The modelling of science language is a powerful teaching technique. An orbit is the circular path that a planet traces out as it goes around the Sun. Similarly, the Moon orbits the Earth. Planets and moons may also rotate or spin on their own axis as they complete their orbits. It is the spin of the Earth (its rotation on its axis) that gives us night and day and its orbit around the Sun is connected with the seasons.

Pupil activity 11.2

Make a glossary

Learning objective: Learn to recognise, use, and know the vocabulary of space.

Resources required: pupils' science books; classroom poster

You can make a class space glossary as a poster and/or ask each pupil to make a glossary at the back of their science book. Include the words from the activity above as well as size, shape, and orientation terms, including massive, sphere, orbit, and rotate. If you have class web pages, the glossary might be included.

Sun, Earth, and Moon
Teacher demonstration 11.3

The size and shape of the Sun, Earth, and Moon

Learning objective: To understand the shape and relative size of the Sun, Earth, and Moon, and the distances between them.

Resources required: beach ball, super bounce ball, tennis ball, football, dry peas, small beads

Many pupils will know that the Sun, Earth, and Moon are shaped like a ball or sphere. Diagrams in books do not show the true difference in size or the distances that these bodies are from each other. Show the pupils a beach ball and tell them this represents the Sun. Ask them to vote for which sphere would be the correct size for the Earth. You may want to show a tennis ball, football, super bounce ball, pea, bead, and so on (as outlined in the resources above). After the vote, reveal that the pea is the correct one! Ask them to vote again for which size the Moon would be. Many of them may know that the Moon is smaller than the Earth and choose the bead. If you haven't got a small enough bead, just use Plasticine™.

Your pupils may be amazed to know that using the scale of beach ball 'Sun' and pea 'Earth', the actual distance would be about 32 metres from the beach ball to the pea! You may like to measure this out in the playground with them. It is small wonder that the diagrams we use in books are so misleading. The Sun is always drawn too small and much too close to the Earth! With the space constraint within a book or internet simulation, we have to live with this inaccuracy, but do discuss it with the pupils.

Pupil activity 11.4

Making models or 'orreries' to show the movements of the Earth and Moon

Learning objective: Learn about the relative movement of the Sun, Earth, and Moon.

Resources required: paper or card, dowelling, wooden discs, wood strip, wire

Pupils can demonstrate and develop their learning by making moving pictures with card or paper to show, for example, the Earth orbiting the Sun (a template is provided for you and your pupils at the end of the book). Three-dimensional models of the planets and moons are called 'orreries'. Schools often purchase these, but pupils can make their own from balls and dowelling. You ought to point out that the size of the spheres and distances are not to scale (see last activity) but that the model helps us to understand the movements of the Sun, Earth, and Moon and therefore is valuable.

The paper orrery (Appendix 1) is quicker to make and assists learning in that it shows the relative movement of the Earth, Sun, and Moon. It requires pupils to cut out the various circles, use split pins to allow the various orbits and to orientate the parts. It will almost certainly help to make one beforehand with the three smaller circles coloured yellow, blue, and grey for the Sun, Earth, and Moon. Directions for a three-dimensional orrery are given in Appendix 2.

Teacher demonstration 11.5

Day and night

Learning objective: Learn that it is the Earth's rotation on its axis that causes day and night.

Resources required: overhead projector or powerful torch, globe, darkened room

Pupils are often confused about how day and night occur. The way we define a day length can be difficult for them too. We might say that a day is 24 hours, but in this definition we include the night as well. Children may think that a day is 12 hours long, and a night is 12 hours long. Day length is also affected by the seasons.

In this demonstration, the overhead projector or powerful torch is used to represent the Sun. It must not move its position at all. Switch on the light so as to illuminate one side of the globe. Ask the pupils which they think the day side is. Ask them which they think the night side is. It might be helpful to place a blob of sticky tack over Britain. Have Britain on the day side and then begin to slowly turn the globe anti-clockwise. Ask the children what is happening. How would the Sun appear in the sky if they were standing on the globe? They can watch as Britain goes into the night side. With a little thought they may be able to identify midday (when Britain is facing directly at the Sun), dusk (as it moves into the dark side), and dawn (as it moves into the light side). Ask them about people in other countries, for example Australia, and explain to them how their day time is our night time.

Common misconceptions

'The Sun moves, not the Earth'

The pupils may think the Sun is moving because it appears to move across the sky. The Earth does not feel as if it is moving, so the pupils may think that the Earth is still.

The above demonstration will go some way to counter this, but much class discussion will be needed. Our language is geared towards the idea of a moving Sun. We use words like sunrise and sunset, which imply movement. We talk about the Sun 'being at its highest point at midday'. We say 'The Sun comes up at 6 o'clock in the morning' and not 'The Earth rotates around to such a point that its horizon no longer covers the Sun, at 6 o'clock in the morning'. Share this problem with the children so that they understand what language can do, and that other people will perhaps hold an incorrect view.

'The Sun goes to bed at night!'

Some younger pupils believe the Sun goes to bed at night or that it goes wherever it seems to disappear. So if it appears to drop behind the local library, they will say that is where it is all night. Related to this is the common assumption that the Sun goes around the Earth. The Sun appears to move across the sky, so therefore they think it just continues on its journey at night and comes around the other side in the morning. By discussion, demonstrations, and internet simulations these ideas can be tackled.

Pupil activity 11.6

What time of day or night is it elsewhere in the world?

Learning objective: To understand that at any given moment different countries and cities experience different times of the day and night to us.

Resources required: internet access to view various webcams from around the world

Have the pupils predict what time of day it is now in various world cities. Ask them to predict if it is light or dark, or near dawn or dusk. They can check their ideas by viewing webcams and looking at the official times for each of the cities. Here are a few suggestions.

http://www.sydney-webcam.com/index.php?nav=cam1 Sydney, Australia

http://www.earthcam.com/usa/newyork/timessquare/ Times Square, New York, USA

http://ipy.org/images/webcams/index.php Antartica, British Antarctic Survey posts

Pupil investigation 11.7

Changes we see in shadows caused by the Sun's light

Learning objective: Exploring how shadows change during the day.

Resources required: shadow sticks (see below)

Light

Before any of these activities are carried out, a warning should be given about the dangers of looking directly at the Sun. As the Sun appears to move across the sky during the day, so the shadows it casts shift their position and length. A simple investigation can be set up to show this using basic shadow sticks. Three possible shadow sticks to use outside are:

Maths

1   A shadow stick can be fashioned out of a pencil standing on a blob of play clay, placed in the middle of a piece of white card. The changing position and length of the shadow can be drawn around each hour.

2   A 'rounders' post in the playground makes an excellent shadow stick for a big demonstration.

3   Children working in pairs, one can stand up straight on a marked spot; the other can draw around the child's shadow.

In each case, repeat every hour or half hour.

After the children have decided on how the shadow will be cast, they can make observations before lunch. Can they then predict:

*   where the shadow will fall in the afternoon (make the prediction in, say, blue chalk);
*   whether it will be longer, shorter or the same as their previous readings.

The Sun is south of the stick behind the observer

Figure 11.7 A pattern of lines showing the position of shadows during a day

Simulations can be found on websites such as that illustrated in Figure 11.8.

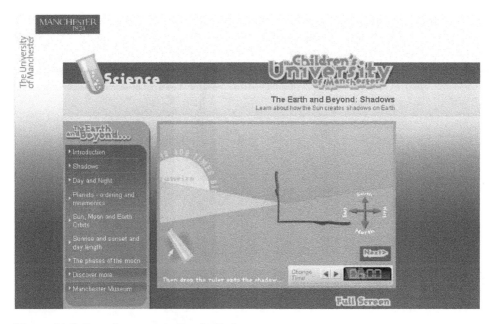

Figure 11.8 Page from a website simulation
Source: http://www.childrensuniversity.manchester.ac.uk

Pupil activity 11.8

Why does the length of the shadow change?

Learning objective: Learn to describe how the Sun moves across the sky.

Resources required: torches, pencils, play clay

Children can mimic the effect they observed in the previous investigation in the playground by setting up their pencil shadow stick on a table in the classroom. Using the edge of the desk as the horizon, they can use a torch as the Sun and make it rise up in an arc and set in a long arc. Looking at the shadow cast, they should be able to note the long and short shadows, and change in relative position. Once again they can note that the 'Sun' is always behind the stick and the shadow in front, just like in the playground.

In the above demonstration, we are in danger of reinforcing a misconception! The idea of the apparently moving Sun is wrong but it is hard to get away from. If we moved the stick instead, would that help? Maybe, but that is not what the children observed outside. Moving the desk (as the Earth) in a convincing but strictly accurate way is out of the question, but it's worth discussing these points with the children. An alternative is to stick an upright matchstick using play clay on to Great Britain on a globe. Hold a torch still as the Sun. Pupils can see the shadow length change as they rotate the globe from west to east. Just after sunrise, the shadow should be long. Can they see it shorten during the morning and lengthen towards dusk?

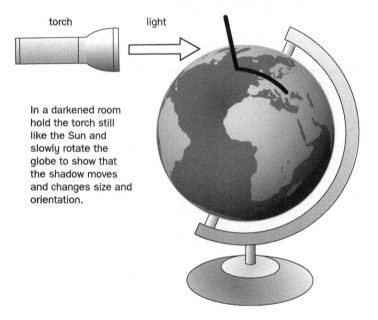

In a darkened room hold the torch still like the Sun and slowly rotate the globe to show that the shadow moves and changes size and orientation.

Figure 11.9 Torch and stick simulate a shadow stick on a globe

Pupil activity 11.9

Make a sundial

Learning objective: To understand how sundials are constructed and used to tell the time.

Resources required: polystyrene cup, pencil, scissors, tape, card, stones or sand, compass to show North

The pupils can build their own portable sundial if they follow these instructions. (See Figure 11.10 for a photograph of the completed sundial.) To make the face of the sundial draw around the mouth of the cup on a piece of card. Draw four small flaps on the outside of the card circle, to help anchor the face in place later. Cut around the circle and flaps. Cut a small hole in the centre of the circle.

Pour some stones or sand into the base of the cup, so that the cup is stable and won't be blown over. Cut a small hole in the side of the cup, about 4 cm from the top. Take a pencil and place it through the centre of the card circle. Push the angled pencil through the hole in the cup, so that the pencil sits at an angle. This will be the gnomon,

Figure 11.10 Sundial – picture was taken at 10am, with the gnomon pointing North

the part of the sundial that creates the shadow. Secure the card face flaps in place with tape. Tape the gnomon if it seems loose.

On a sunny day place the sundial on the ground. Use the compass to find North and point the top part of the gnomon pencil that way.

Challenge the pupils to make three initial readings – at the start of the school day, midday, and end of the school day – and mark these accordingly. When they have finished, can they estimate (in pencil) the intervening hours? On the next available sunny day have them check their predictions and put the final hourly marks for their sundial in place.

Year length and the seasons

Teacher demonstration 11.10

Why is a year 365 days long?

Learning objective: Understand that a year is the time taken for the Earth to complete one orbit of the Sun.

Resources required: beach ball, globe, large space to work in

Have a pupil hold the beach ball, which represents the Sun. Explain that they must not move. A second pupil moves the Earth (globe) around the Sun, tracing a circular path, moving in an anticlockwise direction. When they have completed a complete orbit, ask the pupils how long that would take in reality. Hopefully they know that it would take a year, or 365¼ days to be precise.

Repeat the demonstration, but this time split the orbit into quarters. Beginning in the summer (for Britain), have the pupil holding the Earth trace out a quarter of the circular path around the Sun before pausing. Ask the class what season it would be now, three months later. It would be autumn. Have them trace a further quarter of the orbit. Six months would have now passed and the class should be able to work out that the season would now be winter. Similarly, move on a further three months, pointing out that the Earth had completed three-quarters of the orbit, to reach spring, nine months on from the starting point. Finally, return to its summer position, asking them how long it took to do one complete orbit.

More able pupils may know that a year is actually 365¼ days. Ask them why we have a leap year, and how often they occur. Ask them what would happen if we just stuck to 365 days and never had a leap year. They may know that our calendar would eventually fall behind the orbit of the Earth around the Sun, and our annual celebrations could end up occurring in the wrong seasons!

Common misconception

'It's hotter in the summer because we are closer to the Sun'

It is very common for children to think that we experience seasons because of the Earth's changing distance from the Sun (closer in the summer, further away in the winter). A discussion of this will quickly show that this idea is wrong. Many children know that our winter is Australia's summer, and that Australians are famous for having Christmas on the beach. If the Earth were further away from the Sun in our winter, then how can it be summer in Australia at the same time?

It is the angle of tilt of the Earth that gives us our seasons. Explain to the children that if there was no tilt, then there would be no seasons. The tilt affects the amount of time the Sun spends in our sky each day, and how directly its rays strike the Earth. The following activities may help.

Pupil activity 11.11

Draw the relative path of the Sun for each season

Learning objective: Learn that the Sun follows the path of an arc through the sky, climbing higher in summer than in winter.

Resources required: books on space and/or access to the internet

Pupils will need to do some research using books or the internet to find the relative path of the Sun across the sky in the four seasons. Some books may show the path for each season. Have the pupils summarise this idea in a series of diagrams. They should draw a view from the same window for each season, with the Sun tracing a higher and larger arc in the summer than in the winter. More able pupils may be able to draw it on a month-by-month basis.

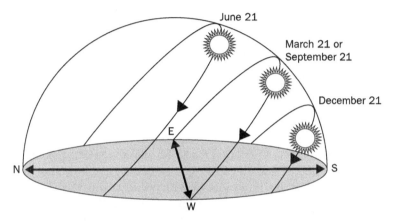

Figure 11.11 The path of the Sun in relation to the seasons

Pupil activity 11.12

Shadows in summer and winter

Learning objective: Understand how the Sun's apparent height in the sky affects the length of shadows in different seasons.

Resources required: shadow sticks, torches, chalk, paper (see the two shadow stick activities, 11.7 and 11.8, earlier in this chapter)

Ask the pupils to set up their simple shadow sticks on their desks, in a darkened room. Once again a torch will play the part of the Sun. The pupils should be able to mimic the effect of a low winter Sun casting long shadows on their desk-bound shadow stick. They can do this by moving the torch in a low arc for winter, noting the length of the shadows. Challenge them to mimic the summer Sun's apparent movement – this should be a larger arc, with the Sun rising up much higher in the 'sky'. Ask them to predict if the shadows will be longer or shorter than in summer. Can they then work out what the shadows will be like in autumn and spring, by tracing the appropriate path of the Sun? Get them to draw their shadow sticks, shadows, and Sun for each of the four seasons.

Can the pupils see that when they mimic the Sun's position in the sky for summer, the light falling on the desk is brighter and concentrated in a smaller area? Similarly, when they place the torch for the winter Sun, they should see that the light is very spread out over the desk and is much dimmer.

Pupil activity 11.13

Internet research on prehistoric monuments as 'calendars'

Learning objective: to understand how prehistoric monuments were aligned for certain annual events.

Resources required: internet access

The prehistoric monuments of Stonehenge in England, Maes Howe in Scotland and Newgrange in Ireland have features that mark the winter solstice, the latter two being very obvious (see below). The winter solstice, 21st December, is the shortest day of the year, when, at midday, the Sun reaches its lowest point for the whole year. The people that built these monuments were the first farmers in the British Isles, and knowing when the shortest day was would have been important information. In our modern world it is easy to forget how a calendar dominates farming – from knowing when the first young animals will be born, to when to plant seeds. The monuments are complex and were clearly used for religious rituals too. Their use as calendars is by no means agreed by everyone, and archaeologists and astronomers are still working together to find out their significance.

Stonehenge: For a panoramic view and interactive map of Stonehenge see: http://www.bbc.co.uk/history/interactive/virtual_tours/stonehenge/index_embed.shtml Its alignments for the winter solstice sunset are still being researched and new evidence has recently just come to light – see: http://www.english-heritage.org.uk/about/news/stonehenge-solstitial-function/

Maes Howe: The winter setting Sun shines directly down a passageway into this impressive chambered cairn, for three weeks either side of the shortest day.

Historic Scotland's details of this monument are at: http://www.historic-scotland.gov.uk

For more details on the monument, video and a live web feed camera (which works throughout the year) see: http://www.maeshowe.co.uk/

Newgrange: The passage tomb captures the Sun rise through a roof box at the winter solstice. The rays travel 19 metres down a passage, to illuminate a chamber. For a discussion of the site and some stunning photographs see: http://www.newgrange.com/

The Moon

> ### Common misconception
>
> ### 'The Moon spins as quickly as the Earth'
>
> Pupils often find it hard to understand that the Earth and Moon spin at different speeds. The Moon turns very slowly relative to the Earth, once in 28 days. The activity below may help.

Pupil activity 11.14

Dance drama to simulate the movement of the Earth and the Moon

Learning objective: Learn about the way the Earth spins on its axis and the Moon orbits the Earth.

Resources required: none

Select two pupils, one to be the 'Earth' and the other the 'Moon'. To begin, the pupil representing the Earth should stand still. The pupil representing the Moon should perform a practice orbit by walking around Earth. Ask this pupil to imagine (or draw) a circle on the floor around the Earth along which to move. The Moon pupil must always have their face pointing towards the Earth. State that this is the face of the Moon we see from Earth. The Moon pupil should move using a crab-like, sideways step, thus the Earth pupil will never see the back of their head, just like we on the real Earth never see the other side of the Moon.

After this practice, they are ready to start. Explain that the Earth pupil's nose is your town and start with them facing one another. So if it was night time and cloud-less, people in your town could see the Moon. Now ask them to move a little faster with the Earth rotating once every ten seconds and the Moon orbiting very slowly but with one side always facing the 'Earth' (the Moon pupil moves sideways and has their face facing the Earth at all times). To avoid dizziness, call out 'freeze frame' when the 'Moon' is one-quarter of its way around its orbit – the Earth should have done seven full rotations by then. Ask as many pupils as possible to explain where the Moon is and check what they are seeing. Then restart and later stop the action when the 'Moon' has reached halfway around its orbit (the Earth will now have done 14 rotations). Ask others to have a go. You could 'freeze frame' and discuss different points in the orbit.

Encourage questions that you can note rather than try to answer there and then. When dealing with a question, try to use the model and get the pupils to try to answer it. Further cement this learning by modelling these movements using balls (see the

'What the teacher needs to know and understand' section at the beginning of this chapter for ideas). When watching simulations, always remember to ask pupils to verbalise and discuss what they see.

The issue of the Moon spinning only once on its axis every 28 days is challenging and too difficult for some pupils. They simply need to know that the Moon has a different speed of spin to the Earth. High-attaining pupils may relish the challenge of understanding that only one side of the Moon ever faces the Earth. The other side of the Moon that we do not see is sometimes erroneously called the 'dark side'.

Common misconception

'The Moon can only be seen during the night'

Children often think that 'the Sun brings the day and the Moon brings the night'. The Moon can often be seen during the day, but it is often faint in the day because the Sun appears so much brighter. Children may just fail to notice the Moon in the day time even when there is a clear sky. Clouds also hide the Moon in the day. The Moon in the day is so faint that it cannot be seen through the clouds when overcast. And you don't need to be reminded that cloudy days are common in Britain! At night though, the situation is very different. The Moon looks bright at night because the starlight reaching the Earth is much weaker in comparison to the Sun's light in the day. The reflected light of the Moon at night easily 'outshines' the stars.

Pupil activity 11.15

How our Moon moves

Learning objective: Learn about the relative movement of the Earth and Moon.

Resources required: internet access

Simulations, many of which are available from the internet, can assist pupil learning. A good example can be found at:

http://www.childrensuniversity.manchester.ac.uk

With the best simulations, the teacher has the option to pause to ask pupils for predictions, explanations, and to emphasise vocabulary and key points.

Pupil activity 11.16

Moon diary

Learning objective: Learn from observation about the changes in appearance of the Moon.

Resources required: table for recording results

Make a Moon diary. Pupils can take a note pad or poster home and sketch the shape of the Moon each night.

You need to check that the Moon is in the sky during this period. Access a website such as:

http://www.moonconnection.com/moon_phases_calendar.phtml

Table 11.1 Moon diary

Week	Sunday	Monday	Tuesday	Wednesday	Thursday	Friday	Saturday
1	7.05pm	6.55 pm	7.01 pm				
2							
3							

Common misconception

'The Moon looks different because of the Earth's shadow'

The apparent changing shape of the Moon is one of the trickiest concepts to grasp. Fortunately, you are not expected to teach it. However, higher-attaining pupils in science may be very interested. A full explanation for the phases of the Moon is given in the teacher's knowledge section at the start of this chapter. The 'phases of the Moon activity' on pages 296–297 could be attempted by higher-attaining pupils.

The Solar System

Pupil activity 11.17

Learning about the planets

Learning objective: Learn about the order of the planets, their size, spin, and number of moons.

Resources required: reference books and internet sites on the planets

Literacy and
numeracy

Ask pupils to write a postcard from a planet. They can imagine a holiday travelling to a planet or around the planets. Postcards can be factual, based on secondary reference material that pupils can access, or more imaginative, focusing on what pupils imagine the planet to be like.

An alternative to this is to produce fact files for each planet. One option is to use a flat file database or a spreadsheet to tabulate data on the planets, perhaps including the data in Table 11.2 and adding other columns such as for circumference.

Table 11.2 Data about the planets

Planet	Distance from the Sun* (km)	Diameter* (km)	Spin period* (most spin anticlockwise)	Time to orbit the Sun* (Earth days)	Number of moons
Mercury	58 million	5,000	58 Earth days	88	0
Venus	108 million	12,000	243 Earth days (clockwise)	225	0
Earth	150 million	12,500	24 Earth hours	365¼	1
Mars	228 million	6,500	24½ Earth hours	687	0
Jupiter	778 million	143,000	10 Earth hours	4,330	63
Saturn	1.5 billion	120,000	10½ Earth hours	10,756	60
Uranus	2.8 billion	51,000	17 Earth hours (clockwise)	30,687	27
Neptune	4.5 billion	49,000	16 Earth hours	60,000	13
Dwarf planet					
Pluto	5.9 billion	2,300	153 Earth hours (clockwise)	90,500	3

* Approximate

Information from NASA available at:

http://solarsystem.nasa.gov/planets/index.cfm

Pupil activity 11.18

Simulating the movement of planets and moons with a pupil 'orrery'

Learning objective: Learn about the relative movements of the Sun, planets, and moons.

Resources required: balls of different sizes, a good torch, a darkened area

The best way to teach the movements of planets and moons relative to the Sun is to make use of a safe light source and balls of various sizes. In the school hall, use the curtains to reduce the light. Two pupils can model the Sun – one holding a beach ball and the other holding a torch which can be pointed at different planets. A third pupil can hold a smaller ball, copying the movement of the planet around the Sun and if possible rotating the 'planet' on its own axis.

Ask the pupils to talk about what is happening as they move. Afterwards, discuss as a class what happened. Pupils might draw cartoons to show their understanding.

Reinforce this teaching by utilising electronic orreries on the web, such as at: http://www.schoolsobservatory.org.uk/astro/solsys/orrery/ or http://www.easytorecall.co.uk/orrery_simulation.htm

Common misconceptions

'Everything goes around the Earth'

Pupils often think that the Earth is the centre of the Solar System (i.e. the planets, Sun, and Moon revolve around the Earth). Simulating the movements of planets in the above activity around the Sun will help tackle this. This belief is an ancient one, and our language reinforces it. We talk about sunrise and sunset, the time the Moon rises, about different constellations of stars 'coming into view' in different seasons, and even about planets such as Venus or Mars appearing over our horizon at different times of the night. All of this language is geared towards a stationary Earth with stellar bodies (or 'heavenly bodies') rotating around it. It is, of course, what we see and how we describe what we see, but not reality. A discussion with the class on what we see from Earth (an 'Earthbound view') and what an astronaut would see from space (an 'Astronaut's view') would help a lot here.

'Every bright object in the night sky is a star'

Most of the bright objects in the night sky are stars but some are planets. Venus, for example, is one of the first bright objects to appear in the sky at dusk, usually just above the horizon. Planets do not produce light, they simply reflect light from the Sun.

Artificial satellites also look like bright points of light and can be seen from Earth. These too look like stars, but they are merely reflecting light from the Sun, like the planets do.

Pupil activity 11.19

Using a virtual observatory

Learning objective: To understand how the night sky changes during the night time.

Resources required: access to computers for the whole class, download Stellarium™ free software

The Stellarium software needs to be downloaded onto each computer the pupils will use. The software is available free at: www.stellarium.org. The software enables the pupils to view the night sky and see the apparent motion of the stars and planets during the course of a night. The software will show the pupils the night sky for the coming night. It can be made to show the names of the stars, planets and constellations. The pupils will see that as the Earth spins at night, so the relative position of the planets, stars and Moon change. They can even see the stars that are in the sky in the daytime, that are normally hidden to us as they are outshone by the Sun.

Pupil activity 11.20

The scale of the Solar System

Learning objective: Learn about the relative distance between the Sun and its planets.

Resources required: beach ball; Plasticine™ balls the size of grains of rice (2), dried peas (2), grain of salt, grapes (2), small tomatoes (2), access to playground and school field, trundle wheel

To help pupils understand the scale of the Solar System, use the information in Table 11.3 to demonstrate scale on the school playground or field (you may only manage to fit in the first four or five planets).

Table 11.3 Data to model the Solar System

Object	Diameter	Distance from 'Sun'
The Sun is a beach ball	30 cm	—
Mercury is a small grain of rice	1 mm	12 m
Venus is a dried pea	2½ mm	23 m
Earth is a large dried pea	3 mm	32 m
Mars is a grain of rice	1½ mm	49 m
Jupiter is a small tomato	30 mm	167 m
Saturn is a small tomato	26 mm	300 m
Uranus is a grape	10 mm	600 m
Neptune is a grape	10 mm	900 m
Pluto is a grain of salt	1 mm	1.27 km (average)

Source: Association of Science Education (1990).

Pupils can use this activity to get a feel for the scale of the Solar System. Take your class onto the school playground or field. Using a trundle wheel, ask individual pupils to stand 12 m, 23 m, and so on, from the class group while holding the requisite Plasticine™ ball. You may only get as far as Mars. Ask pupils to talk about what they see and explain the relationships of the Sun with each planet. Pupils may like to estimate where the further planets would be on this scale, when they would be out of the school grounds. Would they be near a bus stop or a shop further down the street? Pluto may be tricky, but they could always use a local map and measure out the scale! Photograph the scale model and ask pupils to record what happened back in class, using diagrams, cartoons or words.

Teach the pupils the mnemonic: 'My Very Easy Method Just Speeds Up Naming Planets' – Mercury, Venus, Earth, Mars, Jupiter, Saturn, Uranus, Neptune, Pluto.

Pupil activity 11.21

Use of media, stories, and films

Learning objective: Tailored to the story and the science to be learned.

Resources required: access to media

When the opportunity arises, make use of stories in the news, media or from children's literature. Such material can make a great starting point, although you will have to point out inaccuracies, such as there is no sound in space!

Literacy

A number of children's stories feature the Earth, the Moon, and space. These can be used to learn about the Earth in space or encourage more creative writing.

A collection of educational videos is available at:

http://www.nasa.gov/multimedia/index.html

and

http://video.nationalgeographic.com/video/science/

Your pupils might watch a video and write their own commentary that includes science terms.

Scientists who discovered our place in the Solar System – Ptolemy and Copernicus

Claudius Ptolemy was a Roman citizen who lived in Alexandria, Egypt from 90–168 AD. He compiled a star catalogue of over 48 constellations that we still recognise today. He also developed the geocentric model of space. This puts Earth at the centre of everything, with the Sun, Moon, planets, and stars all revolving around it. His order (from nearest to Earth to furthest away) was: Earth, Moon, Mercury, Venus, Sun, Mars, Jupiter, Saturn, all the stars.

To give a sense of the complexity of planetary movement for the Ptolemy system to be true, have a look at the following website: http://astro.unl.edu/naap/ssm/animations/ptolemaic.swf. You can select which planet you are interested in and watch its weird, inaccurate orbit!

Ptolemy's idea of the Earth-centred universe lasted for 1400 years. It was overturned by Nicholas Copernicus (1473–1543) who put forward his Sun-centred (heliocentric) model. His careful calculations showed that the Earth was not the centre of the universe. Bodies such as the planets and stars appeared to go around the Earth merely because the Earth rotated once a day, on its axis. The idea of the Earth moving was revolutionary, but his idea that the Sun was the centre of the solar system, and not the Earth, was to prove even more controversial.

To directly compare pictures of Ptolemy's geocentric (Earth-centred) model and Copernicus's heliocentric (Sun-centred) model, see: http://amazing-space.stsci.edu/resources/explorations/groundup/lesson/basics/g37/

Support for Copernicus's Sun-centred solar system came from Galileo Galilei. His recent improvements to the telescope enabled him to see the four largest moons of Jupiter for the first time. By careful observation he realised that they were orbiting Jupiter, not the Earth, in direct contradiction to Ptolemy's model, in which everything must go around the Earth. In 1616 Galileo was forbidden by the Christian Roman Catholic Church to teach Copernicus's Sun-centred model. In 1632, after he published a book explaining the Sun-centred model, he was brought before the

Inquisition in Rome. He was convicted of heresy and sentenced to life imprisonment, later reduced to permanent house arrest. To avoid torture he was forced to publically state that he did not believe Copernicus's Sun-centred model. The Roman Catholic Church cleared Galileo of any wrongdoing in 1992.

Summary of key learning points

- the Sun is the centre of our Solar System and the planets Mercury, Venus, Earth, Mars, Jupiter, Saturn, Uranus, Neptune orbit around it. Beyond these are the dwarf planets, the most well known of which is Pluto;

- the inner planets are four rocky planets (Mercury, Venus, Earth, Mars). Then come the gas giants (Jupiter and Saturn). Next are the ice giants (Uranus and Neptune);

- all planets have moons orbiting them, and even the dwarf planet Pluto has a moon;

- Other smaller objects in our Solar System include meteorites, comets and asteroids;

- the Earth, Sun, and Moon are broadly spherical;

- the Earth turns once in 24 hours, and this gives us night and day;

- the Moon orbits the Earth every 28 days;

- the Earth orbits the Sun every 365¼ days, that is, a year;

- some prehistoric monuments use the Sun to mark the shortest day of the year, the midwinter solstice;

- the Moon's changing phases are caused by the changing position of the Moon in relation to the Earth, and which part of the Moon is illuminated by the Sun;

- a galaxy is a large collection of millions of stars. Our galaxy is the Milky Way, one of 100 billion galaxies in the universe.

Self-test

Question 1

The Solar System includes (a) planets, (b) the Universe, (c) moons, (d) stars

Question 2

The Sun (a) is orbited by nine planets, (b) is a ball of gas, (c) is not a true star, (d) orbits the Earth once every 365¼ days

Question 3

A year (a) consists of 365 days, (b) includes winter caused by the Earth's distance from the Sun, (c) includes summer caused by the Earth's tilt, (d) is the same for all planets

Question 4

Earth (a) is the fourth planet from the Sun, (b) is orbited by the Sun, (c) spins on its own axis each day resulting in night and day, (d) spins on its own axis as evidenced by the movement of clouds

Self-test answers

Q1: (a) and (c) are correct. The Universe is all of space and so the Solar System is one tiny part of it. There is one star in the Solar System; the other billions of stars are spread throughout the universe, found mainly in clusters called galaxies.

Q2: (a) and (b) are correct. The Sun is a true star and the Earth orbits the Sun once every 365¼ days.

Q3: Only (c) is correct. An Earth year consists of 365¼ days. The distance from the Earth to the Sun varies a little during the year but not enough to cause the seasons; it is the tilt of the Earth that is responsible. The time taken to orbit the Sun is different for each planet, so for example Mercury orbits the Sun in 89 Earth days whereas Venus orbits the Sun in 225 Earth days.

Q4: (c) is the only correct answer. Earth is the third planet from the Sun and is in orbit around the Sun. The Earth does spin on its own axis but cloud movement results from moving air in the Earth's atmosphere and not the spin of the Earth.

Misconceptions

'Is it spinning or orbiting?'

'The Sun moves, not the Earth'

'The Sun goes to bed at night!'

'It's hotter in the summer because we are closer to the Sun'

'The Moon spins as quickly as the Earth'

'The Moon can only be seen during the night'

'The Moon looks different because of the Earth's shadow'

'Everything goes around the Earth'

'Every bright object in the night sky is a star'

Web resources

http://amazing-space.stsci.edu/resources/explorations/groundup/lesson/basics/g37/
    (geocentric and heliocentric views of the Solar System)

http://astro.unl.edu/classaction/animations/coordsmotion/eclipticsimulator.swf
(seasons simulator)

http://astro.unl.edu/naap/ssm/animations/ptolemaic.swf
(geocentric and heliocentric views of the Solar System)

http://ipy.org/images/webcams/index.php
(webcam, Antartica, British Antarctic Survey posts)

http://solarsystem.nasa.gov/planets/index.cfm
(information on solar system)

http://video.nationalgeographic.com/video/science/
(educational space video clip)

http://www.bbc.co.uk/science/space/solarsystem/other_solar_system_bodies/comet
(comets)

www.childrensuniversity.manchester.ac.uk
(simulations on Earth in space, moon and seasons)

http://www.earthcam.com/usa/newyork/timessquare/
(webcam, Times Square, New York, USA)

http://www.easytorecall.co.uk/orrery_simulation.htm
(orrery)

http://www.english-heritage.org.uk/daysout/properties/stonehenge/
(prehistoric sites and winter solstice)

http://www.historic-scotland.gov.uk
(prehistoric sites and winter solstice)

http://www.maeshowe.co.uk/
(prehistoric sites and winter solstice)

http://www.moonconnection.com/moon_phases_calendar.phtml
(the correct Moon phase for everyday of the year)

http://www.morehead.unc.edu/Shows/EMS/seasons.htm
(more on the seasons)

http://www.nasa.gov/multimedia/index.html
(educational space video clip)

http://www.newgrange.com/
(prehistoric sites and winter solstice)

http://www.pbslearningmedia.org/resource/ess05.sci.ess.eiu.totaleclipse/total-solar-
eclipse-animation/
(solar eclipse)

http://www.schoolsobservatory.org.uk/astro/solsys/orrery
(orrery)

www.stellarium.org
(virtual observatory)

http://www.sydney-webcam.com/index.php?nav=cam1
(webcam, Sydney, Australia)

12

Electricity

About this chapter

This chapter looks at what electricity is. It deals with electrical current, conductors, batteries, circuits, resistance, and voltage. It explains how the filament in light bulbs works and how simple circuit diagrams are drawn. The second part of the chapter addresses what pupils need to learn about and the final part some of the best ways to teach pupils about electricity, including common misconceptions.

What the teacher needs to know and understand

What is electricity?

All atoms have a central nucleus which has a positive charge. Electrons orbit around this central nucleus. The electrons have a negative charge.

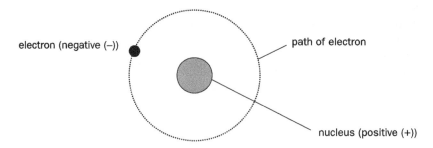

Figure 12.1 Atom showing position of nucleus and electron

Opposite charges attract, so positive and negative charges are attracted to each other. A simple view of electricity is to see it as being made of the negatively charged electrons. If we make the electrons move away from the atoms that they are normally attached to, we can do interesting things with them.

Static and current electricity

There are two types of electricity: static and current. The only difference is how the electrons are made to move. With static electricity, two materials are usually rubbed together (say a rubber balloon on a woolly jumper) as in Figure 12.2. Some electrons are ripped off the wool and stick to the balloon, so the balloon becomes negatively charged with these extra electrons (as the electrons carry the negative charge). Try this yourself.

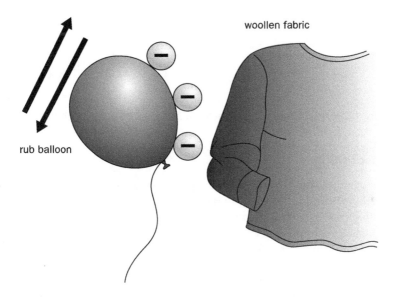

Figure 12.2 A balloon is rubbed on wool, 'ripping off' negative electrons

If the balloon is then placed near a wall, it may stick to the wall (as in Figure 12.3). It does this because the negatively charged electrons on the balloon repel the negatively charged electrons in the wall, making them move away and leaving behind an area of positive charge on the surface of the wall. Remember that opposite charges attract. The electrons on the balloon are attracted to this positive area, and the balloon will stick to the wall.

Eventually, the balloon will fall off as the extra electrons on the balloon 'leak' away into the air. Note that with static electricity, it is usually two insulators that are rubbed together. Insulators are not good conductors of electricity, so the electrons usually stick on the surface of the insulator and do not flow away through the material.

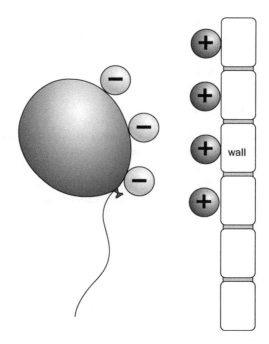

Figure 12.3 Negatively charged balloon attracted to positive charge on wall

Current electricity

Current electricity is the type of electricity that flows through the mains electrical wires in our homes and in the circuits the pupils make at school. Electrical current is the flow of electrons in a wire. The moving electrons carry a negative electrical charge. Current is measured in amps.

Wires usually have a metal inside, with plastic wrapped round it. Metals are good conductors and allow electrons to flow freely through them, whereas plastic is not a good conductor, so all the moving electrons stay inside the metal part of the wire. With current electricity, there is an electrical source, such as a battery or the mains. The electricity flows from the source through a wire, through various components (such as a bulb), and back to the source, forming a circuit. The circuit must be complete for the electricity to flow, as generally electricity is not powerful enough to jump gaps in the wire.

A series circuit

The type of circuit pupils build first in primary science is called a 'series circuit'. A series circuit is a simple loop, with a battery and one or more other components in it. It does not matter in what order the components are placed in a series circuit. Note that there are no branches to a series circuit, meaning that the electricity can only follow one route as it travels around the circuit. In a simple series circuit, the current is the same at any point. The current cannot be used up, the electrons simply flow from one end of the battery through the wires to the other end of the battery. However, the electrons may transfer some of their energy to the components in the circuit while on route.

Younger pupils can draw the components and circuits as they see them to record their work. Older primary age pupils can use the symbols in Figure 12.5 and draw more stylised circuits (Figure 12.4), which show wires to be straight lines, and corners to be at right angles.

Figure 12.4 A simple electrical circuit

| cell | battery | wire | bulb | motor | switch | buzzer |

Figure 12.5 Symbols for electrical components

Batteries and cells

We are all familiar with the different-sized batteries that we use around the home. Small cylinder-shaped ones labelled 'AA' or the even smaller 'AAA' are used in our remote controllers for the TV and DVD player; larger cylindrical ones labelled 'C' and 'D' are used in torches or a radio. Most of these single batteries have a voltage of 1.5 volts. People often think that bigger batteries are more powerful, but they are not. Bigger batteries just last longer than smaller batteries when used continuously. The best guide to the strength of a battery is to look at the label on it, which always shows the voltage of the battery.

A battery provides the 'push' to move electrons around the circuit. Voltage can be thought of in terms of how much 'push' the battery can give the current. By adding more batteries to a circuit, we can create a larger voltage and hence a larger 'push'. By

Literacy

adding more batteries, we can make a bulb glow brighter, a buzzer sound louder, and a motor spin more quickly.

Some devices require more energy to work than others. For example, there are usually two batteries in a remote control, making a total of 3 volts (1.5 V + 1.5 V). A large radio needs more energy to work and often has four batteries inside it, giving a total of 6 volts (1.5 V + 1.5 V + 1.5 V + 1.5 V).

Scientists refer to these single 1.5 volt batteries as 'cells', and this is a word that older primary school children should know. Confusingly, however, scientists use the word battery as well, but only to refer to a collection of cells stuck together and sealed up. You will have seen 9 volt batteries that are rectangular-shaped and have two metal contacts at one end. This is what a scientist means by a battery and it is made up of six 1.5 volt cells inside it (6 × 1.5 V = 9 V). Here, a familiar word used by the public is used slightly differently by scientists, which is not uncommon! In the rest of the text, we will use the term 'battery' to cover both cells and batteries, just as in everyday life, unless there is a need to refer specifically to the concept of single cells.

In primary classrooms, most devices require between 2 and 6 volts to work correctly. Often, the voltage a component needs is printed or etched on to it. It is important to match the voltage of the battery or batteries to the voltage of the component.

Bulbs are commonly 1.5, 2.5, 3.5 or 6 volts, buzzers are 3 or 6 volts, and motors are often 3 volts. The children must know not to put too much voltage into a circuit, or the component can overheat and 'burn out' (this does not present a danger) and thus no longer work.

It is not safe to use rechargeable cells or batteries in pupils' practical work with circuits as these can easily overheat, split apart or catch fire. A rechargeable battery will always have 'rechargeable' printed on the side of it, so if in doubt, check first. Standard non-rechargeable batteries are very safe, but should be disposed of correctly when they no longer work.

Bulbs

When an electrical current passes through a bulb, it causes the wire inside to become so hot that it glows and gives out light. The pupils need to learn that the more bulbs they add to the circuit, the less bright they are. Two bulbs are dimmer than one bulb, and three bulbs are even dimmer than two bulbs. (An explanation for the teacher is provided in the 'Resistance' part of this section.) If they add any more bulbs, they may not give out any light at all. The pupils also need to know that if there are two bulbs in a circuit, both bulbs will be *equally* dim. They often think that one will be brighter than the other, which is untrue. To make sure that they see this, you need to ensure that all the bulbs they use are the same. To ensure the bulbs are exactly the same, you have to check two figures on the bulb. On the metal part of each bulb, there are two figures etched into it. One is in volts (V) the other in amps (A). If two bulbs have the same voltage (e.g. 2.5 V) and the same amp number (e.g. 0.3 A), they will be the same. These two bulbs are rated identically, and so will glow the same amount when put in a circuit together. This is what the children need to see.

If the pupils do add two bulbs with different voltages or different amp numbers (e.g. one is 2.5 V and the other is 6 V), one will be dimmer and one will be brighter as they draw different amounts of power from the battery. This needs to be avoided, as it will reinforce the above misconception! Children *do not* need to know about what happens with differently rated bulbs, but *do* need to see the correct effect from two bulbs rated the same. If there is one bright bulb and one dim bulb in the same circuit, now you know why, and how to take steps to avoid it in the future!

Buzzers

A buzzer is a device that converts electrical energy into sound energy. These devices only work 'one way'. This means that the red wire of a buzzer must be connected to the positive side of a battery, the black to the negative. If connected the other way, no damage is done, they just won't work until they are connected correctly.

Motors

A motor is a device that converts electrical energy into kinetic (movement) energy. A motor normally has two metal contacts on the back of it, each to be connected to a wire, one leading to the positive terminal of the battery, the other to the negative terminal. If this is done, then the spindle of the motor may spin clockwise. To make it spin anticlockwise, swap the wires around, so that they lead to the opposite ends of the battery compared with before.

Conductors

Conductors are materials that readily allow electricity to flow through them. There are three main groups of conductors: metals, graphite, and some liquids.

All metals are conductors. Some are better than others, but in a classroom context any can be seen to work. A metal is a good conductor because it has some so-called 'free electrons' that are only loosely held by their atoms. These 'free electrons' can easily be made to move, as part of an electrical current. Copper is used for wires because it is an excellent conductor.

Pencil 'leads' are conductors (because they contain graphite), but not as good as metals (see later investigation). Water is a poor conductor (compared with metal), and salt water is a better conductor than non-salt water (see later investigation). If children are trying out liquids as conductors, it must be stressed that it is safe to do so with batteries but not the mains, as this could quite easily kill us.

Insulators

Insulators do not conduct current electricity. Plastic, wood, and card are just three everyday examples of electrical insulators. Any electrical charge tends to stick to their surface and not flow through the body of these materials.

Resistance

Resistance is a useful term to understand and to introduce to older pupils. Although the National Curriculum (DfE, 2013a) does not require this term to be used in primary science, a simple grasp of it can help them understand why we cannot put lots of things in a circuit and expect them all to work.

Resistance is a measure of how hard it is for an electrical current to flow through something. Some things, such as copper wire, provide very little resistance, and so the electrons can move through them quite easily. Other things provide high resistance, and so impede the flow of electricity to a greater extent.

Three factors affect the resistance of a wire:

1   The material the wire is made of – is it a good conductor or a poorer conductor?

2   The thickness of the wire – for example, most mains wires are wide to allow the easy passage of electricity.

3   The length of the wire – the longer it is, the harder it is for the electricity to flow through.

An electrical wire is a good example of something that offers little resistance. The material it is often made of is copper, a good conductor. These wires are generally quite thick to allow the easy flow of electrons. They are quite long, which is not as great a disadvantage as you might think, because copper is such a good conductor. Some electrical energy will be converted to heat as the current flows along the wire and the electrons bump into obstructions (atoms in the wire), but most wires don't become noticeably hotter if used correctly.

Contrast this with the filament of a light bulb. The filament is just a special kind of wire. A bulb filament is made of a poorer conductor than copper, such as tungsten. This means that the electrical current will find it harder to flow through it. The filament wire is very thin, making it difficult for the electrons to avoid collisions with obstructions in the wire. It is also very long (it is coiled, so it doesn't take up a lot of space), which means that the electrons will hit more obstructions as they move through. Therefore, a bulb filament has high resistance. However, this is actually useful. When electrons hit obstructions in the wire, they transfer energy to them. These obstructions are atoms, remember. As the atoms are struck by the electrons, they will vibrate and start to emit heat and light. The more the electrons collide with the atoms in the wire, the more they vibrate and the more light and heat they can emit, and thus the hotter and brighter the filament becomes, until it glows very brightly. Glowing brightly is just what we want a bulb to do. The heat is an unwanted by-product.

With this explanation we can see that the more bulbs we add to a circuit, the higher the resistance will become. With each additional bulb we add, the resistance increases, the current decreases, and the bulbs glow more dimly.

All components have resistance. Thus, adding more buzzers to a circuit will increase the resistance, decrease the current, and they will buzz less loudly. Similarly, the children will find that they cannot insert motor after motor and expect them to spin rapidly.

There are two ways around this. The first is to add more cells (or batteries) to increase the voltage. By increasing the voltage, we increase the 'push' and so increase the current. The larger current will enable the bulbs to glow brightly once again. Many of the children will be familiar with the idea that more batteries mean brighter bulbs. The second way to overcome resistance is to use parallel circuits.

Parallel circuits

So far, we have talked only about a series circuit, which has one component after another in a single unbroken and unbranching circuit. However, another kind of circuit – the parallel circuit – has one or more branches on it. If we create a parallel circuit and place a bulb on each branch, the bulbs will remain bright. In Figure 12.6 you can trace the two paths that electricity can follow. The first route goes from the battery through the 'top' bulb and then back to the battery. The second route is through the 'bottom' bulb and back to the battery. Whichever route the current takes, it only has to pass through one bulb and so will encounter less resistance than if it had to travel through two bulbs side by side. Because there is less resistance, the bulbs will be bright.

Some people find this counter-intuitive because they worry that the electrical current is splitting up at the wire junctions. It is, but this doesn't matter. We should think in terms of how easy it is for the electricity to push through a number of components, one after the other. Each branch only has one component, so each bulb will be brightly lit. The only consequence of this circuit is the cell or battery will not last as long and will 'go flat' more quickly than when the two bulbs are dimly lit in a series circuit. This is because electrical energy in the parallel circuit is being converted more quickly to light and heat.

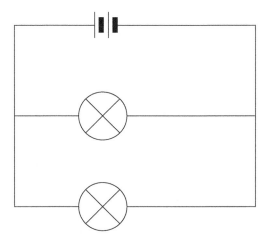

Figure 12.6 A parallel circuit

What pupils need to know at Key Stage 1

Electricity is not a statutory requirement at Key Stage 1. That noted, it would be a great springboard for Key Stage 2 if Key Stage 1 pupils could make simple circuits using batteries, wires, bulbs, buzzers, and motors. This would free up time in Key Stage 2 to deal with the more complex electrical concepts of conductors, insulators, building switches, making useful circuits, and drawing circuit diagrams.

What pupils need to know at Key Stage 2

(ST) denotes statutory requirements.

Lower Key Stage 2

(ST) Identify common appliances that run on electricity

Suggestions for working scientifically:

> To be able to identify whether a machine uses batteries or mains electricity.
>
> Research how to work safely with electricity.

(ST) Identify whether or not a lamp will light in a simple series circuit, based on whether or not the lamp is part of a complete loop with a battery

(ST) Recognise that a switch opens and closes a circuit and associate this with whether or not a lamp lights in a simple series circuit

(ST) Construct a simple series electrical circuit, identifying and naming its basic parts, including cells, batteries, wires, bulbs, switches, motors, and buzzers

Suggestions for working scientifically:

> Use their circuits to create simple devices – for example a fan using a motor; a steady hand game with a buzzer; a night light with a bulb.
>
> Draw the circuit as a pictorial representation (not necessarily using conventional circuit symbols at this stage; these will be introduced in Year 6).
>
> Observe patterns, for example, that bulbs get brighter if more cells are added.

(ST) Recognise some common conductors and insulators, and associate metals with being good conductors

Suggestions for working scientifically:

Discover which materials can and cannot be used to connect across a gap in a circuit.

Upper Key Stage 2

(ST) Associate the brightness of a lamp or volume of a buzzer with the number and voltage of cells used in the circuit

(ST) Compare and give reasons for variations in how components function, including the brightness of bulbs, the loudness of buzzers, and the on/off positions of switches

Suggestions for working scientifically:

Using simple series circuits, answer questions about what happens when they try different components, for example switches, buzzers and motors.

Systematically identify the effect of changing one component at a time in a circuit.

Design and make a set of traffic lights, a burglar alarm or some other useful circuit.

(ST) Use recognised symbols when representing a simple circuit in a diagram

Ways to teach 'electricity' at Key Stage 2

Things that use batteries and things that use mains electricity

The two types of electricity that the children need to be familiar with are batteries and mains electricity. Older children often do not know the word 'mains' and fail to distinguish between battery electricity, as a safe form that we can use to do experiments with, and the mains, which can be dangerous if simple precautions are not taken.

Pupil activity 12.1

What uses batteries and what uses mains electricity?

Learning objective: Understand why different devices need different electrical energy sources.

Resources required: none

Have the children identify, draw or list things in the classroom or school that use electricity. Can they split them into things that use batteries or mains electricity? Can they explain why objects use one or the other type of electricity?

Objects that need a lot of energy use the mains (e.g. school computers and televisions). Objects that don't need so much energy and are not constantly in use can use batteries (e.g. TV remote control, torch). Sometimes there is an overlap, for example laptops can use batteries, but these soon run down and have to be charged up again using mains electricity.

 Mains electricity is dangerous because it is so powerful. Lots of safety materials are available on this topic, for example at: http://www.switchedonkids.org.uk

Common misconception

'Electricity just comes out of plugs'

A discussion of where mains electricity comes from may be revealing. Many children think it comes simply from the plug socket in the wall, not connecting it with underground cables, neighbourhood substations, pylons, and ultimately power stations. Others believe that it just 'comes from underground'.

 Stress how batteries can be used sensibly and safely in experiments. The only real danger with batteries is if they are damaged as the chemicals inside are poisonous and can burn the skin. However, it is difficult to cut one, so this is not too much of a problem. If a battery leaks, it must be disposed of immediately.

Common misconceptions

'Electricity comes from the air'

Where do batteries get their electricity from? Discuss with the children that chemical reactions in the battery produce electricity, as some pupils might think that batteries receive electricity from the air, just as radios receive radio programmes or as wireless devices communicate with each other. Here they are confusing radio waves and other signals with electricity.

'Bigger batteries are more powerful'

A common misconception is that the bigger the battery, the more powerful it is. This is not always the case. Of the batteries commonly used around the home, the cylindrical ones come in four different sizes: AAA, AA, C, and D. The smallest ones, AAA, are often used in remote controls and the biggest ones, D, are often used in torches. The children need to be shown that they are all as powerful as each other: 1.5 volts. The only difference is that bigger cells last longer if used continuously.

Ask the children why they think there are different-sized batteries, and then try the activity below.

Pupil activity 12.2

The right battery for the job

Learning objective: Understand why batteries come in different sizes.

Resources required: a range of batteries and battery-operated items

Provide a range of battery-operated items for the children to look at. Can they match the battery to the device before looking at the place where it goes? Can they explain why some things have small batteries (e.g. remote control, because it is small itself and only used for a second or two at a time) and others need big batteries (e.g. a torch, which needs a lot of energy to work for minutes to hours on end). Can they insert the batteries into the device the right way round? (There is usually printed guidance inside the device, but batteries don't always have *both* the positive and negative signs on them).

Pupil activity 12.3

Constructing simple circuits

Learning objective: To be able to make simple circuits with a range of components.

Resources required: batteries, bulbs, crocodile clips, wires, buzzers, bulb holders, battery holders

From Key Stage 1 to early Key Stage 2 onwards, children should be able to put together bulbs, batteries, buzzers, and so on, and make simple working circuits. The pitfalls of the various components are listed in the 'What the teacher needs to know' section at the beginning of the chapter.

Children need to be able to troubleshoot their own circuit if it does not work, by checking the connections before asking the teacher. Fostering a feeling of self-reliance in this aspect will help later when they make more complex circuits. Frequently, the reason why a circuit does not work is because there is a break in it, which the pupils have not noticed, because they simply have not checked that all the wires are connected properly to the various components.

Common misconceptions

'The electricity comes out of both ends of a battery'

The belief is that electricity comes out of both ends of the battery, flows around the circuit, and meets up at the component. A discussion about a complete loop of a circuit is needed, as electricity flows from one end of the battery, through the circuit, to the other end of the battery. A good whole-class activity is to arrange the children in a big loop, representing wires, with two children acting as either end of a battery. One of the 'battery children' takes a ball (representing electricity) from a box and passes it to the child next to them, who then passes it on. This continues with the balls moving around the loop, with the second 'battery child' collecting the balls and putting them back in the box.

This idea reinforces the flow of electricity in one direction. Other things can be tried, such as breaking the circuit by removing some children. Without throwing the balls, can the remaining children still pass them on? The answer is 'no' and this shows what a gap in a circuit does, effectively stopping electricity from flowing.

'The plastic insulation on wire conducts electricity'

Many children believe that the plastic bit of the wire is the bit that lets the electricity go through, or even that the wire is hollow (like a pipe). Crocodile clips obscure the copper wire inside the plastic, so it is useful to have a stripped-back wire with the copper showing when explaining what happens.

'A bulb doesn't have any connections'

It can be hard to see where the electricity goes in and out of a bulb, at the screw thread on the side and the nodule on the base, so being able to light them up without the use of bulb holders is good practice.

'Put a motor in to make the bulb brighter!'

Some children think that putting a motor in a circuit would make a bulb brighter. Presumably, they think that the motor acts like a windmill or rotor and adds energy to the circuit! The only way to tackle this one is to get them to try it and see that it actually makes a bulb dimmer (see 'Resistance' topic on page 330).

'More buzzers mean more noise'

Putting two or more buzzers in a circuit won't give a louder noise. To challenge their misconception, ask the pupils to put two or even three buzzers in a circuit and listen to them buzz quietly (three buzzers may produce no sound at all). You can explain that the more components we put in a circuit, the harder it is for the electricity to get through.

Although pupils should make circuits with real components when learning about electricity, there are many websites and CD resources offering simulations and demonstrations, including the following:

http://www.hyperstaffs.info/science/work/physics/child/index.html

http://www-g.eng.cam.ac.uk/mmg/teaching/peterstidwill/interact/resources/siliconspies/siliconspieslink.htm

Some suppliers even make high-quality software such as circuit-building software free of charge. See: http://www.yenka.com/en/Yenka_Basic_Circuits/

Pupil activity 12.4

Brightness of different bulbs

Learning objective: Learn how and why bulbs change in brightness.

Resources required: bulbs, batteries, battery and bulb holders, crocodile clips, wires

Ask the children to predict what will happen if one or more bulbs are added to a circuit with a bulb already in it. An investigation into how to make bulbs brighter or dimmer is hard for more children than might at first be expected.

Common misconception

'Adding a bulb will mean both bulbs will be brighter'

Many younger children think that adding a second bulb to a series circuit will either make both bulbs brighter, or they will remain equally as bright as one on its own. Another misconception is that one bulb will be bright and the other will be dim. Older children may know that adding an extra bulb will make things dimmer, but not be able to explain why, or what to do about it.

Introducing the concept of resistance, without actually using the word, is tricky. Stating that 'the more things in the circuit, the harder it is for the electricity to get through' is a good way to start. Thus the more bulbs or buzzers (or any component) added, one after the other, the less electricity gets through, and the less well they work – bulbs will be dimmer, buzzers will be quieter, and so on. It is important that the children see the two or more bulbs are *much dimmer* and are *just as dim* as each other.

Pupil investigation skills 12.5

How we can make bulbs brighter?

Learning objective: To be able to manipulate factors to change the brightness of a bulb.

Resources required: bulbs, batteries, battery and bulb holders, crocodile clips, wires

One of the easiest ways for pupils to make bulbs brighter is to add more cells or batteries. More cells will deliver more energy to the circuit and the children should be able to explain this. The same solution is available for any number of additional components such as buzzers or motors.

Common misconception

'Make the wires shorter to make the bulbs brighter'

This is a very common misconception, but copper wires have very little resistance, and so taking a wire or two out will not make any appreciable difference.

Exploring parallel circuits

Parallel circuits (Figure 12.6) are not in the primary National Curriculum (DfE, 2013a). However, many children know how to build them, or discover how to do so in the course of their investigations. This can be a useful way to challenge more able pupils.

Parallel circuits are a little trickier to make (see page 331 for a full explanation of how they work) and are even trickier to explain to children without the concept of 'resistance'. However, if you explain that electricity finds it hard to go through one component after another (in a series circuit), but easy to go down any branch of a parallel circuit that just has one component, this might suffice. Explain that although the electricity splits up at the branches, it meets up again on the other side of the circuit with electricity from the other branches and can flow back to the battery. More able children will be able to handle this idea, and can trace the various routes from one end of the battery to another along the branches. Parallel circuits are great for design and technology as when making vehicles, for example, as the children can have two bright headlights and a horn, all running from one battery. Children can be challenged to predict what will happen if they add even more bulbs.

Pupil activity 12.6

Can we get mixed components to work properly?

Learning objective: Understand how parallel circuits work.

Resources required: batteries, bulbs, crocodile clips, wires, buzzers, motors, bulb holders, battery holders

Children who have completed the above should be able to tackle this in one of the two ways previously outlined. They may need to be reminded that buzzers only work 'one way'.

Pupil activity 12.7

Building switches

Learning objective: Understand how a switch can control the flow of electricity.

Resources required: paper clips, split pins, foil, plastic-coated wires with stripped metal ends, card split pins each connected to a wire

A switch is simply a means to break or reconnect a circuit. For younger children, the way they achieve it is merely to detach a wire in the circuit. A range of simple switches can be made – two of the most common are illustrated in Figures 12.7 and 12.8.

Figure 12.7 is a paper clip switch. Fasten a paper clip to a piece of card with a split pin. Put a second split pin in the card, within reach of the other end of the paper clip, so that the paper clip can be moved to and fro connecting the two together. Wire or crocodile clips can be connected to each of the split pins and the whole thing inserted into a circuit.

Figure 12.8 is a pressure switch. Fold a piece of metal foil over each end and attach the metal core of a wire to each. Glue each to the ends of a strip of card that also folds

Figure 12.7 Paper clip switch

Figure 12.8 Pressure switch

in half. Connect into a circuit and press to close the switch. This could be used to make a burglar alarm. The fold needs to be strong enough to keep the metal parts apart when the switch is not being stepped on.

Symbols and drawings

Children need to learn that components in a circuit can be represented by symbols, and this is what scientists and electricians use and draw when they are making circuits. The standard symbols are shown in Figure 12.5.

Children learning to draw the correct symbols when illustrating circuits will often draw a mixture of symbols and pictures to represent the components. For example, they might draw a cylindrical cell for the power source, add the symbol for a switch on the other side of the circuit, and then draw a light bulb glowing (instead of the circle with a cross in). It is worthwhile having them draw the components in a circuit as they see them, and then beneath draw the circuit with each component in symbolic form.

Pupil investigation skills 12.8

Conductors and insulators – building and using a simple testing circuit

Learning objective: Learn which materials are conductors and which are not.

Resources required: circuit-making equipment, a range of objects and materials to test

Different materials can easily be divided into conductors and insulators (see page 329). A simple testing circuit can be made to determine whether a material is a conductor or insulator.

The circuit in Figure 12.9 has a deliberate break or gap in the wires, which means that objects can be placed across the gap to test if they conduct electricity. The gap

Figure 12.9 A testing circuit

might simply be two unconnected wires, whose crocodile clips can be connected to the test object or material. If the object or material conducts electricity, the bulb will light up. Alternatively, you could replace the bulb with a buzzer.

The children should be able to predict which materials are conductors (or insulators) and carry out the test. From their results, various conclusions can be drawn:

- that most everyday materials are electrical insulators;
- that all metals are conductors.

Common misconceptions

'Some metals don't conduct do they?'

Some pupils believe that only some metals are conductors. They appear to be muddling the concept of conductivity with magnetism, since only a couple of metals are magnetic. Strangely, many think that copper is magnetic, but it does not conduct electricity. The reality is that copper is not magnetic and is an excellent conductor of electricity.

'The metal door handle doesn't conduct!'

Beware of plastic-coated metals in the classroom such as door handles. The plastic layer can often not be seen or felt, but it will stop electricity from flowing into the metal!

More interesting conductors

Pupil investigation skills 12.9

Do pencils conduct electricity?

Learning objective: Learn that not all pencils conduct electricity.

Resources required: a range of pencils, pencil sharpener, usual circuit equipment

An investigation can be carried out where different grades of pencil are tested, and the amount of conductivity noted, by looking at the comparative brightness of the bulb.

The pencil lead of an HB pencil is a good conductor. Simply sharpen each end of the pencil and attach to the circuit that contains a bulb in the normal way. It will be noted by the children that the bulb does not glow as brightly as it does for metal, indicating that although pencil lead is a conductor, it is not as good as metal.

Common misconception

'Pencils are made of lead, that's why they conduct'

Many children think that pencils will conduct electricity because of the word 'lead', which is also a metal, but there is no metallic lead in a pencil lead! Pencil lead contains graphite and clay, and it is the graphite that is the conductor. Graphite is made of carbon and in this form it is a good conductor.

Art pencils can be sharpened at both ends and tested: try 3B, 3H and 6B, 6H. The ones with the highest clay content do not conduct at all well, but the one with the highest graphite content is an excellent conductor. Challenge the children to work out why the different grades of pencils work differently.

Note that pencils that have been dropped tend to have broken leads inside them and hence the break in the circuit will mean that they won't work!

Pupil activity 12.10

Do liquids conduct electricity?

Learning objective: Understand that liquids can conduct electricity.

Resources required: water, salt, plastic cups, spoons, circuit equipment

Liquids can be tested safely in the classroom, although a discussion on mains and batteries should be conducted beforehand. Water is a relatively poor conductor. Very salty water is a good conductor.

Note that salty water does tend to make steel rust, so wash and dry any crocodile clips thoroughly after use, or attach steel paper clips to them and throw the wet paper clips away afterwards.

The children need to set up a working circuit that includes a bulb that lights up. They then need to make a break in the circuit by disconnecting two crocodile clips. To each crocodile clip attach a metal paper clip. Each clip can be lowered into the liquid and the brightness of the bulb noted. If it fails to light at all, try more salt in the solution, making sure it is well dissolved.

Pupil activity 12.11

Making devices using circuits

Learning objective: Understand how simple components are used in everyday devices.

Resources required: batteries, wires, bulbs, motors, buzzers, switches

Pupils may not appreciate that the simple circuits they build and components they use can be found in everyday appliances. Challenging them to make their own devices can be a fun activity for them.

A simple night light can be constructed with a bulb and bulb holder. They can make a suitable shade to let some light through using cones of thin coloured paper or tracing paper. A fan can be made by attaching cardboard 'wings' to a motor. These can be anchored with Blutac™ or more securely by attaching them to a small plastic wheel from a design technology kit. Pupils could also make colour wheels that spin and mix colours together by attaching a small circular card to a motor. A burglar alarm could be made using a pressures switch and a buzzer (see Pupil activity 12.7). Designing buggies powered by motors would be a great design and technology link.

Using programmable control units, the pupils could make their own traffic lights and programme them to come on in sequence. See Figure 12.10.

Electricity and scientists – Franklin and Volta

Benjamin Franklin proved that lightning was a form of electricity in his incredibly dangerous kite experiment. In 1752, with the help of his son, he drew down electricity in a lightning storm and stored it in a Leyden jar (a jar that can collect and hold electricity). Lightning did not actually hit his kite – if it had done, he would have been killed!

The full details are outlined at: http://www.codecheck.com/cc/BenAndTheKite.html

Alessandro Volta is famous for making the first battery around 1800. He used copper and zinc discs and pieces of cloth which had been soaked in salt water. He then stacked the discs alternating with each other, and with a piece of salty cloth between them, forming a tall pile. Finally, he placed a wire running from the top to the bottom of the pile. Electricity ran through the wire, and he had created the first ever battery. Pupils can do a similar experiment using a 'potato clock kit'. The kit uses copper and zinc metals which are placed in a potato, or apple, or fizzy drink. The juice or drink reacts with the metals to create an electrical current, which is used to make a digital clock work.

You can buy a kit to do this, or make your own as detailed in this link: http://www.wikihow.com/Make-a-Potato-Clock

Figure 12.10 Photo of traffic lights with programmable box (Data Harvest Solutions)

Summary of key learning points

- all matter is made up of particles which include electrons; these carry a negative charge;

- in good electrical conductors, a proportion of electrons (so-called 'free electrons') can move easily; in poor conductors, like plastic, such movement is very difficult;

- resistance is a measure of the difficulty of flow of electrons in a material;

- when a battery (or cell) is attached in a circuit, it provides a 'push' that causes electrons to move in one direction around the circuit; this movement (flow) of electrons is called current (measured in amps);

- current is not consumed and is the same in all parts of a simple series circuit;

- voltage (measured in volts) might be thought of as driving the current;

- electricity is a form of energy that can be easily converted into other forms (e.g. sound from a buzzer, light from a light bulb, motion from a motor);

- as moving electrons collide with obstructions (atoms) in a wire or component, they make the atoms vibrate more;

- these collisions cause components such as a bulb filament to become hot and emit light;

- a circuit, including its components, can be represented by standard symbols in circuit diagrams.

Self-test

Question 1

The following are conductors: (a) all metals, (b) salty water, (c) plastic, (d) pencil lead (HB)

Question 2

In a simple series circuit, bulbs get dimmer if (a) we increase the number of cells, (b) we increase the number of bulbs, (c) we break the circuit, (d) we add a motor

Question 3

When building a circuit from different components, (a) it *does not* matter which order the components are in, (b) it *does* matter which order the components are in, (c) it is important to connect the wires from the buzzer the right way round, (d) the bulbs used should be identical

Question 4

A circuit will not work if (a) there is no battery or cell, (b) the switch is in the off position, (c) there is a break in the circuit, (d) there is no switch

Self-test answers

Q1: (a), (b), and (d) are correct. All metals are conductors; water is a relatively poor conductor in comparison, but its conductivity is improved if salt is dissolved in it. Pencil leads contain graphite, which is a good conductor, and an HB pencil in a simple circuit will show this. Plastic is a good insulator, which is why we use it on the outside of plugs and wires.

Q2: (b) and (d) are correct. If we add more bulbs in a series circuit, we increase the resistance and so decrease the current, making the bulbs dimmer. Adding any other component will also do this, for example a motor. Breaking the circuit will turn the bulbs off altogether, and adding cells will increase the voltage and so the bulbs will become brighter.

Q3: (a), (c), and (d) are correct. Components can be connected in any order in a series circuit, buzzers must be connected with the red wire going to the positive end of a battery and black to the negative end, and bulbs should have the same voltage as each other and the same amp number as each other.

Q4: (a), (b), and (c) are correct. Circuits require a source of electricity to work and should be complete. You don't have to have a switch in a circuit.

Misconceptions

'Electricity just comes out of plugs'

'Electricity comes from the air'

'Bigger batteries are more powerful'

'Electricity comes out of both ends of a battery'

'The plastic insulation on wire conducts electricity'

'A bulb doesn't have any connections'

'Put a motor in to make the bulb brighter!'

'More buzzers mean more noise!'

'Adding a bulb will mean that both bulbs will be brighter'

'Make the wires shorter to make the bulbs brighter'

'Some metals don't conduct, do they?'

'The metal door handle doesn't conduct!'

'Pencils are made of lead, that's why they conduct'

Web resources

http://www.codecheck.com/cc/BenAndTheKite.html
(Benjamin Franklin's kite experiment)

http://www-g.eng.cam.ac.uk/mmg/teaching/peterstidwill/interact/resources/
siliconspies/siliconspieslink.htm
(making more circuits)

http://www.hyperstaffs.info/science/work/physics/child/index.html
(making circuits, circuits in toys, resistance in wires, interactive whiteboard)

http://www.wikihow.com/Make-a-Potato-Clock
(Build a battery, similar to Allesandro Volta's first ever battery)

http://www.yenka.com/en/Yenka_Basic_Circuits/
(register and then download free circuit-building software)

13
Sound

About this chapter

This chapter addresses the science you need to know and understand about sound. It looks at how sound is made and how it travels in a medium from a vibrating source. It covers the range of volume and pitch in sound, human hearing, and echoes. The second part of the chapter addresses what the pupils need to learn. The final part suggests effective ways to teach about sound, including common misconceptions.

What the teacher needs to know and understand

Sound is a form of energy

Sound is a form of energy that is transmitted in a medium. As land-dwelling creatures on planet Earth, we hear sound transmitted in the medium of air. However, if you put your ear to a wooden table and tap on the table at arm's length, you will hear sound that has travelled through the medium of wood. If you swim underwater, any sound you hear will have travelled through the medium of water. Our ears have not evolved to hear in water and so our perception of sound underwater is not as clear as our perception of it in air.

Sound sources

The most familiar instances of sound are when objects vibrate in the air around us. Take a moment to listen; few of us live in a silent environment. Can you identify sounds you can hear from traffic, a computer, your home? Where is that sound coming from?

What is vibrating? Is it vibration of a motor as it spins? Or floorboards vibrating? The loudspeaker in a TV making the air vibrate? A musical instrument? Try saying the word 'science'. Where is that sound coming from? Place your hand on your throat and repeat the word. Can you feel your voice box vibrating? The human voice box, or larynx, produces our voice and consists of special tissue that can be vibrated to produce sound. The vocal chords also adjust the frequency, amplitude, and quality of that sound.

Hearing sound

Biology of
hearing

The human ear is divided into the outer, middle, and inner ear. The parts of the outer ear (the pinna and ear canal) receive and funnel sound towards the middle ear. Vibrating air hits the eardrum and makes it vibrate. The vibration then passes through tiny bones (the ossicles) inside the middle ear. From here the vibrations pass through the cochlea in which tiny hairs pick up the vibrations. These are converted to electrical impulses passing down the auditory nerve to the brain. The ear is highly sensitive and can be damaged by very loud sound. Pupils should know to care for their ears by not exposing them to excessively loud sound, keeping them clean, and not allowing objects to enter into the ear canal.

You should also be aware of the functions of two other elements of the ear. First, the Eustachian tube connects your inner ear to the back of your mouth so that the air pressure in the inner ear can adjust to match that of your environment. You will be aware of this when you increase or decrease your altitude (lower air pressure at higher altitude) significantly and find your ears 'pop', such as when an aeroplane descends. Second, the semicircular canals are situated in your inner ear and their three loops, which are filled with liquid, are responsible for your sense of balance.

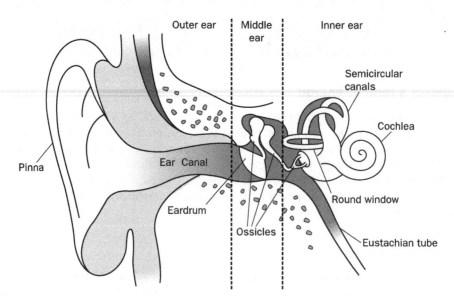

Figure 13.1 The human ear

Sound travels

Sound travels in air when the air molecules are made to vibrate. The molecules bump into each other and form a 'compression wave'. (See teacher demonstration 13.12 and Figure 13.3 for a good model of this.) These waves radiate out in all directions and are perceived by the human ear when the sound enters the ear canal and vibrates the eardrum, middle ear, and cochlea so that messages about the sound are sent to the brain. Sound travels in waves from a source like ripples on a pond but in three dimensions. The sound of a light aeroplane can be heard below, beside, and above the plane. This is the same for all sounds. As sound travels through a medium, it dissipates and becomes fainter. The speed of sound varies depending on the medium. In air sound travels at approximately 340 metres per second (770 miles per hour); in water it travels over four times faster and through iron over ten times faster. The relatively slow speed of sound in air and the much faster speed of light (around 300,000,000 metres per second) account for the delay between you seeing an explosion one mile away and hearing it a moment later. We see and hear this effect commonly with fireworks – a rocket explodes into different colours and a moment later we hear the bang of the explosion. In a vacuum there are no atoms or molecules – that is, no medium – and so sound cannot travel. This is why there is no sound in outer space.

You will have experienced echoes; this is an example of a reflection, but in this case reflection of sound. Large, fairly flat, and hard surfaces will reflect sufficient sound to produce the echo effect that we have all experienced. When walking through a school hall that is empty of other people, you may hear your footsteps echo around you. This is because the sound is bouncing off the hard surfaces around you and being returned to your ears. Interestingly, this effect is not present when the hall is full of people, as their soft bodies help to absorb the sound, preventing it from bouncing around so much and thus reducing the echoes.

Properties of sound

Sound has a number of properties, including frequency (pitch), amplitude (loudness), and quality. The terms used in primary science lessons are pitch and loudness. Frequency or pitch refers to the number of sound waves per second. High-pitched sounds such as a whistle have a high frequency; low-pitch sounds such as thunder have a lower frequency. If you whistle or sing 'la' and vary the pitch, you will change the frequency of the sound – have a go. Amplitude is the volume (or loudness) of the sound and describes the size of the waves; louder sounds are perceived as larger sound waves. If you repeat a word going from very quiet to very loud, you will increase the amplitude and you may sense that more energy is required. The quality of a sound relates to its purity – that is, whether it is, or is close to, a musical note. Interestingly, the same note does not sound the same on different instruments because of slight variations such as harmonics, which give a sound its character. Other noises around us are random mixtures of sounds.

Pupils often confuse pitch and loudness. You need to know that two things affect loudness:

- the amount of energy put in – for example, how hard you beat, blow, pluck or scrape something;
- the amount of stuff vibrating, that is, larger sound boxes make louder sounds – for example, a large bass drum is louder than a small finger drum.

Three things affect pitch: the size, length, and tightness of the thing that is vibrating. For example, large drums make sounds of a lower pitch than small drums.

Shortening or lengthening a string changes its pitch, and there is a similar effect with air columns of different length. Smaller lengths of string or air vibrate more quickly, and so have higher pitch. Finally, a skin drum can be tightened or loosened – the tighter the skin, the faster it vibrates and so the higher the pitch.

> Try playing with a virtual oscilloscope on the internet, such as the simplified one at:
>
> http://www.educationscotland.gov.uk/resources/s/sound/oscilloscope.asp
>
> Alter the volume (amplitude) and the pitch (the frequency).

What pupils need to know at Key Stage 1

Sound is not a topic at Key Stage 1. However, pupils only visit it once as a topic at Key Stage 2, so some input earlier would be of great benefit.

The learning objectives for Key Stage 1 pupils could include:

- that everyday objects, as well as musical instruments, can be used to make sounds;
- how sound can be made in different ways including striking, plucking, blowing, scraping, and shaking;
- that to make a sound louder requires more energy. So a whistle can be blown harder, a drum struck harder, a guitar plucked harder, and so on.

What pupils need to know at Key Stage 2

(ST) denotes statutory requirements.

Lower Key Stage 2

(ST) Identify how sounds are made, associating some of them with something vibrating

Suggestions for working scientifically:

Explore and identify the way sound is made through vibration in a range of different musical instruments from around the world.

(ST) Recognise that vibrations from sounds travel through a medium to the ear

Suggestions for working scientifically:

Pupils might make earmuffs from a variety of different materials to investigate which provides the best insulation against sound.

(ST) Recognise that sounds get fainter as the distance from the sound source increases

(ST) Find patterns between the volume of a sound and the strength of the vibrations that produced it

Suggestions for working scientifically:

Find out how the volume of sounds can be changed in a variety of ways.

Make and play their own instruments by using what they have found out about *volume*.

(ST) Find patterns between the pitch of a sound and features of the object that produced it

Suggestions for working scientifically:

Find out how the pitch of sounds can be changed in a variety of ways, for example, find patterns in the sounds that are made by different objects such as saucepan lids of different sizes or elastic bands of different thicknesses.

Make and play their own instruments by using what they have found out about *pitch*.

Ways to teach 'sound' at Key Stage 2

At all times when teaching about sound, you must stress and repeat the message that ears must be cared for. Very loud sounds must be avoided and objects should not be put into the ear. You could even impart this information at the end of each lesson. Also be sensitive to pupils who have a known hearing loss and be aware that your lessons might reveal cause for further medical investigation of hearing.

PSHE

Pupil activity 13.1

Identifying mystery sounds

Learning objectives: Learn that there are many kinds of sound and that there are many ways of making sound.

Resources required: recordings of sounds (internet based) and/or a large bag; objects for making sounds

This can be done in different ways, including objects hidden in a large bag (avoid plastic bags) or audio recordings made by yourself or pre-recorded. Simply make or play the mystery sounds and ask pupils to identify them. This can be made even more challenging by asking pupils to make the recordings.

Recordings can be downloaded from internet sites, such as:

http://www.crickweb.co.uk/ks1science.html

Common misconception

'I hear only when I listen'

Pupils often have difficulty with ideas about listening and hearing. They sometimes think that they only hear things they are near to. They may even say that very faint sounds have not been heard. Pupils sometimes feel that it is their listening which is crucial, that in some way they direct their ears towards particular sound sources. They seem to be confusing this with the brain's ability to attend to important sounds. These ideas can be challenged by experiencing many different sounds and by making pupils aware of all the many things they are hearing.

Pupil activity 13.2

What was that sound?

Learning objectives: Learn that there are many kinds of sounds and that sounds are heard when they enter your ears.

Resources required: a selection of drums, tambours, tambourines, triangles, rain sticks, tuning forks, bells, whistles, guitars

As in the activity above, pupils love identifying sounds; here they see the object making the sound and can pluck, blow (*note*: children should not share an object touched with the lips) or bang it. Familiar and less familiar musical instruments are ideal for this. Ask them to try to identify the part of the instrument that makes the sound and describe the sound travelling away from the source. Can they identify exactly how the instrument makes the sound – for example, is it banged, plucked, scraped or blown?

Pupil activity 13.3

Sounds from everyday objects

Learning objective: Learn that there are many kinds of sound and ways of making sounds.

Resources required: household objects, a beater, and/or a large blunt nail

Gather together a range of household objects which will be gently struck to explore sounds (avoid glassware being handled by pupils). Ceramic bowls such as plant pots work well, as do items of cutlery. Can they predict the type of sound that will be made? Group those items making a clear sound and those that make a dull sound. You could introduce the idea of vibration, some of which is invisible. All the objects vibrate when struck, but the better ones vibrate to produce a clear sound or sharp note. Note that some objects will only produce a high-quality sound if held in a particular way – for example, a plant pot will ring if suspended by a loop of string through a hole. If pupils are to hold breakable objects, make sure you actively supervise and teach them that these objects need to be held only a few centimetres above a desktop. Stress that different objects may make sounds in different ways if they are used differently. Can they gently bang, pluck, scrape, or blow on any of the objects to make the sound? Plastic bottles without lids can make a sound when hit with a beater, a different sound when blown across the neck (placing the lips near the hole), and a different sound again when scraped with a fingernail.

Common misconception

'Sound cannot go around corners'

Pupils may confuse sound with light here. Light cannot go around corners, but sound easily can. They need their attention drawn to the fact that sound can be heard above, below, and beside a sound source. They can also hear objects that are not in view, which means that the sound is travelling around corners. Can pupils hear a sound made under a table? If a dog barks next door, can all the neighbours hear it? Can they hear people talking around the corner of a building?

Pupil activity 13.4

Faint sounds on the school playground

Learning objective: Learn that sounds travel away from where they are made and get fainter as they travel.

Resources required: access to a large space, a beater and drum or tambour, a trundle wheel (optional)

On the school playground or playing field, ask one pupil to stand a few metres from the class and, at your signal, softly beat the drum. Check that all the pupils have heard the sound. Remind them about the sound source, about sound travelling and entering the ear. Ask a second child to stand 10 or 15 steps away (or measure 10 metres with a trundle wheel). Ask the class to predict what the sound the second pupil hears will be like. Have the class join the second child. The child with the drum then beats the drum softly again. Ask the class to describe how the sound has changed. Keep repeating this activity at regular intervals, increasing the distance between the listeners and the beater until the sound is much quieter.

If you have time, repeat the test with different sounds. It is important that the pupil with the drum knows to beat it the same way and with the same amount of force each time. They may be tempted to hit it harder the further the other pupils are away so that they can all hear it more clearly! You could address why it must be the same each time, introducing the concept of a 'fair test'.

Pupil activity 13.5

Can you hear a pin drop?

Learning objective: Learn that sounds travel away from where they are made and get fainter as they travel.

Resources required: light objects to drop, a means to hide the dropping of the objects

Noisy classrooms and schools can make investigation and demonstrations with sound more difficult. In this activity, you need to produce quiet sounds in one corner of the class. Pupils can then indicate by raising their hand whether they have heard it. Be aware and sensitive to any pupils with hearing difficulties. You could ask them to close their eyes and tell them that they are going to use one of the best sound meters in the world and they all have two of them, their ears! Try doing this out of sight of the pupils, asking them to listen and raise an arm if they hear anything (you can ask them to close their eyes). Pupils could suggest sounds to test. Sounds you might try are dropping objects onto paper – a pin, a match, a small nail, a large nail – clicking a pen open, opening a jar, and sharpening a pencil. Include some very quiet sounds but also some louder sounds that everyone can hear. Make sure you discuss examples of sounds everyone can hear and others that some can hear and some that no one can hear.

Practical activity 13.6

Sound safari

Learning objectives: Naming different sounds and how they are made.

Resources required: access to school corridors and playground

Take the pupils on a sound safari of the school. Before you set off, ask them to predict sounds they might hear and suggest places you might visit. Can they suggest a place that will be quiet and somewhere where there will be no sound? Visit different places in school where there will be different sounds, such as outside classrooms, outside the school kitchen, outside the school office (it is polite to warn colleagues that you are there and what you are doing!), and in the playground. Ask the pupils to be quiet and to listen to the different sounds. Can they say what the sounds are? Can they describe them? Challenge them to name as many sounds as possible.

Pupil activity 13.7

Putting the twang into science

Learning objective: Learn that sound sources vibrate, but that not all vibrations can be seen.

Resources required: collection of different sound-making objects, including instruments, such as elastic, bell, tuning fork, balloon, guitar, rulers or wood strips

Ask different pupils to demonstrate examples of sound sources and to identify the part of the object that is vibrating. Ask them to state whether they can see the vibrations. Ask them whether they can feel the vibrations. Ask them what they sound/feel like. Remind the class about the vibrating source, that sound travels and that they hear when sound enters their ear. Note that sometimes when you blow something you make air itself vibrate. It is the column of air vibrating inside a musical instrument that makes it work, not the wood or metal of the instrument.

Now ask every pupil to 'twang' a ruler or wood strip on the side of a table and ask them whether they can see or feel the vibrations and to describe them. Ask one pupil to demonstrate twanging different lengths of ruler over the side of the table. Can pupils describe the differences in sound? Introduce the term 'pitch'. Ask all pupils to explore the production of different frequencies of sound with the wood. Can pupils see that the frequency of the vibrations increases (they get quicker)? Tell them that we use the word 'pitch' but scientists also use the word 'frequency'. Return to the collection of objects you began with and ask pupils whether they think it is possible to alter the frequency of these.

Websites clips for understanding different types of musical instruments

http://www.bbc.co.uk/learningzone/clips/appalachian-spring-a-performance/7999.html (orchestral performance)

http://www.bbc.co.uk/learningzone/clips/sections-in-an-orchestra/8974.html (short guide to orchestral instruments)

http://www.bbc.co.uk/learningzone/clips/sound-colours-from-everyday-objects/7969.html (more junk instruments)

http://www.bbc.co.uk/learningzone/clips/tuning-junk-instruments/5210.html (large pieces of junk become musical instruments)

Pupil activity 13.8

More energy makes things LOUDER!

Learning objective: Learn that we can make things louder by putting more energy into a thing, such as shaking harder, plucking harder, beating harder.

Resources required: a range of instruments that can be made to produce loud and quiet sounds, a bottle, large elastic stretched over a box

Make a sound by beating something and ask pupils how it could be made louder. Involve pupils in a demonstration to show that beating harder makes the sound louder. Perhaps ask for volunteers to demonstrate plucking, blowing, and scraping sounds. Can they show the class how they make the sounds louder? Can the class suggest how to make the sounds quieter? Give examples of everyday objects and musical instruments.

Remind the pupils about the sound being made by vibrations and what you have taught them about sound vibrations. Can they explain how the energy provided affects the sound waves?

Pupil activity 13.9

A sound box makes things LOUDER!

Learning objective: Learn that by adding a sound box (where there was none before) or replacing a small sound box with a larger one, sounds become louder.

Resources required: large hollow containers including buckets and boxes, musical instruments such as violin and guitar, large elastic bands or long pieces of knicker elastic

Stretch an elastic band over a plastic bin or bucket. Ask a pupil to hold the bucket and pluck the elastic while everyone listens to the sound. The pupil holding it should feel the vibrations. Ask pupils for a description of the sound and vibration.

Compare this with a much smaller container and ask pupils to describe how the sound is different. You might begin to refer to sound travelling in waves. Some pupils will have heard of sound waves and will want to know more. Initially, explain that they are a little like ripples on a pond travelling away from the source.

This can be repeated on a range of large containers and with elastic stretched over boxes and pieces of equipment. Ask pupils to compare the sounds between examples. Can they describe the sounds? Explain that makers of musical instruments use this phenomenon to increase the loudness. Ensuring the container is clean, ask a child to wrap their arms around the container while you pluck the elastic again. Can they hear and feel the vibrations? Again ensuring the container is clean, repeat this with a child's ear to the container. Ask pupils to describe to one another the journey of the sound from elastic, air, container, air to eardrum. You might extend and enrich this and other similar activities by measuring the loudness of the sound in decibels with a hand-held sound meter or with a computer sound sensor.

Music, and DT

Pupil activity 13.10

How can you make sound higher or lower?

Learning objectives: Learn that shortening or lengthening a string changes the pitch. Learn that shortening or lengthening a column of air changes the pitch.

Resources required: a one-string elastic guitar, a recorder or swanny whistle, straws, a large elastic band, pencil

After stretching an elastic band over a strip of wood add a wooden slider to alter the pitch.

Figure 13.2 A one-string elastic guitar

music, DT

Stretch a large elastic band over the end of a classroom table and slip a pencil under it at one end. Invite a pupil to pluck it. Ask the pupil to describe what they see and hear. Ask if someone can suggest a way to change the pitch of the sound. Continue with the demonstration, making progressively higher pitched sounds by moving the pencil. Ask pupils to confer before answering the question 'why is the pitch of the sound changing?'

Emphasise that as the length of string is shortened, so it vibrates more quickly and the pitch becomes higher. Demonstrate the same effect on a stringed musical instrument (guitar or violin work well) and on the one-string elastic guitar. Ensure that as many pupils as possible have a go. Ask pupils to consider the explanation and whether they can draw a sound story to show the sound being made and travelling to an ear.

Either in this lesson or another, demonstrate the same effect with vibrating columns of air. First, you will have to explain that a vibrating column of air makes a sound. Try blowing on a recorder, blowing across the top of a bottle, and across the end of a straw. If a recorder has more fingers on it, the column of air becomes longer. How will this affect the sound? If a straw is cut, it will become shorter. How will that affect the sound? Can the pupils test their predictions?

Now do the same with a row of bottles each containing different amounts of water. Can two pupils put them in order of ascending pitch? Ask them to explain their reasoning, before testing their ideas and blowing across the top of the bottles.

Pupil activity 13.11

Tightness makes sounds higher

Learning objective: Understand that tightening rubber or elastic creates a higher pitch.

Resources required: empty two-litre plastic drinks bottles, balloons, elastic bands

Remove and discard the lids from the bottles. The balloons are going to be stretched over the mouths of the necks of the bottles. First, make a small slit in a balloon and poke the bottleneck through the slit. Then, secure the balloon to the bottleneck using an elastic band wrapped around the neck, ensuring the balloon is tight across the opening of the bottleneck. Place different balloons at varying tightness on different bottles, and label the bottles accordingly (e.g. tight, very tight, slack, etc.). Now the pupils can pluck the balloons and hear a high or low sound (the bottle acts like a sound box). Can they discern the differences between the tighter balloons making higher sounds and the slacker ones making lower sounds? (Ensure the cut balloons are disposed of afterwards, so that they do not present a choking hazard to young children who may put them in their mouths.)

Discuss with the pupils how the same can be done with drums. If you have large drums in school, show the pupils where the drum skin is anchored and can be tightened. Challenge them to think of string instruments that also can be tightened and stretched to make a higher sound. They should be able to think of a guitar or violin. If you have pupils who can play these instruments, ask them to demonstrate playing a tightened or slackened string.

Teacher demonstration 13.12

Slinky spring shows sound travelling

Learning objective: Learn that sound waves travel as compressions of particles in a medium.

Resources required: slinky spring

A slinky spring provides the best demonstration of sound waves travelling in a medium (a gas, a liquid or a solid). Place the slinky on a flat surface, the floor or a long table and ask two pupils to stretch it and hold it throughout the demonstration. Ask one to very quickly move their hand towards the other person by about 15 cm and then quickly return the hand to its starting position, and observe the result. Observers should see a compression wave travel along the slinky and then bounce back, simulating an echo. Repeat this a few times, perhaps allowing other pupils to propagate the

Hearing, see Figure 5.11 on p. 101

wave. Make it clear that the person starting the wave is acting as the vibrating material and that the wave then travels through a medium.

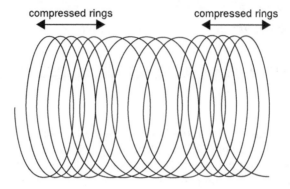

compressed rings   compressed rings

Figure 13.3 Compression wave travels down a slinky spring

Teacher demonstration 13.13

Sound moving away from its source

Learning objective: Learn that sound travels away from a vibrating source.

Resources required: tuning fork, bowl of water, newspaper

With a small group of pupils gathered around the bowl, bang the tuning fork on a scrap of wood and place the vibrating end gently onto the water in the centre of the bowl. Ripples radiate outwards very quickly from the source of sound. If you quickly remove the tuning fork, you may see the vibration 'echoing' back from the sides of the bowl. The children could take turns at doing this in small groups. This is a memorable and effective demonstration.

Ask the pupils to remember a time when they threw a stone into water. A stone thrown into a still pool or large bowl of water will produce waves in rings, which travel away from the source in a way that is similar to the way sound waves are produced and travel.

Pupil activity 13.14

Making ear defenders

Learning objective: Learn that different materials can reduce sound entering the ear and that we call this sound insulation.

Resources required: examples of sheet materials that can include different fabrics, bubble plastic, cotton wool, aluminium foil, papers, cards

This can be used as a teaching activity or adapted to become a pupil-led investigation. You need to identify a sound that you can make consistently, such as striking a musical instrument, shuffling paper, pouring water, or dropping a pin. You can, of course, use several sounds if you wish. Warn pupils never to put objects into their ears. Recap on sound travelling from a source to the ears. Ask a pupil to demonstrate by first listening to the sound and then when holding a material over their ear. Hopefully they will notice a difference. If they find it difficult, remind them to listen with that ear or cover both ears with the material (this is a better test). Discuss these options and fair testing with the pupils. Can they ensure that the fabrics and materials are the same thickness?

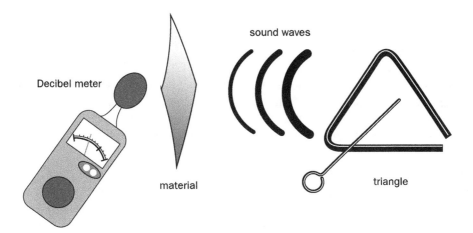

Figure 13.4 Testing sound insulation properties

Folding them can help. Then ask pupils to look at and ideally handle the samples of other materials. Ask them to describe the characteristics of the materials that insulate sound well, then to repeat the test themselves this time making a prediction about the best materials for insulating sound.

An alternative or extension is to repeat the tests but replace the human ear with a decibel meter.

Teacher demonstration and pupil discussion 13.15

How does sound travel?

Learning objective: Learn that vibrations from a source require a medium through which to travel to the ear.

Resources required: a pencil, metal spoon, or nail

Pupils need to be able to hear a quiet, consistent sound such as a pencil being dropped onto a desk from a height of one centimetre. Repeat it a number of times so that several pupils can hear and describe it. Perhaps only those pupils close by will hear it. Then ask a pupil to hold an ear to the table as far away as possible from the noise and repeat; this time the pupil should notice a slightly louder sound as the pencil hits the table. (If it does not appear to work, it may be that the pupil is concentrating on their other ear.) Pupils might repeat this in pairs at their own table.

Explain that we experience sound travelling from a source through air but that sound can travel through other materials such as wood, steel, rock, and water. Ask the pupils if they have experienced any examples. Prompt them with the following examples, if required:

- tapping on metal pipework in a building;
- sound underwater in a swimming pool;
- movement of furniture in a room above them.

Consider these examples and draw the journey of the sound as a simple flow chart, noting that the last part of the journey to the eardrum travels in the medium of air. Emphasise the fact that each medium must vibrate for the sound to travel through it; for instance, in the first example, the metal particles vibrate, which in turn make the air particles around the pipe vibrate.

Source	First medium	Second medium
Plumber tapping a pipe →	The sound travels through the pipe	→ The sound leaves the pipe and travels through the air to the ear
Object dropped in room above →	The sound travels through the floor material	→ The sound travels through the air to the ear

Pupils should understand that sound waves can travel through different mediums and transfer from one medium to another. You can explain that sound travels faster in solids and liquids than in the air around us. Challenge pupils by linking this to what they know about solids, liquids, and gases. The speed of travel of sound is slower in the air because of the gaps between the particles (atoms and molecules) in air. Solids and liquids have fewer gaps between the vibrating particles, so the sound can be passed on more efficiently.

Common misconception

'Sound doesn't travel through solids'

Many pupils are happy with the fact that sound travels through air by making the air vibrate. They may know that sound travels through water, as they have heard sounds when underwater in the swimming pool. Many, however, do not believe that sound travels through hard solids, which it does, very well. Ask them to think about sound in terms of vibrating particles. Air is made of gas particles that can vibrate to transmit sound; water can similarly vibrate, and so can the particles in wood or metal. Only in outer space or another vacuum where there are no particles is there no sound. If you find they are still struggling with the idea, ask them if they have ever put their ear to a door or wall to try to listen to what was happening on the other side of it!

Pupil Activity 13.16

Researching how instruments from around the world produce their sounds

Learning objective: to use their knowledge of how sound is generated, altered, and transmitted to explain how unfamiliar instruments may be played.

Resources required: internet access

By the time your pupils have finished studying this topic they should be familiar with the different ways of making vibrations, ways to change volume and pitch and how certain materials can help or hinder the transmission of sound. With these factors in mind, allow them to research online a variety of unfamiliar world instruments (example websites are listed below). Challenge them to say exactly how the sound is generated (is the instrument plucked, scraped, shaken . . .?), how the volume or pitch might be changed (by shortening a string, lengthening a column of air), and how a sound box may be amplifying the sound (a familiar example is an acoustic guitar) or the sound could be stifled (such as when a trumpet is muffled).

Many of the instruments may look unfamiliar at first, but clicking on and magnifying the pictures, followed by a little detective work, should reveal how most of them work. You may like to take examples from the above paragraph as a prompt sheet.

Many websites have a good collection of images, and are slowly adding sound clips to the instruments, for example:

http://learningobjects.wesleyan.edu/vim/

http://www.asza.com/ihm.shtml

http://www.imit.org.uk/pages/a-to-z-of-musical-instrument.html

http://www.vam.ac.uk/page/m/musical-instruments/ (historical musical instruments of the Victoria and Albert Museum, London, some with sound)

Summary of key learning points

- sound travels through a medium from a vibrating source;

- sound can vary in amplitude and frequency, which affects loudness and pitch respectively;

- the quality of sound is judged by how close it is to a musical note;

- sounds are heard when vibrations from an object enter the ear, causing the eardrums to vibrate and impulses to be carried by nerves to the brain;

- some materials reflect sound;

- some materials act as sound insulators.

Self-test

Question 1

Sound travels (a) faster than light, (b) from a vibrating source, (c) best in air, (d) in all directions from a source

Question 2

Sound waves (a) can differ in amplitude resulting in different volumes, (b) can differ in frequency resulting in different pitches, (c) are only made in the human voice box, (d) are just like waves on water

Question 3

Sound (a) is a form of energy, (b) can only travel in a straight line, (c) can travel through a vacuum, (d) can be dangerous

Question 4

I hear sound because these body parts help me: (a) eardrum, (b) cochlea, (c) Eustachian tube, (d) semicircular canals.

Self-test answers

Q1: (b) and (d) are correct. Sound travels much slower than light and travels faster in solids than in gases. So if best means fastest and travelling over long distances, then air is quite a poor conductor of sound. Because our ears have evolved to work in air, then air appears to us to be quite a good conductor of sound.

Q2: (a) and (b) are correct. Sounds are made by very many vibrating objects. Sound waves are a little like waves on the surface of water but are different in a number of ways, for example sound waves go in all directions at once.

Q3: (a) and (d) are correct. Sound can travel around corners. Sound requires a physical medium that is made up of particles (e.g. air, water, wood) to travel through. A vacuum has no particles.

Q4: (a) and (b) are correct. The Eustachian tube helps less directly because it equalises the air pressure inside the inner ear. The semicircular canals give us our sense of balance.

Misconceptions

'I hear when I listen'

'Sound cannot go around corners'

'Sound doesn't travel through a solid'

Web resources

http://www.crickweb.co.uk/ks1science.html
   (sound recordings)
http://www.educationscotland.gov.uk/resources/s/sound/oscilloscope.asp
   (simple oscilloscope)

Website clips for understanding different types of musical instruments

http://www.bbc.co.uk/learningzone/clips/appalachian-spring-a-performance/7999.html
   (orchestral performance)

http://www.bbc.co.uk/learningzone/clips/sections-in-an-orchestra/8974.html
   (short guide to orchestral instruments)

http://www.bbc.co.uk/learningzone/clips/sound-colours-from-everyday-Objects/7969.html
   (more junk instruments)

http://www.bbc.co.uk/learningzone/clips/tuning-junk-instruments/5210.html
   (large pieces of junk become musical instruments)

World instruments websites:

http://learningobjects.wesleyan.edu/vim/

http://www.asza.com/ihm.shtml

http://www.imit.org.uk/pages/a-to-z-of-musical-instrument.html

http://www.vam.ac.uk/page/m/musical-instruments/
  (historical musical instruments of the Victoria and Albert Museum, London, some with sound)

14
Light

About this chapter

This chapter looks at light sources, how light travels, reflection, shadow formation, and how we see things. Transparent, translucent, and opaque materials are also dealt with. Coloured light occurring in rainbows, soap bubbles, and coloured filters is touched upon, as is diffraction – the bending of light. The second part of the chapter addresses what the pupils need to learn. The final part suggests effective ways to teach about light, including examples of common misconceptions.

What the teacher needs to know and understand

Light sources

Light sources are things that *make* light and are usually very hot, such as the Sun, other stars, a burning match, lightning, the glowing wire filament of a light bulb, and a firework. Children often think of the Moon as a light source, but it is not because it does not make light, it merely reflects the Sun's light. Chemical light sources produce light through the reaction of different chemicals and are not hot. These are seen in nature; for example, glow worms and fire flies use chemical reactions to make light. Chemical light sources are much less common than other light sources, although you can buy cheap chemical 'light sticks' (worn by children at parties) in toy shops. These operate at room temperature and are safe to use (but should not be broken open to release the chemicals).

Earth in space

Light sources are easier to see when there is little extraneous light around them. This is why candles appear brighter in a darkened room than they do in sunlight. You can see the meagre light that candles produce in a dark room 'lighting up' the wall, but in direct sunlight you don't notice this as the Sun's brighter light masks the candle's light. Stars cannot be seen in the daytime, because the light from our Sun is so great it obscures the weak light from the stars. At night time, when we have no sunlight, we can then easily see the light from the stars.

White light is made of different colours

Art and design

Most light sources give out white light. Sunlight is mostly white light. White light is in fact a mixture of colours, the colours of the rainbow. Isaac Newton was the first to prove this conclusively by splitting white light with a glass prism. He called the resulting colours the 'spectrum', which has its roots in Latin, meaning 'ghost'. White light is split into its constituent colours of red, orange, yellow, green, blue, indigo, and violet (see Figure 14.1). The mnemonic 'Richard of York Gave Battle in Vain' can help adults and children remember the sequence of colours. When a rainbow occurs, the white light from the Sun is being split up into its constituent colours as it passes through droplets of rain.

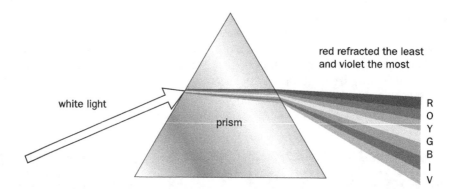

Figure 14.1 White light split into its constituent colours

Soap bubbles also show the different colours inside white light, through a process called 'interference'. This is where beams of light are mixed or mingled together to produce different colours. This is a very complex phenomenon and we will only give a simple explanation here. Most light hitting a bubble will pass through it (because the bubble is transparent), but some does not go through and is reflected back. A soap bubble has two surfaces that can reflect light. It has an outer soapy surface and an inner soapy surface, with water sandwiched between them. If light bounces back off the outer soapy surface and combines with light bouncing off the inner soapy surface, then different colours can occur as the light beams mix back together. This process gives rise to the different rainbow colours seen in bubbles. The colours change before our eyes depending on the angle the light hits the bubble and the thickness of the bubble, which cause the beams to recombine in different ways.

You will have observed similar colours in car oil spilt on a wet road, where the surface of the oil on top and the surface of the water below are both reflecting light rays. It is mingling back together of these rays from the two different surfaces that produces a range of colours. Compact discs show a similar effect, as light bounces off the different plastic layers and recombines to make the colours we see.

All the pupils need to know at this stage is that white light is made up of the colours of the rainbow and transparent objects can reveal the colours through either splitting up the white light as it passes through (e.g. in the prism) or mingling it together as it is reflected off different surfaces (e.g. bubbles or oil on water.)

Light travelling

Light travels in a straight line from a light source. Each light source produces millions of beams in all directions, but it is often useful to think of a single straight line beam travelling away from a source to explain the properties of light.

Shadow formation

A beam of light can be blocked by an opaque material. This means that behind the object a shadow will appear, which is simply a lack of light.

Reflection

Light is reflected from most surfaces, but how it is reflected depends on how smooth or rough the surface is. When incoming beams of light hit a rough surface, they scatter in many different directions. This is sometimes called 'diffuse reflection'. In contrast, when incoming light beams hit a smooth surface all the light beams are reflected in the same direction, forming a clear reflected image on the smooth surface. Mirrors are both shiny and smooth, and are therefore very good at forming perfect images. Other objects can form clear images too, although not as well as a mirror. For example, you may have seen your own image reflected in a metallic fridge door or on a laminated piece of paper.

Dark and dull colours (such as black) tend to absorb light rather than reflect a lot of it. This is why dark surfaces get hot on sunny days. Dark surfaces absorb the light (and its heat energy) and so warm up.

Because light travels in a straight line, it cannot go around corners. The only way to make it do so is to reflect it at an angle with a mirror.

Seeing colours

When light hits any object containing a colour pigment, the entire spectrum of colour in the light is not reflected. Some colours in the spectrum are absorbed by the pigment and as a result we only see the reflected colour. For example, a red object absorbs all the colours except red. Only the red light is reflected, and when this enters your eye you see the red object. Colour reflection is actually more complex, but this simple explanation will suffice for our purposes and is one that primary pupils can readily understand. This effect is illustrated in Figure 14.2.

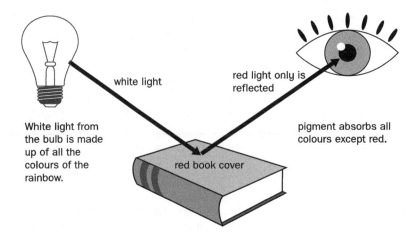

Figure 14.2 How we see coloured objects

Transparent materials

Transparent materials allow most of the light hitting them to go straight through. Usually, 98 per cent of the light passes through, with just 2 per cent being reflected, allowing us to see glass windows (or not, as anyone who has walked into closed patio doors knows). Because a small amount of light is blocked, transparent materials give a very faint or pale shadow, compared to the black shadow of an opaque material.

Colour filters

A colour filter is transparent, but only lets its own colour through while absorbing all the other colours. Imagine a blue plastic filter. This only lets blue light through. The other colours from the spectrum are absorbed by the filter so don't pass through. If you look through the blue filter, objects appear blue (or black if they don't reflect back any blue light at all).

Translucent materials

Translucent materials allow light through them but tend to scatter it internally first. A good test is to hold the material in front of a page of text. If you can read the text, the material is probably transparent; if you can see that there is text but it is difficult or impossible to read, the object is probably translucent. If you can't see through it at all, the material is probably opaque! Note that translucent materials give fairly dark shadows, though not as dark as opaque materials, because they do allow some light through.

Refraction of light

Refraction of light occurs when light beams are 'bent', as they pass from one medium to another. Example of mediums are the things light travels through, such as air, water, and glass. The denser the medium, the more the light is slowed down and the more it is bent. You may be familiar with the optical illusion called the broken straw. When a straw is placed in a transparent beaker of water and looked at from the side, the top part of the straw does not appear to be properly connected to the bottom part. This is because the more dense water is slowing down and bending the light, giving the straw its odd appearance when viewed from the side. Glass is denser than water, so can bend light even more. Glass lenses are able to bend light so that it can be focused onto a point. An everyday example would be a magnifying glass, which can focus the Sun's rays onto a leaf and cause it to smoulder at a single point. Telescopes, spectacles, and microscopes all use glass lenses to focus light to magnify or reduce images.

Light is a form of energy

Energy comes in many forms and light is one of them. This means that it can be produced from other forms of energy. For example, the chemical energy released when wood is burnt produces both light and heat energy. Electrical energy from a battery can be transformed to light energy in the coiled wire of a bulb (the filament). Light is also sometimes referred to as a kind of radiation. Radiation includes visible light (that allows us to see objects), infrared (this is heat, produced from anything warm), ultra-violet light (the kind of radiation that comes from the Sun to give you a suntan), and radio waves. These kinds of radiation are called electro-magnetic radiation by scientists.

Energy

What pupils need to know at Key Stage 1

Light is not a topic in the National Curriculum at Key Stage 1. However, in preparation for its appearance at Key Stage 2, some initial knowledge would be useful for younger pupils so they can build on these concepts later. Learning objectives could include:

- that certain things produce light – usually from burning or being made hot from electricity. Burning things include the Sun, stars and bonfires. Electrical things include light bulbs in lamps, car headlights and street lights;

- shiny materials do not make light, but are good at reflecting it so that they appear bright. Examples include mirrors, foil, silver paper;

- shadows are caused when certain materials block light. Pupils should be able to sort materials into those that block light (opaque) and those that let the light through (transparent). (See Chapter 8, 'Materials', 'Key Stage 1', 'What the pupils need to know' section.)

What pupils need to know at Key Stage 2

(ST) denotes statutory requirements.

Lower Key Stage 2

(ST) Recognise that light from the Sun can be dangerous and that there are ways to protect their eyes

Suggestions for working scientifically:

> Research why it is important to protect their eyes from bright lights and that it is not safe to look directly at the Sun, even when wearing dark glasses.

(ST) Recognise that they need light in order to see things and that dark is the absence of light

(ST) Notice that light is reflected from surfaces

Suggestions for working scientifically:

> Explore what happens when light reflects off a mirror or other reflective surfaces, including playing mirror games to help them to answer questions about how light behaves.

(ST) Recognise that shadows are formed when the light from a light source is blocked by a solid object

Suggestions for working scientifically:

> Find out how shadows are formed.
>
> Measure shadows, and find out what might cause the shadows to change.

(ST) Find patterns in the way that the size of shadows change

Suggestions for working scientifically:

> Look for patterns in what happens to shadows when the light source moves (i.e. the shadow moves too – always appearing directly behind the object, relative to the light source).
>
> Look for patterns when the distance between the light source and the object changes (i.e. the size of shadow changes).

Upper Key Stage 2

(ST) Recognise that light appears to travel in straight lines

(ST) Use the idea that light travels in straight lines to explain that objects are seen because they give out or reflect light into the eye

(ST) Explain that we see things because light travels from light sources to our eyes or from light sources to objects and then to our eyes

> Decide where to place rear-view mirrors on cars.
>
> Design and make a periscope and using the idea that light appears to travel in straight lines to explain how it works.

(ST) Use the idea that light travels in straight lines to explain why shadows have the same shape as the objects that cast them

> Investigate the relationship between light sources, objects and shadows by using shadow puppets.

Other effects with light:

> Extend their experience of light by looking at a range of phenomena including rainbows, colours on soap bubbles, objects looking bent in water and coloured filters (they do not need to explain why these phenomena occur).

Ways to teach 'light' at Key Stage 2

For all demonstrations and hands-on practical work, the room needs to be darkened to stop outside sunlight from interfering with the light sources the children are trying to use. The school hall is often a place that can be easily darkened and the children can spread out to do their work. A classroom or work area that can be darkened sufficiently for experimental work is ideal. We must stress that a darkened area is essential. Trying to do the experiments with bright sunlight entering the room will not work. It may be worth considering teaching light in the autumn term or early spring term, as there are several light festivals at this time of year.

Ensure that you have good torches for pupils to use. Weak torches or those with virtually flat batteries are useless. These confuse results and can cause misconceptions (e.g. no obvious shadow may be formed by an opaque object).

R.E.

Light sources

Pupil activity 14.1

A light source hunt and discussion

Learning objective: To identify light sources.

Take the children on a walk around the school on a 'light source hunt'. Ask them to identify indoor and outdoor light sources. After discussing and adding light sources they already know to the list, have them draw those they can remember or categorise them as say 'safe' and 'dangerous' (there are very few safe light sources for children – mainly toys and torches). Make sure you discuss non-light sources (i.e. reflective materials) and explain why they don't make light, but can look bright.

Earth in space

Explain how the Sun gives us light. Many children find this hard to grasp, as the Sun is not always visible in the day. Explain that even when the sky is cloudy, still a lot of the Sun's light gets through. Talk about the dangers of the Sun and how we must never look at it directly. If they ask about night time, you must be clear about the Earth turning and that our part of the Earth is not lit up by the Sun at night. A demonstration with a turning globe and a torch is the best way to show them this idea. Further cement their understanding by asking the children to explain it to one another.

Pupil investigation skills 14.2

Hands-on with torches and an investigation

Learning objective: An exploration (and/or investigation) of the amount of light emitted from each torch in a set of torches.

Resources required: a range of different-sized torches, white card or paper

Ask the children to use different types of torches. They should shine them onto a piece of card to see how bright they are. Warn about not looking straight at the torches or shining them in their own or others' eyes. Can they use comparison or describing words

such as brighter or dimmer when using them? Can they order the torches from brightest to dimmest? How will they ensure it is a fair test? For example, always shine the torch at a set distance from the card. Can they devise a way to test if the brightest torches have beams that travel the furthest? These questions can be considered on the basis of simple exploration but only confidently answered after an investigation. It is useful to judge torches qualitatively – that is, using descriptive superlatives such as bright, brighter, brightest, dim, dimmer, dimmest.

Teacher demonstration 14.3

Lighting up the wall with bright sources, looking directly at dimmer light sources

Learning objective: Observing, describing, and comparing light sources in dark and light rooms.

Resources required: light sources (as detailed below)

Some light sources get hot very quickly and should not be handled by children, but a whole-class demonstration can initiate useful discussion. The light from table lamps and overhead projectors can be shone on a wall. Do this, switch them off, and then darken the classroom before switching them on again. The children will notice a big difference – that is, light sources seem brighter to look at (see safety point below) and seem to produce more light in their surroundings when viewed in the dark. Even a torch beam on a wall demonstrated in this way will show this effect. Can they explain this?

Ask the children to look at dimmer light sources more safely, such as Christmas lights, novelty light-up toys or, easiest of all, a candle. These again look much brighter in the dark, as light from elsewhere is not negating their effect (see page 367 for more on this). You should follow this with a discussion of what are safe and unsafe light sources in the home.

Common misconception

'Shiny things are light sources'

A common misconception among younger children is that all shiny objects are light sources, because they look bright. There are two approaches that can be used to challenge this idea, outlined below.

Pupil investigation skills 14.4

Shiny objects

Learning objective: Explore shiny materials to see if they are shiny in the dark.

Resources required: a range of shiny objects, such as metal foil, pie dish, plastic mirrors, and fluorescent plastic

If the children are familiar with the fact that light sources look brighter in a darkened environment (such as fairy lights at night), try this with the shiny object. Ask them to observe the shiny object in the normal class setting and then in a darkened setting. It will be harder to see the object in the darkened setting, not easier. And the darker the setting the better. You could simply close the blinds or curtains. Or, using fabric, you could make a dark 'cave' or use a stock cupboard. Try placing light- and dark-coloured toys in the darkened room or space. Ask the children to state which toys are easy to see. Try repeating this with torches. Children can also try shining torch light on the shiny object, which will make it brighter. A problem you may experience is that complete darkness is hard to achieve; if any light gets in, the children will be able to see! Also note that some children may be fearful of complete darkness.

Another effective approach employs a shoe box viewer. A shoe box viewer can be easily made from a box with a lid on, with a small hole cut into the side to look through. Place the shiny object inside and with no external light sources the child will not be able to see it. For further uses of the box, see below.

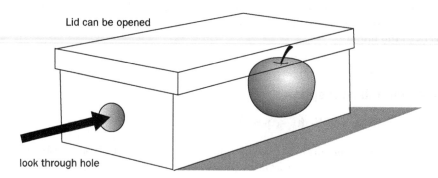

Lid can be opened

look through hole

Figure 14.3 A shoe box viewer

Common misconception

'But we can see in the dark, can't we?'

Most children have not experienced complete darkness, particularly in cities; it is hard to do so. The darkest time they experience is probably bedtime with the lights off, and they will comment that they can still see 'a bit'. Some children may also believe they can 'see in the dark' because they eat carrots, since they have been told that 'carrots make you see in the dark'.

Pupil discussion 14.5

We cannot see in the dark as our eyes require light to see things

Learning objective: Learn that we need light to see.

Resources required: none

Initiate a class discussion about where the light is coming from that enables the pupils to see in bed. Perhaps the bulb at the top of the stairs sends light through the gap underneath the bedroom door, or light enters through the gap in the curtains from the street lights outside, or even through the thin fabric of the curtain. This small amount of light enables them to see things. Outside, the light sources are more obvious such as street lights. However, as starlight, the Moon's reflected light, and distant street lights are relatively weak, we still feel that we are in the dark.

Pupil activity 14.6

What can we see in the box?

Learning objective: Observing what we can see in dull light.

Resources required: a shoe box viewer

A shoe box viewer is a good way to show that we need light to see. Use a shoe box with a small hole cut out of it in the side, large enough for a child to put their eye up to look in, but not too large or light from the outside will get in too. Objects placed inside at the far end cannot be seen.

If a small opening is cut into the lid to make a flap, and the flap is covered by a thick piece of card glued onto it, then varying amounts of light can be let in, and as more light is let in the easier it is to see the object.

Pupil activity 14.7

Where are the darker parts of school?

Learning objective: Explore the school for places that are darker.

Resources required: the school grounds

Pupils could list and visit the darker parts of school and view an object held in their hands at the different locations. How clearly can they see the shape or colour of it at different locations? Ask them how much they would be able to see of the object if they had no light at all.

Shadow formation and light travelling from a source

To understand shadow formation, it is important that the children know that light travels away from a source and strikes things. But how can we show light travelling from a source? The following demonstration can help.

Teacher demonstration 14.8

Light travelling away from its source and moving in a straight line

Learning objective: Understand how light travels.

Resources required: darkened room, good torch, board duster, and chalk (or talcum powder)

In a darkened room, place a torch on its end on a table so that it is pointing at the ceiling. Switch it on and the children will observe the beam on the ceiling. Now ask them if they can see the light as it travels through the air from the torch to the ceiling (they won't be able to, as air is invisible and you can't light up an invisible thing!). Now bang the chalk-laden duster with your hand just above the torch bulb (or squirt the talc bottle in the same place) and move it up while creating more dust to reveal the beam. The light beam can now be seen, illuminating the chalk, spreading out but travelling in a straight line towards the ceiling. (Warning: beware of dust – check that pupils are well away and that asthmatics are at some distance, and try not to inhale the dust yourself.)

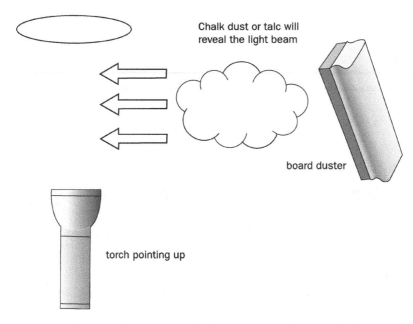

Figure 14.4 Demonstration of light travelling in a straight line

Shadow making

Pupil activity 14.9

Drawing our own shadows

Learning objective: To be able to draw an accurate shadow representation.

Resources required: drawing materials

A good starting point is to get the children to draw a small picture of themselves and their shadow. The common errors the pupils may make are discussed in the 'Common misconceptions' box below.

Common misconception

'Do shadows have faces? Are they connected to us?'

Two misconceptions commonly occur. First, many children want to draw faces on shadows, and sometimes other features. Here the children may be mixing up notions of a shadow, which has the same shape as them, and their reflection, which also has the same shape *as well as* other features. This mix-up often occurs throughout Key Stage 2, with some children even referring to a shadow as a 'dark reflection'. Gradually, they learn to distinguish between the way a shadow is formed (as light is blocked) and when reflections occur (as light bounces off something).

Another common error made by pupils is that the shadow they draw is not joined to their feet, but floating away from them.

Pupil activity 14.10

Where are our shadows?

Learning objective: To understand that a person's shadow is connected to them.

Resources required: none

Discussion of the above errors with the whole class is an excellent way to tackle these notions, but if this is reinforced on a sunny day with examination of their shadows in the playground, all the better. Sunny days can be hard to come by, so you may have to be patient!

Ask the children to examine their shadows in the playground. Do they see any facial features when the sun is behind them? (They may see their nose in profile but never their eyes!) Do their legs connect with the bottom of the shadow? If they jump up in the air, then they don't. This can lead to a discussion on how flying things such as clouds and aeroplanes are not connected to their shadows. They may not find it obvious that for something to be connected to its own shadow it must be on the ground itself.

Teacher demonstration 14.11

Can you see the features?

Learning objective: Understand why a shadow shows certain features, but not others.

Resources required: overhead projector, a simple card silhouette of a head without facial features and a second card silhouette of a head with features stuck on (e.g. eye, nose, and mouth)

It is easy to show that features such as the eyes and mouth of a person do not appear in shadows. Make a shadow by placing the simple card silhouette on the overhead projector and get the children to observe the shadow. When you place the card with features on the projector, there should be no discernible difference in the shadow created.

Pupil activity 14.12

How can we change how shadows look?

Learning objective: Explore and talk about shadows and how we can change them.

Resources required: torches, different objects

Let the children experiment with making simple shadows using a torch and a range of materials (this section is expanded later on). Ask them to see if they can change the size of the shadow, or change the shape of the shadow, by moving the torch to a different position. Both the shape and size of a shadow offer possibilities for an investigation.

Pupil investigation skills 14.13

How can we change the size of a shadow?

Learning objective: Understand how and why a shadow can be of different sizes.

Resources required: torch, small opaque object, screen, ruler, white card for screen

First, set up the torch, shadow-making object, and white card screen in a straight line, as shown in Figure 14.5.

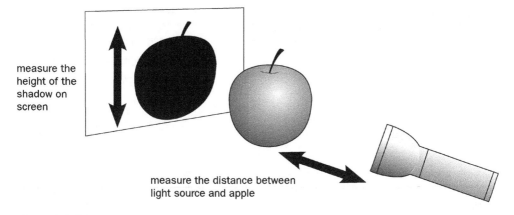

measure the height of the shadow on screen

measure the distance between light source and apple

Figure 14.5 Investigation of changes in shadow size

When setting up their experiment, the children need to decide to change *only one thing*, while keeping *the other things exactly the same*. Pupils should keep the light source and screen fixed in the same positions and *only move the object* that makes the shadow. This idea of changing only one variable (or factor) is fundamental to science. The variable in this case is the distance between the light source and the object. Have them measure the distance between the torch and the object each time they change it.

The pupils need to make a second measurement of the height of the shadow each time they change the distance. Can they work out the relationship between the size of the shadow and what they are doing? Pupils may find it difficult to know what to move and what to keep the same – some may want to move the screen and some may want to move the source. Some may wrongly try moving more than one thing at a time. Many pupils will be able to correctly describe what happens as they move the object to change the shadow size, but will find it difficult to explain the relationship between moving the object and the size of the shadow that forms on the screen.

Pupil investigation skills 14.14

Do all materials block light?

Learning objective: Explore different transparent and non-transparent materials.

Resources required: torches, good selection of fabrics and objects: transparent, opaque, translucent (milk carton, greaseproof paper, tracing paper), and coloured transparent acetates. (For more suggestions see Table 14.1.)

Table 14.1 Objects and materials for light investigations

Transparent	Opaque	Translucent
coloured and colourless drinks bottles (plastic)	food cartons (card) magazine (paper)	tracing paper (paper) greaseproof paper (paper)
CD case (coloured plastic)	lolly stick (wood)	thin paper tissue (paper)
sandwich bag (polythene)	stick of chalk (chalk)	plastic milk bottle (plastic)
cling film (polythene)	spoon (metal)	
	stone (rock)	

Ask the children to sort the materials into groups that will or will not let light through based on their predictions before they test them. Children should be able to come up with their own ways of testing the materials, ensuring that they set up a fair test each time.

As adults, we know that materials can be classed as transparent, translucent, and opaque. Starting with the idea of transparent and opaque, children can make predictions about which materials will fall into different categories. They should be able to test a material in the following three ways:

- Can you see through it?
- Can you shine a light through it?
- Does it make a dark shadow?

They may be able to come up with the following:

- An opaque material blocks light so that we can't see through it, can't shine a light through it, and it makes a very dark shadow.
- A transparent material allows light through it, we can see through it, and it makes a very faint (or pale) shadow.
- A translucent material allows only some light through; you can't see anything through it except bright light sources, and it makes a fairly dark shadow.

Common misconception

'If it's got colour it can't be transparent'

Children often think that transparent things have no colour, such as 'clear' glass. They can be confused with a coloured acetate sheet, because colourful things are often opaque. By looking through a coloured acetate or green wine bottle, shining a light through it, and reading text from a book through it, they should be able to reach the correct conclusions.

How we see things

From previous work, children should be familiar with the idea of light travelling in straight lines from a light source (see Teacher demonstration 14.8). We only see things when light enters our eye. This may be easy to state, but it is hard to demonstrate and although many children may nod with agreement at the statement, when questioned more closely they are less clear and they tend to hang on to their misconceptions.

Common misconception

'Light comes out of the eye when we see'

Many children believe that the light comes out of their eyes when they see things. Our language does not help as we say 'I saw you the other day', which sounds like an active process, rather than 'light reflected off you and entered my eye, the other day'. This can encourage children to think that in doing the seeing they are being active, but it is really a very passive process.

Pupil discussion 14.15

How do we see things?

Learning objective: That light must enter our eye for us to see.

Structure
and
function of
the eyes

You might discuss with the children what it would be like if light really did come out of their eyes. For one thing, the pupils of their eyes would be bright white and glow like a torch bulb, not be black. When they looked at a wall, there would be two bright spots on it from their glowing pupils! The reason the pupil of the eye is black is because light goes in and does not come out. If pupils cover the end of a cardboard kitchen roll tube with the palm of one hand, and look in the other open end, it appears dark because light goes in and does not come back out again. It is like the eye's pupil, or a dark cave.

Teacher demonstration 14.16

Light travelling into our eyes

Learning objective: Learn that light travels in straight lines.

Resources required: metre rulers or garden canes, triangles of card

Take some metre rulers or garden canes and stick card triangles on one end of each to make long thin arrows. These will be 'light beams'. Ask the pupils to hold them so that they point away from a light source heading in different directions. Have one beam physically travelling across the room and going into a teddy or doll's eye. If you use a pupil as the person that sees the light beam, don't forget safety goggles for them!

These 'pretend light beams' are also great for showing how light cannot go through an opaque object and also for demonstrating reflection. Have the light beams leave the light source, travel across the room, hit a book, bounce off, and go into the teddy's eye, saying 'at the moment the light enters his eye, he sees the book'. Such a concrete, active demonstration reinforces the fact for older children, who should be asked to draw diagrams of beams to represent how we see, how shadows are formed, and how reflection occurs.

Concrete demonstrations of pupils doing the following with the light beams will help their understanding:

- seeing light sources – light goes straight from the source to their eyes;
- seeing objects – light travels from a light source, reflects off an object, and goes into their eyes;
- seeing objects that are behind you – holding a mirror in front of a pupil, ask them how could they see an object behind them, without turning their head.

Ask them to act out these scenarios in front of the class (remember to use safety goggles for the person 'seeing the beam' or stop the beams getting too close to the children's eyes).

Reflection

Light is reflected off all surfaces. Smooth and shiny surfaces tend to reflect light at the same angle, so that we may see an image in them. Rough surfaces will reflect light, but they tend to disperse and scatter the light beams in different directions, so no clear image is formed. What we call 'reflectors' tend to be materials with shiny, smooth surfaces.

Pupil investigation skills 14.17

Which surfaces make the best reflectors?

Learning objective: Study surfaces to find the one that is most reflective.

Resources required: good torches, darkened classroom, small white card screen, light meter (optional), a range of flat fabrics/materials that are rough, smooth, shiny, and dull

This simple investigation can reveal some surprising results for children. They will know that mirrors are good reflectors, but other materials and fabrics can be surprisingly good too. There are distinct material properties at play here, most significant of which are how shiny is the surface (or how dull) and how smooth is the surface (or how rough). Ask the children to look at and feel the fabrics and materials. Which do they think will make the best reflectors, and which the worst? They may immediately know to look for their reflection in the best ones, but how could we test ones that don't show our reflection to see how good they are?

A simple set-up (see Figure 14.6) using a white card screen will allow a qualitative measurement (bright, very bright, dim, etc.) to be done. Using a light meter will allow a quantitative measure of reflection and children can draw a graph. The light meter can be a hand-held device or one linked to a computer for data logging.

Working in pairs or threes, hold the mirror at an angle to the small white card screen, touching at one end to form the top apex of an imaginary triangle. When the torch beam is shone at the mirror, it can be seen on the small white screen.

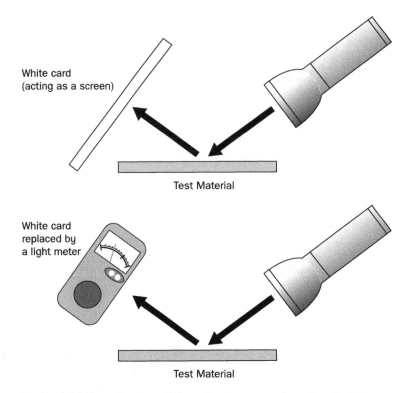

Figure 14.6 Investigation of the reflective properties of materials

Replace the mirror with the different fabrics. How much light do they reflect – some, none, a lot? Is there any colour reflection on the white screen? Children should understand that two characteristics of materials that influence light reflection are *shiny or dull* and *smooth or rough*. They should be able to rank the materials in order of 'reflectivity'.

Pupil activity 14.18

What is the difference between a shadow and a reflection?

Learning objective: Tell the difference between a shadow and a reflection.

Resources required: metre rulers or garden canes, triangles of card

Shadow and reflection can be modelled easily in teacher demonstrations using the large metre ruler or garden cane 'light beams'. We have outlined some scenarios above for how light travels and how we see things. When the light bounces (reflects) off an object, ask the children where the shadow will appear. It should always be directly behind the object. The problem is that a shadow cannot always be seen behind an object, because light from another light source could be illuminating the area that should be dark! In classroom settings, the many ceiling lights shoot light out in all different directions. Sunlight through the windows also cuts down the number of shadows. Ask the pupils to draw two labelled diagrams, one showing how reflection works and the other showing how shadows form.

Common misconception

'Is it a shadow or a reflection?'

This was discussed earlier, but after doing work on reflection and shadow-making, children should see that the two are very different processes. A shadow is made when light is blocked by an opaque object, the shadow appearing behind the object, in line with the light source. Reflection occurs when a light beam is reflected (bounced) off an object and changes its direction. Even older primary pupils muddle these two concepts up.

Activities with mirrors

Pupil activity 14.19

Making a periscope

Learning objective: To know how angled mirrors can change the direction of light beams.

Resources required: small plastic mirrors, Blu-Tack™, ruler, cardboard tubes, scissors

By actively manipulating mirrors, and drawing imaginary light beams moving between and being reflected off mirrors, pupils can get an idea of how they are used for everyday purposes. For example, a periscope has two mirrors, angled at 45 degrees to allow an observer to see over a wall, or around a corner.

The mirrors can simply be attached between two rulers, using Blu-Tack™ to hold them in place at the right angle. A more impressive periscope can be made using a card tube, such as one for a kitchen roll or even better a tube from a roll of wrapping paper. Challenge the pupils to cut the holes in the correct places, and to position the mirrors at the right angle.

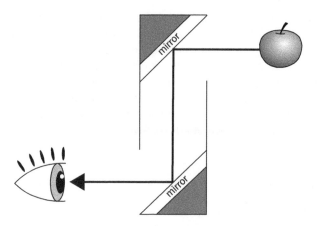

Figure 14.7 How a periscope works

Templates for making periscopes can be found at: http://www.webinnate.co.uk/science/week8.htm or at: http://www.nasa.gov/audience/foreducators/5-8/features/F_Construct_a_Periscope.html

Pupil activity 14.20

Measuring angles of reflected light beams

Learning objective: To understand that light travels in a straight line and mirrors can change its direction in predictable ways.

Resources required: pencils, white paper, plastic mirrors, light boxes with slit openings, rulers, protractors, darkened room

Pupils need to draw a ruled line and label it 'mirror line'. Next, they should put a line going through it at 90 degrees. This is called the 'normal'. Now place the mirror on the mirror line. If they send a thin light beam towards the mirror (using the slit setting on the light box) they will see a beam reflected back. Ask them to send their beam at 45 degrees to the normal (see Figure 14.8) and then to measure the angle of the reflected beam relative to the normal line. The reflected beam should also be 45 degrees. Challenge them to try some different angles, and see if they can confirm that the reflected beam always travels back at the same angle as the angle of the beam that they send towards the mirror.

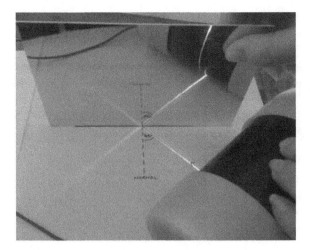

Figure 14.8 Reflecting a light beam

For virtual games using reflection from mirrors see this BBC website:

http://www.bbc.co.uk/schools/scienceclips/ages/10_11/see_things_fs.shtml

Pupils can get an appreciation of how these ideas are used in architecture and interior design by viewing mirrors to lighten up a room at:

http://www.bbc.co.uk/learningzone/clips/use-of-mirrors-to-light-a-room/247.html

White light is made up of the colours of the rainbow

Teacher demonstration 14.21

What colours are inside sunshine?

Learning objective: To know that sunlight contains all the colours of the rainbow.

Resources required: sunny day, hosepipe connected to a tap

Have the pupils assemble outside on a sunny day. They and you should stand with your backs to the Sun. Hold the hosepipe in front of you and have a helper turn on the tap. When the water comes out, the sunlight travels through the water droplets and is split up into its rainbow colours, and you will see a rainbow form in front of you. Have the pupils look closely and name the colours they can see. Notice the shape of the rainbow. With no horizon to cut it off, you should be able to make a full circular rainbow, not just the semicircle we normally see. If you struggle to see it, try to put the rainbow into a shadier area, still keeping the Sun at your back.

Pupil activity 14.22

How can we split up white light?

Learning objective: To know that white light contains different colours.

Resources required: bubble mixture and loop wands to blow the bubbles, different compact discs (some show the effect better than others, recordable discs are often the best)

Certain objects can reveal the presence of colours inside white light through a process called 'interference' (see the 'What the teacher needs to know' section for an explanation). Pupils do not need to know exactly how the phenomenon occurs, just that coloured light is contained within white light.

On a sunny day, the pupils can blow bubbles outside. Ask them to observe closely what they see. What colours are there? Do the colours in the bubbles change as the bubbles fall?

Similarly with compact discs, if they look at the back of a CD and tilt it, this can often cause them to see colours from white light hitting the disc and different beams being reflected and mingling together to make varying colours. Can they see the colours grade into each other as they tilt the disc? Can they see the whole spectrum?

Coloured filters

When light passes through a filter, the filter only lets its own colour through. So blue filters let through blue light, but block the rest. Red filters let through red light but block the rest. Cheap filters aren't always effective at blocking all but one colour – but even coloured transparent sweet wrappers should give the pupils some ideas of how filters work.

Pupil activity 14.23

Making tinted spectacles

Learning objective: To know that different filters block out different colours of light.

Resources required: different colour plastic filters, card to make spectacles, scissors

Challenge the pupils to combine different colour filters to block out as much light as possible, with the minimum number of filters, to make indoor tinted spectacles. They may find that blue and yellow filters combined make the world appear green, but green and red filters are really effective at blocking out light.

The pupils must not look at the Sun, using their tinted spectacles or even real sunglasses. They will need to be reminded of this fact.

Diffraction

When light passes into different mediums such as water and glass, it is bent. This causes optical illusions of objects looking broken or magnified.

Pupil activity 14.24

Optical illusions with light

Learning objective: To know that light can be bent by water, and this causes optical illusions.

Resources required: clear beaker of water (full or nearly full), pencil, marker pens and postcards

Pupils can place the pencil in the beaker full of water and view it from the side. Ask them to describe carefully what they see. Can they draw the 'broken' pencil? Get them to observe the pencil in the beaker without water, and then to observe what happens as the water is added. When does the broken pencil illusion become the most impressive?

Pupils can make a simple lens using a glass tumbler full of water. First they need to draw a letter of the alphabet on one side of a postcard, similar in size to the height of the glass. Place the tumbler on the table and place the postcard and the letter against the glass, and look at the letter from the other side. The letter will not look much different. Now fill with water and view again. What difference can they see? They should be able to see the letter is magnified and perhaps distorted. The shape of the glass holds the water to produce a lens, which can bend light. Water is much denser than air, so bends the light more to distort and magnify the letters.

Summary of key learning points

- light sources are objects that emit light;
- light travels in a straight line from its source;
- when light hits a material, it is reflected off the material;

- smooth shiny materials reflect light beams all in the same direction so that a clear image is formed, for example, in a mirror, or on a polished floor;

- rough materials reflect light beams but disperse them in different directions and at different angles and so no clear image can be seen in them, a so-called 'diffuse reflection';

- we see light when it is reflected off an object and then enters our eye;

- shadows form when light cannot pass through an object;

- materials can be classed as transparent, translucent or opaque depending on how much light they let through;

- white light is made up of the colours of the rainbow and can be separated with a prism or by raindrops; bubbles and compact discs also can reveal the spectrum from white light;

- coloured objects tend to reflect the colour of light that can be seen, for example red objects absorb all the colours of white light except red, and reflect back red light;

- colour filters stop all light going through, except the colour of the filter – so red filters only allow red light through;

- light can be bent as it passes through different mediums. This leads to optical effects such as a straw in water appearing broken, and a penny in a glass of water looking larger than it actually is.

Self-test

Question 1

A shadow made using a torch and a stick figure can be made larger by (a) moving the light source towards the stick figure, (b) moving the stick figure towards the light source, (c) moving the stick figure towards the shadow, (d) moving the light source away from the stick figure

Question 2

Examples of light sources are (a) the Moon, (b) stars, (c) glow worms, (d) sparkler fireworks

Question 3

Properties of light include (a) that it travels in a straight line only, (b) that light beams spread out from a light source when they travel, (c) that it can pass through transparent objects with only a small percentage of beams being reflected, (d) that it travels much faster than sound

Question 4

The best reflectors of light that allow the clearest images to be seen are (a) rough and dull, (b) smooth and dull, (c) shiny and smooth, (d) colourful and shiny

Self-test answers

Q1: (a) and (b) are correct. Anything that shortens the distance between an object making a shadow and the light source will make the shadow larger. This is because as light spreads out from its source, it makes a cone shape. The closer the stick figure is to the light source, the more of the cone of light it can block and hence the larger the shadow it can make.

Q2: (b), (c), and (d) are correct. The stars are the same type of thing as our Sun, burning gas and emitting a lot of light. They appear feeble to us as they are so far away. Glow worms use chemical reactions to make light. Sparklers are burning chemicals that emit light. The Moon appears very bright because it is able to reflect a lot of light from the Sun. This reflected light makes a moonlit night surprisingly bright, but without the Sun the Moon would be completely dark.

Q3: All the answers are correct.

Q4: Only (c) is correct. The rougher a surface is, the more it disperses the reflected light in different directions at different angles. Hence a smooth shiny surface is the best reflector.

Misconceptions

'Shiny things are light sources'
'But we can see in the dark, can't we?'
'Do shadows have faces? Are they connected to us?'
'If it's got colour then it can't be transparent'
'Light comes out of the eye when we see'
'Is it a shadow or a reflection?'

Web resources

http://www.bbc.co.uk/learningzone/clips/use-of-mirrors-to-light-a-room/247.html
     (mirrors to lighten up a room)
http://www.bbc.co.uk/schools/scienceclips/ages/10_11/see_things_fs.shtml
     (virtual light games)
http://www.webinnate.co.uk/science/week8.htm or http://www.nasa.gov/audience/
     foreducators/5-8/features/F_Construct_a_Periscope.html
     (periscopes)

Appendix 1: Paper Sun, Earth, and Moon model or orrery

Cut out the 5 discs and obtain three split pins. First of all put a split pin through the middle of the Sun (x) and then through the middle of the Sun's path disc (xs). Then push another pin through the middle of the Earth, through the middle of the Moon's path disc (x) and through the 'e' in the Sun's path disc. Finally glue the Moon onto the 'm' on the Moon's path disc (gluing it means that one side will always (correctly) face the Earth).

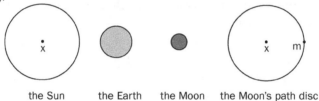

| the Sun | the Earth | the Moon | the Moon's path disc |

disc

Sun's path

e •

xs

NB The orrery is not to scale

Appendix 2: Simple three-dimensional orrery that can be made by pupils

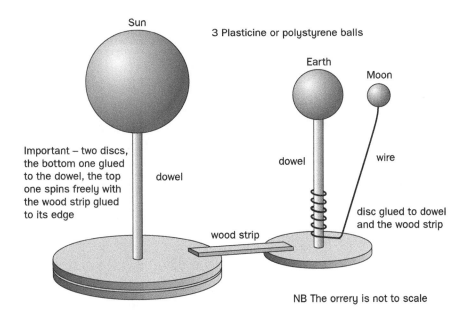

Sun

3 Plasticine or polystyrene balls

Earth

Moon

Important – two discs, the bottom one glued to the dowel, the top one spins freely with the wood strip glued to its edge

dowel

dowel

wire

wood strip

disc glued to dowel and the wood strip

NB The orrery is not to scale

The three-dimensional orrery requires dowelling to be glued upright into the centre of two wooden discs (see Figure A2). A further wooden disc with a pre-drilled centre hole is then dropped down onto one of the glued discs. This second disc must turn freely as this is the base for the Sun. A lolly stick or wood strip is then glued to the free-moving disc and at the other end to the other (Earth) disc and dowel. You can now add suitable balls or spheres of Plasticine™ to represent the Sun and Earth. The Earth should now orbit the Sun. The last feature to add is the Moon, held in place by a stiff wire coiled around the Earth support dowel and shaped to place the Moon in position. The Moon should, as long as the wire is not too tight, move so that it orbits the Earth.

Appendix 3: My science development diary

My science understanding		
Date	Target	Action taken/date completed

My science teaching		
Date	Target	Action taken/date completed

Bibliography

Ahlberg, J. and Ahlberg, A. (1993) *Funnybones*. London: Picture Puffin.

Alexander, R. (2004) Still no pedagogy? Principle, pragmatism and compliance in primary education, *Cambridge Journal of Education*, 34(1): 7–33.

Association of Science Education (ASE) (1990) *The Earth in Space*. Hatfield: ASE.

Association of Science Education (ASE) (2010) *Be Safe!* (4th edn). Hatfield: ASE.

Barnes, D. (1976) *From Communication to Curriculum*. Harmondsworth: Penguin Education Books.

Baud, D. (1987) *Developing Student Autonomy in Learning*. London: Kogan/Page.

Brown, M.W. (2007) *Goodnight Moon*. New York: HarperFestival.

Cole, J. (1992) *The Magic School Bus Gets Lost in the Solar System*. London: Scholastic Publications.

Cole, J. (1995) *The Magic School Bus Gets Lost in Space*. London: Scholastic.

Cross, A. and Board, J. (2014) *Creative Ways to Teach Primary Science*. London: McGraw-Hill.

Darwin, C. (1872) *The Origin of Species by Natural Selection*. London: John Murray.

Department for Children, Schools and Families (DCSF) (2008) The Assessment for Learning strategy (available online at: http://webarchive.nationalarchives.gov.uk/20130401151715/https://www.education.gov.uk.

Department for Education (DfE) (2013a) *The National Curriculum for England*. London: Department for Education.

Department for Education (DfE) (2013b) *Teachers' Standards*. London: Department for Education.

Driver, R. (1983) *The Pupil as Scientist?* Milton Keynes: Open University Press.

Elstgeest, J. (1985) The right question at the right time, in W. Harlen (ed.) *Primary Science: Taking the Plunge*. London: Heinemann.

Flavell, J., Miller, P. and Miller, S. (1977) *Cognitive Development*. Englewood Cliffs, NJ: Prentice-Hall.

Freedman, C. and Cort, B. (2007) *Aliens Love Underpants*. London: Simon & Schuster.

Gipps, C., McCallum, B. and Hargreaves, E. (2000) *What Makes a Good Primary School Teacher?* London: Taylor and Francis.

Goldsworthy, A. and Feasey, R. (1997) *Making Sense of Primary Science Investigations*. Hatfield: ASE.

Goldsworthy, A., Watson, R. and Wood-Robinson, V. (1999) *AKSIS Investigations: Getting to Grips with Graphs*. Hatfield: ASE.

Gott, R. and Duggan, S. (1995) *Investigative Work in the Science Curriculum*. Buckingham: Open University Press.

Harding, T. (2003) *That's Science: Learning Science Through Songs*. Stafford: Network Educational Press.

Harlen, W. (1999) *Effective Teaching of Science: A Review of Research*. Edinburgh: Scottish Council for Educational Research (available online at: http://www.scre.ac.uk/pdf/science.pdf).

Harlen, W. (2006) *Teaching, Learning and Assessing Science 5–12* (4th edn). London: Sage.

Hattie, J. (2009) *Visible Learning: A Synthesis of over 800 Meta-analyses Relating to Achievement*. Abingdon: Routledge.

Heller, J.R. (2007) *How the Moon Regained Her Shape*. Mount Pleasant, SC: Sylvan Dell.

Hodson, D. (1998) *Teaching and Learning Science: Towards a Personalised Approach*. Maidenhead: Open University Press.

Howe, A., Davies, D., McMahon, K., Towler, L. and Scott, T. (2006) *Science 5–11: A Guide for Teachers*. London: David Fulton.

Jelly, S. (1985) Helping children raise questions – and answering them, in W. Harlen (ed.) *Primary Science: Taking the Plunge*. London: Heinemann.

Marzano, R., Marzano, J.S. and Pickering, D. (2003) *Classroom Instruction That Works: Research Based Strategies for Increasing Student Achievement*. Alexandria, VA: ASCD.

McGuigan, L. and Schilling, M. (1997) Children learning in science, in A. Cross and G. Peet (eds) *Teaching Science in the Primary School: A Practical Source Book of Teaching Strategies*. Plymouth: Northcote House.

Mercer, N. (1995) *The Guided Construction of Knowledge*. Clevedon: Multilingual Matters.

Naylor, S. and Keogh, B. (2000) *Concept Cartoons in Science Education*. Sandbach: Millgate House Education.

Ofsted (2013) *Maintaining Curiosity: A Survey into Science Education in Schools*. London: Office for Standards in Education.

Peacock, G.A. (1998) *QTS Science for Primary Teachers: An Audit and Study Guide*. London: Letts Educational.

Pekmez, E.S., Johnson, P.M. and Gott, R. (2005) Teachers' understanding of the nature and purpose of practical work, *Research in Science and Technological Education*, 23(1): 3–23.

Petty, G. (2009) *Evidence-Based Teaching: A Practical Approach* (2nd edn). London: Nelson-Thornes.

Piaget, J. (1973) *Memory and Intelligence*. New York: Basic Books.

Roden, J. (2005) *Achieving QTS: Reflective Reader in Primary Science*. Exeter: Learning Matters.

Rousseau, J.J. (1979) *Emile or On Education* (trans. A. Bloom). New York: Basic Books.

Schulman, L.S. (1987) Knowledge and teaching: foundations of the new reforms, *Harvard Educational Review*, 57: 1–22.

Sharp, J. (ed.) (2004) *Developing Primary Science*. Exeter: Learning Matters.

Sharp, J., Peacock, G., Johnsey, R., Simon, S. and Smith, R. (2000) *Primary Science: Teaching Theory and Practice*. Exeter: Learning Matters.

Smith, R. and Peacock, G. (1995) *Investigations and Progression in Science*. London: Hodder and Stoughton.

Stenhouse, L. (1975) *An Introduction to Curriculum Research and Development*. London: Heinemann Education.

Turner, J., Keogh, B., Naylor, S. and Lawrence, Liz (2011) *Its not Fair – or Is It?* Sandbach: Millgate House.

Vygotsky, L.S. (1988) *Thought and Language* (3rd edn). London: MIT Press.

Wellington, J. (1998) Reasons for doing practical work now and their limitations, in *Practical Work in School Science: Which Way Now?* London: Routledge.

Wellington, J. and Osbourne, J. (2001) *Language and Literacy in Science Education*. Buckingham: Open University Press.

Wenham, M. (1995) *Understanding Primary Science: Ideas, Concepts and Explanations*. London: Paul Chapman.

Yore, L., Bisanz, G. and Hand, B. (2003) Examining the literacy component of science literacy: 25 years of language, arts and science research, *International Journal of Science Education*, 25(6): 689–725.

Index